Moral Foundations

Moral Foundations
An Introduction to Ethics

Alexander F. Skutch

AXIOS

Axios Press
P.O. Box 118
Mount Jackson, VA 22842
888.542.9467   info@axiospress.com

Distributed by NATIONAL BOOK NETWORK.

Publisher's Cataloging-in-Publication Data

Skutch, Alexander Frank, 1904-2004.
    Moral foundations : an introduction to ethics / Alexander F.
Skutch.
        p.   cm.
    Includes bibliographical references and index.
    LCCN 2005935717
    ISBN-13: 978-0-9661908-9-2
    ISBN-10: 0-9661908-9-0

    1. Ethics.   I. Title.

BJ301.S58 2007   170

                                              QBI07-600149

Contents

Six: The Innate Foundations of Morality

Seven: Conscience and Moral Intuitions

Eight: Pleasures and Happiness

Nine: The Determination of Choice

Ten: Moral Freedom

Eleven: Right and Wrong

Twelve: Goodness

Thirteen: Ethical Judgments and Social Structure

Fourteen: Duty

Fifteen: The Relativity of Good and Evil

Sixteen: Characteristics of Ethical Systems

Seventeen: The Foundations of a Universal Ethic

Preface

IN THIS BOOK I relate morality to earlier stages of the cosmic process of which it is an advanced development, interpret moral sentiments and ethical concepts in the light of this relationship, and by giving due weight to all pertinent motives, lay the foundations of an ethic both comprehensive and congenial to our spiritual aspiration.

Morality is essentially the conscious effort to cultivate harmony in our individual lives, with the people around us, and at its best with the wider realm of nature and the planet that supports us. Ethics is the division of philosophy that studies morality in all its diverse expressions. Both analytic and constructive, it not only tries to fathom the springs of moral action and the meanings of the words it uses, but from its birth in ancient Greece it has examined the ends of human life and the means for their attainment. These ends have been as diverse as the temperaments of the people who taught or wrote about ethics, but most have been concerned

with the cultivation of a firmly established happiness, contentment, or sense of fulfillment. It is hardly an exaggeration
to call ethics the quest of felicity. Fascinated by the peculiar
features of our moral life, philosophers have given too little
attention to the close connection between morality and its
antecedents in the animal kingdom and, beyond this, in
the Universe at large. Even Herbert Spencer, a thinker with
interests as wide as Aristotle's, failed to articulate his ethics
with his evolutionary philosophy as closely as he might have
done.[1] In this book I try to achieve a closer union.

When we view morality broadly as the effort to increase
harmony in all that concerns us, we recognize its resemblance to a widespread cosmic process. From its prime
foundations in space and matter, the Universe is pervaded
by a movement that unites diverse entities in patterns of
increasing amplitude, complexity, and coherence—the
process of harmonization. On a vast scale it has created
the solar system, in which Sun, planets, and their satellites
move in a pattern so stable that it has endured for the long
ages needed to cover Earth with abundant life—a system
that might serve as a paradigm for an orderly society. On
a very small scale, a similar process unites atoms in molecules and both in crystals that are often both beautiful
and enduring. On an intermediate scale harmonization
is evident in the growth of organisms both vegetable and
animal, wherein a greater diversity of components are
more closely integrated and interdependent than in any
inorganic creation of whatever magnitude. When, after
countless generations of slow advance by the crude, gam-
bling methods of biological evolution, harmonization
brought forth minds sensitive to the process that perme-

ates them, they use their capacity to foresee and choose to promote harmony in the living world—they become moral agents. Because biological evolution has been opportunistic rather than planned, and the excessive intensity of a primarily beneficent process has overcrowded Earth with living things that too often compete fiercely for what they need, the task of these agents has not been easy; but realization that their efforts are in the direction of a cosmic movement that creates order and beauty and increases the value of existence—a movement that impels them forward—should encourage then to persevere.

Prolonged study of free animals, especially the more social birds, has impressed me with the broad similarity of their problems to ours. Their welfare, like ours, depends upon concord with others of their kind. They have developed patterns of behavior that promote cooperation and mitigate interindividual conflict. A major difference between them and us is that their behavior is largely innately controlled whereas ours is largely learned. Hence we become more conscious of our conduct than we suppose other animals to be, but our habits are less strongly impressed upon the nervous system. This circumstance, in restless minds able to choose between alternative courses of action, is responsible for all the vagaries of human behavior. It has made morality a human need, as compensation for our loss of integrated patterns of behavior that are innate rather than learned. Our wandering thoughts and all the temptations that solicit us in a complex civilization have made us more prone to go astray than we suppose other animals to be; but they, too, are not guiltless of aberrations from the pattern of behavior that safeguard their survival as individuals and as species. Differences between them and us should not blind us to fundamental similarities. They might be said to have a protomorality such as our remote prehuman ancestors possessed, and from which our more self-conscious morality evolved as innate behavior was gradually superseded by learned behavior.

To support a favorite theory or achieve expository neatness, philosophers have too often tried to derive the whole of morality from a single motive, such as self-preservation, the pursuit of pleasure or happiness, duty, or something else, neglecting other motives that might support our moral endeavor. Although this course may be intellectually satisfying, it commonly fails to achieve an ethic of ample breadth and inclusiveness. Only by giving voice to all our innate resources of moral relevance can we establish an ethic that satisfies a wide moral vision. By this course we may expand our moral endeavor beyond humanity to the creatures around us, now so afflicted by our activities, and to the abused planet that supports us all. An ethic established firmly on all pertinent motives, from the strongest to the weakest, should immensely encourage our growing efforts to save Earth from the disaster that increasingly menaces it. The environmental movement is of great ethical relevance because the possibility of a firmly established, enduring morality depends upon its success, but it is still much too weak to accomplish its aims on a global scale and needs all the support, practical and intellectual, that we can give it.

Chapter One

The Science of Ethics

1. Delimitation of the Subject

ETHICS IS THE study of morality in all its varied manifestations. Morality is one of the higher or more advanced modes of harmonization, which can occur only after the earlier modes have prepared for it through a long evolution. It is the endeavor of intelligent, foreseeing beings to bring order and stability into their individual lives and to dwell in concord with the innumerable creatures of their own and other kinds which share Earth with them. Moral beings realize this goal in the measure that they succeed in arranging all the details of their lives in a coherent system, and in adjusting the resulting individual patterns of conduct in a comprehensive social pattern, which reduces to a minimum the strife between living things and, as far as possible, permits each of them to attain the perfection natural to it. Thus, broadly viewed, morality is the effort of harmonization to mitigate, by means of self-conscious agents, the conflicts which spring up everywhere as a secondary effect of the very universality of the impulsion toward harmony or order. Ethics is the study of the impulses which lead to this endeavor, the methods it employs, and the phenomena to which it gives rise.

At the outset, it seems necessary to delimit morality from certain other of the higher modes of harmonization, and to define its relation to them. This is no easy task, for they are closely associated. On one side it merges into the arts, while on the other it is joined by the closest bonds to religion. But no particular art, nor all of them together, is competent to effect that articulation and coordination of all our activities without which our most devoted efforts in limited fields may lead to discord and frustration rather than to the prosperity and happiness which they are intended to promote. This attempt to regulate and coordinate is essentially a moral endeavor; hence the science of morality ranks above any special art, and must assign to each of them its place in the whole scheme of human life.

Just as it stands above the arts, so morality ranks below religion in the hierarchy of human activities. For while moral endeavor, when most inclusive, strives to bring harmony into our relations with all the beings which surround us, religion attempts to attune our inner life to an encompassing whole. The primary goal of morality is practical harmony, that of religion spiritual harmony; yet these two are so closely linked that it is difficult to disentangle them. Restrained by fear of statute law, social censure, or supernatural retribution, a person may act with perfect correctness toward another whom he or she hates and desires to injure; yet such conduct, for all its superficial rectitude, is, in the opinion of many philosophers, not truly moral. And if it is difficult to cultivate irreproachable conduct in the absence of a right attitude of mind, it is impossible to attain that pervasive inner harmony which is religion's goal without harmonious external relations. Thus morality has ever been a major concern of all the more advanced religions, and a morally blameless life has been considered the indispensable prelude to the higher reaches of religious experience.

Because morality is so intimately linked with so many other human endeavors, in the midst of which it stands as a director and moderator, it is scarcely possible to circumscribe in any direction the subject matter of ethics. On one side it merges into physiology and hygiene, for unless we preserve health we cannot fulfill our obligations and do good deeds. In other directions it blends into the fine arts and all the sciences, for these enhance life's value, and morality is concerned with the realization of values. This is especially evident in Nicolai Hartmann's ethic of values, for some of those which he recognizes, as, for example, that of personality, seem to pass beyond the province of morality; yet in a wider sense they remain within it.[1] It is useless to attempt to narrow the field of ethics by confining its attention to acts and dispositions which enhance the strictly *moral* worth of a person; for, if we take a liberal view, one's love of beauty or of knowledge, or proficiency in an art or science, seem to increase moral no less than total worth.

Yet to include within the study of ethics everything which is somehow pertinent to it would expand it to unwieldy proportions. One way of keeping it within manageable bounds is to center its attention on the structure of situations in which living beings can by their own efforts increase their perfection and advance toward the fulfillment of their highest aspirations. Hence the present work is dedicated to the development of a *structural ethic*, or ethic of relations.

In taking this course, we do not overlook the supreme importance of character. Although character and conduct are conceptually distinct, actually they are so closely joined that it is scarcely possible to disentangle them. One's character is most adequately revealed by behavior, by the nature of the relations we strive to maintain with the beings around us, while one's dealings with one's fellows have in turn a strong influence on character. Thus to perfect character and to improve external relations are two aspects of the same endeavor. We cannot advance toward one of these goals without drawing nearer to the other, and our choice of a route is largely a matter of practical convenience.

2. Can Ethics Be Classified as a Science?

Students of ethics have been perplexed whether to classify their subject as a science, an art, or otherwise. The objection to including ethics among the sciences is that, whereas science deals with what is, ethics, it is said, is concerned with what ought to be. This, at the first glimpse, appears to be a valid and useful distinction; but mature reflection reveals that it is superficial and not wholly true. Much of the confusion and disorientation in contemporary ethics may be traced to just this refusal to recognize that ethics, no less than physics, is concerned with actually existent situations and with energies that cause clearly demonstrable effects. In the first place, our opinion of what ought to be lacks authority if it ignores what already exists. Any one of our most fanciful dreams might with equal force command our present efforts, unless we insist that our notions of what ought to be are somehow related to present realities. Even from this point of view, ethics must be more than the consideration of imaginary states that might satisfy our highest moral aspirations.

If the world is pervaded by an energy or activity that produces order of the sort that we recognize as good or moral, ethics must become aware of this active principle and its effects that have moral relevance. A single process, harmonization, pervades the Universe, building up its manifold contents into patterns which tend to increase indefinitely in complexity, amplitude, and coherence. Operating on a small scale, harmonization arranges the finest particles of matter in atoms, molecules, and crystals, each of which has a definite organization; while on a vast scale it creates the admirable order and regularity in the movements of great bodies that the solar system displays. The harmonies achieved by this activity on a cosmic scale, in the rhythmic revolutions of Sun and planets with all their satellites, are revealed to us by the science of astronomy. At the other extreme, chemistry discloses the regularity and order in the behavior of the elements of matter, in all their varieties and combinations.

This same creative process, operating in the realm of life, gives rise to the harmonies in form and function which biology investigates and describes. And when animals reach a certain high degree of organization, when they acquire minds capable of sympathy, of foreseeing the future and comparing alternative courses of action, of deliberately striving to increase their concord among themselves and with the surrounding world, we recognize the continued action of harmonization, which now presents certain special modes of operation made possible by the new instrument, foreseeing intelligence, that it has produced.

The investigation of these special phenomena falls within the province of ethics, as the movements of the heavenly bodies come within the purview of astronomy. These two sciences are equally necessary for the complete description of our world, and the omission of either of them from the august company of the sciences would leave our picture of the whole cosmic process fragmentary and defective. For ethics and astronomy, along with physics, chemistry, geology, biology, and psychology, are all alike concerned with successive stages in the same grand movement. They are equally dedicated to the study of actual processes going on in our world, and describe for us the modes of operation and the effects of the same creative energy at its several levels of accomplishment. Since we ourselves are intimately involved in that particular phase of the world process which ethics treats, and can do much to accelerate or retard its advance, ethics is above all a study of *what is coming to be*, and of the means to hasten its advent.

Although ethics resembles the physical and biological science in dealing with actual constituents of the world and demonstrable processes within it, it differs profoundly in its methods of investigation. A partial history of the moral development of humanity might conceivably be written from wholly external observation. If we could collect sufficient records, made preferably by observers who remained themselves unseen, of the conduct of people of different races and epochs, taking account of such points as their treatment of wives and children, of dependents, servants or slaves, of animals domestic and free, their honesty in business and their care of the sick and aged, we might write a history of the moral growth of humanity as impersonal and objective as the studies we now make of the behavior of insects or birds. But available records give us pictures of the daily conduct of ancient races that at best are fragmentary. And even if they were somewhat complete, they would give us an imperfect and distorted picture of the operation among humans of that creative activity which is essentially a moral power. For the differences in the moral development of individuals of the same culture and epoch are far greater than the differences in the general moral level of cultures separated by thousands of years and thousands of miles, and a study of the common practices in Greece in the first century of our era would tell us as little of the moral aspirations of a Plutarch or an Epictetus, as acquaintance with the behavior of the masses of humans of our day reveals to us the moral stature of a Gandhi or a Schweitzer.

To supplement the deficiencies that would remain in the most complete record of peoples' external activities, we must turn to their direct statements of the ideals which inspire them and the maxims by which they strive to guide their conduct. Or we must look within ourselves and feel the stirrings of the moral impulse in the depths of our being. But when we turn to these sources of information, we employ methods of investigation radically different from those of astronomy, physics, or biology. Yet ethics need not because of its special methods of investigation cease to be a science. Psychology, long considered to be a branch of philosophy, has gradually won for itself a place among the sciences, although it depends in part on methods of obtaining information fundamentally different from those of the other sciences.

3. The Divisions of Ethics

The primary datum of ethics is the presence within ourselves of impulses, sentiments, or aspirations of the sort that we call moral. If we have felt a desire to perfect ourselves, to make our happiness stable and enduring rather than fitful and undependable, to live in greater harmony with the beings around us, we have in our personal experience a starting point for the study of ethics. If we have wished to bring happiness to others or to share it with them, or have striven actively to ease the pains or improve the condition of some other being who is not expected to repay us for our trouble, we have a more valuable, because more developed, datum for beginning our ethical investigations. These and many other expressions of our moral nature are facts as certain and real as any that come within the range of our experience. They provide material for scientific study as solid as the phenomena which physics and chemistry strive to explain.

From this initial datum, two lines of departure are apparent. In the first place, we may wish to analyze and explain the primary moral fact. How do we happen to have this moral impulse within us, or why did we perform this act that we call moral? We wish to know its antecedents, how it arose, how it is related to other phases of the world process. Likewise, we may wish to analyze it psychologically, to understand its psychic components and its relation to other contents of our minds. These endeavors give rise to the *science* of ethics, of which two major divisions may be recognized. The first of these is Historical Ethics, or the history of morals, which attempts to trace the development through the ages of moral ideals and practices. The second is Analytic Ethics, which studies the innate foundations of morality, above all its motivation. And just as criminology can be studied by a person who has never known a criminal impulse, or pathology by one who has never been sick, so these two branches of ethics might be cultivated by one who had never felt a moral impulse, but was instigated by detached curiosity alone. Such a person, however, would even as a scientific investigator be at a disadvantage in having to look to others for some intimation of the peculiar character of moral impulses and aspirations, which are most readily observed as they occur within oneself.

Most writers on ethics have undertaken their task in response to something more intimate and urgent than detached scientific curiosity. Although they have often begun with an analysis of the innate or even the cosmic foundations of morality, they have thence proceeded to the elaboration of an ideal of character and conduct, which they aspired to practice themselves and disseminate among their fellows. All the great "systems" of ethics, such as Platonism, Stoicism, Utilitarianism, or that of Benedict de Spinoza, have had this inclusive scope. And in passing from detached observation to active endeavor, they have crossed the boundary between ethics, the study, and morality, the dedication to certain rules or ideals of life. Thus, in addition to a science of ethics it is necessary to recognize an *art* of ethics or, if one prefers, a pure and an applied science of ethics. The second stands in the same relation to the first as scientific horticulture to botany in its several branches. And just as scientific horticulture represents an advance in many ways over plant growing by unexamined traditional methods, so ethics as an art or applied science is capable of advancing beyond conventional morality, with its inadequately examined foundations and often crudely articulated practices. Ethics as an art is something more than commonplace morality.

Thus the art of morality grows up when from the initial datum of ethics, the presence within us of moral impulses or aspirations, we follow the second line of departure, or both together, and instead of merely trying to analyze and explain moral aspirations we strive to bring them to fruition. When we take this course, we wish to discover what kinds of activities will most fully express or satisfy our moral ideal, what arrangements in the external world will best comport with it. This gives rise to Applied Ethics, which deals with the concrete effects of conduct. It attempts to answer such questions as: When, if ever, is it permissible to depart from strict veracity? What are the effects, immediate and remote, of almsgiving? How soon should I forgive one who has deliberately injured me? What are the moral effects of asceticism and to what extent should it be practiced? Applied Ethics differs from casuistry in that it takes a general view of moral problems, while casuistry is concerned with the minute, and often far from disinterested, analysis of particular situations.

Moreover, since hardly anybody is wholly self-sufficient but requires the cooperation of others to achieve a satisfying life, we soon discover that we accomplish little, except schooling ourselves in cheerful resignation, without the help of others who share our ideals. Not only is it, as a rule, far easier to inculcate these ideals in the plastic minds of children than in less receptive minds of people of mature age; unless we accomplish this, the ideals which have inspired our lives will perish with us, and this for many people is a distressing prospect. Thence the necessity for the second branch of practical ethics, which might be designated Hortative Ethics, and which is concerned with the formulation and dissemination of moral ideals as well as the moral education of the young.

Although some writers, as, for example, T. H. Green in his *Prolegomena to Ethics*, have depreciated the practical value of ethical theory and disclaimed the responsibility for generating a "moral dynamic" or enthusiasm in their readers,[2] the perusal of their works sometimes leads the reader to suspect that they have taken too modest a view of their office as moral philosophers. At any rate, to go to vast pains to develop an ethical doctrine without trying to present it in such a way that it will win adherents and help others to achieve a more satisfying life, without even hoping that it will have this effect, seems to be a rather barren endeavor. Certainly, the diffusion of moral ideals is as much a part of the moral philosopher's task as the provision of aids to navigation and the accurate measurement of time is of the astronomer's. What could be more pitiful and futile than an ethical doctrine that was not intended to be put into practice?

Thus we have recognized four major divisions of Ethics, as follows:

1. Historical Ethics, which traces the growth through the centuries of moral ideals and practices.
2. Analytic Ethics, which studies the innate foundations of morality.
3. Applied Ethics, which deals with the concrete effects of conduct.
4. Hortative Ethics, which is concerned with the formulation and dissemination of moral ideals and the moral education of the young.

Of these four major divisions of ethics, the first two will occupy our attention in the present book, which is above all devoted to the analysis of the innate foundations of the moral life, the meanings of moral terms, and the characteristics of ethical systems.

4. Problems of Historical Ethics

Historical Ethics is the most objective, and in that sense the most scientific, branch of the subject. It displays to us the actual growth of moral sentiments and practices through the centuries, and this growth is as well established as the shape of Earth's path around the sun, and as independent of one's favorite ethical doctrine as the mathematical figure described by Earth is independent of our explanation of the mystery of gravitation. In following the moral history of humanity, we witness the subtle working of harmonization in the complex field of human conduct and the relations of people to the beings that surround them.

The history of morals is concerned with two distinct but related phenomena, peoples' expressions of their ideals and their actual practice in a given community. Between the highest ideals of a culture and its concurrent practice there is often a great gap, at times so wide that one suspects that moral aspirations have little influence on daily conduct; and the more advanced the culture, the wider this gap becomes. But if we examine the practice of a later age in the light of the expressed ideals of an earlier period in the same cultural tradition, we sometimes find that common practice has advanced toward the aspirations of the earlier epoch; and this is especially true when a period of peaceful and orderly development has intervened, without great reversals caused by the invasion of rude hordes at a lower stage of culture. Dropped into the minds and consciences of humans at some remote period of the past, a moral aspiration may seem to decay and vanish like a seed buried too deeply in the soil; but with great vitality it sends its shoot slowly upward through the dark loam, until at length it emerges and flowers in the sunshine. An unfulfilled ideal, if a genuine expression of our moral nature, will never let us rest until we have brought it into current practice, or exhausted ourselves in the effort.

Because of the vast gulf which separates the ideals of thinkers of greatest moral insight and the current practice of their neighbors, the historian of morals, eager to demonstrate the slow growth of morality, will be perplexed as to the best course to pursue. If we include ideals and practices in the same view, we will be forced to admit that the common practice of our day falls far short of the loftiest teachings of two or three millennia ago, and then it will be difficult for us to demonstrate that there has been growth and progress. If, on the other hand, we focus on the ideals of a period with no mention of its social conditions and actual practices, our story will lose much of its instructiveness; for it is precisely against the background of the prevailing habits of their times that the moral aspirations of exceptional individuals acquire greatest significance. How can one appraise the Messianic visions of Isaiah without some understanding of the contemporary situation of the Jews, or fully appreciate the grandeur of the ethical ideals developed by the Hellenic philosophers if we know nothing of the selfishness, duplicity, ingratitude, and puerile sectionalism which fill like a nauseating stench the pages of Greek history? Whatever method of exposition we choose, the historian of morals must use great skill to give a balanced picture of the growth of morality.

It is necessary to distinguish sharply between moral history, as we here understand it, and the history of theoretical ethics. For the latter, Euripides, who so far as we know had no special theory, is far less important than Plato and Aristotle, whose ethical doctrines, worked out in great detail, were firmly established on cosmological and psychological foundations. But as an expositor of the highest moral ideals of his age, the dramatist is certainly no less important than the philosophers, whom he perhaps excels in his moral sensitivity, as expressed in his sympathy for women and slaves, his advocacy of conjugal fidelity, and his yearning for an ideal justice. When we compare Euripides' misgivings about slavery with Aristotle's warm endorsement of this institution in the *Politics*, or his views on marital fidelity with the arrangements for the procreation of the governing class in Plato's *Republic*, it seems clear that, for all their careful analyses of moral questions, the great philosophers had on many points failed to reach ideals so advanced as those of the dramatist of an earlier generation, whose views were perhaps determined by his natural sympathies more than by formal theories.

5. The Early Flowering of Moral Ideals

From at least the time of Herodotus, historians have recognized the difficulty of learning, from the often fragmentary and conflicting reports available to them, what actually happened in history. In one respect the historian of moral ideals enjoys a great advantage over the historian of political events, economic or social customs; for, as compared with the complexities of diplomacy or economic interactions, the ideal is usually simple, clear, and capable of succinct expression. In many instances, the historian of ethics enjoys the immense advantage of possessing the actual statements of their principles made by people of outstanding moral stature, either as set down in writing by themselves or as recorded by their disciples. Thus, while we know what Pericles did and said only through the biased accounts of his contemporaries or the imaginative reconstruction of his speeches, as by Thucydides, we have the direct statements of their views on moral questions by individuals like Plato, Aristotle, Seneca, and Epictetus.

On the other hand, the historian of moral ideals is handicapped by the very rapidity of their growth in relation to the general cultural advance of humanity. While the improvement of a person's actual condition had to wait on the slow accumulation of experience in such fields as social organization, education, government, agriculture, and industry, the growth of his or her moral nature was not so limited by external factors, with the result that aspirations could soar in relative independence of the physical state. Some of our noblest moral ideals shine forth to us from the dawn-mists of history, against a background of barbarism, disorder, and great social injustice. This situation led Charles Gore to remark that "the broad consideration of the history of religion and morality . . . leads to an interesting conclusion, that at each stage where conspicuous advance is made the best comes first."[3] Perhaps it would be truer to say that only the highest expressions of moral ideals have been preserved for us from the earlier epochs, while the stages that led up to them have been, for the most part, lost from our view. Sympathies so wide as those of the Buddha or Lao Tse point to a long period of development, a tradition already mellowed by age; but the earlier growth, of which these are the flowering, can at best be followed in an imperfect and fragmentary fashion. The first moral teachings were given orally, while the earliest written records have failed to withstand the corrosion of time.

In studying the growth of moral ideals, we must distinguish between their breadth and their altitude. What beings do we intend to include in our moral community and consider to be bound to us by ties of duty or sympathy? What relations do we strive to establish among these beings, and what is our conception of the perfect character? Under the head of comprehensiveness, neither East nor West can point to any general or sustained progress in the development of the moral ideal during the last two millennia. In the Stoic system, classic antiquity elaborated an ethical concept, which recognized the brotherhood of all humanity, with its corollary that all people must be accorded equal justice and kindness. The Stoics cherished an ideal of virtue and devotion to duty which has scarcely anywhere been surpassed. Strict conformity to the doctrines of the early Stoa would cramp the emotional and esthetic sides of human character; but later exponents of the system, whose writings alone have been preserved entire, reveal an admirable broadening of sympathies; and even in the earlier period other Classic philosophies, as those of Plato and Aristotle, served as a corrective for the Stoic narrowness. Moreover, in Athens at least, the whole social atmosphere tended to prevent a lopsided development of human personality.

If no single Classic system included all that seems desirable in the moral ideal, even as comprised within an ethic limited to our own species, the same is true of nearly all modern systems of ethics. Here and there in the Pagan world voices like those of Pythagoras, Plutarch, and Porphyry cried out for the extension of sympathy and justice to nonhuman creatures, just as in the modern West isolated thinkers like Schweitzer have made a plea in the same direction. But, in general, modern Western philosophers, like their predecessors in the ancient Mediterranean world, have taught an ethic rather narrowly limited to humanity; with Stoicism, perhaps more than any other system of wide influence, founded on principles which, by a liberal interpretation, should transcend these limits. Perhaps the growth of the Christian doctrine that love is a primary moral force is the greatest advance in ethical idealism rather than in detailed practice to which the West can point since the decay of the Classic schools; but except with a few poets and dreamers, this love has rarely been diffused as wisely and as freely as it should be.

In India the moral ideal was in ancient times, by both Jains and Buddhists, made as comprehensive as it could well be, and the same is true of the Taoists in China. When one is solicitous for the life and welfare of the least creature that flies in the air or creeps in the dust, when one vows to delay their own entrance into bliss until every living thing has been freed from the wheel of existence, further expansion of the moral ideal is scarcely possible. But even when the ideal has become as comprehensive as it can be, there may still be room for improvement in the relations which it contemplates and in its concept of the perfect character. Despite the admirable sympathy of these Eastern religions with all that lives and breathes, their strong ascetic leanings precluded an ideal of the fullest development of human capacities. I am not aware of any Indian religion or philosophy, not obviously influenced by the modern infiltration of Western ideas, which formally corrected this deficiency; but the splendid development of art and literature in ancient India points to a general practice not constricted by the too narrow formulation of some of its leading creeds. Indeed, even within the bosom of these creeds, the arts flourished grandly.

6. The Slower Advance of General Practice

When we turn from the consideration of moral aspirations to that of moral customs, such as might be studied even by an intelligent observer who could not communicate with the objects of his or her investigation, we omit the distinguishing feature and lose the peculiar flavor of human moral endeavor. It is possible to demonstrate among nonhuman animals long-continued and definite advances of the very sort that we commonly look upon as moral when exhibited by ourselves; but as far as we know, these advances were not made in pursuit of an ideal which when first expressed seemed often to be visionary, never to be realized in practice. Yet it is precisely in the field of moral practices, rather than of ideals, that the historian is in possession of materials which permit him or her to trace a steady and persistent progress through the centuries. The chief reason for this is the lag of general practice behind the ideals of the moral elite, which has brought some of the most important advances in the former closer to our own time.

How can we explain this contrast between the early and apparently sudden advent of high moral ideals and their slower, more gradual realization in practice? The reason seems to be that the first is largely personal, while the second is more closely dependent on social conditions. Inspired by the yearning for inner peace or for union with the source of one's spiritual strength, the earnest seeker strives to divest his or her mind of all the blinding passions, all the disruptive attitudes that veil from the inner vision the true nature of the primary determinant of being. Purified of this obscuring fog, our mind becomes sensitive to the influence of that inner creative force which steadily impels us to work toward the attainment of the amplest and most satisfying harmony that we can conceive; for only in the realization of this inclusive concord do we express our inmost nature and slake our spiritual thirst. Thus, we form the ideal of living at peace with all creatures and harming nothing. Already the moral aspiration has reached its widest possible scope. Although the ideal itself springs from the depth of our being, to realize it in our actual life will require long ages of observation and practice, the laborious working out of innumerable details.

Unlike the ideals of the most enlightened individuals, which may expand vastly in a short period, the moral practices of a community depend on so many complex factors that their improvement is necessarily gradual. One of these factors may be, as Alexander Sutherland contended, a gradual shift in genetic constitution, resulting from the more rapid multiplication of the more sympathetic individuals, whose more tender care of wife and children ensure that, on the average, they will leave more progeny than people whose sympathies are poorly developed. But it is scarcely possible to disentangle the possible effects of such differential reproduction from the cumulative effects of education, and the gradual diffusion of lofty ideals from those finer minds which conceived them through the rank and file of society, who although perhaps incapable of ever forming such ideals for themselves, are not wholly blind to their beauty when presented to them by others.

Then, too, there is the development of the means of putting these ideals into practice, which includes such things as the accumulation of useful inventions, which until recently came slowly, and the resulting improvement of economic conditions. Thus, to take a single example, the abolition of slavery, and of conditions of labor no better than those of slaves, was brought about not only by the growth of sympathy and the slowly dawning conviction that it is wrong to hold one's fellows as chattels or to exploit them mercilessly, but also by the increasing use of mechanical power and the invention of labor-saving machinery. These same practical improvements have made possible the lightening of the burdens of those domestic animals who with scant recompense have long shared our heaviest tasks. Although the saint and the dreamer will deprive self of comforts and endure hardships in order to express in his or her manner of living convictions which spring from the inmost self, the average human is reluctant to deny comforts and pleasures for a moral purpose; so that the improvement of relations with other beings depends largely on the development of morally more acceptable means of providing the satisfactions that people crave.

This situation leads us to question whether we are here dealing with an improvement that can properly be called moral. Because people prefer to work their farm with machinery rather than with driven slaves, we cannot immediately infer, without further investigation, that they are morally or spiritually at a higher level than their ancestors who did not scruple to exploit bondsmen. Their preference for machinery might be caused merely by its greater productive capacity and the economies it effects. Deprived of mechanical servants they might, if they could, acquire human chattels and treat them as harshly as any ancient slave driver. Perhaps the only way to test this point would be to destroy machinery, revoke the laws prohibiting slavery, and observe subsequent developments. Yet even in the absence of such experiments, I think it evident that a certain proportion of the advances which we are tempted to classify as moral are not that at all, but merely economic; they result from altered external circumstances rather than from heightened moral sensitivity. At the same time, I am convinced that this is by no means the only factor involved in the advances we are now discussing. There seems to have been a concomitant general elevation in moral tone, brought about by the very improvements in economic and social arrangements, although, as we have already seen, among the moral nobility of humanity it long antedated these improvements. All that we can do is to call attention to these two contrasting factors involved in apparent moral advances; it is impossible to assess them with accuracy.

It is not my purpose here to repeat the oft-told tale of the slow but steady infiltration of moral ideals into the social practices of humanity. Lecky,[4] Sutherland,[5] and others have traced the gradual advance of moral sentiments in Western civilization in such matters as the treatment of women and children, the condition of slaves and the abolition of slavery, the care of the sick and aged, the administration of justice, the treatment of convicted criminals, the fate of captives in war, and many other departments of social and individual practice. This progress has not been uniform and continuous in all parts of the world, or even in its most favored regions; but many relapses have been caused by barbarian invasions, civil strife, or the deterioration of economic conditions. Yet there can be no doubt that humanity has advanced a long way even in the five or six thousand years that separate us from the dawn of history—a short period as geologists and paleontologists measure time. In order to be assured of the reality of this improvement, it is only necessary to reflect upon the contrast between the condition of the lowest savages dwelling in small bands of related individuals, who viewed with deep distrust or implacable hatred the members of every other group, and our own ability to travel in safety over immense stretches of territory, through millions of people personally unknown to us, finding everywhere the protection of law and often help when in need.

If we are filled with shame and disgust by the contemplation of the political history of humanity, with its endless tale of treachery and deceit, carnage and destruction, the moral history of our species has an opposite effect, bringing a note of solace and promise. Whether we pay attention to the expression of moral ideals or daily practices, we discover much to raise our courage and give us hope for the future. Although we are far, very far, from the perfect realization of the best teaching of more than two thousand years ago, we have risen high above the lowest stages of savagery. If in the present century we witness on the whole a decline in the world's moral tone, a survey of the past gives us reason to hope that this is only another of those periodical depressions in a slowly rising curve of which history affords us other examples. For when we consider the whole breadth and depth of moral phenomena, the wide diffusion of moral endeavor in space and time, we can be sure that we are not dealing with sporadic outbursts of zeal nor with the expression of irrational whims, but that we witness a steady evolution brought about by a creative energy that pervades the whole of humanity and the whole realm of living things. And if its advance has not been more rapid, it is because of the countless obstacles and resistances which it must slowly and painfully overcome.[6]

7. Analytic Ethics, Its Limitations and Value

The second major branch of ethics is interpretative rather than constructive, theoretical rather than practical. It is concerned less with the description of moral conduct than with understanding its causation, and it stands in much the same relation to practical morality as the atomic theory to the observable phenomena of chemistry and physics or as psychological doctrines to human behavior in general. Thus, it is more closely allied to science than to art, although it ranks with the interpretative rather than the descriptive departments of science. But its closest affiliation is with philosophy and psychology, and the most important contributions to the subject have been made by philosophers who felt the necessity to round out and give point to their system or world view with some consideration of moral phenomena, deriving them by preference from their favorite cosmological or psychological theory.

Western philosophers who have discussed ethics have not, on the whole, been people of outstanding moral sensitivity, nor have they possessed a moral vision much in advance of the more enlightened section of their contemporary society. To find the highest expression of moral ideals in Western civilization, we must turn to some of the poets and religious writers rather than to the authors of ethical treatises, for the philosophers who wrote them have in general been more eager to explain the moral phenomena that their society displayed than to rise to hitherto untrodden heights of moral grandeur.

Thus it happens that Western ethical thought has, by and large, been analytic rather than synthetic, explanatory rather than constructive. Western moral philosophers have been more interested in discovering how it happens that people have certain moral notions and why we consider certain things to be right, than in developing a higher concept of rightness or goodness. They have been more concerned with investigating the anatomy, the physiology, and the genealogy of morals than in visualizing the form and stature they will ultimately attain, more eager to define such moral terms as "good" and "right" and "duty," and to provide a rational or logical foundation for the prejudices they happened to receive from their social ambience, than to widen the scope of moral endeavor. This is clearly revealed by David Hume, who wrote: "The general opinion of mankind has some authority in all cases; but in this of morals it is perfectly infallible."[7] In the final acceptance of conventional modes of thought and practice, Hume followed the usual course of skeptics; but other philosophers, while not so frankly avowing their adherence to conventional morality, have on the whole been equally content to follow it.

This conclusion is readily confirmed by a survey of Occidental ethical thought. For all their intellectual penetration, Plato and Aristotle hardly rose above a municipal concept of society; their moral outlook was in effect circumscribed by the narrow boundaries of the Greek city-state to which they were accustomed from childhood. If mere force of intellect could have fashioned a more comprehensive moral ideal, certainly these masters of thought might have accomplished this. In the seventeenth and eighteenth centuries, when cities had merged into nations and enlightened individuals began to think of themselves as "citizens of the world," the prevailing moral concept was one that embraced all humanity. This concept was the outgrowth of the best thought and feeling of the age rather than the creation of an individual thinker who reached it through the consideration of the essential nature of morality. Even one so incisive as Immanuel Kant busied himself establishing a rational foundation for the moral notions he received from his ambience rather than developing a wider and nobler moral ideal.

If, on the contrary, we examine the highest moral ideals that humanity has achieved, we find that they are not the deliberately reached conclusions of the most penetrating thinkers, nor arrived at by the most profound trains of thought. The later Stoics cherished a moral concept far superior to that of the earlier Greek philosophers, yet they were in general less fertile thinkers. Albert Schweitzer in two steps reached a moral vision far superior to that which resulted from the laborious synthesis of Spinoza or the penetrating analysis of Kant.[8] India produced at an early date a moral outlook broader in scope than anything which has until quite recently emerged in the West, yet the steps by which it grew are lost in the mists of antiquity. They supported their moral teachings by the doctrine of the transmigration of souls, yet Schweitzer managed to reach a rather similar position without reference to this ancient belief.

It seems fair to conclude that a moral ideal is not, or not primarily, a product of deliberate philosophizing. The germ of it is already within us when we begin systematically to think about the subject. Our moral philosophy is an effort to provide rational support for an intuition which is not itself the child of reason. We strive to build up a foundation beneath an image which is already present, floating vaguely through our minds. No ethical theory which fails to support this vision of the good life, no matter how closely it may be reasoned, will finally satisfy us. Philosophical investigation serves to define, to clarify, to make consistent and articulate our moral ideal—and this is an immense advantage—but it does not create it. The germ of all morality is an intuition. The Intuitive School of ethics has been striving toward a fundamental truth, but one most difficult to seize.

Even if we were to conclude that our growth in moral vision owes nothing to the painstaking psychological dissections and laborious reconstructions of philosophers, it would be wrong to cast aside analytic ethics as worthless. That for at least several millennia some humans have cultivated ideals which rise far above the current practice of their time is a well-substantiated fact; and if we have faith in causation and the continuity of the world process from the primal nebulae to the highest aspirations of humans, this fact must have causal antecedents. Although one who cherishes a moral vision will doubtless continue to hold it sacred whether or not its origin can be explained, he or she might find some satisfaction in understanding how it arose and how it is related to one's whole nature. Such knowledge may bring one confidence and a feeling of stability in the moments of doubt and hesitation, which are the common experience of everyone who has striven to advance a few steps beyond the supporting crowd. Moreover, insight into the psychological foundations of morality should be valuable to those who seek to communicate their vision to others.

If moral philosophers have so often been content with a narrow concept of the scope of morality, perhaps one reason for this is inadequate exploration of human nature and their consequent failure to discover all the motives which converge to support our moral endeavor. Or perhaps they preferred neatness of construction to moral grandeur; and for the satisfaction of showing their skill in deducing their whole moral system from a single first principle, they deliberately ignored a good share of the wealth of our moral nature. In order not to be guilty of the same narrowness, I shall in this book attempt a thorough survey of all those motives and psychic traits which seem to have significance for morality, and to clarify the meanings of the moral terms we must employ.

It is obvious that the immediate or primary object of ethics, as of any other science or study, is knowledge. But we desire some kinds of knowledge for their own sake, while other kinds are sought chiefly for their practical application. To know about the stars, the geological history of our planet, or the habits of the animals and plants that surround us, is satisfying in itself, even if it does not in any way alter the course of our lives. On the other hand, to learn carpentry if one does not intend to build houses or make furniture, to study pathology if one has no intention of applying the information in curing diseases, seems a wasted effort. Similarly, there appears to be little point in studying ethics unless one is prepared to modify one's conduct in the light of investigations. Although it may be gratifying to trace the orbit of a planet even if we cannot alter it by a hair's breadth, there can be little satisfaction in knowing that it is possible for us to live better and more harmonious lives if we take no steps to do so. Quite the contrary, the man or woman who is spiritually alive would find it intolerable to be assured that his or her conduct might be improved yet do nothing to improve it.

Hence, ethics is a dangerous study. As with any other investigation, we embark on it without knowing just where it will lead us. It may well be that we shall reach conclusions which will make it impossible for us to persist in our comfortable but morally unsatisfactory habits. Those who undertake the serious study of ethics should be aware that they incur the risk of making discoveries that will demand their strenuous exertion; and even if they refuse the challenge thus held forth to them, they will never, unless morally insensitive to an extraordinary degree, be able to continue in their old, easygoing ways with the same complacency as before. It seems but fair to warn those who approach this study of the risk they incur.

Chapter Two
The Moral Quality of the Cosmos

1. The Objective Criterion of Morality

WHEN WE VIEW the peculiar features of the moral life as we know them in ourselves, they appear to us altogether unique, without counterpart in the nonliving world, possibly even without close parallel in other animals. Indeed, it is only in our individual selves that we can taste the full flavor of moral experience and detect all the subtle feelings associated with moral endeavor. In what other way could we know that insistent pressure, seeming to surge up from the depth of our being and often impelling us to perform some act which goes against our spontaneous inclinations, which we designate by the word "duty" or some similar term? Where else than in our own minds could we follow all those complicated maneuvers of thought, those marches and countermarches of anticipation, which precede a decision on some difficult question whose consequences are momentous to self or others? How could we know the full significance of words like "foresight" and "choice" if not ourselves endowed with these faculties? Could we ever imagine the sentiments which impel us to forgo some pleasure or personal advantage for the benefit of another being, if we had not felt them in our own breast?

The distinctive subjective features of the moral life have strengthened the view that morality is peculiar to humanity and there is nothing corresponding to it beyond humanity—save possibly in the angels, of whom we lack positive information. This view has two unfortunate consequences, one theoretical, the other practical. In the first place, it discourages the endeavor to trace the course by which the moral consciousness arose and to discover its intimate connection with widespread cosmic processes. This failure to recognize the deeper roots of morality makes us draw a sharp and scarcely passable boundary between humanity, which has the glory and the burden of the moral sense, and all other forms of being, in which we can detect no corresponding sentiments. Hemmed in by this high wall raised by our own prejudices, we feel isolated and solitary in a world which reveals nothing comparable to that which often seems the most significant peculiarity of humanity.

Isolation leads to estrangement; presently we come to suspect that this larger nonhuman world, wherein we detect no trace of morality, is not only indifferent but actually hostile to our moral aspirations. Hence arises a feeling of depression, of hopelessness, of futility and even despair, which robs us of much of our moral force. Some thinkers have stubbornly defended the uniqueness of humanity and above all of its moral sense, feeling that by emphasizing the differences which separate humans from the other animals they exalt our worth and lift us to a higher level. But this is mistaken zeal. Our first duty is to learn the truth, whether it prove agreeable or the reverse. But we should be happy if the facts point to an intimate connection between our highest moral aspirations and universal processes, for if thereby our egregious human pride is humbled—a wholesome experience—our moral energy will be greatly enhanced by the mere recognition of its cosmic foundation.

But in order to trace the connection between human morality and cosmic processes, we must view both from the same side. We find the greatest difficulty in recognizing the similarity of phenomena which we know only subjectively to those that we know only objectively. Until we examine from the same standpoint human morality and parallel developments in the larger world, we shall never reveal their close relationship. Since we cannot know other animals, and far less inanimate systems, from the subjective point of view, our only recourse is to examine our own behavior and that of other components of the world, lifeless no less than living, from a wholly external standpoint. Only after we have decided what, objectively viewed, is the distinguishing feature of human morality, can we look for resemblances between it and certain nonhuman phenomena. When we have done this, it will be proper to examine the subjective features of our morality and to surmise—we can do no more—how far they are represented in nonhuman animals or even in lifeless systems.

How then could an intelligent observer, unable to communicate with us in any way, possibly with an affective life so different from ours that he could not even imagine the emotions and aspirations that stir our breasts—how could such an observer recognize the presence among humans of that which we designate by moral goodness or some equivalent term? What are the objective criteria of morality? I believe that the observer we have imagined would look above all for *continuing harmonious association*. Wherever he discovered that two or more individuals, more or less intimately associated with each other, continued to thrive, he would recognize what we designate as moral conduct, and when in their interactions one suffered injury or loss, he would suspect that morality was imperfect or lacking. Continued study would reveal that whenever two individuals who have much to do with each other continue to prosper, there is a certain reciprocity in their intercourse. Although it may not be necessary that in every transaction between them there is an equitable exchange of services or goods, in the long run what A does for B tends to be balanced by what B does for A, whether the benefits that each receives from the other are given directly or flow from one to the other by a circuitous course, perhaps with a number of intervening links in the cycle. The chief exceptions to this *reciprocity* would occur when the first individual differs greatly from the second in strength or resources, as in the case of a parent and a little child, or a healthy person and a sick one. In such a situation, the flow of benefits may be almost wholly from the stronger to the weaker; but in the measure that the latter approaches his or her benefactor in strength, the relationship between the two would pass from one of dependence to one of reciprocity.

Closer observation would reveal that all the activities of those who dwell together in harmony tend to form a coherent pattern. The various occupations of the same individual are adjusted to each other with measure and proportion, and no single activity is continued to the point where it obstructs other necessary activities and perhaps so seriously disturbs the vital equilibrium that death ensues. Likewise the whole course of life of one individual would be such that surrounding individuals would be benefited rather than injured by his or her presence. Thus the several individuals who compose any moral community form a coherent system in which each strengthens the whole, while at the same time his or her own life is enhanced by inclusion in this whole. And the wider this system, the greater the number and variety of individuals embraced by it and the more perfect they become, the higher the grade of morality which the observer would recognize.

2. Examples of Continuing Harmonious Association

If we look about us in the nonhuman world for examples of the continuing harmonious association which we take as the objective criterion of a moral society, we find an almost embarrassing wealth of material. Each more complex living thing is itself such a system in miniature, for it contains a large number of cells and a diversity of organs which cooperate closely together for the benefit of the whole, upon the prosperity of which the existence of each part depends. Since each organism is a sort of community, an animal society might be regarded as a community of communities; and we find, especially among insects, numerous examples of populous societies, which may endure as long in terms of the life span of their members as human nations, and in which the harmony and cooperation among individuals is certainly no less than in most human societies.

But the grandest example of the sort of association we are now seeking is the solar system, which is the largest coherent system that we know in some detail. This far-flung association consists of many bodies, ranging in magnitude from the Sun itself through the planets of various sizes to their numerous satellites and the even smaller asteroids. Although separated by distances vast in comparison with their own diameters, the several members of the solar system do not move in independence of each other but are linked together by the closest bonds, so that the course of each is determined by the presence of the others to such a degree that the existence of hitherto unknown planets has been revealed by irregularities in the orbits of those that were already under observation. The whole system displays that combination of freedom with order which is the aspiration of a rational life. While each swiftly moving planet and satellite follows a set course, it is never thwarted or opposed by any of its neighbors, but for immeasurable ages has circulated without impediment in the wide space available to it; so that doubtless if, as the ancient philosophers believed, the stars and planets were divine sentient beings, each would feel itself perfectly free and unconstrained in all its movements. Thus, while dwelling in harmony with all its celestial neighbors, each planet has been able to express its potentialities without interference from the others.

Because of their great distance from us, we can hardly surmise what forms the creative energy has brought forth on the other planets. On the Earth it has produced sublime mountains and wide oceans, the loveliness of clouds, the constantly renewed splendor of the rainbow, and innumerable beautiful crystalline formations. But it is chiefly by means of the living things that it has engendered that Earth has succeeded in covering its broad surface with countless graceful forms. This rich development of life is wholly dependent on the radiant energy which the Sun, from its immeasurably greater resources, continues to pour forth without stint to its attendant planets, as a generous parent showers benefits upon his children. Our satellite the Moon, and the nearer planets, contributes each within its means to the beauty of Earth by embellishing the nocturnal sky with their shining forms, to which are added the contributions of myriad distant stars. And Earth itself is a brilliant luminary in the sky of the neighboring planets.

It would be difficult to find a more perfect model of a moral community than the solar system itself. The observer unable to detect the motives or follow the subjective processes which underlie human conduct could hardly fail to be struck by the great resemblance between this system and a human community which had achieved the most admirable morality; for we have supposed that our observer is too discerning to permit differences in size and duration to distract his or her attention from fundamental similarities. We to whom our difficult decisions, and the severe restraints we must at times impose on strong impulses, seem to constitute the distinctive features of the moral life might take exception to this comparison, insisting that the resemblances between the solar system, or any lifeless system, and a moral community are superficial, because only in ourselves can we detect the peculiar flavor of moral endeavor. We might agree that the sun and planets furnish a schema of what a moral society should be, even if there is no real connection between them. But if it could be demonstrated that the order in the cosmos at large and that in a human community are outcomes of the same process, we would be constrained to admit that their resemblance is more than accidental. Although it would still be true that we must strive to fulfill our moral aspirations by means peculiar to ourselves, we might then be fortified in our devotion to these ideals by recognition of their venerable ancestry and wide connections.

3. Harmonization

A single process, harmonization, activates the Universe from it prime foundations in space and matter to its highest expressions in the realm of mind, building from discrete entities patterns which tend to increase indefinitely in amplitude, complexity, and coherence. Harmonization is not the same as biologic evolution, whose course has been immensely complicated by collisions between patterns growing from separate centers; but it is the moving force in evolution, and without it there would be no progressive development. Although certain forces recognized and measured by physicists, such as gravitation and electromagnetic attractions and repulsions, have contributed to the creation of these patterns, the connection between them is not evident; we have not yet succeeded in explaining gravitation in terms of electricity, nor electricity in terms of gravitation. The basic similarity of the process in all its phases points to a single unitary cause, whose ultimate nature still eludes our scientific investigations; and this source of harmonization appears to be the divine or godlike component of the Universe. Although this is not the place for a full exposition of harmonization, it seems necessary to call attention to some of its salient features. Without a clear comprehension of the process we may fail to understand the close connection between moral endeavor and its antecedents in the living and lifeless worlds.

Whether the ultimate constituents of matter are particles in any clearly conceivable meaning of this word is an unanswered question. Yet it is certain that fruitful attempts to understand the structure, behavior, and transformations of matter take the form of atomism, and the great value for experimentation of some of the newer versions of this theory has firmly established its position in scientific thought. Whatever matter may be in itself, we can hardly think profitably about it without visualizing it in the guise of minute particles with definite properties that are constant for each variety of matter. According to the widely accepted modern view, atoms are not the solid, indivisible bodies that Leucippus and Democritus visualized, but compound entities comprised of three basic units:

protons that bear positive electric charges, much smaller electrons that are negatively charged, and neutrons about equal in mass to the protons but electrically neutral. Each elementary substance like hydrogen, carbon, or gold is a collection of an immense number of atoms, each of which contains, within narrow limits, the same number of each of the three kinds of particles. Those whose chemical behavior is the same, but whose slightly different atomic weight suggests that they contain a somewhat different complement of the ultimate particles, are known as isotopes of the same substance.

The three kinds of particles in each atom appear to be arranged in a definite pattern, with the smaller electrons circulating around the relatively massive nucleus composed of protons and neutrons, somewhat as satellites revolve about a planet or planets about the Sun. It seems permissible to think of an atom as a miniature solar system, repeating on a scale inconceivably small certain salient features of the pattern, which the solar system presents to us on a scale whose vastitude staggers our imagination. If, as seems not unlikely, the three sorts of ultimate particles were not at first combined in definite structures, but at a later stage altered conditions permitted them to associate in the form of atoms, this formation of coherent patterns from discrete entities is an example of harmonization. It was the first step in building up the cosmos, and all the more complex forms are dependent on this primal order.

The next step in harmonization is the synthesis of molecules from the atoms. Although simple molecules, like those of atmospheric oxygen and nitrogen, are composed of two or more atoms of the same kind, the more complex molecules are formed of several kinds of atoms, and sometimes of a large number of each kind. It appears that each chemically pure substance, whether water, or cane sugar, or a particular kind of protein, is a collection of molecules, each of which contains the same number and kinds of atoms joined together in the same pattern. All the more complex sorts of molecules require for their formation moderate temperatures and concentrations of matter. Hence they cannot arise in the terrific heat of the incandescent stars; and in the denser of these stars, whose specific gravity far exceeds that of any matter known on earth, it is probable that even complete atoms, with their full complement of electrons, cannot persist. The more complex molecules are even less able to arise in interstellar space, whose vast amount of matter is very thinly diffused and at extremely low temperatures. The surface and outer layers of a cooling planet offer, as far as we know, the conditions most favorable for the genesis of complex molecules.

Hence it is evident that harmonization had an immense preliminary task to perform before it could produce molecules of the size found in the more complex inorganic salts. First, the atoms themselves had to take form as the ultimate particles fell into definite patterns under the influence of their own electrical forces. Then the matter contained in our solar system was rounded off into Sun, planets, and satellites by the energy that we call gravitation, which is primarily a property of space. Only when some of the members of the solar system had acquired suitable temperatures could harmonization produce the more complex molecules. Many of these molecules, as those in a variety of mineral salts, are highly stable at temperatures such as prevail at Earth's surface. In them each atom seems to have its definite position and function in relation to the whole, yet to maintain its individuality in the little orderly society which it helps to form. Such a molecule, which may have existed unchanged in some rock that was laid down hundreds of millions of years ago in the Cambrian era, offers us an excellent example of that continuing harmonious association which is the only objective criterion of morality.

From atoms like those of carbon and sulfur, or more often from molecules like those of water and common salt, crystals are built up. In them the constituent particles are aligned in a definite order like bricks in a wall; and they preserve this arrangement with great constancy, which is what distinguishes the crystalline state from gases, liquids, and amorphous solids, in which the atoms or molecules move more or less freely in relation to each other. If formed in favorable conditions, each crystal has a definite, geometrical shape, which is often of great beauty, as in the endlessly varied hexagonal crystals of snowflakes. Many crystals when shattered fall apart in fragments each of which has the shape of the original mass, affording a vivid demonstration of the structural regularity, which pervades the whole formation.

Since atoms and molecules are individually too small to be seen even with a microscope, crystals are, on the ascending scale, the first products of harmonization that are visible to the human eye. In a vast variety of glittering, colorful gems, in the frost flowers that form on a window pane in freezing weather, in snowflakes, they show us that harmonization tends to produce beauty on a small scale no less than in the clouds, the rainbow, and the starry heavens. As we follow it upward from crystals to more complex organic forms and the things they make, we find that the creation of beauty is one of its outstanding accomplishments. From ancient times the good has been compared with the beautiful. If we ask what moral goodness and sensuous beauty have in common, this seems to be unity in multiplicity, the arrangement of the parts of a complex pattern in such a way that they harmonize with each other and with the whole. Since we recognize beauty in evanescent things like a rainbow and a song, it does not, like a moral order, require a *continuing* harmonious association; yet its value is greatly enhanced for us when it is enduring.

Long after the older crystalline rocks were formed on the cooling surface of our planet, living things appeared and left their traces in the sedimentary formations. How life arose is a question for which at last we are beginning to have probable answers. But it is obvious that in living things harmonization, the process which had been going forward since the cosmos began to acquire form and regularity, entered a more intense phase; and this more concentrated activity of harmonization is what chiefly distinguishes life from lifeless matter. Even the smallest and simplest of living things contains a greater variety of atoms, arranged in more complex patterns, and the continued existence of each compound part is more closely dependent on the whole, than in any lifeless system of comparable extent. The molecules in organic bodies, especially those of proteins, are of a size and complexity without parallel in nonliving matter; and nowhere else in nature will one find such a variety of chemical compounds in so small a compass as in a living body, whether vegetable or animal. Moreover, the great variety of activities carried on by all these heterogeneous parts working in closest cooperation distinguishes a living organism from all lifeless systems. The harmonization that gives form and coherence to a living body might be called its enharmonization.

The attributes, which sharply distinguish a living from an inorganic body, are found in the simplest organism visible under the microscope; but the larger multicellular animals and plants, with their great variety of distinguishable parts, give us a more vivid apprehension of what harmonization accomplishes. Such an organism is composed of a vast number of cells, each in itself a formation of great complexity, conjoined in tissues of many sorts; and of these tissues a variety of organs are formed. All of these cells, tissues, and organs must work together in closest harmony to carry on the vital activities of the organism and preserve its life. Perfect balance between all its parts and functions is the condition of health; and when any one of the many constituents of an animal exceeds or falls short of its allotted task, sickness results, perhaps death. Thus the prosperity of the whole organism depends on the harmonious association of its parts, and the continued existence of each part is bound up with that of the whole; for when the animal dies, if only through the failure of a single one of its many organs, every other part ceases to function, and as a rule the whole complex fabric promptly decays.

If ever we are in doubt about the meaning of morality, we need only think of our bodies when in fullest health, how arms, legs, eyes, ears, mouth, stomach, heart, lungs, and kidneys work together in concord for the benefit of a whole, on whose welfare the continued prosperity of each of them depends. The very diversity of these cooperating organs reminds us that sameness in all its members is not a necessity of a moral community. On the contrary, unlike units can work together no less than similar units, and indeed their very differences, whereby one complements another, often facilitate their cooperation. Perhaps the close dependence of all its movements on a single will would seem to make the animal body an unsatisfactory prototype of a moral society, which is the more admirable in the measure that its members enjoy freedom yet preserve harmony. But only a minor part of all the body's manifold activities is controlled by the will; and, originally at least, these activities were just those in which subordination to the central nervous system was most necessary for the prosperity of the whole community of organs which compose the animal body.

Wherever minds occur, they are built up and enriched by a process which closely parallels that which we have traced in lifeless and living matter. The most elementary content of consciousness appears to be a sensation, which may originate either in the external sense organs or in deeper portions of the body. When we view an object, each point on its surface sends off trains of light waves, which jostle each other in a disorderly crowd as they swarm through the pupil into an eye. Spread out by the crystalline lens to form on the retina an inverted image of the object, the light waves excite many separate rods and cones. Yet the countless independent vibrations, stimulating so many different nerve endings, produce in consciousness a single impression, in which, moreover, the slightly differing images in the two eyes are united into one figure that reveals solidity or depth.

However many details our subsequent analysis can pick out in the tree, person, or mountain which lies in our field of vision, we first become aware of it as a whole, which for consciousness is usually prior to its parts. In the instant of time which elapses between the excitation of our retina by the light and our awareness of the object which sent forth this light, and in a manner we do not understand, a multitude of discrete vibrations have been gathered together to produce a single impression. This is a typical example of harmonization, which everywhere fuses discrete entities into a coherent whole. Similarly, when we hear a noise, whole trains of aerial vibrations stir up complicated movements in each ear, yet we become conscious of all this disturbance as a single sound. By a still higher synthesis, which is wholly independent of the hearer's will, the multitudinous notes of an orchestra are presented to consciousness as a melody, which has for the mind a unity that a physical analysis of the sound waves might fail to detect. Likewise in tasting, smelling, and feeling with the fingers, many separate physical events on a microscopic scale are reported to consciousness as a single sensation.

But each developed mind contains more than a multitude of discrete sensations or memories of them. By the further exercise of its synthetic activity, similar impressions are grouped together, giving rise to universals or general ideas to which we apply names like "tree," "house," or "person." Further synthesis gives us concepts of a higher order, as when from experience of many different sorts of animate creatures we form the idea of an animal, and by recognizing certain similarities in both animals and vegetables we arrive at the notion of a living thing. Ceaselessly driven by its own creative energy, the active mind is constantly uniting its impressions under ever more inclusive headings. It forms theories to account for the manifold particulars of experience and tries to achieve a comprehensive worldview or system of philosophy. In all these creative endeavors, the mind is impelled by a demand to give coherence to its contents, and in the measure that it succeeds in this attempt it is satisfied and claims to have found truth. Where this coherence is obviously lacking, it is discontented and stands self-accused of falsehood. The building up of a coherent pattern of thought is an instance of harmonization not unlike the construction of a living body from materials which were at first scattered through the environment without any organic unity. Coherence is necessarily the criterion of truth, because the thirst for truth is simply the demand for the coherence of its contents imposed upon the mind by the process which constitutes it. Truth is the counterpart in the intellect of a moral order in a human community; in one case we have harmony among ideas and in the other among persons.

4. Moral Endeavor a Special Mode of Harmonization

Our conscious moral endeavor carries a step farther the process we have traced from the simplest constituents of matter to complex organisms and their intellectual activities. The ultimate particles join together in a smaller or larger community called an atom, which is conceived as a patterned structure whose existence depends on the harmonious integration of its component parts. Atoms of the same or more often of different kinds band together to form molecules, which are frequently of great complexity yet made up of units so well adjusted to each other that they may endure for ages. A variety of complex molecules form a living cell, and of many such cells, tissues, organs, and organisms are composed. As in this long series we advance from level to level, the structural units become increasingly complex, but from beginning to end the process consists in the joining of separate entities into a coherent, harmonious whole, in which the component parts support rather than clash with each other. When minds arise, they are furnished by a process which closely resembles that which we have traced in the physical world, and which at its lower levels, as in the synthesis which results in the perception of an external object and even that which gives us generic concepts, is just as independent of the conscious will as the growth of our bodies. Only at the higher reaches of thought does harmonization become a deliberate, conscious endeavor to achieve a coherent grouping of the mind's contents.

It has become evident, I hope, that our moral endeavor is a continuation at a higher level of a process which has gone forward since the world began to acquire form and order. We whose life and health depend on the harmonious cooperation of the manifold parts of our bodies, whose peace and clarity of mind depend on the harmonious integration of the teeming contents of thought, are driven by the very movement that created us to strive ceaselessly to cultivate with the beings around us the same sort of harmonious relations that we find within ourselves when body and mind are at their best. We bring to this task faculties that were perfected by this very process of harmonization but which are not evident in the lifeless world, and whose presence even in the animals which most resemble us is not easy to demonstrate. Human moral endeavor demands above all intelligence, foresight, and deliberate choice, in the absence of which the distinctive features of the moral life would vanish. And since we cannot be sure that these particular mental capacities occur together anywhere save in ourselves, we do well to insist that morality is, strictly speaking, a purely human phenomenon, as far as we can tell. And yet at the same time it is necessary to acknowledge the close connection of our moral endeavor to those earlier phases of harmonization which prepared the way for it, and of which it is a continuation. We may do this by recognizing a *moralness* which pervades the cosmos from its prime foundations, and which leads, as will be shown in the following chapter, through the *protomorality* of nonhuman animals to the *morality* of humans. Our morality is, then, a particular mode of the universal moralness, in the absence of which it could never have arisen, and without whose continuing support it would be ineffective.

But the presence of intelligence and deliberate, foreseeing choice are not in themselves sufficient to constitute any animal a moral being. We know only too many instances of the application of this endowment to the pursuit of ends the reverse of moral. It is only when foresight and choice are dedicated to the increase of harmony that true morality begins to exist. Moral endeavor depends above all on the presence of a good or moral will, which uses intelligence as its instrument. The will to increase harmony is not created by intelligence but rather is an expression of the same movement which builds up a mind; for, as we have seen, the coherence which makes the mind an effective instrument of thought is a result of harmonization. The moral will, then, is the pressure upon consciousness of that very movement which gave order to the crude materials of the world, which constructs our bodies of particles of matter at first widely scattered through our environment, and which from many discrete sensuous excitations builds up clear perceptions and coherent systems of thought. We are moral because we are formed by a process which from its earliest beginnings produced that harmonious association which is the goal of morality.

In tracing the advance of harmonization, we learned that each synthesis served as the foundation for a further synthesis. Atoms, which we now believe to be complex entities, are the building blocks of molecules. These in turn serve to form crystals or, in a divergent line of development, the far more complex structures of living things. The earliest living things apparently consisted of a single cell, but cells eventually became structural units of the higher animals and plants. This movement continued until it created animals whose bodies could perform a great variety of operations and whose minds could reason, anticipate the future, and choose freely between alternative courses of action: a moral being was born. Such a being sometimes considers itself to be an end in itself, even the end of all ends. Yet, whenever it ceases to strive beyond itself, it becomes a prey to confusion and lassitude, which belie the assumption it has too carelessly made. If, from one point of view, it is an end in itself, from another it is an agent for carrying harmonization to yet higher levels.

In producing beings endowed with intelligence, foresight, and a moral will, harmonization provided for itself a powerful instrument of a sort which, as far as we can be sure, it previously lacked. At all earlier stages of the world process, harmonization seems to have worked wholly within the patterns it was forming; and although always directed toward the increase of concord, there is no evidence that it foresaw the form this harmony would eventually take. When two expanding patterns, each infused with harmonization, came into contact with each other, neither could appreciate in what direction the other was tending, or what it was striving to achieve. Frequently they clashed violently together; or at best they might accommodate themselves to each other in response to mutual pressure, as when two trees grow up close together; for neither could know the other's needs. But an intelligent being can survey itself and some other being from a single point of view, foresee at what points it and this other being are likely to collide, and plan a course of action which will eliminate, or at least diminish, conflict. Or it can so guide two or more other beings that the discord which threatens to arise between them is avoided or even converted into harmony. Moreover, without sacrificing its happiness or perfection, it can restrict its own activities on certain sides where conflict appears inevitable, to develop itself in some other direction where it will compete with nothing. By uniting discordant elements in a higher synthesis, the moral being can promote the advance of harmonization with an efficiency, which it hitherto lacked, thereby becoming a willing collaborator in this aeonian and beneficent process.

Chapter Three

The Protomorality of Animals

1. Transition from Cosmic Moralness to Human Morality

THE LAST CHAPTER demonstrated that the moral endeavor of humans carries forward at a higher level, in the peculiar circumstances of human society, and with the aid of minds able to foresee the future and compare alternative courses of action, a process which has been at work in the world from the earliest period that we can gropingly reconstruct, and which pervades the contemporary Universe from the smallest particles of matter to stars and planets. This is the process of arranging the components of the world in coherent patterns, in which alone order, relative stability, and growth are possible.

If current views of the structure of matter are sound, there is a fundamental similarity between the disposition of protons, neutrons and electrons in an atom, where each preserves its own identity yet behaves as an integral part of a larger whole, and the arrangement of planets and their satellites in the solar system, where each major body enjoys freedom of movement and the possibility of indefinitely continued existence yet acts as part of a coherent system. And without making a strained comparison, we can recognize a close resemblance between the behavior of the planets and satellites and that of people in a free and orderly society, where each leads his or her own life and works out his or her own destiny, yet avoids violent clashes with others, precisely because behavior follows a pattern whereby the needs of the individual have been adjusted to the welfare of the community. Thus we may recognize a moralness pervading the Universe, from atoms to stars and from crystals to humans; and of this cosmic moralness our conscious morality is one particular development.

If this view of a moralness pervading the whole creation is correct, there must have been a gradual development of our human morality, with all its peculiar features, through the whole series of simpler forms of life that connect us with the primitive bit of protoplasm that seems to have been our earliest ancestor. And it is reasonable to suppose that the successive stages of moral growth, through which our own lineage has passed, are represented more or less adequately by contemporary animals at various levels of development.

Either human morality grew gradually, or it was suddenly given to us, by some agent and in some manner that we can hardly imagine, at some definite date in the past. Not only the moral history of humanity, which traces the slow growth of moral sentiments and practices in the human species, but our knowledge of evolution and the principle of continuity, make us prefer the first of these alternatives. Admitting this gradual development, we are tempted to ask: When did our ancestors first become moral beings in the narrow meaning of the term? At precisely what point in the evolution of life does the moralness that pervades the Universe acquire the specific features of human morality? But, as in all slow and fairly uniform processes, such as a sharply defined turning point probably never occurred. Even if we could reconstruct in all details the moral development of the animals that evolved into humanity, it might be difficult to designate the date when human morality was born. At best, we might say, "Here is scarcely a trace of typically human morality," and then, viewing a stage many generations later, "Here the peculiar features of human morality are distinctly recognizable."

It is, of course, impossible to reconstruct the whole course of development of human morality. Even the bones of our subhuman ancestors have been too seldom preserved in geological formations, or too infrequently found, to enable paleontologists to follow in satisfactory detail the evolution of the physical features of *Homo* from the earliest primate stock. The monkeys and apes that today inhabit the warmer regions of the Earth are not our ancestors so much as our collaterals. Recent decades have brought forth a number of excellent studies of their habits by dedicated naturalists who have watched them for months or years amid the discomforts and hazards of the wild regions where they dwell.

Despite their forbidding aspect, the Mountain Gorillas with whom George Schaller lived proved to be gentle, peaceable animals, more amiable than chimpanzees, whose brutal slaughter of young baboons or, rarely, human babies and rampant sexuality reveal distressing tendencies in our closest extant relations.[1] Although on the whole, less intelligent than monkeys and apes, and farther removed from us in the evolutionary sequence, birds in their immense diversity provide some of our best examples of what protomorality can achieve in social relations. Often, even in the free state, living in close association with humans, and lending themselves readily to observation, they have been more widely and thoroughly studied than other terrestrial vertebrates. Accordingly, they will chiefly occupy our attention in this survey of the protomorality of animals.

2. Can the Conduct of Animals Ever Be Designated as Moral?

Before proceeding with our inquiry, we must, in the interest of the accurate use of terms, decide whether we can apply the designation "moral" to the conduct of animals, or any of it. In ancient times, Plutarch undertook to show, in an amusing dialogue, that animals, not devoid of reason, surpass humans in some of the moral virtues, including fortitude and temperance.[2] In the eighteenth century, Hume supported his psychological and moral views with brief discussions of the reason of animals, their pride and humility, their love and hatred.[3] Later, Spencer wrote a chapter on "animal ethics,"[4] and Alexander Sutherland contended, in an elaborate study, that morality is not exclusively human.[5]

One of the most strenuous and sensitive of modern field students of animal behavior, Fraser Darling, wrote of "the growth of a code of behavior which may have ethical qualities" among Red Deer and other higher animals who live in societies.[6]

Despite the long and imposing tradition that assigns moral qualities to at least the warmblooded animals, there is widespread reluctance to concede that the behavior of animals ever exhibits morality. Much of this resistance to the recognition of morality in animals is due to nothing more than our overweening pride, and the feeling that to recognize in other creatures attributes that we please to consider specifically human is to degrade ourselves to the level of the brutes. As though the worth of any being depended on anything except its own inherent attributes and the nobility of its conduct! Those who are led by empty pride to deny that animals can be moral may be dismissed without further comment.

But even sympathetic observers, with wide experience with free animals, often deny that they possess any sort of morality. "The moral being of man," wrote Viscount Grey of Falledon, "stands outside and apart from the wild life of nature. It is just because this wild life is amoral, not troubled by questions of right and wrong, that we find it so refreshing and restful."[7] After describing how the newly hatched European Cuckoo throws its foster brothers from the nest, E. A. Armstrong added: "The fact that humans can realize, as the birds cannot, the havoc wrought by the infantile impulses of the cuckoo, brings home to us more poignantly the loneliness of our status as the only beings on earth who enjoy the blessings and suffer the penalties of a knowledge of good and evil."[8] And Edmund Selous asked: "*Is* there right or wrong in anything? That is a point which the intensive watching of birds often raises. Established and unestablished—is it really more than that?"[9]

With so many respected names supporting opposite views, we shall be in good company whichever we accept. The solution of the dilemma depends wholly, I believe, on whether we judge by objective or subjective criteria. If we imagine an intelligent visitor from another planet who observes us and other animals in just the same way, without being able to communicate with any of the creatures studied, hence without knowing that for some thousands of years humans have earnestly discussed questions of right and wrong and written tracts and learned volumes about them—an observer, in short, who would perforce judge morality wholly by overt behavior—such an observer would, I am convinced, decide that many kinds of animals are no less moral than humans, and that not a few are more moral than the majority of people.

Ethics deals not only with the description of conduct, but even more with how it is determined. For us, who view the effort to achieve coordinated and integrated behavior not merely externally but also internally, the essential feature of morality is the choice between alternative possibilities of action. And this is more than being simultaneously aware of conflicting impulses or motives. We can be sure that animals are often torn between opposing motives, as when hunger draws them to food while fear or caution impels them to retreat; as when parental devotion is brought into sharpest conflict with self-preservation by the advance of some more powerful creature toward their nest or young. Diligent observers of animals have witnessed such conflicts of motives more often than they can recall. But what they can never witness is the internal play of feelings or thoughts at such critical moments, or on any other occasion. They can never know whether a bird or quadruped looks even a short way into the future, tries to foresee the consequences of the alternative courses open to it, weighs them against its own feelings and desires, and reaches a decision by this process. I know that certain philosophers, some of respected name, have confidently declared what animals think or feel, or what they can never think or feel; but however competent these philosophers may be in other spheres, when they make positive assertions on these questions that transcend human experience, they speak without knowledge.

However admirable the behavior of animals may appear to us, however irreproachable their conduct as parents or conjugal partners or members of a group, we can never be sure that their behavior at critical junctures is determined in the same manner as our own when we make moral decisions rather than blindly follow established custom or a momentary impulse. In view of this uncertainty, we do well to refrain from calling their conduct "moral," for thereby we assert the similarity of processes which may be quite different. On the not improbable assumption that the objectively moral behavior of contemporary vertebrate animals is determined, not in the same way as our own, but in the manner of our remote ancestors, that it represents a stage through which our lineage once passed, let us designate it as "protomorality."

This distinction should not make us undervalue the worth of many of the acts of nonhuman creatures. When we see an animal of whatever kind perform a service for its fellows or risk its life defending its young, we are filled with warm admiration. Such a deed, especially if it departs from the routine behavior of the species, strikes a responsive chord deep within us and reminds us of our brotherhood with this creature outwardly so different from ourselves. But presently a student of animal behavior tells us that the subjective state of the animal who performed this admirable act was probably quite different from what we spontaneously imagined; perhaps it neither foresaw the end of its action nor felt the sentiments of love and devotion which would have inspired us in corresponding circumstances. And a moralist further dispels our romantic illusions by reminding us that unless the deed was done with prevision of its end and after overcoming contrary impulses, it lacked merit. Where we saw a noble act that allied the doer to our own higher selves, we now see only the operation of a mechanism in which we might take a scientific, but never a moral, interest.

But this is to take hold of the matter by the wrong end. If our moral purposes had created for themselves organisms capable of performing devoted services for children and friends, we would be justified in regarding animals able to perform similar services without the corresponding moral sentiments as radically different from ourselves. The analogies in structure and behavior would in this case be accidental rather than indications of a common source. But the reverse is the true account: it is because we are, in the first place, organisms capable of performing acts of devotion for offspring and companions that we have developed these moral sentiments, which are the last refinement of a long evolution. Whether the bird or quadruped who did the deed that made us feel more akin to it had such sentiments or lacked them does not greatly alter the situation. The similarity between it and ourselves was real rather than fancied, and our spontaneous response was more revealing than our rational dissection. For the generous or heroic act of the mammal or bird stems from the same deep source in animal nature as our own generous and heroic acts. The two are identical in all save the distinguishing features of our peculiarly human morality, ability to foresee distant ends and to obey the better motive while pulled contrariwise by the worse.

3. Intraspecific and Interspecific Morality

As a further preliminary to our inquiry, we must emphasize a distinction which, although it seems obvious enough, is frequently overlooked, leading to much confusion in our thinking about the moral aspects of the behavior of nonhuman animals. Not only people of little education, but even most philosophic moralists, commonly judge a person's moral stature almost wholly by his or her conduct toward other human beings. Even the insistence that we treat with equal justice and compassion all members of our own biologic species is a relatively recent development in human ethics; except at the higher stages of culture, people have one code for members of their own group, and a sharply contrasting one for outsiders—the "law of amity" and the "law of enmity," to use Spencer's expressive terms. Even today, among the most enlightened nations, the undiscriminating treatment of all people, of whatever race or color, is a pious aspiration rather than a consistent practice. In dealing with other biologic species, few people do not even profess to apply the same standards that govern their relations with other humans. Indeed, they may stubbornly oppose the suggestion that moral principles are binding in this sphere. Although they may condemn wanton and pointless cruelty to animals, the majority of people see nothing wrong in killing or maiming them, even in torturing them, if they can allege some small practical advantage to themselves, or even if it affords brief amusement.

In our moral appraisals of the behavior of animals, we commonly fail to make this distinction of kinds. We judge their treatment of individuals of other species by the same standards that we apply to their treatment of individuals of their own species. We measure their behavior by a scale more rigorous and exacting than all but a few of the most sensitive moralists have ever thought of applying to our own conduct. When people see a jay plundering a sparrow's nest and devouring its young, they vehemently condemn the predator; yet, an hour later, they may with no qualms of conscience eat veal or lamb, forgetting that a cow or a sheep, as mammals like themselves, bear much the same relation to them as a sparrow to a jay. To avoid this surreptitious and confusing shift in the ethical criterion, we must distinguish an intraspecific and an interspecific morality, and confess that among ourselves only the first is much cultivated.

Some discerning naturalists have not failed to recognize the distinction that in all fairness we must make between an animal's treatment of others of its own biologic species and its treatment of members of a different species. In *The Charm of Birds*, Grey of Falledon told of a Great Tit who had entered a cage trap set in his garden for rats and "other small nuisances." In the same trap a Dunnock had also been caught; and the tit, probably entering later, had killed the other prisoner and eaten its brain. When visited, the trap contained the mangled remains of the Dunnock and the live Great Tit, "a patent and thriving murderer."

"What did you do with the horrible tit?" the Viscount was asked.

"Madam, I set him free, not feeling competent to assess his moral responsibility in the matter."[10]

The tit was certainly neither more nor less a cannibal than the human who eats the flesh of a monkey, a cow, or any other mammal.

When we decide which actions are right and which wrong among animals, we are perforce limited to objective criteria. We must judge them by what they do, not by what they say. It is as though we visited a land whose people spoke an unknown language. We could neither read their laws nor understand them when they recited their decalogue; but, by prolonged observation, patient and discerning, we might acquire a fairly clear notion of what these people held to be right and what wrong. If we saw that movable property, left unguarded, remained undisturbed until the owner returned for it, we would conclude that theft was considered wrong by them. If we surprised people in the act of stealing, their furtive manner might strengthen our confidence in this conclusion rather than lead us to suspect its accuracy. If we saw them caught in the act and attacked by indignant bystanders, or dragged off to be punished, we could no longer doubt that stealing was considered wrong. If, on the contrary, we learned that it was common for one person to enter another's dwelling and carry away whatever took his or her fancy, that this was done boldly and openly, we would conclude either that there was no individual property, or that theft was not regarded as a serious misdemeanor.

The wholly objective method of inquiry to which we are limited will not permit us to judge whether among animals there is such a great divergence between what they profess and what they do as with ourselves. But I wish to avoid even the implication that animals possess formal rules of conduct, either transmitted orally or impressed on their consciousness in some way that we do not understand. For them there are neither tablets nor scrolls of the law. For them—or at least in our judgment of them—behavior and code of behavior are identical.

Right and wrong conduct, in most human societies, canter about property, the relations of the sexes, the treatment of dependent young, the performance of specific obligations, the truth or falsehood of the spoken or written word. We might also add moderation and its opposite, excess in personal habits, and kindness or cruelty toward animals of other kinds. Moral codes are multitudinous and diverse, and a much more detailed analysis of their contents might be made; but this summary treatment of moral categories will be adequate for our present purposes. Animals are, in many ways, simpler than our-selves, and act in a more direct fashion. Besides, without being able to exchange thoughts with them, it would be difficult to sort questions of right and wrong according to their finer shades.

4. Respect for Property and Stealing

Animals, like ourselves, may possess property of two kinds, real and personal. Their real property consists of their living areas or territories which they defend from others of their own species, and their nest sites, dormitories, or lairs when these are holes in trees, burrows in banks, crevices in rocks, or of other immobile forms. The personal or movable property of most kinds of animals is limited to the straws, sticks, feathers, or other materials that compose their nests. A few species, notably the bower birds of Australia and New Guinea, and certain crows, jays, and magpies, own what we might call articles of luxury, such as shells, fragments of glass or china, small metal objects, flowers, colored fruits, and other bright and glittering baubles, which they arrange artistically in the "bowers" where they mate, place in their nests, or hide in secret caches. Certain woodpeckers, jays, nutcrackers, titmice, and nuthatches among birds and rodents and carnivores among mammals, possess reserves of food that they have stored away.

The same plot of land may belong to a human, a thrush, a sparrow, a warbler, and other birds, as well as to the quadrupeds and insects who may likewise claim it. The human ownership is certified by a deed registered in the public archives. The bird proclaims possession with song poured forth from a conspicuous perch. The mammal marks a domain with secretions. Doubtless the claim of each is equally valid, save as brute force makes one stronger than another. Each of the several owners may, in fact, exercise all the prerogatives of dominion without infringing upon the rights of another. The thrush that nests in my garden neither recognizes nor rejects the claims of the wren, the flycatcher, and the tanager to the same property; one mostly ignores the other. Likewise, I am generally ignored when, in the exercise of my proprietary rights, I gather the oranges or prune the shrubbery. But the thrush cannot afford to ignore other thrushes of the same species, because neither by the customs of people nor of birds can the same plot of ground have simultaneously two independent owners of the same kind. For each truly territorial bird, sole possession of an adequate area is of the utmost importance for winning a mate and raising a brood of young. Most exceptional is the behavior of the Red-backed Shrike, who, according to S. Durango, in Scandinavia attacks almost every bird of whatever kind that enters his territory.[11]

As H. Eliot Howard and many later observers have amply demonstrated, each male territory holder knows the boundaries which separate his own from neighboring plots and tends to respect them.[12] Trespassing is relatively rare, for if discovered the trespassing bird will be chased, and, if he resists, he will have to fight. In the conflicts that arise over violations of territorial boundaries, the bird on his own land nearly always wins. If he in turn invades his opponent's domain, the apparent relative strengths of the two are reversed, and the chaser becomes the fugitive. Were we in the birds' situation, we would say that when our rights were violated our sense of rectitude lent us force, whereas when we trespassed, our feeling of guilt made us cowards.

In an intensive study of the Horned Lark, Gayle Pickwell observed this vacillating behavior.[13] After the male larks have established well-defined territories, they fight each other only on the invisible boundaries which separate them. At the boundary line, two males "frequently strut before each other and often peck the ground furiously, like barnyard cocks, but all fighting is in the air. . . . Up they go, dash against each other, tumble over and over, an animated bundle of struggling feathers. Having indulged in wing to wing combat for a moment, they finish off with a most curious game of tit for tat; one chases the other for a few feet in the air, invades thus the flying one's territory; the pursued promptly turns pursuer and gets into his neighbor's territory, when the game is again reversed." The superiority of each combatant depends not so such on his intrinsic prowess as on whether he is on his own or the other's side of an imaginary line. On the snowy tundras of Greenland, N. Tinbergen watched similar pendulum like duels between male Snow Buntings, as they settled down on their breeding grounds in the spring.[14] Sometimes the battle, which seemed more like a game, would swing back and forth over the boundary line for nearly an hour without pause.

Likewise, M. M. Erickson found that in Wrentits in California "in all disputes observed, the one in possession has been the victor."[15] Since it is highly improbable that the one in possession was invariably the physically stronger individual, some other, non-physical force must come into play here. It is sometimes said that a bird on his own land is invincible by others of his kind. Although exceptions have been noticed in Red-winged Blackbirds and other species, this is approximately correct.

The same phenomenon has been observed in animals less highly organized than birds. K. Lorenz found that when two male stickleback fishes meet in battle, it is possible to predict with a high degree of certainty how the fight will end; the fish farther from his nest will lose the contest.[16] In the immediate neighborhood of his nest, even the smallest stickleback will defeat the largest one. Here again, psychic factors, far different from mere fighting ability, come into play and affect the outcome of the duel.

In matters of land tenure, birds and certain other animals appear to have something closely resembling our human feeling for right and wrong. Among diminutive Yellow-faced Grassquits in Costa Rica, fighting seems never to occur. Nevertheless, each male insists upon the inviolability of a small area around his covered nest and invites trespassers of his own kind to leave simply by flying toward them. They need no stronger notice that their departure would be appreciated. Other animals settle their differences by voice alone, as we shall see in section 6 of this chapter.

Although real or landed property is, on the whole, respected by birds and certain other animals, with what we have called personal or mobile property the situation is different. The theft of materials from occupied nests is widespread among birds. It is least likely to occur among members of the same territory-holding species, for the simple reason that before one individual can steal from another's nest it must invade the other's land, and it is likely to be attacked as a trespasser before it can become a thief. But, since the same area may be simultaneously held by a number of pairs of birds of diverse kinds, the territorial system is, in itself, no safeguard against the loss of nest materials to other birds.

I believe that the majority of nest-building birds are more or less guilty of such petty larceny, but some species are more addicted to it than others. A still unfinished nest is more likely to suffer depredations by neighboring builders than one that has been completed and contains eggs, because it is less constantly guarded, and, even more, because its materials, still loose and readily detached, are more easily removed than materials which have been carefully worked into a finished structure. Whether the presence of eggs ever causes a would be pilferer to desist from her intended depredations, I cannot say; but I know for a fact that Rufous-tailed Hummingbirds, when for some reason the females build exceptionally close together, will pull apart unguarded nests of others of their kind even when they contain eggs.

Among birds that breed in crowded colonies pilfering is rife. Almost everyone who has studied colonial-nesting birds, from penguins, herons, and terns to oropendolas, grackles, and rooks has commented on the habit. One might suppose that such wholesale larceny of the materials of nests would so diminish the reproductive efficiency of the colony that it would long ago have been suppressed by natural selection. Its very widespread prevalence among colony nesters points to the conclusion that, on the whole, it cannot be as harmful as it appears at first sight. Among Montezuma Oropendolas, weaving their long pouches in crowded clusters in a lofty treetop, one frequently sees a female try to pull away a strip of palm leaf or a fiber that dangles loosely beneath the unfinished nest of a neighbor. Sometimes, grasping the free end firmly in her sharp bill, she closes her wings and throws all her weight upon it in an effort to detach it. The hens' covetousness at times drives them to take an even bolder step. While a bird newly returned to the nest tree from a material-gathering expedition rests with her hard-earned fibers hanging from her bill, a lazy neighbor may seize the end of one and try to wrest it away. This creates a ludicrous situation: the rightful owner cannot even open her mouth to protest this outrageous behavior, for at the moment of doing so she would lose everything!

Such neighborly banditry seems never to lead to direct retaliation, although doubtless most members of the colony are by turns both robbers and robbed. No lasting enmity among neighbors appears to spring from it, and the thief does not lose status in the community. This habit of pilfering is not without certain beneficial consequences. It is not easy to detach a strong fiber that has been properly woven into the fabric of an oropendola's nest. This is attested by the fact that oropendolas, unlike many other birds, do not often use their own abandoned nests as quarries for material to build new ones. They find it easier to fly afar to strip fibers from green palm fronds and banana leaves. Accordingly, only carelessly attached strands are likely to be stolen, and slovenly builders are the chief victims of the practice. Thus, the prevalence of thievery discourages slipshod work and promotes careful finish just as, no doubt, the existence of thieves has made us humans more orderly and careful of our property.

In colonial-nesting birds whose cruder nests of sticks, straws, or stones are not woven into a tough fabric like the oropendolas' pouches, the need for one member of the pair to keep almost constant guard, from the time the nest is begun, to prevent the loss of materials, may be a positive advantage because it promotes the early establishment of a system of sentry duty, which later will be of the utmost importance in safeguarding eggs and nestlings, from the crows, gulls, skuas, and other marauders that commonly lurk around nesting colonies.

Allied to the pilfering of nest materials by birds that breed in colonies is the stealing of food. When a tern returns from the sea with a fish for its nestlings, another of its kind may swoop down and snatch it from the parent's bill, often succeeding in bearing away the prize, despite angry protests. This kind of thievery appears to be rarer than the theft of sticks and straws from nests, and apparently does not occur among land birds that nest in colonies, such as oropendolas, caciques, grackles, and weaverbirds, possibly because such birds bring to their nests items of food that are smaller and less conspicuous than fishes, and not so easily snatched away. Frigate birds, some gulls and sea eagles, habitually harass fishing birds until they drop or disgorge their food, but this comes under the heading of interspecific rather than intraspecific morality.

5. Relations of the Sexes

Day after day, I found five Red-capped Manakins in a certain spot amid the lowland forests of Panama, each on their customary perch. With their scarlet heads and vivid yellow eyes contrasting with their velvety black bodies, they were conspicuous despite their diminutive size; but by brisk calls, loud snapping sounds made with their wings, and bizarre antics, they did their best to make themselves more obvious. Much of their dancing and posturing displayed their bright yellow thighs, scarcely visible while the manakins perched in repose. The purpose of all this showmanship was to attract the modest olive-green females of their kind. Unlike most birds, manakins never pair. To the neutrally colored females alone falls the whole task of building the nests, incubating the eggs, and raising the young. The one reproductive function of the males is to fertilize the fe-males' eggs at the proper moment and, meanwhile, so to advertise themselves that they may be readily located by females who need them.

Then, one afternoon in March, I had the good fortune to be present at the exciting moment when a female arrived. She alighted unobtrusively on the slender horizontal branch where one of the five males regularly performed, and stirred him to frenzied exertions. Perching close beside her, he executed an amazing series of rapid about-faces. At each swift turn he flapped his wings loudly, and all the time he kept his lemon-colored pantaloons conspicuously exposed. After this acrobatic exhibition, he moved off a way and then began, with mincing dance steps, to slide along the branch toward his visitor, tail foremost, with his body inclined forward and his legs straightened to expose those yellow thighs. At his approach, the female sidled away; whereupon he flew out, looped about in the air, approached her flying with a loud flourish of wings, alighted upon her back uttering a high, shrill *eeeee*—and in a trice accomplished the vital purpose of all this acting.

And what were the four rivals doing while the favored one was engaged with the female? Did they rush in and try to wrest her from him? Nothing of the sort! Each was on his own perch, obviously greatly excited, calling and performing for all he was worth, but abiding rigidly by the "rules" of this courtship assembly and keeping out of the fortunate one's way. The female visitor had made her choice among the several males who tried to entice her to their perches, and that choice was final. Among free birds, the female nearly always selects her partner without coercion.

As I walked off through the high forest, I marveled at the self-control of these little manakins even when excitement was at its highest pitch. Many other birds have essentially similar systems of courtship, among them numerous other species of manakins, the Prairie Chicken and Sage Grouse of North America, the Ruff and Blackcock of Europe, many hummingbirds and birds of paradise. The nuptial exercises of the male Ruffs, once considered to be wild and desperate struggles, were shown by Selous[17] to be, in fact, well-regulated tournaments, in which the males display, meet each other momentarily in dashing but harmless encounters, and abide meekly by the choice of the females, called Reeves, at the end. Most naturalists who have carefully watched birds in these courtship gatherings, whether of little Golden-collared Manakins at their bare dancing courts beneath the undergrowth of tropical forest, or big Sage Grouse performing several hundred together on high, arid plains, have reported that, with rare exceptions, the most decorous order prevails, each rival acting his part in the conventional manner. Indeed, without strict adherence to the established pattern of behavior, such assemblages would degenerate into mad scrimmages that would defeat their purpose.

F. M. Chapman described the punishment that awaits a male Golden-collared Manakin who violates the etiquette of his kind by intruding upon the court where another displays.[18] A mounted "skin" of a male, set on a perch above a court, was at times attacked with such fury by the outraged owner that, if not promptly removed, it would soon have been demolished. But to demonstrate such behavior, Chapman was obliged to resort to the stratagem of the stuffed effigy. He never saw a living bird provoke a neighbor to such violence by remaining on the latter's court.

At the first glimpse, we are impressed by the strangeness of these mating systems so different from our own and from those of more familiar birds. More worthy of our wonder and admiration is the self-control that they demand. They presuppose a long period of development, an ancient culture that has contributed to the prosperity of a species. They would not be feasible without a corresponding morality, or something closely allied to it. They remind us how diverse self-perpetuating patterns of behavior may be, and that individuals should be judged by how well they conform to the pattern of their own species or culture rather than by standards alien to them.

Monogamy is the matrimonial system most common among birds. Migratory birds may mate for a single nesting, as in the Northern House Wren, or, more commonly, for the duration of a single breeding season, in which several broods may be raised. At its termination the pair is, as a rule, dissevered by the migratory journeys, in which the male usually precedes the female.

In the absence of the disruptive effect of long migrations made necessary by seasons of severe weather and scarcity of food, the nuptial bonds of birds are more enduring. A great many kinds of nonmigratory birds of the tropics, and not a few of extra tropical regions, are found in pairs at all seasons. Many of them take partners when only a few months old, long before they will breed. Although it is obviously not impossible that they should change mates frequently yet always have one, to all appearances these birds who are nearly always seen in pairs are constant to each other as long as they live; and this has been confirmed by a growing number of prolonged observations of identifiable individuals in families as diverse as albatrosses, geese and swans, crows and jays. The avian class as a whole tends strongly toward that lifelong constancy of nuptial partners which we regard as ideal. The chief obstacles to its attainment are the necessity to migrate and the numerical inequality of the sexes in the breeding population, which, arising from obscure causes in certain species, would with strict monogamy deprive many individuals of the more numerous sex of a share in reproduction.

Bigamy occasionally arises in species normally monogamous. A nesting female who loses her mate may attach herself to the already mated male on a neighboring territory. A temporary or local excess of females may lead males to contract alliances with several of them simultaneously. Although the males of species that are regularly polygynous seldom attend the nests, males who more or less accidentally acquire several mates may feed the young of all their partners.

Monogamous birds, of certain kinds at least, are guilty of occasional lapses from matrimonial fidelity. Among birds who guard nesting territories, the female, wandering beyond the boundaries of her mate's domain (of whose exact position she may be ignorant), may engage in an illicit affair with a neighboring male. Statistics of the frequency of such "stolen matings" are rarely available; obviously, such information would be difficult to gather for any kind of animal. In many tropical finches, tanagers, wood warblers, wrens, and other birds, of which the mated male and female are almost inseparable at all seasons, I would not expect these lapses to be at all common. Each female Laysan Albatross accepts only her own mate, fleeing from other males who rudely try to rape her. Common Eiders, and Herring Gulls appear to be equally chaste. "Stolen matings" appear never in themselves to cause the disruption of families. The jealousy of birds is not retrospective but is limited to the present moment. The temporarily unfaithful partner does not acquire a moral stain that makes him or her undesirable as a partner.

6. The Settlement of Disputes without Violence

Like humanity, species of animals differ in cultural level. Many are still in that barbarous stage, exemplified by humans in the twentieth century, in which they settle their differences violently. Notable among these are certain carnivores, ungulates, rodents, and gallinaceous birds. But many kinds of animals have learned to compose their quarrels by voice and posturing alone—by arbitration, we might say. This method of settling disputes is widespread among birds. E. V. Miller's careful study of Bewick's Wrens in California revealed that their conflicts over territorial boundaries are logomachies devoid of violence.[19] Long ago, Edmund Selous thought that among Oyster-catchers vocal duets were replacing fighting as a means of settling differences.[20]

The birds that I have most often watched contending nonviolently with others of their kind include antbirds, trogons, woodpeckers, and honeycreepers. Among the lovely little Blue Honeycreepers of tropical America, the disputants appear always to be of the same sex, either two azure-crowned males, or, more often, two modest greenish females. If other individuals are present, they are interested auditors who take no active part in the proceedings. The causes of the disputes have seldom been evident to me, but they seem very important to the diminutive protagonists. Facing each other close together, they repeat over and over again their nasal notes, at intervals punctuated by a clear monosyllable. They turn rapidly from side to side, flit their wings, and twitch their tails. Their debates appear to consist, like many of our own, largely of the monotonous reiteration of the same point. Finally, one of the two weakens and retreats; the other may then lunge at the vanquished, or pursue it in flight; but I have never seen them clash. Once I watched two female honeycreepers dispute in this manner for an hour.

What fascinating glimpses into the avian mind these purely vocal disputes give us! Monotonous they at times undeniably are; but human disarmament conferences are the same; and they have not, like these avian conferences, the redeeming virtue that they eliminate violence. Since in these disputes between birds a victory is won with never a test of physical force, we must regard it as a moral victory, or something closely similar.

A protracted discussion, such as I witnessed between the female honeycreepers, may, without a clash of bodies, reveal important differences in the protagonists. It was clear to me that the winner displayed greater energy and endurance than her opponent; she called more frequently and continued more persistently to repeat her notes and to posture. Energy and endurance are qualities of great moment in rearing a brood of young birds, as in the struggle for existence in all its aspects. An advantage of a purely vocal and demonstrative contest over violent fighting is that the contestant who happens to be slightly weaker comes off unscathed, fit to reproduce its kind. Although it may be inferior to the victor in certain aspects, it may, nonetheless, possess attributes worthy of perpetuation in the species. Thus, biologically no less than morally, the formal contents widespread among animals are preferable to brutal fighting. Few species are so firmly established that they can afford the needless sacrifice of individuals.

Among lizards, especially brightly colored diurnal species, contests between males often take the form of display and bluffing, so that injuries are rare. Among the nocturnal geckos, however, bright coloration is lacking, voice and hearing are well developed, and fighting at times becomes so violent that one of the contestants is killed. Among mammals, tiny shrews engage in noisy contests, and many disputes are settled by screaming alone. Howler monkeys of tropical American forests settle territorial conflicts by voice, in this respect having advanced considerably beyond their fellow primates who wear clothes and read newspapers. The male howler's larynx is so enormously developed that scarcely any other existing animal can produce so loud a vocal sound. Apparently, in the whole group of primates volume of noise adds to the cogency of arguments; whereas among birds, sweetness of tone and musical excellence are more effective. Even in animals that do not compose their differences by voice and posturing alone, much so-called fighting is merely formal, so that they might be said to fence with foils. In the intraspecific contests of animals, formality tends to replace relentless ferocity as evolution advances, with the notable exception of humanity.

7. Parental Behavior and the Question of Duty

We can imagine an animal no less conscious than ourselves, no less susceptible to discomfort and pain, yet in mind and body so perfectly adjusted to the normal conditions of its life that, without ever feeling perplexity, strain, or compulsion, it invariably follows the course which the most exacting morality would approve. It would be difficult to decide whether beings so closely resembling Wordsworth's:

> Glad Hearts! without reproach or blot
> Who do thy work, and know it not,

possessed anything corresponding to our morality, rather than blind hereditary adjustment to their circumstances. Only by observing their conduct when some accident upset this happy adjustment, so that they could not persevere in their accustomed paths except under the stress of weariness or pain or the clash of conflicting motives, could we throw light on this point. Similarly, with free animals, whose less rapidly changing lives have resulted in more perfect innate adjustment to recurrent situations than we find in civilized humans, only in exceptional circumstances do we detect adumbrations of a sense of duty. And it is chiefly in the breeding season, when, above all, other individuals are strictly dependent upon them, that we might gather evidence on this matter.

One who has watched many birds build their nests hardly doubts that, as a rule, the task is not burdensome. The male often sings as he works, and sometimes his mate also voices songful notes. In the tropics, where permanent residents can afford to devote a month or more to nest building, many kinds make their structures much larger and more elaborate than appears to be necessary for the accomplishment of their primary purpose, then continue to add to them throughout the period of incubation, until the eggs hatch and the young need to be fed. Evidently, they find building an agreeable activity. Incubation of the eggs may be a less enjoyable occupation. For creatures as active as birds, these intervals of motionless inactivity in the nest might become irksome. Nevertheless, I suppose that, on the whole, they find it not unpleasant. Male and even female birds of certain species sing while they sit upon the eggs; and at times the individual on duty is reluctant to relinquish its place to the mate who comes to relieve it. Bringing food to the young, up to a certain point, and when it can be easily found, also seems to be an agreeable occupation. This is suggested by male birds who are so eager to begin feeding that they bring food to unhatched eggs, or proffer to their sitting mates morsels that are rejected.

Thus, when all goes well, we have little reason to infer that nesting birds are held to irksome tasks by something corresponding to our sense of duty. But often all does not go well. Although nest building normally appears to be a happy occupation, sometimes when one is lost and the bird hurriedly constructs another to receive eggs soon to be laid, she appears to labor with a grim determination that must be wearisome. While studying Brown Jays, I often imagined that females, who cried loudly and, to human ears, complainingly while they incubated, were bewailing the disagreeable necessity that nature had imposed on them. Doubtless, such active birds would rather be foraging with their companions than sitting in dull immobility on their eggs.

Sometimes, especially in inclement weather, incubating birds continue to cover their eggs while hungry, and even when they would appear to be suffering acutely from a long-continued fast. Many marine birds, especially of the penguin and petrel families, remain on their nests for days or even weeks without eating; and some Emperor Penguins, who incubate single eggs on the ice in the frigid gloom of midwinter at the edge of the Antarctic continent, pass about two months in an absolute fast. Must not birds at times experience gnawing pangs of hunger, while they slowly become emaciated from lack of nourishment? Although in seasons of plenty to feed nestlings may be a pleasant occupation, during storms and at times of scarcity parent birds deprive themselves of food in order to nourish their young. Their actions, such as swallowing the excrement sacs voided by the nestlings instead of simply carrying them away, often strongly suggest hunger. Moreover, birds often lose weight while attending offspring.

If an activity is either enjoyable or mechanical, it may involve no feeling of duty or obligation; and no element of morality, in the narrower sense, need enter into it. But if strain, discomfort, or weariness arise, we must explain why the animal persists in its disagreeable task when it might do something more pleasant. Obviously, we cannot then apply the theory that to seek pleasure and avoid pain is the ruling principle in animal behavior, and that this system ensures the continuance of the species because, by means of natural selection, the pleasures have been adjusted to reinforce behavior that in normal circumstances contributes to this end, while the pains discourage harmful activities.

The only alternative to this explanation suggested by our human experience is that the painful or unpleasant activity is performed from a sense of duty or respect for a principle. When a human denies himself or herself some readily accessible pleasure or performs a disagreeable task without being the direct beneficiary, he or she does so from a feeling of obligation, or in conformity to social or religious mandates or personal standards of conduct. And it may be that he or she is able to follow the course that is less immediately gratifying only because of foreseeing that thereby his or her pleasures, happiness, or sense of fulfillment will be ultimately enhanced—a point that we must reserve for later consideration. At least, it seems obvious that strong allegiance to duty or principles of conduct implies foresight.

Nonhuman creatures, it is widely held, take no thought of the future but act solely in response to present factors, internal or external. If we accept this view, we cannot claim that when, despite hunger and cold, a bird remains sitting on its nest it does so because it foresees that its eggs will chill if left exposed, or that it deprives itself of food for the sake of its young because it knows that, if not adequately nourished, they will not develop into sturdy fledglings. Thus, we seem to be deprived of the only two explanations of the bird's observed behavior that have so far occurred to us.

But, in addition to a highly developed sense of obligation that takes account of remote consequences, I believe that we may recognize a simpler, more primitive feeling of duty which reveals itself by faithfulness to the present task or steadfastness in distressing circumstances, without thought of the future. Many of us are capable, in greater or less degree, of just this stubborn service to the obvious demands of the present situation, regardless of consequences to self or others—a most valuable trait, for too much thinking about the uncertain future begets wavering irresolution and unstable conduct. Animals are capable of this loyalty to present commitments, whether undertaken with foresight or blindly, thus revealing a rudimentary sense of duty, from which our human feelings of obligation gradually evolved.

Where we recognize a feeling of duty, even rudimentary, we must likewise acknowledge the presence of something akin to conscience. In the conflicts that sometimes, especially in inclement weather, arise between self-regarding and parental impulses, what determines which will prevail? When a hungry bird passes food from its own bill to the gaping mouth of a nestling, does it experience greater pleasure in watching the baby eat than it would find in assuaging its own hunger? To assert that it sacrifices immediate gratification in order to avoid the foreseen prickings of a troubled conscience would exceed the limits of our knowledge. The bird's choice, I believe, must be between feelings that are immediately present. If, to satisfy its hunger, it deprives the nestling of needed food, it violates the pattern of behavior that made and preserves its kind. If it places the food in the nestling's upraised open mouth, it continues to be hungry but fulfills one of its strongest impulses, so that it preserves a feeling of wholeness, of organic if not moral integrity, that is somehow satisfying. It is to this sensitivity to the conformity of the single act or series of acts to the whole inherited pattern of behavior that we must look for the origin of that unique way of feeling that we call conscience.

When we trace the determination of conduct that we recognize as moral to the deepest source that introspection can discover, I believe that we must acknowledge that this source is the feeling of inward calm and integrity which we enjoy when we obey our most enduring motives, or are faithful to maxims of conduct that from early childhood have been impressed upon us, or to those that we have subsequently adopted; and, on the other hand, the sense of frustration and unrest, of incompleteness and inadequacy, which we from time to time experience as a result of having, in a moment of weakness, permitted the gratification of appetite, or the pursuit of some transitory desire, to interfere with the performance of duty as we saw it. The second state of mind is so distressing, so like a vague but persistent pain, that the former is by contrast a positive satisfaction; and we learn by experience to avoid conduct which, by causing this sense of inner fragmentation, destroys the peace of mind that is the foundation of all solid felicity.

The more advanced animals, with complex patterns of behavior and impulses that are often brought into conflict by circumstances, must occasionally experience similar feelings. And feelings of this sort, at times mildly pleasant, but in ourselves perhaps more often distressing, are just what we call conscience. Therefore, I cannot agree with those who confidently assert that conscience is the exclusive possession of humans and all other animals are devoid of it. In my view, it is not the presence of this sensitivity to behavioral integrity or its absence that gives its distinctive character to our human morality, for we share it with other animals. Our morality differs from that of nonhuman animals chiefly because, with our more developed minds, we can look farther into the future, carefully compare alternative courses of action, and choose between them. Whatever moral superiority we may have over the other animals we owe primarily to our greater intelligence, and to the wider sympathies that it generates, rather than to the presence of some special moral principle which they lack.

Like ourselves, animals are guilty of more or less frequent lapses from what we take to be the strict path of duty. Certainly, erring humans will not, on this account, deny that they have something like morality; on the contrary, this capacity to pursue divergent courses suggests that moral conflicts might arise in them. One of the sins most often charged against birds is the desertion of their eggs or nestlings. Occasionally we find their babies lying dead in the nest, with no apparent cause for their decease save cold and starvation. Sometimes we can assure ourselves that the parents still survive, but we rarely know enough to pass judgment on the seeming delinquents. The mother may have been frightened from the nest early on a cold, wet night; and, before she could find her way back at daybreak, the nestlings, deprived of the parental coverlet, succumbed to exposure. Scarcity of food, such as may occur toward the end of a long breeding season, may also cause birds to abandon their nests. Swallows sometimes migrate southward, leaving their young to die.

Stern moralists may maintain that, in spite of cold and dearth, parent birds should stay to starve with their nestlings. However, the causes of the loss of eggs and nestlings are so numerous, the enemies of birds on the whole so much more powerful than themselves, their environment so little subject to their control, that if parent birds often sacrificed their lives for dependent offspring, their species would be in danger of extinction. Except in the relatively few species that practice cooperative breeding, the death of the parents would inevitably be followed by that of their helpless young, so that nothing would be gained by their sacrifice. In the animal kingdom as a whole, natural selection tends to repress parental devotion that would impair the reproductive efficiency of a species, which might become extinct by excess of parental zeal no less than by its waning.

As seems fitting to us and is biologically sound, parent birds often take greater risks to save their young than to save their eggs. Considering all the dangers they run, my impression is that the parental devotion of birds, taken all in all, is about as strong as is consistent with the preservation of species. When feathered parents, frenzied by the peril of their nestlings, attack a large snake or powerful mammal, they exceed the bounds of prudence and, by endangering themselves, jeopardize the existence of their kind.

8. Animal Protomorality and Human Morality

From the foregoing survey, necessarily much less detailed than it might be made in a book devoted to this subject alone, I believe that we may fairly conclude that animal behavior is often influenced by a feeling not unlike conscience in ourselves, so that, without placing too much strain on the terms, we may speak of right and wrong conduct among them, although this is obviously not the same in all species, nor the same as with us. When we reflect that in humans, usually considered to be a single biologic species, there is scarcely anything which has not at one time and place been held to be right, and at another, wrong, we are not surprised to find such differences among the multitude of animal species.

Among birds, the invasion of another's station in a courtship assembly, or of another's breeding territory, is in many species evidently wrong. Either it is not done at all, or the individual guilty of the transgression is furtive in manner and readily put to flight by the aggrieved party, even if the latter be physically weaker. But the theft of the materials of a nest is not wrong; many birds, especially those that breed in colonies, do it quite openly, excite no enmity that endures beyond the act, and do not lose caste among their fellows. The relations of the sexes vary enormously from species to species; but even in certain monogamous species occasional lapses from nuptial fidelity do not appear to be wrong, since they do not disrupt the pair nor prevent the successful rearing of a brood. The feeding of nestlings other than their own, often those of a different species, as birds of many kinds occasionally do, seems to spring from the same instinctive or emotional root as our own spontaneous charity, although this has undergone great complication in the finer human minds. We have good reasons to believe that birds are motivated by feelings cognate to our sense of duty, even if they do not look so far into the future as we do. Birds do not punish offenders except when they are caught in the act. Although the contrary has been claimed of certain crows and their allies, the evidence is not convincing.

Sin, in the widest sense, is incurred when an appetite or desire seeks satisfaction by escaping from the comprehensive pattern of behavior that governs the life of an individual or its species. Although at times the appetite or desire is itself corrupted (e.g., appetite for opium or narcotics), often it is sound and healthy, so that it is not its satisfaction per se, but its escape from the pattern, which governs a life, that constitutes sin. From this point of view, an animal sins when its passions drive it to violate the innate pattern of behavior of its species, no less than a person sins when transgressing the moral or religious code that he or she recognizes as binding.

The wild life of nature, regarded simply as woodland glades, murmuring brooks, fragrant flowers and songful birds, or the tranquil emptiness of a seascape in calm weather, is restful and refreshing after the clangor and turmoil of human existence, especially in the crowded centers of population. Its myriad shapes and colors divert the fevered mind from its too-absorbing problems. But viewed with a more penetrating and philosophic eye, what spectacle could be more hideously revolting than that of countless animals, each busily stuffing itself with as many other living things as its maw can hold? Were this all that we could detect beneath the seemingly tran-quil face of nature, some who now turn to it for spiritual comfort and refreshment might shrink away in horror.

What redeems the world of animals, regarded with the philosophic rather than the sensuous eye, is the effort that nearly every individual makes to create something beyond its puny self, to project life beyond its own ephemeral bit of clay. It is not the ravening bird or the veracious beast that inspires; such spectacles can hardly uplift dejected spirits or dispel black misgivings. It is the ant beneath the upturned stone, ignoring her own peril while she feverishly drags the callow brood to safety; the beaver toiling to build the dam that will protect its home and progeny; the fingerling fish boldly attacking whatever menaces its tiny brood; the weak and fearful birdling valiantly defying the serpent that creeps up to engulf her nestlings. Often, despite ourselves, we acknowledge the magnificence of these mostly ineffectual displays of devotion. We learn that effort and strife, struggle against discouraging obstacles, are not our peculiar lot but as widespread as life itself.

And on every side, we behold living creatures, weak and transitory, often hardly more than mechanisms driven by an insatiable need of nourishment, spurred on by some mysterious force to risk and wear out their little lives in the service of something beyond themselves. From generation to generation, in endless cycles, they persevere in the endeavor that at long last, in favored lineages, lifts life to higher levels of organization, awareness, and spirituality. Intuitively, we recognize in this effort something akin to our own moral nature—for what is the highest morality but the impulse to dedicate our brief span of mundane existence to some more enduring good?

By far the greater part of human moral effort is dedicated to stabilizing the life of the individual, bringing harmony into society, and ensuring the continued existence and prosperity of our species. In many kinds of nonhuman animals, we see these same ends accomplished in ways that excite our wonder and admiration. Indeed, whereas among ourselves frequent lapses from the norms of conduct are expected, when discovered in free animals such aberrations hardly ever fail to arouse surprise and indignation in everyone except, perhaps, experienced and reflective naturalists. The "instincts" of animals are popularly held to guide them undeviatingly and infallibly in the behavior proper to their kind. In Crèvecoeur's *Letters from an American Farmer*, we find an amusing account of a wren who drove a swallow from its nest on his porch, then carried off the swallow's straws to the nest box that he had made for her.[21] "Where," he asked, "did this little bird learn that spirit of injustice? It was not endowed with what we term reason! Here then is proof that both these gifts [reason and instinct] border very near on one another; for we see the perfection of one mixing with the errors of the other!"

Although the habits of bees, ants, birds, and other animals often appear so perfectly adjusted to their needs that they are held up as examples for us to follow, their patterns of life were not developed by criticism of existing customs, the examination of various proposals for improvement, and the choice of what appears the better way. This method of determining conduct is, as far as we know, exclusively human and the distinguishing feature of our morality at its best. But where similar effects are achieved by different means, we should ask whether the underlying cause is not the same. May it not be that animals' innate patterns of behavior, which in certain respects closely resemble the kind of conduct that we regard as ideal, are expressions of the same process that impels us to create an ideal and to exert ourselves to realize it? Harmonization is not narrowly limited to a single method but may proceed by diverse means, employing always the most adequate instruments that it has thus far created for itself. At one stage, working in the obscure depths of living substance, it may make use of genetic variations; at a later stage, it may operate by means of minds that can foresee and compare. But always it acts to bring harmony into the manifold of existence, to create the most comprehensive and coherent patterns that available materials can form and the environment support. If this view be correct, then the protomorality of animals and the deliberately achieved moral conduct of thoughtful people are equally results of the moralness pervading the Universe, and their common source should be acknowledged.

This conclusion may be rejected by biologists who remind us that the innate behavior of animals has been evolved by a process of trial and failure. Genetic mutations cause changes in ancestral patterns of activities. When these mutations improve an animal's adaptation to its environment and make it more successful in propagating its kind, they persist and spread through the population; when they have a contrary effect, they are eliminated. Thus, in the course of generations, the most complex patterns of behavior are built up by the natural selection of random mutations.

To attribute the whole process to chance is to lose sight of the essential point—a widespread failure of current evolutionary doctrine. It is not by chance that the apparently random genetic mutations, or the activities which they determine, are articulated into a pattern as coherent as the included elements will permit, so that the behavior of the animal may be tested for fitness as a whole rather than as a sequence of discrete and unrelated acts. It is these integrated patterns, variously modified, which compete with each other in the circumstances of the animal's actual existence; and that the one that best fits the organism to survive and prosper will prevail over the others is a fact almost too obvious to mention. And it is just the process, which welds all the details of an animal's behavior, as all the multitudinous constituents of its body, into a coherent, adequately functioning whole, which also causes it and ourselves to exhibit the kind of conduct that we call moral.

Chapter Four

Instinct, Reason, and Morality

1. Appetites and Aversions the Springs of All Voluntary Activity

WHEN, AS IN the last chapter, we survey broadly the lives of the more pacific birds or some other class of nonhuman animals, noting how well their inherited modes of behavior equip them to carry on their necessary activities, adjust themselves to others of their kind, and even to achieve in their relations with other species a degree of harmony that we can hardly contemplate without being ashamed of humanity's conspicuous failure in this sphere, we are moved to ask certain searching questions. If, without ethical studies and moral maxims, other warmblooded animals arrange their lives on the whole so well, what is the advantage of our self-conscious morality, with its ideals and standards that we hold before ourselves only to violate, so that they become a source of shame and sorrow to us? Why must we have this sort of morality, when other creatures do so well without it? Would it not be better to abandon the strenuous effort to live in conformity to moral rules that we succeed only in breaking and follow our natural impulses, as other animals appear to do?

Viewing the situation still more broadly, we may ask whether the abandonment of the kind of regulation of behavior which prevails in other animals for that which we find in ourselves, the transition from protomorality to morality, has been a true advance. When we contemplate, as Cicero did two thousand years ago, all the disorder and suffering that reason misused has brought into the world,[1] we may question whether the growth of intelligence and the sort of morality that goes with it does not represent a miscarriage of harmonization, which might have borne creation to a higher level by continuing to perfect protomorality, without all the complications for which humanity has been responsible. How can morality, in the narrow sense of the word, advance the cause of harmonization? To these questions we now address ourselves.

In all animals, whether we classify their behavior as "instinctive" or "rational," the springs of activity are essentially the same. They are the desires and appetites which drive them to seek certain objects or to place themselves in a certain relation to their environment, the fears and aversions which impel them to avoid other objects or conditions which might be injurious or unpleasant to them. Perhaps it would not be an exaggeration to say that appetite is the sole effective cause of spontaneous animal activity, and that it may be positive, leading the creature toward certain objects or into certain situations, or negative, impelling it away from other objects and out of other situations, insofar as it is free to act. This analysis permits us to make an instructive comparison of the appetites of animals with the tropisms of plants, which also are positive and negative. Thus, upright green shoots are as a rule positively phototropic and negatively geotropic; they bend toward the light and away from the pull of gravity. A primary root, on the contrary, is negatively phototropic and positively geotropic, turning away from a source of light and toward the center of Earth. These movements, intimately related to the vital functions of each organ, are an expression of organic tensions homologous to the appetites and impulses which cause all spontaneous activity in animals. In all living things, the ultimate springs of activity are similar.

How, it may be asked, do the purely intellectual or spiritual activities of humans fit into this scheme? The mind, as it becomes emancipated from its primitive condition as a servant ministering to the needs of its body, comes to resemble in certain aspects an independent organism, yet one whose welfare is intimately linked with that of the animal body in which it resides. A mind has its own life more or less distinct from that of its body, its appetite for knowledge, which we call curiosity, its desire for understanding, its dread of falling into error, its aversion to ugliness. These appetites, positive and negative, are related to the life of the spirit in much the same way as hunger and thirst, fear of falling and efforts to avoid great heat and cold, are related to the life of the body. Without them there would be no purely intellectual or esthetic activity, just as without the animal appetites there would be no physical activity beyond, for a time, such involuntary functions as respiration, circulation, secretion, and the like. The mind, like the body, has appetites which are primary and cannot be resolved into anything simpler. These appetites, organic and intellectual, are the impulses or drives responsible for all voluntary activity.

2. A Comparison of Instinctive and Rational Guidance

By itself, an appetite is as helpless as a newly hatched sparrow. It can only lift up, widemouthed, its blind head and wait until its parents drop something into it. The stomach calls for food, but knows not where to find it; it craves water, but must be carried to the spring; even the mind's thirst for knowledge requires other faculties for its satisfaction. Considering animals as a whole, and leaving aside those simple and direct reactions which we call reflexes, there are two ways in which appetites are satisfied: by instinctive and by rational activity. The fundamental difference between instinct, insofar as we understand it, and reason lies in the degree of rigidity of patterns of behavior. Instinctive patterns tend to be fixed and inflexible, rational patterns more yielding and fluid. Viewed on the plane of conscious mental activity, the difference between instinct and reason appears to lie in the degree of freedom in the association of ideas. Instinct might be called the fixed association of ideas or their cerebral equivalents, reason the free association of ideas. Since there are many degrees between strict fixation and perfect freedom in mental activity, we can hardly draw a sharp boundary between instinct and reason. Animals as low in the zoological scale as the flatworm can learn after a fashion, indicating some degree of freedom in the association of ideas or their equivalents;[2] humans' stubborn adherence to old errors, even after the truth has been demonstrated to them, proves that their mental processes fall far short of perfect freedom.

Instinct guides impulse into action in ways determined by heredity; it canalizes effort, regiments activity. Whether or not it foresees the ends of activity is a question we need not attempt to settle here, but it is clear that it guides activity much as the tracks guide a railroad train. Where intelligence is well-developed, it feels here the appetite or need, visualizes there what will satisfy this need, passes in review all the available means, and finally decides which course will lead most easily and rapidly to the desired objective. The contrast between instinctive and rational behavior may be illustrated by considering the relative advantages of travel by train and on foot. If the object of appetite happens to be situated on an established railroad line and the tracks are clear, the instinctive train will probably take its passengers there with the least effort in the shortest time. But if the direct line happens to be blocked by a landslide or a derailment, the rational pedestrian will somehow make a detour around the obstruction, reaching his destination ahead of the stalled instinctive train. And if the objective is at a point not served by the system of instinctive tracks, intelligence alone can bring us there.

The implications for morality of this difference between instinct and reason are momentous and have never, as far as I know, received the attention they merit. Instinct strictly limits the means by which an appetite or desire can be satisfied. These methods, the innate patterns of behavior, are in general genetically controlled; so that, like other heritable characters, they change by mutations and are subject to natural selection, whereby deleterious innovations may be eliminated, while those favorable to the species will be preserved and diffused through the population. For example, in some species of birds in which it is customary for the female alone to warm the eggs, we find occasional aberrant males who take turns sitting in the nest. If it were advantageous to the species to have the male parent help with incubation, we should expect that the stock in which he acquired this habit would gradually replace lineages in which he failed to do so, with the result that incubation by the male as well as the female would eventually prevail in the species. Or, to take the reverse case, if, in one of those numerous species of birds in which both parents share the task of warming the eggs, certain males lost this habit, they might leave few descendants, so that this harmful change in behavior would not be perpetuated.

Thus instinctive behavior, all without moral maxims or exhortations, conforms fairly closely to Kant's Categorical Imperative: "Act only on that maxim that you could will to become a universal law." That is to say, act only in the manner that you would wish every other individual of your kind to imitate in corresponding circumstances. Animals guided by instinct do in general behave as though they willed their conduct to become a universal law, at least of their particular species. These innate patterns of behavior are, indeed, the "natural laws" or rules of conduct which the naturalist strives to discover when studying the life history of any kind of free animal.

3. How Instinct Limits Harmful Activity

The limitations of instinctive behavior are curious and instructive. Among the Buff-throated Saltators, big, olive-green finches widespread in tropical America, nests are usually scattered through thickets and plantations rather than concentrated in particular spots. Once, however, I found two nests, both containing eggs, only eight feet apart in neighboring coffee bushes—a most unusual discovery. One of the incubating females was clearly dominant over the other, who had somehow lost her tail feathers. Each time that the dominant saltator approached or left her own nest, she would look into the other's nest, and if the tailless saltator happened to be present warming her two blue eggs, she would chase her rapidly through the plantation and into the neighboring thicket. This happened dozens of times each day. But the timid saltator was persistent, and, despite innumerable interruptions she managed to hatch one of her eggs, after an unusually long period of incubation. The more belligerent bird, as she passed to and fro to her two offspring, continued to chase her neighbor from nest and nestling, and sometimes she would look into the nest. Then the sight of the gaping red mouth of her absent neighbor's baby might stimulate the dominant saltator to place in it the food which she had brought for her own family. From time to time she even sat in her tailless neighbor's nest, brooding the nestling whose mother she had chased away.

This was most inconsistent behavior. Had the belligerent saltator succeeded in causing her timid neighbor to abandon the nest, the eggs would have spoilt, or the nestling would have died of starvation and exposure. Had she broken the eggs or killed the nestling, the unwanted neighbor would have deserted her nest and then in all probability would have gone farther off to build another—the very result that the belligerent one was apparently trying to achieve. Why, then, did not the dominant saltator easily and swiftly accomplish her purpose by destroying the contents of her neighbor's nest? Either something similar to a moral inhibition prevented her from committing infanticide, or it never occurred to her to do so. [Since the accomplishment of her apparent purpose of causing her neighbor permanently to abandon the nest would have had precisely the same effect as the more direct destruction of the contents of the nest, we may conclude that the belligerent one never thought of doing so.] It could not have been that she wished to adopt her tailless neighbor's family, for unless her mate had helped to incubate and brood, she could not have adequately warmed the eggs and nestlings in separate nests; and male saltators regularly restrict their participation in parental duties to feeding the young.

This is a single example of the general rule that the inflexibility of an animal's mental associations limits the number of ways in which it can be harmful. We witness the same limitation in those many species of birds, mentioned in section 6 of the preceding chapter, which apparently never fight among themselves. They do indeed engage in disputes over mates or nest sites, but these are settled by logomachies and posturing into which violence does not enter. It seems never to occur to these little birds that their bills would serve to pull out their adversary's feathers, or even to destroy an eye. They are certainly not as destructive as they might be.

The inflexibility of their mental processes, which prevents nonhuman creatures from being as harmful to each other—and to themselves—as they might be, if they had a human mind and human capacity for hatred, may also operate to their disadvantage. How many times while watching a quadruped or bird vainly trying to accomplish something, as to reach food, build a nest, or escape an enemy, have we not wished that we might demonstrate what *our* intelligence might accomplish with the means at *their* disposal! Sometimes I have watched faithful parent birds diligently carrying food to nestlings that were doomed to die, because their poorly attached nest would fall before its occupants could fly. I felt sure that with only a bill for a tool and readily available vegetable fibers for thread, I could have sewed up those nests far above my reach and saved the youngsters. But these birds built once for all; after their nestlings had hatched, they were mentally incapable of returning to an earlier stage of their cycle and making repairs, no matter how badly they were needed.

Similarly, some animals display amazing inflexibility in their manner of eating. An experimenter, whose curiosity exceeded his humanity, demonstrated that certain birds, whose normal diet consists of insects and other small creatures caught in motion, would in captivity starve to death rather than eat dead and immobile food of the same kind. "Stupid!" "Blind instinct!" we exclaim. Yet when humans submit to torture and death rather than deviate from their ancestral customs or commit some act which they believe to be wrong, even in what seems to most moderns so trivial a matter as making an obeisance to an idol or eating some forbidden food, we admire them, often in spite of reason. Is not faithfulness to mores as admirable in one species of animal as in another?

4. How Reason Increases the Range of Harmful Conduct

Where instinct sees one or a few well-tried ways of satisfying an appetite, a developed intelligence sees many ways, which vary endlessly with the shifting circumstances of life, and in novel contingencies may be without precedent in the history of the species. The appetites of animals are to a high degree mutually exclusive; now hunger, now thirst, now desire for warmth and shelter, now the sexual urge occupies the center of consciousness and enlists all the faculties to aid in its satisfaction. When intelligence is free and ample, yet controlled only by appetite, it will lead the animal to the fulfillment of the dominant desire by the easiest and shortest route, regardless of the whole welfare of the individual or its kind. The most superficial reflection makes it clear that nothing could be more perilous to any animal than suddenly to endow it with an active mind, capable of the free association of ideas, without at the same time providing a means to prevent each new desire from taking possession of this intelligence, and using it for the attainment of satisfaction without regard for ultimate consequences.

The present existence of humanity is testimony that there has never since humans arose been a time when the intelligence of each individual was not subject to some check or control which limited, in the interest of the species or of a society, the degree to which it could be enlisted in the service of each of one's shifting appetites. Strength of habit and social pressure seem to be the forces which have been chiefly responsible for the preservation of humanity through its long and perilous period of transition from the instinctive to the rational control of conduct. Even when reason points out a new and intrinsically easier mode of satisfying a desire, habit often makes us continue to follow a well-tried method.

In a highly social and imitative animal like humans, society acts even more powerfully than personal habit to preserve traditional patterns of behavior and restrain the individual from satisfying his or her desires by procedures injurious to the community. Among all the higher animals, individuals vary considerably in intelligence. One of unusual mental alertness who discovers a novel method of satisfying desires may antagonize more stupid or conservative neighbors, whose disapproval may be strong enough to ensure conformity to conventional procedures, or at least to delay the general adoption of the innovation. And whenever, in directing all the resources of mind and body to the satisfaction of a single dominant appetite, the individual causes inconvenience or injury to a neighbor, he or she must expect retaliations proportioned in their severity to the degree of the injury. Thus, at an early stage in the history of humanity, we find taboos and laws intended to restrain socially deleterious behavior, or that which appeared to be so.

A large share of the misery and shame which, throughout the historic period, have weighed so heavily upon humanity, must be attributed to the difficulties of effecting the transition from the instinctive to the rational control of conduct. With innate patterns of behavior fast disintegrating and reason so imperfectly developed, is it surprising that humans should at times reach depths of degradation that we rarely see in creatures guided by instinct alone? In our present troubled epoch of transition, social pressure is by far the most powerful agent for enforcing conduct held to be right, yet it is pitifully inadequate. In the first place, the generally accepted ends of human activity are still narrow and partial, falling far short of the ideals held two or three millennia ago by individuals of the highest moral insight. In the second place, people escape social coercion by concealing their acts from society, by becoming enemies of society, or by raising themselves above society: they satisfy their appetites at the expense of the best interests of their kind by hiding their sins from their neighbors, by becoming outlaws, or by becoming tyrants and dictators. The first of these categories is the most numerous; but the last is the most dangerous, because the few who comprise it can compel great masses of people to serve the ruler's selfish craving for power, wealth, or adulation. As long as people continue to make intelligence the servant of single appetites, without regard for the whole welfare of themselves and their kind, then the higher the development of this intelligence, and the greater its control of nature, the more perilous will the situation of humanity become.

In purely instinctive behavior, the strongest desire can, as a rule, find fulfillment only by means of a pattern of behavior which continues to exist because it is beneficial to the species, or at least not definitely harmful to it; in rational behavior, unless adequately controlled by morality, the unbridled wish may seize upon the highest achievements of intelligence and turn them to its own nefarious ends. *The ways in which instinct can be harmful are limited by the number of inherited modes of behavior; the ways in which reason can be mischievous are indefinitely multiplied by the free association of ideas.*

5. Disruptive Effects of Nascent Rationality upon Human Life

As we read the story of primitive humans, in whatever part of the world, our first reaction is likely to be a feeling of anger, of indignation at manifold cruelties. Next, perhaps, we view with amusement or scorn the muddled thinking and absurd beliefs. Or we may be filled with revulsion or nausea by the contemplation of an existence so brutish, so undisciplined according to our own standards, so inconsiderate of the feelings of other beings. But if we continue to study and ponder the ways of the savage, our final attitude is profound pity; for we contemplate a life which has been thoroughly upset and in many aspects disintegrated by the beginnings of free intellectual activity. At times the disruption of earlier instinctive patterns seems to result in a mental state little short of madness. We ask ourselves: Can beings who act like this be sane?

But as we reflect maturely on the nature of instinct and reason, we see that it could not have been otherwise: the intrusion of free mental activity into a life once regulated by instinct inevitably brought profound disorders—disturbances so severe that to establish anew a harmonious pattern of thoughts and conduct would require hundreds if not thousands of generations.

Although accounts of the feasts and orgies of savage tribesmen may lead us to conclude that they were thorough hedonists while their treatment of the prisoners destined to supply the flesh for their cannibalistic feasts suggests that they were hedonists of the most callously selfish sort, a consideration of their whole life convinces one that this view is untenable. Hedonism is one of the most difficult of civilized arts; to practice it with satisfactory results we need much science and much philosophy. Savages lacked the first rudiments of Epicureanism; they were too close to the strong, primal currents of life deliberately to make pleasure their goal. For them, merely to survive and reproduce their kind was the serious business of existence, but they were often profoundly confused about the best ways of attaining these ends. And their inability to be even moderately kind to themselves was at the root of all their cruelty to others. Until we have learned to be good to ourselves, how can we be beneficent to those about us?

We read of Brazilian Indians who take a prisoner of war, give him land to cultivate and a maiden of the tribe to wed, treat him as one of themselves; yet they and he know all the while that at the end of some months, or perhaps years, he will be killed in a fearsomely cruel manner, to provide a cannibal feast whose hideous details had best remain unmentioned. A Carib father for months secludes himself, fasts, allows his skin to be gashed and irritant substances to be rubbed into the wounds, submits to a hundred hardships and restrictions and inconveniences, in order that his first-born son may become strong and brave; and the baby's net benefit from all this excess of laudable parental devotion is, so far as science can tell—absolutely nil. A Chaco Indian, almost exhausted by the fatigue of the chase, pricks his limbs with a jaguar bone awl to draw blood and thereby strengthen and refresh himself! At a more advanced cultural level, a sick Inca emperor orders the sacrifice of a hecatomb of human victims to the sun, to ensure his recovery. This is not the behavior of beings who are either selfish or cruel, so much as of beings whose thought and life have been profoundly disorganized by a new and intricate tool—reason—whose use baffles and confuses them.

Compared with the troubled and confused lives of savage and perhaps even of civilized humans, that of an animal with a well-knit pattern of instinctive behavior seems stable, balanced, integrated. Means are, on the whole, well-adjusted to ends, with no vain fluttering after the unattainable, and little striving to reach vital objectives by unrelated or obviously futile procedures. For the logic of facts and events, on which instinctive patterns are established, humans have been striving to substitute another kind of logic, that of ideas and words. But it requires a vast number of ideas, and profound insight into the relations between them, to create a body of knowledge capable of guiding us through this immensely complex and perplexing world. A few ideas, a partial insight into the relations between events, merely confuses and stultifies us; as when the savage, having correctly observed that whenever it rains, drops spatter the foliage, now believes that he can cause a shower by sprinkling water on green leaves. Only when the mind has created a whole new world that is a facsimile, or at least a symbolic representation, of the material world, does it become somewhat competent to deal with this world. Superstition springs from our failure to understand causality—whether in the realm of physics or that of morals and religion.

When we contemplate the tremendous disorientation of life for which free mental activity is responsible, we can understand the mystic's conviction that to attain wholeness and unity he or she must liberate the mind from the disturbing action of rational thought. Since life at the instinctive level appears to be better integrated and in closer contact with its source, it is not absurd to suppose that if we could return to an earlier stage, perhaps by sinking far into the depths of our own "unconscious mind," we might recover the wholeness which humans have lost, and experience that perfect bliss which can be won only by complete integration of the self and its flawless union with that which supports and embraces it.

But the biologist knows that to retrace the course of evo-lution is a vain endeavor. Even when an animal succeeds in returning to an earlier mode of existence, as when a few mammals readjusted themselves to life in the sea, whence their remote ancestors had emerged, that which returns is profoundly different from that which set forth. Having lost the vital wholeness which belonged to our distant, nonhuman forebears whose minds had not yet become restless, there appears to be no salvation for us save by establishing a new integration at the rational level. In this new synthesis, the vital impulses which we share with all animals must be preserved, but regulated and moderated by adequate intelligence and keen appreciation of our relation to the whole. Few people, perhaps none, have ever achieved perfect integration on the rational level. We, who still experience the countless evils which spring from imperfect unification of the self, should be profoundly compassionate of humans at a still lower stage of culture, whose recovery from the terrific shock of the impact of free mental activity on the old instinctive life has been perhaps even less complete than ours. All human history, no less than all pre-history, is but the clinical record of the birth-agony of intelligence, which again and again threatened to be stillborn.

6. The Fallacy of Naturalism

It is understandable that contemplation of humanity's story, with its record of the consistent failure of social conventions, religious teachings, and moral doctrines to make most of us good and happy, should lead some thinkers to conclude that the only remedy for this painful situation is to cast away all these human creations as so much worthless trash and return to the wholesome ways of nature. Yet the resulting ethical naturalism, as that of the Cynics or Rousseau, could only appeal to people who have not adequately studied the natural world. Neither the careful observer of free animals, who sees them satisfying their needs by means of well-tried inherited procedures, nor the anthropologist, who knows that the "savage" is far more a formalist than most "civilized" people, is likely to agree that people can become good and happy simply by following their uncorrupted natural appetites. Unless guided by instinctive patterns of behavior, social custom, or rationally constructed systems of conduct, such impulses drive us into painful situations. Since humans have lost all effective innate patterns of behavior, they must rely on either social or rational control—or some-times, in advanced cultures, a combination of the two—to avoid disaster.

Although rigid imperatives and crystallized rules can never be adequate guides to right behavior, on the whole we do best to follow them, if only because few of us have the leisure and wisdom to decide every problem in conduct by rational deduction from general guiding principles. What we need is not so much the relaxation of established patterns of conduct as their improvement and amplification to cover whole provinces of activity in which at present guidance is lacking or inadequate. And apart from intelligence, we have nothing that can help us improve behavior. We could wish that social arrangements would not so often thwart or distort sound vital impulses, yet to give these impulses free rein without rational guidance would not improve our situation. On the contrary, it might result in more frequent and severe frustrations, because without intelligent coordination they would so often oppose and cheat each other.

The germ of truth in ethical naturalism is that most human impulses, even today, can trace their descent from animal appetites that promoted the welfare of the individual and his or her kind, and that intelligence, still immature and subject to countless aberrations, has in many instances led these impulses astray. The remedy for this distressing situation is not to distrust intelligence and the guidance it gives us, for this would leave us more naked and helpless than the meanest instinct-guided "brute;" it is to use reason more thoroughly and conscientiously to create a society wherein a larger proportion of our sound vital impulses may attain fruition without discord and conflict. The "original goodness" of humans, as of other living beings, is that innate capacity to organize discrete elements into coherent patterns which is the most characteristic feature of life. This faculty accomplishes its end by whatever means evolution has provided for it. In humans, it has no agent superior to the intellect and its moral judgments. Thus it is evident that the cause of our trouble provides the means of curing the trouble. Reason, by making it possible for us to satisfy our appetites by procedures not tested and approved by long ancestral usage, makes moral guidance a necessity; and reason alone can supply that guidance.

Yet I doubt whether the rational control of behavior, at its present level of development among people, serves the whole interest of humanity as well as instinctive control, with all its limitations, promotes the welfare of many another species of animal. Our single hope is that human reason will some day attain a stature which will prevent its degradation to the service of single appetites, without considering how their indulgence effects the whole life of the individual and relations with other beings. We earlier saw that instinctive behavior is in general adjusted to the welfare of the species, that it conforms rather closely to Kant's Categorical Imperative. Hence we might set as the goal of rational activity that it rise to the level of instinctive behavior in promoting the prosperity of life as a whole, rather than prostituting itself to the satisfaction, successively, of single appetites.

7. Ultimate Moral Advantages of Reason over Instinct

Since the conduct of beings endowed with reason, as we witness it in the contemporary world, is still far from achieving that admirable integration of activities which we find in instinctive behavior at its best, what, we may justly ask, is the advantage of free intelligence? How can it benefit life as a whole? What shall we gain if we successfully complete the long and perilous transition from one mode of control to the other? Leaving aside, for the present, the question of whether intellectual activity may be regarded as an end in itself, and considering it merely as an instrument for bringing harmony into the world, there are, I believe, three outstanding advantages which can be achieved by the substitution of reason for instinct.

First, reason is capable of fine discriminations over a broader field than instinct covers. Instinctive patterns of behavior are in general adjusted to the average or prevailing situation; reason, when adequately developed, may adjust to the unusual situation with tremendous moral advantages. Thus animals, as a rule, make no effort to attend or provide for the sick and wounded of their kind. Even social and gregarious species appear to recognize no intermediate stages between life in all its fullness and death. Either their adult companions are treated as normal members of the group, able to hold their own in every way, or they are ignored like those which death has finally and permanently removed from their midst. Or else, as in cattle, the sight or smell of a wounded companion confuses and upsets them, making them behave in strange and unaccountable ways. A few kinds of birds have, indeed, been known to feed their disabled fellows, but even among them such solicitude is rare.

The reason for this neglect of the sick and wounded by animals that are guided by instinct seems obvious. To adjust their behavior to the many stages between the plenitude of health and the final stillness of death, to know how to deal with the innumerable varieties of injury and sickness to which the flesh is liable, would require finer discriminations, and greater flexibility of conduct, than we can expect in any animal governed by innate behavior patterns. Moreover, in animals subject to predation, as the majority of them are, concern for the weak and the lagging might be fatal to the strong and jeopardize the existence of the species. It remained for rational animals to distinguish between the ailing and the dead and to develop, slowly and blunderingly, methods of attending their sick and injured companions.

The second important superiority of reason is that its beneficent innovations may be spread more rapidly and widely than those of instinct. Since an improvement in an instinctive pattern seems usually to result from a genetic mutation, it is available only to the direct descendants of the animal which first exhibits it; and often it is at first, until it becomes fixed in the species, transmitted to only a portion of these descendants. But when a rational being endowed with language has made a helpful innovation it can, by teaching and example, diffuse this improvement widely among its contemporaries, and through writing or oral tradition make it available to remote generations not its own progeny. Unfortunately, the harmful innovations made by rational animals can be diffused in the same manner as the beneficial ones; frequently they are more eagerly accepted by contemporaries; and in the absence of rigid control by natural selection they often become established with alarming rapidity.

The third and outstanding advantage of reason over instinct is its capacity to distribute benefits over a much wider area, to increase the breadth of the moral community to an almost unlimited extent. Innate patterns of conduct are adjusted primarily to secure the prosperity of a single biologic species; and the factors which govern their origin, survival, and transmission are such that it is difficult for them to become more inclusive. Yet instinctive behavior cannot be wholly insensitive to the claims of other forms of life. Each living creature is a member of a complex community of animals and plants, and its welfare is subtly linked with that of neighbors of the most diverse kinds. At least, it is unlikely that its instincts will continue to cause the deterioration of the community of which it is a part, for this may lead to its own decline.

Although reason still often falls short of instinct in the scope of its beneficence, it is intrinsically capable of extending its kindly influence far more widely. The rational animal can benefit by experience broader and more varied than that of its direct ancestors, and it can in turn transmit the treasures of its wisdom to rational beings other than its own progeny. It can take as its aim the welfare not only of its own immediate community but of all communities and all life. Yet it must be exceedingly careful how it proceeds, and not vaunt too lightly its superiority over instinct. Instinctive patterns are formed gradually by natural processes; they are, in most instances, the carefully yet unconsciously weighed conclusions of experience garnered over a period so long, an area so wide, and by so many individuals, that reason is bewildered when it attempts to collate and draw deductions from so vast an array of diverse data. Let our intellect become as powerful as it may, it will not easily improve upon millennial instincts.

When we review in broad terms the whole history of the relation of intelligence to the old, instinctive life upon which it supervened, we find a gradual reversal in the direction of reason's march. Although, at first, it leads us away from nature, finally it guides us back to her. Thus, dawning intelligence attempts to improve or adorn the human body, as also sometimes the bodies of dependent animals, by all sorts of grotesque deformations, distortions, scarifications, discolorations, and the like; but finally the maturing mind recognizes that, at its best, the body in its natural form is more comely than human ingenuity can make it. Art follows these same shifts in the standard of beauty. At first, dawning intelligence beguiles humans into cruel practices, for which nature provides no precedent; but, as it matures, reason suppresses these revolting excesses. Or reason may lead humans to attempt the extirpation of innate appetites and emotions, but at last it discovers that it is better to regulate than to suppress them. An early effect of rationally directed activities is the unhealthy agglomeration of millions in great cities, but finally intelligence demands a return to a more natural environment.

Similarly, the imperfectly rational mind permits itself to be dominated and unbalanced by particular appetites; but, as it improves, reason controls the appetites and animal impulses, ordering them in a system which resembles an innate pattern of behavior, although its origin is different. Finally, when it escapes wholly from domination by secondary determinants of activity and, penetrating more deeply into the core of our being, establishes contact with the primary determinant and becomes sensitive to it, reason strives to make the moral community as harmonious and extensive as possible, including all things within its beneficent scope. When we have been led back by maturing reason into closer concord with the creative energy of the Universe, we may proudly claim with Wordsworth:

> By grace divine,
> Not otherwise, O Nature! we are thine. . . .

Chapter Five

The Structure of Moral Relations

1. The Nature of Prohibited Acts

IF ASKED WHAT morality is, people whose moral instruction consisted in learning a list of prohibitions would, I believe, answer with a negative rather than an affirmative statement. They might tell us that it is not lying, not stealing, not killing, not coveting, not cheating, nor in any way injuring one's neighbor. If further asked what common feature unites all these interdicted activities, they would find it difficult to answer. They might say that all these forbidden actions cause people pain, bodily or mental, or are injurious to them. This is true enough, but not adequately discriminative. For competition in trade or the professions brings much loss and sorrow to those who fail in it; and the punishment of children makes them unhappy; and the practice of medicine and dentistry are abundant sources of pain even to those who are ultimately benefited by these arts; yet, as far as I am aware, such activities are nowhere prohibited by the moral code.

The common feature which unites the activities most consistently forbidden by the moral codes of civilized peoples is that by their very nature they cannot be both habitual and enduring, because they tend to destroy the conditions that make them possible. For some prohibited acts, this statement will immediately be clear; for others, its truth is not so obvious. A case of the former sort is stealing. That which people steal is wealth, and wealth is produced or accumulated by human labor. People are willing to toil and endure privations in order to obtain wealth only because they have some prospect of holding onto and using it. In proportion as the probability of keeping their material goods is diminished, they relax their efforts to create or procure them. As an extreme case, we might imagine a population so aggressively predatory that nobody is likely to hold until tomorrow what is earned today. In such circumstances, nobody would sow and till the soil, no one would manufacture clothes or dwellings or useful tools, none would even bother to claim land without a prospect of keeping it. All would live from hand to mouth on food gathered in the wilderness and devoured as soon as found. It would be impossible to steal, because there would be no property of any sort. The condition that we have imagined does not exist even in the most primitive human tribes of which we know, nor among animals of many sorts, which control parcels of land that are respected by others of their kind. Stealing is a self-defeating activity.

Or take the case of lying. Language serves as a medium for the communication of ideas, because in general we consistently use the same sound to designate the same object, and the same combination of words to signify the same relationship or activity. This is the indispensable condition for that association of sounds with definite things or ideas which is the foundation of language. Further, we on the whole give credence to the statements we hear, because on the whole we find them trustworthy. Now suppose that lying were to become more prevalent than truthful speech. In the first place, people would then habitually use, when speaking to another, not the word or phrase which would convey to the hearer's mind the object or situation in the speaker's mind, but one that suggests some other object or situation. There could be no constancy in the use of a wrong word for a given thing; for then this wrong word would finally, through habit, become the accepted word, and come to mean what the speaker desired to conceal. In the second place, nobody would believe or pay attention to what he or she heard; for no one wishes to be deceived, and we are supposing a society in which people are deceived by what they hear far more commonly than they are enlightened by it. In these circumstances, language would become a hodgepodge of meaningless sounds; and no one could be misled by false statements, because no one would either understand or give credence to them. Lying, then, if sufficiently prevalent, would destroy itself. The distinction between falsehood and truth would be lost, and it would no longer be worth anybody's while to speak falsely. In actual circumstances, the liar succeeds in deceiving us only because most people tell the truth more often than they lie.

Next we may consider covetousness, which springs from admiration for another's possessions and may express itself in two ways. It may stimulate us to try to win or create similar possessions by legitimate activities. Although such emulation is deplorable when we are led by another's example to set our hearts on things that are foolish and vain, it is salutary when we are inspired to strive for things of real worth. In its other manifestation, admiration grows into envy and leads us to brood over some particular possession of another person, either vainly hoping that some unforeseen stroke of good fortune may make it ours, or else scheming to acquire it by unlawful means. In the first case, covetousness becomes a deterrent to active endeavor, in the second, an incentive to crime. In proportion as covetousness became general, it would cause a diminution of possessions worthy to stir envy.

It would be tedious to demonstrate in detail how each of the acts forbidden by the accumulated wisdom of humanity tends to defeat itself; but I believe that it can be shown that each of such activities, if rife, would either directly undermine the basis of its own existence, or would lead indirectly to the same result by the disintegration of the society in which alone it could be carried on, or more commonly, it would operate in both of these manners simultaneously. We conclude, then, that *advanced moral codes prohibit activities which are intrinsically incapable of becoming prevalent and enduring.* As a self-perpetuating process, life tends to impose its own character on each of the activities of living things, for only such activities can continue to sustain it. We condemn conduct which cannot be enduring because it is incompatible with life itself.

2. The Reciprocity of Enduring Relations

Now that we have decided what kinds of activities are prohibited by moral codes and in what their wrongness consists, it will be easier to discover what kinds are moral and why they are so designated, and likewise what sorts of conduct are beyond the sphere of morality, being extra-moral or perhaps supra-moral. It will become evident that certain kinds of behavior, not generally conceded to be pertinent to morality, are its very foundation, whereas others, often stressed as fundamental to morality, have little to do with it.

Since activities which, by their very nature, cannot become both prevalent and enduring are immoral, it follows that moral behavior must be enduring, or at least have the possibility of becoming enduring. *Moral relations between finite beings are, insofar as the limited existence of these beings permits, enduring relations, and to be lasting they must be reciprocal.* Reciprocity is the very life-blood of a moral order; as justice, which is the concept of reciprocity in human relations is the foundation of a stable community. Thus, moral conduct is not the mere absence of wrong behavior. If we simply desist from lying, stealing, coveting, murdering, and other proscribed acts, we do not thereby become moral beings. For we might avoid every wrong deed by becoming perfectly quiescent, abstaining from all activity of any sort and having no dealings with anybody. Thereby we should indeed avoid harming our neighbors, but a moral order is something more than the absence of injurious acts. Morality consists in arranging entities in a harmonious pattern, and such a pattern can exist only with relations to bind these entities together. For living beings, these relations take the form of activities, which to be lasting must be reciprocal; and the more equitably reciprocal they become, the longer they are likely to persist.

That an enduring pattern can be established only by means of reciprocal relations becomes clear when we examine some of the great, stable systems, which our planet displays. The millennial circulation of the waters, on which all terrestrial and fluviatile and even much marine life depends, is maintained by reciprocity; the oceans do not over a long period yield up to the clouds more water than is returned to them either directly by rainfall or through the discharge of rivers. A small but persistent inequality in either direction would, in the course of ages, result either in the drying up of the oceans or the desiccation of all the lands. Similarly, a forest flourishes from century to century because of the reciprocal exchanges between the vegetation and the soil, the latter supplying water and salts, while the plants return to it the organic matter and the minerals contained in their dead tissues. If the plants yielded up nothing to the soil, it would soon become impoverished and unable to support further growth.

The fabric of a moral order is not woven of the acts of exceptional abnegation and outstanding virtue that win our praise and at times excite our emulation, but rather of those reciprocal relationships by which a society is constituted, and without which there could be no stable community. Because such relations are so commonplace, as long as they remain undistorted we rarely think of them as moral. Our moral consciousness is almost wholly focused upon deviations, in one direction or another, from the norm: on one side, upon acts of injustice and infractions of the accepted rules, on the other, upon persistence in righteousness in the face of exceptional difficulties.

What, then, is the stuff of which morality is made? It is the relation between husband and wife, when they love and are loyal and each does his or her share in maintaining their home. It is the relation between parent and child, when graced by devoted care and fond obedience, so that the parent fulfills his or her own nature in bringing to flower all the best qualities latent in the child. It is the relation between teacher and pupil, when the one imparts knowledge gladly and the other learns eagerly, with respect and gratitude to the preceptor. It is the relation between friends, who must mutually amuse, instruct, support, console, or ennoble each other; else friendship becomes an empty form. It is the relation between the state and the citizen, when the former gives in protection and services a fair return for the devoted efforts and the contributions of the latter. In a commercial society, it is the relation between buyer and seller, when there is no misrepresentation or dishonesty on either side, and each is by means of the transaction enabled to obtain certain desired goods with greater facility than would otherwise be possible. And it is the relation between employer and employee, when the wages and conditions of labor are a just recompense for honest work. These relationships are the threads of which a moral fabric is woven; without at least some of them, no pattern could be preserved and there would be no social morality. They are all reciprocal relations; and to the extent that they deviate from just reciprocity, they become precarious and tend to disintegrate.

It is evident that relations of this sort are by no means confined to humanity, but some of them exist among all social and even among comparatively solitary animals. Hence these animals possess a form of morality, even if they never discuss their duties; just as birds who sing beautifully practice a form of art, although they lack artistic canons. Since, as was earlier suggested, people are as a rule made aware of their morality chiefly by deviations in one direction or the other, and animals, whose patterns of behavior are largely innate rather than learned, conform to them more consistently, it follows that they should for this reason alone be less conscious of them.

The awakened spirit never desires exclusive possession. To give, or at least to share, is more in keeping with its nature. Although it hungers for truth, beauty, and love, it never wishes to take these things from any being in the sense of depriving it of a possession; for it is the peculiarity of spiritual goods that an indefinite number of minds can each possess them entirely. The spirit also yearns to give whatever goods it may have and to help all struggling creatures. But the body must take exclusive possession of things for its own use; if it fails to acquire a sufficiency, it perishes. Thus, as beings compounded of body and spirit, we are moved by two contrary impulses: as bodies we must take; as spirits we would give. A compromise between these two is necessary: we will not take more than we give. Hence we strive to make our dealings with other beings reciprocal, taking no more than we can give in fair exchange, yet giving more than we take whenever we can.

As helpless infants, we must take everything and can give nothing. In childhood and adolescence, we slowly acquire the capacity to give, but not as much as we receive. As we grow old, we need less and have more to bestow. Although when young our greatest pleasures come from what we receive, in later years we find it far more satisfying, because more in harmony with our spiritual nature, to give.

3. Reciprocal Relations between Organisms of Different Species

How far can animals of one species cultivate moral relations with those of another species? Just to the extent that it is possible to establish relations which, because they are reciprocal, are enduring. Such relations may exist between people and their domestic animals, as, for example, the horse and the cow. Horses serve us by transporting us and our possessions, or by drawing the plough and the harrow. In return, they receive food, shelter, and medical attention when sick. With a kind and considerate master, they may lead what appears to be a happy and contented life, and the association can last as long as the animal. In return for pasturage, salt, subsidiary rations, and shelter in rigorous climates, cows produce enough milk to rear calves with a generous surplus for their owner; and again the relationship is reciprocal and enduring, hence moral in nature. The exchange of services is, in general, the indispensable foundation of these associations; for few people, no matter how kindly disposed toward horses and cows, are wealthy enough to support them unless they in turn aid their owners in providing the necessities of life; and no matter how greatly attached to their master they might be, no horse can continue to work, nor any cow to yield milk, without adequate food and care.

These associations between people and dependent animals are, however, surrounded by dangers inseparable from the exercise of arbitrary power. If the master is cruel and grasping, the poor animal has no adequate means of defense and redress. And in any case, it can hardly communicate its feelings to us, so that we can never be certain whether, from its point of view, it is receiving a fair return for what it gives. It is hardly necessary to add that if the animal is slaughtered, the owner's relationship with it is neither reciprocal nor enduring.

A somewhat analogous relationship is, in our day, becoming increasingly common between people and birds. The feathered tribes brighten our lives with song and lovely plumage and sprightly ways; and, moreover, many of them protect our shade trees, orchards, and gardens from the ravages of insects. As people become more aware of the values to be derived from birds, they make greater efforts to attract them to their gardens, by planting trees and shrubbery that provide edible fruits or serve as sites for nests, by protecting them from enemies of various sorts, and often by placing seeds, fruits, or other foods on trays or tables set among the trees specially for them. It is improbable that the birds are conscious of the pleasure they give to their human admirers; it is even doubtful whether many of the latter are aware that in feeding and protecting them because they enjoy their presence they are entering into a moral relationship. Yet if we deny that a relationship is moral merely because there is no awareness that it is so, we exclude from this category many of the most beautiful and spontaneous of relations, and reduce morality to self-conscious acts performed in obedience to maxims and calculations.

Another reciprocal relationship moral in form is that between insects and the flowers whose pollen they transfer. The very existence of many kinds of plants, as well as of many insects whose whole economy is established on the pollen and nectar from their blossoms, is dependent on the continuance of this exchange of services. Yet it is improbable that either of the associates is aware of what it owes to the other. The same considerations apply to the hummingbirds and other small birds which pollinate flowers while they gather nectar from them. When, as happens occasionally with hummingbirds and regularly with the flower-piercers of the highlands of tropical America, the birds extract the sweet fluid through a perforation which they make in the base of the blossom and thereby avoid touching the stamens and transferring the pollen, the transaction loses all reciprocity and likewise its moralness.

Numerous other reciprocal relationships, which the biologist calls mutual symbiosis, are known in both the animal and vegetable kingdoms. A widespread and notable example is afforded by the lichens so abundant in most parts of the earth, growing on rocks and trees and barren soil. Each lichen is composed of two distinct organisms, one a fungus, the other a green alga. The latter alone is able, by virtue of the green pigment in its cells, to synthesize organic compounds with energy contained in the sunlight, hence it provides the elaborated food for both members of the partnership; while the fungus protects the alga within its enveloping filaments. Although some botanists have regarded this association as an example of helotism or the exploitation of the self-supporting alga by the dependent fungus, lichens are abundant in so many situations where algae could not thrive without the fungus, that it seems evident that both members benefit by their symbiosis.

4. Direct and Cyclic Reciprocity

It is far from my intention to teach a bookkeeping morality, for which a ledger with columns for debits and credits would be an indispensable adjunct. Indeed, the purpose of the present book is not to advocate any form of behavior, but to analyze and understand the innate foundations and structure of morality and the meaning of moral terms. The present chapter is devoted to demonstrating the reciprocity of all genuinely moral relationships, which involve an interchange of kindly influences, or benefits of some sort, and that this reciprocity is the condition of their permanence. But it does not follow that in every such relationship, the benefits which pass in the two directions must be exactly equivalent. The services, material and spiritual, which humans render to each other are so heterogeneous that it is impossible to measure their value by a common scale and keep a numerical record of them; and even if it were feasible to do so, the practice would introduce a subtle poison into such relationships as that between friends, or parents and children, or even good neighbors. All that I maintain is that some current in both directions is necessary to preserve a healthy circulation and keep the relationship alive. Moreover, if we sincerely believe that it is more blessed to give than to receive, we should in all fairness permit others to obtain their due share of the higher blessedness.

But in addition to these direct and immediate interchanges, the world contains many indirect ones, which are, if possible, even more important to our welfare. We receive from all sides benign influences no less than material advantages which we have done nothing to merit or to earn. They flow to us unsolicited from a general fund of goodness and bounty which pervades the world at large no less than every healthy human society. And precisely because we receive so much from sources hidden from our view, we must be willing to give much even when no return is in sight. For this general fund, although vast in terms of our own capacity, is not inexhaustible, and its maintenance depends on our returning to it, on the average, about as much as flows from it. Yet our own limited resources would be far more speedily depleted if we gave much more than we receive. Thus we must still preserve some reciprocity, but it may take a cyclic course rather than be direct and immediate. Instead of an exchange of service, interest, or feeling between A and B alone, it may take the form of A to B to C to D ... to A; and the number of intermediate links may be very large. Cycles of this sort are common in the natural world no less than in human affairs, where they are important not only in commerce but likewise in the intellectual realm.

5. Charity, Apparent and Real

Since moral relations are reciprocal, to have something to offer in return for what is received is of the greatest importance. From this point of view, to be able to perform a large variety of activities, and to serve the community in manifold ways, is a moral advantage which humans enjoy in greater measure than any other animal; for this versatility permits the continuance of reciprocal relations in circumstances where this would be impossible for a less adaptable being. Thus, one who has lost the use of his or her legs may take up some sedentary occupation, and so make some return for the food and other prime necessities produced for him or her by his more active fellows. Even a blind person may be taught to fabricate a number of useful articles. Civilized societies are increasingly successful in finding productive occupations for all sorts of handicapped people, except the insane. To be usefully and agreeably employed not only promotes the self-respect and happiness of these unfortunates; the services they perform for others, however slight, bind them to the community and increase its capacity to support its sick, crippled, and otherwise handicapped members. For no society, however rich and industrially efficient, can feed and attend an unlimited number of unproductive individuals.

In primitive cultures with little division of labor, and few special services by which the crippled and the handicapped could make some return to their fellows for the heavy burden of supporting them, the maintenance of the maimed, the chronically sick, and the aged cannot be long continued. With what appears to their civilized descendants the most brutal callousness, our savage ancestors frequently abandoned or killed their failing parents or incurable brothers and sisters, as the one possible method of relieving themselves of an encumbrance they could hardly support. If our solution of this problem is morally superior to theirs, this is not only because our sensibilities are finer and our compassion greater. Equally important is the fact that we have been able to diminish the burden by giving special employments to the handicapped. Thereby they continue to be united to the remainder of the community by that reciprocal relationship which is the foundation of morality rather than dependent on charity for their support.

The maintenance of a moral relationship with our domestic animals is rendered more difficult by the narrow specialization of the services they can perform for us. A horse, for example, can only haul or carry burdens, and if seriously crippled, becomes useless for such labors. There is scarcely anything that the lame horse can do to repay us for the time and expense of caring for him, which in some parts of the world is no slight outlay. Similarly, a cow whose diseased udder no longer yields milk can perform no useful service, except possibly in those few mountainous regions where cattle are employed to carry loads over rough trails. Compassion, or gratitude for past services, may impel us to continue to care for these animals whose usefulness has ended; but the burden may be heavy and even beyond our means. Were it possible to give them alternative tasks, whereby they could contribute something toward their own support, it would be far easier for us to cultivate the kind of relationship with them that the highest morality approves. In all our dealings with the living things that surround us, we should strive unremittingly to foster the reciprocal relations which we recognize as moral; for these can be indefinitely continued and extended; whereas our capacity to maintain the nonreciprocal relation of charity is limited and soon exhausted.

Much so-called charity, or almsgiving, brings us indirect benefits, at least of a negative sort. By taking care of the indigent and the helpless sick, we preserve the health of the social body and shield ourselves from many ills which might spring from the presence of masses of penurious people, as by the spread of disease, the increase of crime, and possibly even mob violence by starving multitudes. Hence beneficence of this sort brings reciprocal advantages and falls properly within the province of morality. But when purest, active charity is always wholly disinterested and nonreciprocal; at least, it can bring no recompense beyond that glow of feeling which spontaneously arises from the satisfaction of a generous impulse. Pure charity is nonmoral or perhaps even supra-moral. Those who recall the large role that almsgiving assumes in much religious morality, as the Christian, Mohammedan, and Hindu, may be inclined to contest this appraisal. But they need only remember that both Jesus and Mohammed promised large rewards to the almsgiver, in paradise if not on earth. Indeed, the disproportion between the eternal benefits that were offered and the precariously held wealth with which they could be bought, placed the advantage all on the side of the dispenser of alms. Although the kind of "charity" that we first considered comes properly within the province of morality, this last kind might with greater justice be classed as commerce—and of an extremely lucrative sort. No wonder that Sir Thomas Browne wished that there might never be an end of the eleemosynary poor! But, when pure, charity is neither morality nor business but, as Santayana pointed out, one of the least alloyed forms of spirituality.[1]

6. Analysis of Some Reciprocally Beneficial Relationships

That moral relations are necessarily reciprocal follows as a corollary of the highest ethical ideal, no less than from a consideration of the structure of enduring patterns. This ideal, which will be developed in detail in the second part of this work, is the creation of a system of harmonious relations of the greatest possible breadth and inclusiveness, wherein the maximum number of beings can attain the greatest possible fulfillment. It is hardly necessary to argue the point that we—each of us individually—are among those beings whose completeness and perfection the ideal contemplates. Indeed, since we are in a better position to improve our own nature than that of any other creature, the moral community would lose rather than gain if we dedicated all our strength to the service of others, while wholly neglecting ourselves. Not only is it undesirable that we make such a sacrifice; it follows from the reciprocal nature of moral relations that it is in practice impossible for us to do much for others without at the same time improving ourselves; just as it is hardly possible fully to develop our own potentialities without helping others to unfold theirs. We may indeed so arrange our activities that while serving others we fail to develop ourselves as much as we should, but we cannot help others without in some measure improving our own nature.

Egoism and altruism, which mean no more than service to self and service to others, are too often regarded as competing moral interests, yet at their highest they are but complementary aspects of the same conduct. It is this empirical fact that makes ethics so profitable a study. If the structure of the world were such that we could not benefit others without diminishing ourselves, nor improve ourselves without harming others, a moral community would be impossible.

This truth will become clearer if we analyze some of the reciprocal relationships mentioned in section 2 of this chapter. Let us begin with one of those most fundamental to the perpetuation of any species of mammal or bird, the relation between parent and offspring. In the nurture of children, in helping them to unfold their innate capacities, the parent simultaneously develops sides of his own character which might otherwise remain imperfect. In bearing with their weakness, slowness of comprehension, and at times their inevitable refractoriness, one grows in patience and forbearance; in guiding their games and sports, one stimulates one's own imagination; in watching their growth in mind and conscience, one finds a deeper insight into the nature of the human spirit; to fulfill parental obligations intelligently and well, one must strive to see things with a child's vision, thereby fostering the growth of that rare, precious faculty, imaginative sympathy. In adding an intelligence to the world and a worthy citizen to the community, parents bind themselves to the social fabric by closer ties at the same time that they enrich their own nature. To unite more perfect entities by closer, more harmonious relations is the alpha and omega of morality.

The relation between teacher and student, when felicitously adjusted, likewise results in mutual improvement. It is obvious that the pupil gains immeasurably by having a preceptor capable of opening his or her mind and training powers of observation and reasoning. But by teaching we clarify our ideas and give precision to our meaning. This occurs when we teach by means of the written word; but the process is more effective when master and student meet face to face, and the former is constantly exposed to the questions, the criticisms, and the uncertainties of the latter. The intellectual life is hardly rounded and complete without a constant interchange of ideas. In its absence, the continued absorption of facts leads to erudite dullness.

The relation between employer and employee gives ample scope for self-improvement on both sides. It is sometimes said that one cannot be a good master unless one has first been a diligent apprentice, or a competent officer unless one has been a disciplined soldier. The employee all too often, in these days of assertive trade unionism, forgets the economic advantages that are owed to a master whose talent for organization, or thorough understanding of certain technical or agricultural procedures, makes the labor of the former produce more than it could without skillful and closely coordinated management. Both employer and employee, by restraining their acquisitiveness and trying to understand the other's problems, grow in insight, justice, and moderation. But it is evident that to be of continued service to workers, employers must not lose sight of their own interests. If, in solicitude for worker's comfort and welfare they pay more, or demand less, than an often severely competitive trade allows, they ruin themselves and through bankruptcy becomes unable to continue benefits to their dependents. The truest and best philanthropy consists in enabling others to help themselves under favorable and rewarding conditions. Unfortunately, a large share of all that passes by this name consists in giving to a third party a portion of what has been extorted from an often more deserving second party; in employing one per cent of our energy to counteract some of the mischief wrought by the other ninety-nine per cent, as Bertrand Russell remarked.

The cultivation of moral relations is more than the establishment of physical or even vital equilibrium by balancing the intake and outflow of materials and energy. The objective situation has its subjective counterpart in the attitudes that correspond to it. Although a good will must be present in the first place to impel us to cultivate moral relations, the reverse process is also at work: the appropriate external situation helps to develop and fortify those qualities of mind in which, it is often held, all moral worth resides. Thus, a kindness performed for a spiritually receptive person arouses the sentiment of gratitude, which if adequate tends to equalize the moral worth of the doer and the beneficiary of a generous deed. Habitual veracity generates faith among one's associates, while honesty in matters of property is answered by trustfulness. Without the complementary sentiments of gratitude, faith, and trust, the virtues of generosity, veracity, and honesty seem to lead a frustrated existence, forever lacking those responsive attitudes that add immeasurably to the wealth of the moral world. Similarly, unselfish love generates an answering love, while outstanding goodness is acknowledged by reverence. These sentiments may long outlast the situations which stimulated their development, hence are rightly held to possess greater moral value than any purely external relation. Yet in the moral history of humanity, as of each individual, the sentiments appear to be the outgrowth rather than the cause of the corresponding objective situations; hence the practical importance of establishing moral relations, even when we can yet detect no trace of the sentiments which alone give them spiritual significance.[2]

It would be unfortunate to leave the impression that we can improve our nature only by means of relations with others of our kind. This is one of the pathetic fallacies of an age in which humanity's horizon is increasingly restricted by the growing, closely pressing crowd of fellow humans. Because of the more complete mutual understanding and the freer exchange of thoughts made possible by the possession of a common language, our relations with others of our kind are more complex and richer in meaning; but not for that reason does association with creatures of other species fail to enhance our spirit, and perhaps also theirs. By taking a friendly interest in birds, beasts, insects, trees, flowers, ferns, rivers, clouds, mountains, and similar things, we cultivate aspects of our nature that are too often neglected, and bind ourselves to a larger whole by subtle yet far-reaching bonds. This also is a part of positive morality.

It has become evident, I hope, that the first great desideratum of the moral life is to cultivate relations which are, or are capable of becoming, reciprocally advantageous, not merely in a narrow commercial sense, but in the realm of the affections and the intelligence. Or if not directly reciprocal, the relations should be cyclic, involving continued beneficent interchange between ourselves and a larger whole. Although we may within our means, enjoy the spiritual satisfaction of almsgiving, we should otherwise avoid relations in which reciprocity is intrinsically impossible.

7. Virtue as the Stubborn Adherence to the Form of Moral Relations

To certain philosophers, as well as, to many other people, morality has appeared to consist not of the cultivation of reciprocal relations, but of conduct that benefits others, to the complete sacrifice and submergence of personal interests and inclinations. And duty is all too often interpreted to imply the performance of acts which are burdensome and distasteful. The highest virtue of moral fortitude is, in this view, exhibited in the most complete abnegation. How much truth is contained in this interpretation of morality, and if true, how can it be reconciled with our present doctrine?

We may begin our inquiry by the examination of examples of conduct into which the motive of personal advantage, on however lofty a plane, does not enter, or enters to a very subordinate degree. In the first rank many people would place the sacrifice of self to country. This assumes its noblest form not when made in the public eye, for then it is rewarded by popular acclamation and the prospect of lasting fame, always a strong incentive to ambitious spirits; nor yet in the heat of battle, wherewith there is the chance of inflicting injury upon the hated enemy, winning glory, and coming off unscathed. It is most admirable when done in secret, or in the presence of one's enemies alone. Nobody displays patriotism in a more heroic form than the spies, who are often mistaken for a renegade or at least regarded with suspicion by compatriots, and are an object of special opprobrium to the enemy. They perform arduous service under the constant threat of an ignominious death. If captured, they cannot, even as much as the common soldier, count on support or even recognition by the country they serve. They must constantly dissemble and make of their whole life a lie. They may be cruelly tortured if suspected of having information of value to the army on which they spy. Only the most exalted patriotism, it seems, could steel people for such a life; and it appears impossible that they could ever experience a reward commensurate with the sacrifices they make.

The history of Regulus has become the classic example of the highest regard for veracity coupled with unswerving devotion to the public interest. If, on returning to Rome, he had urged the Senate to return the Carthaginian prisoners whose exchange he had been sent to arrange, he would have redeemed his pledge to his captors and might have stayed at home, an honored citizen. Or, even having recommended the retention of the prisoners, he was under no compulsion save that of his plighted word to return and endure torture by the Carthaginians, for in Italy he was beyond their reach. Yet he chose death of the cruelest sort rather than break faith with either his country or its foes.[3]

In ancient civilizations, scarcely any duty ranked higher than that of filial obedience; and neither legend nor history affords a brighter example of stern adherence to this obligation than that of Rama, the hero of the Indian epic, the *Ramayana*. King Dasa-Ratha had arranged for the succession of his eldest son to the throne of the Kosalas; but on the morning set for the coronation, in fulfilment of a promise he had long before carelessly given to one of his wives, who now became jealous of the preferment of another wife's son, the aged monarch reluctantly sentenced Rama to fourteen years of exile in the forest. Without demur or complaint, the hero went forth to a hermit's lean life in the wilderness, accompanied by his ever-faithful wife, Sita, and his younger brother. Soon after banishing his son, the old king died of grief and remorse. Rama's mother and his brother Bharat, who had succeeded to the throne, found their way to his sylvan retreat and implored him to return and assume the kingship that was rightfully his. But Rama unswervingly obeyed the command reluctantly given by a father who no longer lived to revoke it, and only after the expiration of the fourteen years returned to claim his inheritance.

It is doubtful whether anyone chooses friends because of their misfortunes; on the contrary, we contract friendship with those who are agreeable to us, and can in one way or another enrich our lives or advance our aims. Yet after a friendship has been cemented, it is considered by most people, savage no less than civilized, disgraceful to abandon friends in adversity. Their circumstances may be such that, beyond mere gratitude, they can make no return for our efforts in their behalf. It may even happen that merely to manifest an interest in their welfare would jeopardize our life or fortune, while they are so situated that they cannot even learn what we do and risk for them. Yet both fiction and sober history record instances of the highest devotion to unfortunate friends. It may happen that, far from being victim of unmerited disaster, friends have by their own misconduct deserved all the ills that have befallen them, at the same time making themselves unworthy of our friendship and giving ample cause for its termination. Yet there are some who hold that the highest virtue demands our devoted service to them even in these circumstances.

What common feature is displayed by these examples of persistence in virtuous conduct when the moral relation ceases to be reciprocal, or even ceases to exist, and continued faithfulness to a rule of conduct can bring only pain and loss to the one who persists in it, and perhaps benefit nobody? In all the cases cited, and many another of kindred nature that it seems needless to mention here, we recognize a relationship which, in average or normal conditions, is mutually beneficial, as that between citizen and country, between father and son, or between friends. Peculiar circumstances, as the hazards of war, a careless promise coupled with a court intrigue, unforeseen and unmerited misfortunes of many sorts, may so alter the conditions of the relationship that it ceases to be reciprocal and virtue then consists in steadfastly preserving its form, even amidst the greatest hardships, so far as is possible in the altered conditions. But it is important not to overlook the fact that such relations originally arose, whether deliberately or by spontaneous evolution, because they are mutually satisfying and promote the best interests of both parties. If they had failed to fulfill this condition, they would never have won widespread recognition and approval; and no one would detect any merit in striving to preserve them at the price of pain and loss. Even moralists who hold that virtue consists in following a maxim of conduct in circumstances where all personal advantage is absent, would find it difficult to deny that, ordinarily, conduct of the sort they recommend yields reciprocal advantages, and this is the reason why it is universally esteemed. Failure to discern or to remember this important fact gives rise to the ideal of a morality which is untenable because it could not be self-perpetuating.

8. Virtue in Daily Life and Heroic Predicaments

Although to act virtuously when benefit to self is remote or uncertain or wholly absent is not the only expression of virtue, it is the best test of virtue's strength. Aristotle taught that moral virtue is fostered by the habitual performance of virtuous acts. There can be no better test of the strength of a habit than its persistence in difficult circumstances. If filial obedience is a virtue, it is certainly no less a virtue when practiced in a home overflowing with the happiness and love which are its recompense than when it brings loss and suffering; but it is necessary to remove the advantages which flow immediately from obeying one's parents in order to prove the strength of this disposition. If devotion to a friend is a virtue, it is so when the relation is a source of constant gratification no less when it is maintained at the price of sacrifice and peril; but perhaps it is necessary to remove the immediate advantages in order to demonstrate beyond doubt that our protestations of devotion spring from something deeper than self-seeking calculation.

Many acts to which the severest moralist could take no exception bring a prompt reward of one sort or another; and in these instances the behavior of the virtuous person and the unscrupulous opportunist might be the same, except as they differed in needs or values. But life is such that we must often forgo immediate for more distant satisfactions, and purely personal for generally diffused advantages—the need of ethical doctrine has grown out of this circumstance. As the gap widens between inclination and satisfaction, between wholly personal and generally diffused benefits, the difference between the virtuous and the unprincipled character becomes increasingly evident in action. The extreme case is reached when one faces the choice between committing a wicked deed with impunity or even profit and adhering to principles when they can lead only to suffering. At this point the contrast between the virtuous person and the vicious becomes most pronounced. In this sense only can it be maintained that to follow the path of duty when it can bring no personal benefit is the only criterion of virtue. But many righteous people may never be brought to this extreme test, because in all the more usual circumstances of life moral relationships are reciprocally advantageous.

Such people are not less virtuous because the strength of their virtue is unknown.

The morally valuable qualities which support the daily life of an orderly community greatly exceed in mass those displayed in heroic predicaments, yet only in the latter is the tenacity of virtue fully revealed; as the strength of steel is put to far greater use in constructions and machinery than in the engineer's testing laboratory, where alone it can be adequately measured. Perhaps all of us should wish that once or twice in our lifetime we should find ourselves in circumstances which strain our moral fortitude almost to the breaking point and provide a demonstration of its strength. But to live constantly just short of the limit of our moral endurance would be as injurious to the will, as to engage daily in labor which strains our muscles to the point of exhaustion would be ruinous to the body.

Not only is existence at the highest pitch of endurance apt to cause permanent lesions, whether in mind or in body; the display of moral fortitude in nonreciprocal situations is likely to engender pride and a feeling of superiority which can hardly arise in more normal situations. For true goodness is the capacity to enter into harmonious mutual relations with others, so that it can be fully revealed only where it finds a responsive goodness in some other being. Hence virtuous conduct in its most desirable context is a revelation of equality rather than of superiority. Insofar as a child or an animal can respond to our love or kindness or confidence and repay it with the same, it is in this respect our equal. Unless with reference to its internal coherence, to call a wholly isolated entity either good or bad would be meaningless. Except in fruitless gestures which may be more valuable for their example than for their effects, virtue flowers only when it encounters some answering virtue in others. Even the form of the gestures is determined by past experience of this reciprocal relation.

It is fortunate for humanity that some individuals are of such tough fiber that they can stubbornly preserve the form of moral conduct even when its usual reciprocal benefits are impossible. Most of us are from time to time called upon to act in these circumstances, in small matters if not in great; and we should be grateful if we are then strong enough to remain steadfast to our principles. And in periods of social chaos when the usual moral relations are distorted or dissolved, the salvation of culture rests with the few who succeed in preserving rectitude when this can bring them only ridicule and persecution. But these admissions do not invalidate the conclusion that in a well-constituted society moral relations are, and should be, reciprocally rewarding.

Morality grows out of our needs—our need to draw upon our environment natural and social for the materials and services that support our lives; our need to give no less than to take. Were we self-sufficient monads, we would have no needs and enter into no relations with other beings. In such circumstances, morality, except possibly as an ethic of self-perfection, could hardly arise. Our needs might be satisfied by forceful or surreptitious taking, or by cooperation. Of these two methods of acquiring what we must have, only the second is likely to be successful over a long interval, and only this is moral. Cooperation is at first practiced within small groups hostile to neighboring groups; and, so precarious. Moral advance consists in reducing strife by the indefinite expansion of the community within which harmonious, reciprocal relations prevail.

Chapter Six
The Innate Foundations of Morality

1. Origin of the Self-regarding Virtues in the Stresses of Animal Life

IN CHAPTER III we saw that nonhuman animals, who do not discuss rules of conduct nor questions of right and wrong, have developed certain behaviors that we find morally admirable. Indeed, these animals sometimes appear to have reached heights of goodness which our own stumbling feet can hardly reach. These patterns of behavior, which no one, however one may interpret their motivation, can deny to be moral in form, point to a natural or innate foundation of morality widespread in the animal kingdom. Since our hereditary endowment, despite all the great modifications it has undergone during many generations of social life, may be traced back at last to roots that we share with other vertebrates, our morality must ultimately rest on the same natural foundation. No ethic is likely to stand firm unless it is securely built on this innate foundation, and before we can build on it we must trace its outlines.

Virtues and duties fall naturally into two great divisions: (1) those which have reference primarily to self and only indirectly to others; and, (2) those which have reference primarily to others and only indirectly to self. This separation is convenient rather than profound. Everything that we do to self modifies in greater or less degree, for better or worse, our own character, and through this our impact on those around us. How we treat others is not only an expression of our own nature; it in turn modifies this nature, making it better or worse. Moreover, what a social animal does to its associates affects them; and this alteration, great or small, is reflected back in their relations with itself. Every animal, even of kinds we call solitary, is in some measure social, for it lives and moves amid a large, complex community composed of other organisms of its own and other species, which its activities can hardly fail to affect, and which in turn reacts on its own welfare.

The self-regarding virtues include prudence, temperance, continence, patience, fortitude, and the like. Among these that refer primarily to others are justice, benevolence, charity, compassion, tolerance, and veracity. These terms overlap: to be intemperate, as in eating and drinking, shows a failure of prudent regard for one's health; and to be unjust is certainly to be lacking in benevolence. Nevertheless, these conventional terms show well enough the range of the qualities we have now to consider, beginning with those that refer primarily to self.

From ancient times, philosophers and religious teachers alike have so extolled the beauty of temperance, fortitude, and prudence, have so strongly insisted upon their indispensability as foundations for a rational or holy life to be acquired through perseverance, that we tend to view them as special accomplishments rather than as natural attributes of living beings. Yet no view could be farther from the truth. Although some of the refinements of these virtues, such as the temperance which leans toward asceticism, the prudence which looks to the distant end of life or even beyond it, the fortitude which holds us to a self-elected course in disregard of consequences to health or comfort—although some of these refinements are indeed elaborations by a reflective mind, the roots of these virtues sink deep into our animal nature.

Prudence, which has also been called rational self-love, was defined by Henry Sidgwick as "impartial concern for all parts of our conscious life;" and again, as the determination "that Hereafter *as such* is to be regarded neither less nor more than Now."[1] Stated still more simply, the maxim of prudence forbids us to seek present pleasures with no regard for future consequences. The natural foundation of this virtue is one of the most fundamental and widespread of all the springs of behavior in animals: that care for self-preservation which inhibits them from needlessly throwing their lives away, especially while they may still propagate their kind. In elevating this deep vital principle into concern for the experience of living and the enjoyment of happiness or well-being that transcends physical survival, reflective people have elaborated an innate attitude inherited from remote, sub-human ancestors.

No one can give much attention to the behavior of free mammals and birds, or even domesticated ones whose lives have not been thoroughly deranged by artificial conditions, without becoming convinced that prudence is a wholly natural principle of conduct. Free animals must be hungry indeed to be drawn, even by the most tempting food, into situations, which they know, or even suspect, to be dangerous. And even sexual ardor, that overmastering passion, does not often drive them to disregard their own safety in the face of known or recognized perils. In laying up stores of food against periods of scarcity, many mammals, birds, and insects exhibit a sort of constitutional prudence, which for all that we can prove operates without foreseeing the end that it serves.

As with prudence, so with temperance, which is its constant coadjutor and support. Although animals may eat heavily, they are rarely gluttonous, if by this we mean devouring enough to cause sickness or eventual loss of fitness through obesity or physiological derangements resulting from excess of food. Their intake of nourishment is on the whole nicely adjusted to their needs. When an animal has eaten enough, it stops, often leaving a tempting fruit half-consumed. Civilized people, who have devised so many ways of titillating appetites corrupted by habitual indulgence in unnatural foods and stimulants, experience more difficulty than many nonhuman animals in practicing prudence in eating.

The innate foundation of the prudent behavior of animals in the face of competing enticements or opposing drives is to be found in the hierarchical organization of the nervous system which places lower centers under the control of higher centers; or, to view the matter from the side of conduct rather than from that of physiology, its foundation is the integration of every aspect of instinctive behavior into a comprehensive pattern, wherein each reflex and each separate activity is subordinated to a whole which promotes the continued welfare of the individual and its kind.

Fortitude is an equally necessary attribute of animals which must often persevere in the face of perils and obstacles to attain some vitally important objective. The little bird hunting through the snowy woodland for enough nourishment to keep it alive through the long winter night, the land bird migrating over a vast expanse of open ocean, the salmon struggling to ascend long miles of a tumultuous mountain stream to deposit her eggs in the headwaters—in activities like these the fortitude of animals was developed, and without this long ancestral preparation we might lack the innate foundation of this virtue. We, who live in societies which shield the sluggish and the wavering from the full consequences of their own weakness, frequently find it necessary to hold fortitude and perseverance before ourselves as an ideal to be cultivated for its own sake; but in a state of nature something very like fortitude is indispensable for survival.

To be convinced that these self-regarding virtues are of natural origin and not inventions of philosophers who needed them to complete a favorite theory of the components of the soul, nor of theologians eager to establish an imposing scheme of salvation, should strengthen our determination to perfect ourselves in them. For it is helpful to be assured that the perfection we strive to attain is not an arbitrary choice nor a grace incompatible with our nature, but a habit of life whose roots lie deep within us—not so much an adornment of our conduct as a necessity of our existence.

We shall leave to another book the consideration of the ends of life; but whatever we may set as the highest goal of our existence, the rule of prudence is equally applicable. Whether we seek pleasure, wealth, knowledge, fame, or to perfect ourselves in virtue, we cannot disregard prudential considerations without abandoning our claim to rationality. Yet most prudential calculations are weakened by a factor to which no one can assign a definite value, and which we will assess according to our personal experience and temperament; for nobody is certain what the morrow will bring. Prudence bids us set equal value on our welfare today and ten years hence; yet we cannot be sure that we will be alive at the end of a decade, nor can we know with certainty what our circumstances will then be, even if we survive. Hence all future benefits are at a discount when set against those immediately available. In matters of money, we can sometimes give a numerical value to this discount, based on the rates of interest and insurance, which in turn are determined by the statistical calculation of risks. In other considerations, as of future pleasure, future health, or future knowledge, the calculation of the rate of discount will necessarily be less exact;

and it will be more difficult to prevent our judgment from being unduly swayed by immediate desires.

Prudential considerations are perhaps least troublesome to those who make self-perfection their supreme goal. Although hedonists must again and again decide whether they should enjoy a small pleasure today at the risk of losing a much greater one in the future; those who strive above all for moral perfection find a certain conduct appropriate to each situation which life presents, and that the perfect deed has a timeless quality which is largely independent of future contingencies. Yet they cannot wholly ignore its more remote consequences to themselves and others, and every ethical doctrine must find a place for prudence.

2. Origin of Benevolence in Parental Solicitude

Turning now to the altruistic or other-regarding virtues, all of which might be subsumed under benevolence in the fullest meaning of the term, we find a widespread tendency, even on the part of moralists who consider benevolence as no less incumbent on us than prudential regard for our own welfare, to view it as somehow derivative from the self-regarding virtues or motives. This was not so evident in Plato, Aristotle, and other ancient philosophers, who wrote at a period when individualism was less rampant than it became in the West after the Christian Reformation, and who could hardly conceive a good life apart from a city of people bound together by common ancestry or the fiction thereof. But the apparent necessity to find the roots of altruism in egoism has posed a perplexing problem to many modern philosophers, including Spinoza, Hobbes, Bentham, Sidgwick, and in fact nearly everyone who aspired to the neatness of a closely articulated ethical theory, with the notable exception of the Intuitive School.

The derivation of the *duty* to promote the welfare of others from the supposed *fact* that, as originally constituted, our human nature leads us to care only for our own happiness, was a problem with which the Utilitarian moralists struggled valiantly but in vain. "Each one," wrote Sidgwick, "is morally bound to regard the good of any other individual as much as his own, except insofar as he judges it to be less, when impartially viewed, or less certainly knowable or attainable by him." As in the case of prudence, this principle would appear to be equally valid regardless of our definition of the highest good—whether it be pleasure, knowledge, virtue, or something quite different. If we concede that each individual has the right to establish a personal criterion of the good, then the highest benevolence would seem to consist in helping all humans or all living creatures to attain the ends toward which they strive, how diverse soever they may be, insofar as their goals may be won without inflicting an incommensurate loss on other beings, including ourselves.

Rationally to distribute our benevolence, we shall need some common denominator, some method of comparing one good with another, so that we may consistently apply our efforts where they will be most productive. The attainment of an agreeable state of consciousness, call it pleasure, happiness, or something else, appears to be the one element common to all the diverse ends that people pursue. Hence universal benevolence readily takes the form of "Universalistic Hedonism," as Sidgwick called the Utilitarian doctrine.

The Utilitarians taught that right conduct is that which, in any given circumstances, will produce the greatest quantity of happiness in the world. It is the doctrine of the *Good Universal*; and whatever faults their theories might possess, it is to the lasting glory of thinkers of this school that, at least in principle, they considered, in their attempts to appraise the moral results of any particular course of action, the feelings not only of humans but of all beings sensible to pleasure and pain.

The Utilitarians taxed their ingenuity to prove the soundness of this fundamental principle. Taking as primary and self-evident the rightness or moral validity of each individual's effort to promote his or her own happiness, they strove to deduce from this an obligation to advance the happiness of all sentient beings, so that, regardless of how felicity is distributed among individuals, it would always be at a maximum. Although a skillful writer or preacher may with no great difficulty effect the emotional transition from self-interest to universal interest, it appears impossible to make logically unassailable the proposition that, because we wish to be happy ourselves, it is our duty to make all the world as happy as we can make it. To self-interest, the most convincing arguments in favor of universal, or at least somewhat widely diffused, benevolence are two empirical facts: first, that individuals often experience great happiness, at times their highest happiness, in working for the welfare of others; and second, that each individual's felicity is intimately bound up with the prosperity, in the widest sense, of the world in which he or she dwells, and is likewise to a high degree dependent on the good will of neighbors. But these discoveries do not in themselves make the satisfactions of altruism more incumbent on us than the pleasures of eating, listening to music, or playing games. Yet the fact that we are often made happy by giving unselfishly to others suggests the true origin of benevolence.

To attempt to derive our benevolent impulses from our purely selfish motives is like trying to explain the origin of the right hand by the existence of the left. In us, benevolence is no more derived from self-interest than one hand from the other. Both are original components of our nature, which we discover in ourselves as soon as we are able to turn an inquiring glance within us and analyze our motives. Only a vicious education or a wrong theory could blind us to this truth. It is as natural that in appropriate circumstances we should spontaneously serve others as that we should exert ourselves to satisfy our own appetites.

With a few curious exceptions, in all the vast host of warm-blooded vertebrates, the young are more or less dependent on their parents for food or protection, or more commonly for both. This makes it indispensable for the parents to have motives directed to the welfare of individuals other than themselves. Moreover, in a great many of these mammals and birds, especially the latter, the attraction between the male and female parents long survives the period of sexual ardor, and leads them to work together for their offspring; in many instances, such cooperation in parental care is essential to the survival of the progeny. And even after their offspring have outgrown the need of their ministrations, the parents, all of whose sexual impulses have become quiescent, may remain for many months in closest association, as happens in numerous non-migratory birds. This enduring companionship of male and female suggests that they are held together by an effective bond which makes the welfare of one of some concern to the other. Thus, in practically all birds and mammals, the perpetuation of the species depends on two radically different sets of impulses: (1) those directed toward self-preservation, and (2) those which ensure the care of offspring and often also the persistence of pairs. From the first are derived all the self-regarding virtues; from the second, the other-regarding virtues or benevolence.

Yet from the fact that we find within ourselves, as original and coordinate components of human nature, both self-regarding and altruistic motives, it does not follow that the second could exist or have significance in the absence of the first. Regard for the welfare of others would be futile in the absence of beings whose existence and prosperity are momentous to themselves. In a world where no creature cared for its own life or happiness, altruism could have neither purpose nor meaning. Hence it is foolish to depreciate concern for oneself in relation to concern for others. Hence also the logic of the Stoics and of Spinoza in taking the endeavor to preserve one's own being as the foundation and starting point of morality. The self-regarding and other-regarding motives are not only biologically but logically complementary; and the task of ethics is not to vilify either of them, but to discover in what proportions they must be blended to advance the ends that it approves.

Moreover, only after an animal has reached a rather high degree of complexity, largely by the action of processes internal to itself, can it become aware of the needs and aspirations of others and devote its strength to satisfying or furthering them. If we felt within us only impulses to gratify or improve ourselves, we would be constrained to regard ourselves as end-products of the process which formed us. Each individual would then represent the terminal point of a creative movement which stopped with himself or herself, hence would be wholly a creature and in no sense a creator. But this is contrary to our experience; we are aware of the very energy that made us acting through us to increase the perfection not only of ourselves but of beings which surround us. Our altruistic endeavors prove that we are active participators in harmonization, not its passive products.

3. Comparison of Self-regarding and Other-regarding Motives

It will introduce clarity into some of our later discussions if we pause at this point to draw attention to certain similarities between motives which impel us to perform acts that benefit ourselves and those which lead us to promote the welfare of others, whether our own offspring or creatures unrelated to us; in the first place, I am aware of a motive of either kind as an inclination or at times a strong desire to act in a certain way. And since it is *my* impulse which I strive to satisfy, whenever my act accomplishes its intended end I experience pleasure or contentment; just as I feel frustrated or ill at ease when any strong impulse is thwarted, no matter whether it is directed toward my own welfare or that of some other being. Hence it follows that I cannot benefit any creature without giving myself a measure of gratification, although this is at times fleeting, and succeeded by sadness or a sense of futility when I see how little my efforts are appreciated or how ineffectual they are. Naturally, at the level of sensation the results to myself of my self-regarding activities, such as eating or sheltering myself or increasing my possessions, are utterly different from those of my altruistic activities, as when I feed or clothe another. Yet at higher psychic levels we find a fundamental similarity between them, for both yield contentment.

This fact, that we cannot do good deeds for others without at the same time gratifying ourselves, has led some people to regard human nature as essentially selfish. They think that whenever we are deliberately rather than impulsively benevolent we have calculated the pleasure our action will bring us and this is the real *reason* for it. If they would probe a little more deeply into human nature, they would see that unless we were originally endowed with altruistic motives, we could not gratify ourselves by giving play to them. While I freely admit that I can never help a person or animal without feeling a little better for what I have done, and that this is an added incentive for my deed, I do not consider this a defect in myself, but rather an excellent quality; although I cannot claim any merit for it, as it was implanted in me by nature rather than won by my own effort. And it seems necessary that an animal endowed with both self-regarding and other-regarding impulses should gain much the same sort of satisfaction, at the higher level, from the fulfillment of either; for in the endlessly varied circumstances of life, impulses of the two sorts will frequently be brought into competition with each other, and it must choose between them. If satisfaction of both kinds of impulses did not yield feelings of the same general character, although varying in quality and intensity, it would be impossible to compare one with the other for lack of a common measure; and it is difficult to understand how in this case a choice could be made.

It is most difficult to assess the relative masses of our selfish and altruistic motives. Frequently, when we survey the people around us, or even scrutinize our inmost self with fearless honesty, we suspect that human nature is predominantly selfish, with perhaps here and there a gleam of disinterested benevolence. But there is another way of viewing this question which will perhaps lead to a different conclusion. The world is crowded with people, most of whom are alive only because during a long period of helpless infancy and dependent childhood they received the devoted care of parents or fosterers; and whatever education and culture they have, they owe almost wholly to the efforts of those who preceded them. Of all the humans who ever lived, the vast majority are now dead. Their efforts were directed in part to preserving and gratifying themselves and in part to passing on the torch of life and culture. It is scarcely possible to separate these two kinds of activities and measure the quantity of each; but aside from certain enduring artifacts and minor changes in the Earth's surface, only those of the second kind have left lasting results. And the generation now living, with all its culture and knowledge, represents a vast expenditure of other-regarding effort by the majority that has ceased to be. The same applies to every species of mammal, bird, or animal of whatever kind that is dependent on parental care.

Although devotion to family and offspring is certainly not the most advanced form of altruism, it is the root whence all more widely diffused benevolence has sprung.

It may be not out of place to call attention to an apparently inevitable defect in nearly all moral discourses and analyses of motivation made in the interest of morality. Even when most intended to defend or incite altruistic conduct, they tend to exaggerate our selfish motives. Humans, like many another animals, are endowed by nature with impulses which reach out beyond and aim at the welfare of others, usually of their own kind, exceptionally of different kinds of beings. As with most native impulses, those that we call altruistic are stronger in some individuals than others. Although it would be folly to maintain that ethical philosophers or moral preachers love their fellow creatures more than many another person whose benevolence takes the form of action rather than of theorizing or sermonizing, I think that we may safely assume that their interest in the welfare of their fellows and sensitivity to their happiness are above the average. When such persons try to influence others whose character is dominated by egoism, what will they do? Their analysis of the motives and effects of human actions makes it clear that what one does for others can bring many and varied advantages to self, and they try to stir egoistic individuals out of their selfishness by calling attention to the benefits and satisfactions which will accrue to them through altruistic endeavor. This is the obvious and easiest course. Thus, moralists develop theories, and deliver exhortations, which make people, including themselves, appear more selfish and calculating than we actually are.

The being wholly untainted by hedonistic calculus scatters its beneficence as spontaneously as the flower its fragrance and the bird its song. Yet moralists are reluctant to admit that such unpremeditated goodness is moral; they insist that the essence of moral choice is the recognition of alternative courses of action and the deliberate selection of one of them. How shall we escape from this contradiction? Perhaps by recognizing that morality appertains not to beings who have achieved perfect goodness so much as to those in the process of becoming good. And as our chief task in life seems to be the formation of character through moral and other endeavor, moral discipline is particularly necessary and appropriate to us.

When we contemplate the life of any animal, of whatever kind, who nourishes and defends its young, how at one moment it gives hard-earned food to its little ones, or risks its life in their defense, how a minute later it may be in desperate straits to save its own skin or satisfy its gnawing hunger—when we pay attention to these sudden alternations of conditions in all the higher animals, it should not surprise us to discover self-regarding motives lurking amidst our most altruistic endeavors; or to find ourselves indulging, at the very moment when we need most urgently to improve our condition, in unpremeditated acts of pure generosity which delay the attainment of our own legitimate aspirations. It would be irrational to permit ourselves to be distressed by this mixture of motives that we so often discover deep within ourselves. The selfish no less than the altruistic impulses spring from our inmost depths; they are equally necessary and equally defensible. The function of reason is not to suppress one or the other, but to blend both into a harmonious whole. In establishing this felicitous balance of the self-regarding with the other-regarding virtues, ordinary conscientious individuals are as likely to exceed due measure on the side of altruism as on the side of egoism; for with imposing authority society presses claims against which they may fear to oppose their own more modest rights. "It is easy," wrote Montesquieu, "to regulate by laws what we owe to others; but it is very difficult to comprise all we owe to ourselves."[2] And his contemporary Joseph Butler contended that we have not too much self-love but rather too little of it, at least of the sort that is intelligent and understands its ends.[3]

4. Adumbrations of Sympathy in Nonhuman Animals

Although we share with simpler animals blind organic urges which drive us to exert ourselves in producing and nurturing offspring who will one day replace us, our more thoughtful and deliberate efforts to promote the welfare of other beings are in large measure motivated by sympathy. Hume, Adam Smith, and other writers of the seventeenth century called attention to the moral importance of this component of human nature, and later Alexander Sutherland made a long and elaborate study, tracing the development of sympathetic feeling in the animal kingdom and the derivation of our moral sentiments from parental sympathy.[4] Although his conclusions are in the main sound, he overemphasized the role in the development of sympathy of the elaboration of the nervous organization, particularly the so-called "sympathetic system," to the neglect of those higher mental factors in which Hume had found the basis of this extremely complex psychic phenomenon. The investigations of more recent students of animal behavior, particularly those of the entomologist W. M. Wheeler, make it necessary to revise Sutherland's account of the origin of sympathy.[5] Although to do this in adequate detail would require a separate volume, sympathy occupies so important a place among our moral resources that we can hardly avoid tracing its growth, at least in broad outlines.

Everyone who has devoted attention to the ways of the social insects, including ants, bees, wasps, and termites, has been impressed by the close cooperation of the few or many individuals which compose a colony, their industry, their devotion to the common welfare, and apparent forgetfulness of self. From ancient times, the prudence and self-abnegation of ants and bees have been held up by moralists as examples for wayward humanity to imitate. The close attachment of each individual to the community as a whole is the inevitable result of its own incompleteness. Although in some of these social insects, especially the ants, the young, newly fecundated female is capable of providing a usually poor and inadequate diet for the larvae which hatch from her earliest eggs, she soon relinquishes this task to the workers into which they develop; and with advancing age she may, as in termites, become hardly more than a swollen sac for the production of eggs, unable to provide for her innumerable progeny, or even for herself. The workers in turn are, in general, unable to engender the larvae they so assiduously attend; and where there is a special warrior caste, the soldiers with huge mandibles or syringe-like heads may be incapable of nourishing themselves and depend, like the larvae, on the ministrations of the workers. Because functions which in most animals are united in a single individual are in these insect communities divided among diverse individuals, the whole colony is sometimes called a superorganism—a sort of social organism composed of incomplete individuals.

What binds together these heterogeneous individuals capable of going their separate ways and performing their diverse tasks, yet unable to survive apart from their society? Is it their feeling of dependence on the whole, or a sense of duty to the mother colony perhaps akin to human patriotism, or self-interest, or sympathy with their fellows, or mere blind habit? When one watches them sharing food with their companions, gently stroking each other with their antennae, licking each other, carefully feeding and nursing the helpless larvae, or dutifully attending their queen, it is easy to imagine that they are moved by sentiments of sympathy and tender sisterly affection. But Wheeler advanced many reasons for believing that the chief bond between the members of a colony is the food they are constantly exchanging, and the pleasant sensations, which we can compare only with tastes and odors in ourselves, that they provide for each other. He applied the term *trophallaxis* (exchange of food) to the concept of a society held together by the reciprocal passage of food, tastes, or other agreeable sensory stimulants.

The facts which support this view are so numerous that only a few can be given here. The larvae of certain wasps, including those of the widespread genera *Vespa* and *Polistes*, after receiving food from a worker, or even when their oral region is otherwise stimulated, secrete from their salivary glands drops of a thin, sweetish liquid which are eagerly sucked up by their nurses. Obviously, the nutritive value of the secreted drops cannot be equivalent to that of the food which the larva receives, else it could not grow; but it may be that the worker so craves these dainties that she relinquishes to sacrifice for them a far greater bulk of the food that she has collected on her foraging expedition; just as the peasant who takes crops to market may pay the value of several pounds of nutritious grain or vegetables for delicacies which as food are worth far less. The mouths of the larvae of certain African ants are surrounded by relatively enormous glands that exude a substance attractive to the workers which nourish and attend them. Even in less specialized ants, the helpless larvae appear to secrete from the surface of their bodies substances, probably of a fatty nature, which are highly attractive to their nurses and provide the stimulus for all the handling, licking-over, and careful removal in the face of danger, which these helpless white grubs receive.

Not only do the larvae provide enticing chemical stimuli for the adults, the latter are in much the same way attractive to each other by means of secretions which their companions lick from their bodies. Moreover, in many of these social insects the workers frequently feed each other, either with regurgitated food or, as in termites, with faecal matter; so that Maurice Maeterlinck was led to characterize a termite society as a "collective coprophagy." The workers of a Ceylonese termite are so eager for the exudate of their huge, physogastric queen that to reach it more readily they tear little strips from her cuticle leaving her body marked with scars. But perhaps the most convincing evidence for the soundness of Wheeler's views is found in the bewildering variety of parasites, belonging to different orders of insects, which lurk in many ant colonies. Not only do these highly specialized beetles, crickets, and other insects nibble exudates from the bodies of their myrmecine hosts; they themselves provide, from special glands, secretions so highly agreeable to the ants that they win for themselves not only toleration but tender care, such as the ants bestow on their own companions and helpless young.

In vertebrates, we observe relations so similar in outward form to those established among social insects by the exchange of food and attractive chemical stimuli that we may, with T. C., extend to them the term trophallaxis, even when neither gustatory nor olfactory sensations are involved in them. In birds, mutual preening of the plumage by members of the same flock is found chiefly in the highly social species, including anis and wood quails. In some less social birds, including certain doves, crows, toucans, and cactus wrens, this mutual attention appears to occur chiefly between members of a pair; while a great many kinds of birds seem to preen only their own plumage. The free sharing of food that has been found by one member of a flock, possibly as the reward of vigorous scratching, is likewise observed only in the most social birds, and the same applies to sleeping in close contact for greater warmth. As a rule, even birds who forage in flocks do not willingly share what they find; and those which roost in large companies preserve a space between themselves and their neighbors.

We do not know whether the smooth shells of the eggs yield agreeable sensations to an incubating bird, who presses the bare skin of the brood patch on its breast against them, or whether similar contact with the soft bodies of nestlings or chicks is pleasant to the parent; but analogy with mammals suggests that this may be so; and such agreeable sensations may serve as an incentive to cover and protect the eggs and young. But there can be little doubt that mutual preening, sharing of food, or sleeping in contact is a bond which holds together the most highly social birds, which display the greatest affection for their companions. In other avian species, which although gregarious are less intimate with their flock mates, as in many mammals, the forces which draw individuals together are opposed by others that keep them apart. Domestic hens and other birds peck at companions who crowd them too closely, those of higher social rank directing their blows at individuals of lower status, who do not return the pecks they receive but treat still lower individuals as they themselves are treated, until the lowest-ranking member of the group is pecked by all but pecks none. In many species, the spacing of the members of a foraging or roosting flock results from opposing forces of attraction and repulsion.

In mammals, similar bonds hold together the members of a herd, and draw the mother more closely to her suckling. Often one sees two horses simultaneously scratching and nibbling each other with their teeth, a performance which appears to yield great satisfaction. Among ungulates, the sight and probably even more the scent of companions grazing or resting close by is necessary for the contentment of each; and by calls and restlessness they reveal their distress when separated from their comrades. Between the mother and her helpless offspring the ties are necessarily even closer. There is no reason to suppose that the gratifying sensations produced by sucking at her breasts are confined to the human mother. Not only does this tugging at the nipples, by no means always gentle in a vigorous young calf, appear to yield positive pleasure to mammalian dams of the most diverse kinds; it also affords relief from the discomfort of a breast or udder distended with milk. The licking of her calf or colt or cub appears to bring the female quadruped agreeable sensations, such as the human mother derives from kissing and caressing her baby, suggesting that a kiss may after all be only a reduced or symbolic form of licking with the tongue, a practice far more widespread among mammals as a whole. Thus the tender care bestowed on their progeny by animals so diverse as the social insects and the higher mammals is not the product of a wholly selfless devotion. The material advantage is all on the side of the helpless young, but the attendant adult receives a fair return in satisfying affective states; and the reciprocity inherent in moral relations is seen to be achieved, in the first instance, by natural means.

5. Analysis of Sympathy

It is easy for the imaginative and sympathetic human observer to read sympathy into these so intimate and apparently affectionate relations between the members of a swarm or a herd, between parents of the most diverse kinds and their callow young. But sympathy is more than the mutual induction of pleasant sensations or affective states by social companions, more even than the most tender and exquisite feelings of devotion of a parent for its offspring. Sympathy is the production in one individual of feelings corresponding to those of some other individual by the awareness of this second individual's condition. We can hardly be sure that these induced feelings are truly sympathetic unless they contrast with, or at least differ from, those which would ordinarily be produced in the first individual by his or her own immediate circumstances. If my companion and I are both in high spirits on a fine, sunny morning, this affords no proof of sympathetic feeling; we may both be responding in the same way to the same external situation. But if some mishap that befalls him or her alone and affects me directly not at all, suddenly changes my elation to sadness, we have an example of true sympathetic induction. If in the midst of grief or misfortune I can be lifted up by another's happiness, arising from some circumstance which brings no direct benefit to me, we have an even stronger proof of sympathetic feelings. Similarly, if two ants stroking each other's antennae, or two horses nibbling each other's shoulders, are both enjoying the exchange of attentions, we have no proof of sympathetic feelings; they are merely reacting in the same way to the same stimulus. Nor can we be sure that a mother's tender regard for her baby is always sympathetic; her devotion to it may be largely a response to the delicious feelings it stirs up in her.

True sympathy appears to depend on complex processes in a rather highly developed mind, no less than on a nervous organization capable of being stimulated by perceptions or representations, themselves of a purely cognitive order, to yield emotional states usually accompanied by definite somatic changes. We have no evidence of the existence of such sympathy in the insects, and very little in the case of birds and nonhuman mammals. Closely as the members of a colony of social insects cooperate with each other, sharing their labors and their food, they seem indifferent to their comrades' misfortunes. Sir John Lubbock placed ants in a variety of situations such as would have aroused the concern, if not the active assistance, of more sympathetic animals who discovered their companions in similar plights; but the free ants passed heedlessly by comrades which he had stuck in honey, buried in sand with only their heads exposed, half drowned and left to recover by slow degrees, chloroformed, or intoxicated. It could hardly be that they failed to notice their unfortunate fellows; for alien ants, placed equally close to them, were set upon with fury and promptly killed. Sutherland experimented with seventeen species of ants, in each case pinning near the entrance of a nest two or three nestmates, which were held down with little pieces of wire bent into the shape of a hairpin.[6] These tests were repeated until at least ten individuals of each species had been treated this way; but in no instance did their free companions, who for hours passed close by in endless streams, show signs of sympathy or make a move to help the prisoners. Yet if a fly or a strange ant were dropped in the same place, the ants at once crowded around to kill and dismember it. Far from remaining indifferent to their injured nestmates, the harvesting ants studied by R. W. G. Hingston in the Himalayas rushed upon them with every sign of anger. He believed that they behaved in this strange fashion because they associated the crippled state of their companions with the presence of enemies as the cause of this, and not finding such enemies, they vented their hostile feelings on their dead and wounded comrades.[7]

Even mammals commonly display a similar disregard for the plight of sick, wounded, or suffering fellows. The horse who all day calls eagerly for the companion who has gone out to work, who neighs with apparent delight as the friend returns, will if stronger push the traveler away from its rations, no matter how tired and hungry the latter may be after a long journey. Cattle who are distressed apart from their herd do not hesitate to horn their weaker companions away from choice food. Dogs give more obvious signs of sympathy, at least with their masters, whose sickness or grief often seems to bring them genuine distress.

Among birds, I have watched Purple Martins and Black-capped Chickadees fluttering excitedly about a comrade who had become entangled in a strand of nest material or a cobweb and hung helplessly beneath the branch of a tree. But despite their obvious interest, they made no intelligent efforts to release the prisoner, who seemed to fear rather than to welcome the close approach of its free companions. And it is well known that many parent birds who carefully attend their young while in the nest quite neglect them if they fall out before they are feathered and can hop about and call, although the unfortunate nestlings lie in full view. Yet in many of these instances the mishap is irremediable; for the unfeathered young cannot be properly attended unless returned to the nest, and this feat appears to be beyond the power of most small birds, whose bills are poor instruments for lifting a tender and relatively heavy nestling without injuring it. Natural selection would operate against a habit so dysgenic as showing much concern for an irretrievably doomed nestling. Young who have fallen from the nest prematurely, yet at an age when it is possible to keep them alive, are often solicitously attended; and the annals of ornithology contain reliably reported instances of birds bringing food to captives of their kind, or nourishing a companion whose blindness or deformed bill prevented its feeding itself.

Although it is most difficult for the human observer to assess how much true sympathy exists among nonhuman animals, we can hardly doubt that we have discovered, even among creatures as callous to the plight of their companions as ants appear to be, the sort of relationship which must be established before sympathy can grow. There must in the first place be a bond between two or more individuals, who are either social equals or stand in the unsymmetric relationship of parents and young; and this close association, so far as it is conscious and not maintained by mere automatic reflexes, must be pleasurable or satisfying. But as long as the relationship affords gratification to both parties, there is no need to postulate the presence of sympathetic feelings, for immediate stimulation by the companion is sufficient to produce agreeable sensations. If one of the companions is injured or hungry or in any way distressed by a cause which does not affect the other, its immediate or direct effect on this other should, in the absence of sympathy, remain the same, except insofar as the less active or less responsive state resulting from its plight fails to yield the usual pleasant stimuli. For the distress of the unfortunate companion to be communicated to the other, who has no immediate cause of unhappiness, requires a somewhat complex mental organization, capable of imagination or something closely akin to it.

Whether the parent animal who shows obvious signs of distress when its calf or cub or nestling is lost or injured or in danger is in fact moved by sympathetic feelings, or whether its perturbed state is due merely to the disruption of habitual activities or to the absence of the pleasant stimuli which its offspring normally affords, is a question which we cannot answer with assurance. But surely in these cases we are nearer to true sympathy than in the ants who show no concern for the plight of their captive or mutilated fellows. Although we cannot be sure in any specific instance how much sympathy actually exists, it is certain that when a parent, itself unhurt and unmenaced, shows distress for the plight of its offspring, we have the kind of situation in which sympathy first arose. It seems obvious too from their mode of origin that the earliest sympathetic feelings, properly so-called, must have been painful or distressing, in contrast to the agreeable feelings *directly* produced by social companions. The sympathetic sharing of pleasure or happiness seems to represent a further elaboration of a process which was originally developed with reference to painful situations. Perhaps this explains why in general we are so much more readily moved to sympathy by the contemplation of the pains of other beings than by their pleasures.

One of the earliest rudiments of sympathy appears in that intuitive awareness, widespread among animals, that flesh is tender and sensitive, that the too vigorous use of teeth, bills, nails, or hoofs will cause pain. Puppies and other young animals at their play, parent mammals of various kinds when they fondle or carry their young, horses and other animals when taking food from their master's hand, act as though they knew that living creatures feel pain, and do not use their teeth as hard as they might. Moreover, some animals behave as though aware that certain organs are more delicate and vulnerable than others, and refrain from attacking these regions of their companions. Of all the countless times that I have watched domestic hens peck their flockmates on the head, I have never seen nor heard of their injuring an eye; and I am fairly certain that this immunity does not result from the avoiding movements of the pecked one, but rather from the forbearance of the pecker. A similar respect for the eyes of their companions has been observed in ravens and other social birds that peck the heads of their subordinates. I once watched a mare use a hind leg to push gently away a newborn calf that had become confused and attempted to suck from her udder instead of its mother's. The mare might well have kicked, but she desisted from using violence. It is impossible for us to know anything about the subjective aspect of these restraints, but it is hardly possible to doubt that in them we witness some of the earliest glimmerings of sympathy and moral inhibitions.

6. The Complex Mental Processes Involved in True Sympathy

As analyzed by Hume, sympathy arises through a rather complex mental process, involving a double and parallel association of ideas and impressions, or to use a more modern terminology, between mental representations and direct presentations.[8] The first and indispensable association is that between the external object which arouses sympathy and oneself. We sympathize only with beings in which we detect some resemblance to ourselves; and the strength of our sympathy is directly proportional to the closeness of this resemblance, or at least to the closeness of our identification of ourselves with the object of our sympathy. Thus, in general, members of one's family arouse more vivid feelings of sympathy than strangers, members of one's society stronger feelings than members of a different society. Similarly, it is easier to feel sympathy with vertebrates who like ourselves have warm blood than with cold-blooded vertebrates; with cold-blooded vertebrates than with invertebrates, which differ from us in so many essential ways. And we can feel sympathy with minerals and other lifeless objects only if we adopt the hylozoic view and invest them with feelings which somewhat resemble our own.

Secondly, it is necessary that the object of our sympathy convey to us in some way its own affective state; and this seems possible only when it expresses its emotions more or less as we do. As little children we cried when we were unhappy, with the result that tears and sobs are in us firmly associated with distress; just as smiles and laughter, by which we ourselves express satisfaction and happiness, are for us indications of agreeable feelings. But the affections of others are never directly presented to us; we merely infer them and form an idea or representation of them at the suggestion of certain sensuous impressions of a very different sort, as the sound and sight of weeping or laughter. And such a representation of another person's affections is never sympathy; we can represent or imagine another's sufferings without in the least sympathizing, or even gloat over his or her misfortunes.

How, then, does sympathy arise? For Hume, as for many other philosophers, the chief difference between an idea and an impression, between a memory image and an immediate sensuous presentation, lies in the superior strength and vividness of the latter. Now our awareness of ourselves is always very strong and vivid, and by association this intensity is imparted to our idea of another being in proportion to its closeness or similarity to ourselves. The closeness of this association affects in a parallel manner the corresponding affective states, so that our idea or representation of the other person's feelings is intensified until we experience within ourselves feelings similar, or to use Hume's terminology, we have an immediate impression of these affections—keeping in mind the fact that impressions may be of two sorts, either of external objects which excite our senses or of our own internal states. Thus it happens that the idea of a friend's sorrow becomes an actual sorrow for us, and his or her joy becomes our joy.

The foregoing argument, necessarily somewhat long and involved, can be presented more succinctly by the use of symbols. Let A stand for one person and B for some other person. Let b be the second person's affective state, while a is A's sympathetic reproduction of it. Because of B's resemblance to A, the latter forms a vivid apprehension of him or her, and likewise through certain signs (e.g., tears or laughter) becomes aware of B's emotion. At first this awareness is purely cognitive, but the vivid strength of A's idea of B affects the associated idea of b, until the latter, from being simply the notion that B is happy (or sad) grows into a, the actual sympathetic reproduction of the happiness (or sadness) of the other. We might represent the final situation as a proportion, $a:b::A:B$.

Such, as I understand it, is Hume's theory of the origin of sympathetic feelings through the double relation of ideas and impressions. We know now, far more thoroughly than was possible for a philosopher early in the eighteenth century, to how large an extent our emotions are correlated with somatic changes, such as the discharge of hormones by the ductless glands, variations in the tension of the blood vessels, and muscular contractions; so that it is evident that the mental processes we have been describing produce important changes in the body, which in turn alter the quality of our affections. Thus it seems evident that the growth and refinement of the nervous system, and especially of nerves that initiate internal and visceral changes, is, as Sutherland contended, of great consequence to the development of sympathy; and one of the factors contributing to this advance in nervous organization is doubtless the practical advantage to a species of animal of being susceptible to stimulation by offspring or by social companions. But without the higher mental processes discussed by Hume, these advances in nervous organization seem in themselves incapable of producing true sympathy.

We need not stop here to follow Hume in the analysis of the role of his "double relation of ideas and impressions" in the production of pride and humility. Even in its simplest form, as when it gives rise to sympathetic joy or sorrow, the process described by Hume may seem too complex and involved to account for the origin of feelings which surge up so swiftly as sympathy often does. When we recall that babies considerably less than a year of age give evidence of the rudiments of sympathy by their different responses to the smiles and scowls of adults, so much association of ideas may seem a gratuitous assumption. A further difficulty lies in the fact that our sympathetic feelings are usually not an exact copy of the feelings which induce them, and may even bear little resemblance to the original feelings, save in their general tone as pleasurable or painful. To some people, the sight of the cutting or tearing of living flesh causes the whole body to tingle with distressing sensations, yet these bear little resemblance to the actual pain of a cut or a laceration. Perhaps in this instance we are dealing with an innate reaction not dependent on present mental associations. On the other hand, the sight of a hungry person or animal, even if extremely emaciated, does not so spontaneously produce distressing feelings in ourselves; and, at least for one who has not personally experienced starvation, it requires a stronger mental effort to share the sufferer's distress, than in the case of immediate violence to the body. In this, and many other examples of sympathetic feeling that it would be superfluous to examine here, it seems impossible to frame an adequate explanation simpler than that of Hume.

Analysis of the psychic foundations of sympathy raises the suspicion that cruelty is closely allied to it and requires mental faculties of much the same order. How could one enjoy the sight of another creature's pains unless one had a vivid apprehension of them, and how could one imagine them save by recognizing the sufferer's similarity to oneself? Yet if this is what actually happened, the cruel person would be pained by the contemplation of another's agony rather than gloat over it, so that unless we suppose that one takes a morbid pleasure in torturing oneself, one could not continue to be cruel. Otherwise stated, if the psychic processes involved in cruelty are the same as those underlying sympathy, the results must be the same, and cruelty becomes impossible except to one with a pathological thirst for suffering. In most cases, cruelty must be otherwise engendered, and it appears to have two sources: (1) the emotional discharge of the hatred a person feels toward enemies who have injured or at least threaten, or else the discharge upon some scapegoat of hatreds and frustrations for which the latter is not responsible; and (2) vulgar delight in a display of any sort, no matter what its source, as, for example, the cries and contortions of an agonized victim. These are reactions of a mind somewhat above the level of purely instinctive behavior but not yet so finely organized as to be capable of much sympathy. The growth of sympathy suppresses these barbarous feelings.

7. The Flowering of Sympathy

The moral importance of sympathy is twofold. In the first place, if the distress of another being induces corresponding feelings in self, we have an immediate and personal incentive to relieve that distress; and if the other being's pleasures please us, we have a similar reason to promote them. On the narrow view, action so motivated by sympathetic feelings is selfish, directed toward the diminution of our pain or the increase of our pleasure but deeper insight will discover an inherent altruism in a being so constituted that it must, by the laws of its nature, seek its own relief by helping others. Moreover, the ultimate fate of these spontaneous sympathetic responses is to a high degree dependent on volition. We can, by so willing, habituate ourselves to view with callous indifference the sufferings of others, or we can make our sympathy more sensitive and ample. Even if a rigid moralist should contend that our sympathetic responses are of little moral worth because they are so largely automatic, he or she cannot deny that what we finally make of our sympathy is as dependent on our deliberate choice as almost anything else that we do.

In the second place, it is sympathy alone which imparts life and feeling to the forms presented to us by our external senses. Without this marvelous faculty, we would take the living beings which surround us just as sensation presents them to us, as colored forms which move and gesticulate and emit noises, never as sentient beings capable of joy and sorrow; for our senses never directly reveal consciousness or affective states. Without sympathy, we would have no reason to consider any feelings but our own, for we would have no warrant for the existence of any sensations external to ourselves. And even if analogy should convince us that creatures who so resemble us in form and actions must possess sensations and affections like ours, this cold, speculative conclusion might lack sufficient vividness and force to influence our conduct, especially on those numerous occasions when some strong impulse in ourselves, of whose reality we can have no doubt, is restrained only by the thought of how our act will injure another being. Without sympathy, the other-regarding impulses would remain within the narrow context in which they originated, and serve only dependent young or at most the members of an inter-breeding group; sympathy leads these impulses forth into an ever-widening realm.

In all stages of development, from its primitive root in that nervous organization of animals which makes them susceptible to agreeable sensations from close association with dependent young or social companions, sympathy is of the greatest moral importance, but this importance increases in the measure that it becomes intellectual and imaginative. The broadening of sympathy depends on the recognition of the resemblances of other beings to ourselves no less than on their differences from ourselves. Without the first, our sympathies are too narrow; without the second, they color their objects with mistaken hues. To our animistic forefathers, the resemblances between widely dissimilar living things masked their differences; they even found in such lifeless objects as wind and cloud and stream psychic qualities like their own consciousness and will. Children, too, exaggerate the resemblances of their animal friends to themselves, overlooking important differences. Hence, when love prompts them to treat these dependents just like one of themselves, the result is often disastrous, for different natures imply different needs. But the opposite tendency, engendered by our pride in our awakening intellectual faculties, to regard ourselves as essentially different from all other forms of life, has even more disastrous moral consequences. The very foundation of a beneficent sympathy is the correct understanding of the likenesses and differences between ourselves and other beings.

Our sympathy with the beings most akin to ourselves is purely imitative, and although even this implies a wonderfully complex mental and nervous organization, it requires no reflective thought. The sensitive person responds to the emotional states of close companions, mirroring their joys and sorrows, by a process almost as independent of intelligence and will as a muscular reflex. But in the measure that other beings are unlike oneself, imagination is required to picture their affective states and to sympathize with them; and this imaginative construction must be guided by a just estimation of resemblances and differences. The highest imaginative sympathy is that which recognizes that beings very dissimilar from ourselves may possess sentiments and cherish values quite unlike our own, and respects the bare possibility of the existence of these so alien feelings. As the resemblances diminish and the differences from ourselves grow greater, this imaginative sympathy becomes increasingly liable to error, but it does not for this reason cease to be morally precious; for the whole possibility of a wider ethic depends on it. Thus, in our noblest moral aspirations, as in our highest religious aspirations, we follow a perilous course, overshadowed by the dreadful possibility of being mistaken in the very matters of greatest consequence to us. Yet those who refuse to take risks never achieve.

8. Love as a Moral Force

The grand objective of moral endeavor is to join all beings in a comprehensive fabric of harmonious relations; and as Empedocles recognized long ago, the greatest binding force is love. Love is distinct from sympathy; for one can feel a touch of sympathy even for a fallen enemy whom one hates; and dull, unimaginative natures may have little sympathy with those whom they most love. Yet, in general, sympathy is strongest where love is strongest; for love promotes that intimate association with another, and close attention to all his or her changing moods, which is the foundation of sympathetic feeling. The greatest resources of our moral nature are sympathy and love; or perhaps it would be better to say loving sympathy or sympathetic love; for the two are closely bound together, and either would lose much of its effectiveness without the other.

Ever since the Greek idyllic poets, and even more the medieval troubadours, sang of romantic love, we have come in the West to look upon the attachment of a youth and a maiden and that of husband and wife as the most intense and typical expressions of this affection. And it is logical to suppose that in the history of the species, as in that of the individual, love between the sexes preceded that of parent for offspring; for until the sexes have been drawn together there can be no offspring, and we commonly say that love impels an animal to seek a mate. But this does not appear to be the course of the evolution which love, in the higher meaning of the word, has actually followed. A passion which bears slight resemblance to tender, sympathetic devotion is sufficient to bring together a male and a female animal and effect the procreation of the species. It appears to have been not in the relation of parent to parent but in that of mother to offspring that love which was something more than transient passion first grew up in the vertebrate stock.

Among birds and mammals, the helpless offspring's need, over a period of weeks, months, or even years, of a parent's tender, watchful, self-denying care, amounting at times to heroic sacrifice, provides the ideal situation for the growth of sympathetic love. When, as happens in a great many birds and not a few mammals, the two parents work together to feed, shelter, and protect their progeny, both are likely to develop similar feelings toward them. At the same time, the affection directed primarily to the offspring may attach itself to the other parent so closely associated with these offspring, until one becomes as dear as the other. In many birds, male and female are inseparable during that large portion of the year when their sexual impulses are quiescent, and they give every indication of tender affection.

Among humans, the growth of love appears to have taken a somewhat different course. In primitive cultures and early civilizations, marriage was often hedged about by rigorous and complicated regulations, which severely limited the young people's choice and would seem to discourage the spontaneous flowering of the affections. In forming alliances, considerations of lineage, property, and inheritance frequently had greater weight than the personalities and sympathies of the bride and bridegroom. Even in Athens at the height of her culture, two marriages might be rudely dissolved in order to permit the nearest kinsman to take possession of the property and person of a married heiress who suddenly succeeded to the family estate.[9] In all those cultures where the transmission of name and property is deemed of more importance than the preferences of the bride and groom, friendships between members of the same sex tend to evoke deeper affection than courtship and marriage.

The conclusion that, in the evolutionary sequence, the parent's love for its offspring preceded love between the sexes is supported by observations on the development of this affection in individuals; for as is well known, the developmental history of the individual more or less closely recapitulates, in many features, the evolutionary history of its stock. Little children, too young to feel the attraction of the opposite sex, are capable of intense loving devotion to a doll, an animal pet, or a younger brother or sister placed in their care. They are heartbroken if any mishap befalls the object of their parental solicitude. In a number of birds, immature individuals, often only a few months old, diligently feed and more rarely warm the nestlings of their parents' next brood. At times, when the nest is threatened, they become more excited and are bolder in its defense than the parents themselves. And one may see half-grown heifers fondling little calves just as the cow does.

But whatever route it takes from its first feeble stirrings in the animal mind, the important point about love is its capacity for indefinite expansion. Beginning in the tender solicitude of a mother for her helpless young, it finally attaches itself to the other parent, thence spreads outward to all who resemble this parent and becomes social affection. But it need not stop with one's own species; one may love an animal, a tree, a flower, anything beautiful or beneficent, lifeless no less than living. That which one loves one strives to join firmly to oneself by harmonious relations, blending the other's life closely with one's own, so that wherever possible there may be a constant interchange of kindly feelings and helpful acts, and all discords between the loved being and oneself are avoided. The greatest creative endeavors are prompted by love: the philosopher strives to build up a coherent body of knowledge because out of a love of truth; the artist is impelled by love of beauty; the moral life is inspired by love of righteous acts harmoniously ordered. The creative energy at the core of our being makes itself felt in consciousness as love, which in its highest and most purified form drives us to cultivate harmony with all things that come near us. Of all the innate springs of moral endeavor, love is the most powerful.

Hatred is the opposite of love; and as the latter unites and consolidates, so the former, as Empedocles also saw, disrupts and scatters; so that it is the chief impediment to moral advance, and the most dangerous ingredient of our nature. Yet the emotion of hate, no less than that of love, grew out of our vital need to live in a complex of harmonious relations; we hate a thing because it tends to disrupt the concord of our existence. But hatred is habitually blind and hurries to drive away or crush the offending object without first considering whether it be possible, through modifications and mutual adjustments, to improve its relations with oneself. Since life is a process of constant change and adaptation, love itself is preserved only by the occasional readjustment of the relations between the loved beings. When these efforts to compose and adapt become too numerous or too difficult and fail to achieve their end, love turns to indifference or even to enmity. Conversely, a radical revision of the relations between the loathed object and oneself may cause one to tolerate or even to love it. This capacity of intelligence to transmute hatred into love is not the least of our moral assets. Likewise, the moral will must diligently guard against the first movement toward settled hatred, which is swiftly springing anger. Where anger is quickly suppressed, hatred is unlikely to arise.

Deeds inspired by unselfish love tend to be of the sort that morality approves; the more comprehensive this love and the more carefully it is guided by far-seeing intelligence, the greater the probability of rightness. But deeds prompted by hatred are almost invariably wrong; and the more this disruptive passion is supported by intelligence, the more terrible its consequences become.

9. Reason and the Universality of Moral Imperatives

Self-regarding motives, altruistic motives, sympathy, and love are our primary moral resources, in the absence of which we could hardly be moral. Yet they are not in themselves an adequate endowment for a moral being; if they were, we would have to admit that nonhuman animals are moral rather than merely protomoral; for we find these same springs of action more or less developed in many of them. What constitutes a fully moral being is the play of these innate motives under the guidance of reason and a foreseeing intelligence. Wickedness and destructive fury are caused by the weakness of these moral motives, faulty intelligence, or both together. When beneficent motives are weak, they may be overpowered by the hatred and other disruptive passions which were fostered in animals by the long, intense struggle for existence, and are often brought to the surface by the many frustrations of civilized life; and these, seizing control of the intelligence, make humans more capable of evil than any other creature.

A purely rational being, without impulses, appetites, or passions of any sort, would probably be neither moral nor immoral, since he or she would lack incentives for action. Yet even such a being would have a moral principle within; for knowledge and coherent thought are produced by harmonization; and harmonization, as was earlier demonstrated, is the primary source of all morality. Since coherence and order are the foundation of rationality, they are pleasing to a purely rational mind, which, insofar as it was capable of volition, would will to preserve or increase them. But for all intense moral endeavors, the impulses that spring from the nonrational part of our nature which we share with other animals, are the motive power. It is the presence of these plus foreseeing intelligence that makes us truly moral.

When an intelligent being reflects on moral questions, one of the first conclusions one reaches is that moral rules must be of general application, rather than a matter of personal convenience. This principle is independent of the specific content of the rules and might be reached while they were still unknown. This was the method of Kant in the *Critique of Practical Reason*, wherein he deduced the rule to which moral rules must conform—the celebrated Categorical Imperative, which declares that ethical maxims must be as universal in their application as the laws of nature, although it tells us nothing about the content of these maxims. But just as people were able to reason before Aristotle enunciated the principles of certain kinds of reasoning in the *Organon*, so they were aware that moral rules must be generally binding before Kant published *Critique*. This, indeed, is what distinguishes a genuine moral principle from expediency, which varies endlessly to take advantage of shifting opportunities.

Nevertheless, the rigid application of general rules, without regard to attendant circumstances, can have unfortunate consequences. Even the most universal of the natural "laws" rarely act in isolation, but in conjunction with other forces which modify their effects. No natural principle is more universal or invariable in its operation than gravitation; yet the bodies we actually see fall rarely take the course which they would follow if obedient to gravity alone, but they trace a more complex trajectory in response to the simultaneous action of wind or other forces. Thus, while it is true that people who try to be moral may not set up for themselves rules of conduct different from those that they believe others should follow, this does not imply that I must always act precisely as I believe that my neighbor should act in a similar situation. There may be real and important differences between my neighbor and myself: in our needs; in our abilities, which bring us special obligations; or in our disabilities, which give us special exemptions. But insofar as I am like my neighbors, true morality demands that I act as I expect them to act in corresponding circumstances. I have no right to allow myself liberties and indulgences which I would condemn in them, merely because they are they and I am I. Virtuous persons set as their standard of conduct those rules which they believe everyone else should follow when all pertinent factors are the same.

Chapter Seven

Conscience and Moral Intuitions

1. The Role of Conscience in the Moral Life

WE CONTAIN, AS original constituents of our being, two sets of impulses, the first of which leads us to promote our own welfare; the second, to serve others. It is inevitable that in the endless permutations and stresses of life these two kinds of motives should at times be brought into conflict. And even motives of the same category often pull us in diverse directions, as when we recognize mutually incompatible means of advancing our own interests, or when others make more claims on us than we have time and strength to satisfy. Placed in such circumstances, we would squander our vitality in endless futile beginnings, had we not been endowed with some arbiter for judging between these so diverse solicitations and deciding which has the strongest claim on us, how several of them can be reconciled in a consistent plan of action, and which of the demands made by others or our own appetites must be vetoed. This inner mediator is called the conscience, which is by general consent that faculty or process of the mind which determines what we should do and what we should not do, which tells us what is right and what is wrong.

The importance assigned to conscience varies with the diversity of ethical doctrines, but no theory of morals whatever can quite dispense with it. It ranks highest in systems of moral autonomy, which make the individual the final arbiter of his or her acts and assign the role of supreme judge to conscience. But even in doctrines of moral heteronomy, which look to some external authority, some lawgiver divine or human, for the distinction between right and wrong, the conscience cannot be brushed aside as superfluous. The rules of conduct issuing from this external source are nearly always stated in general terms and apply to classes of acts rather than to definite instances. To adjust to the universal rule our behavior in the particular case, with all its subtle complications and all the counterclaims which may simultaneously assail us, often requires the strenuous exercise of moral judgment and some principle within us which approves our decision. This principle often comes into play even when our duty in a particular instance is pointed out to us by some authority that we recognize as supreme, as when a child is assigned a definite task by a parent. If the child obeys unquestioningly and mechanically, without feeling the competing attraction of some other course of action, such as a frolic with playmates, moral considerations do not arise; but if torn between the voice of duty and the lure of play, the child faces an ethical dilemma, whose solution implies the activity of that moral determinant which we call the conscience; without it he or she can hardly be called a moral being. It is no wonder that conscience is so often held to be a unique possession of humanity, divinely implanted in the human breast.

Conscience is not the faculty of judging moral problems so much as the peculiar feeling which hovers about such judgments. For the validity of this distinction we can trust to everyday language: we speak of our conscience as troubled or tranquil, but of our judgments as sound or unsound. The solution of a moral puzzle is an intellectual process, differing from any other practical problem in the points it considers and certain formal requirements, rather than in the way the mind operates. We draw conclusions from premises and forecast the consequences of acts in the light of experience or with the aid of accepted forms of reasoning. Conscience may trouble one even when one acts upon a decision reached through no logical errors nor wrong deductions from accepted facts. A bad conscience is distinct from bad reasoning. Conscience might be called the judge of our judgments; it approves or condemns our decisions on moral questions, and our consequent conduct, from a standpoint higher, or more central to ourselves, than the intellect.

Since conscience is above all a mode of feeling, we can know it only immediately in ourselves, never in others. Like all feelings, like every shade of color, it is in all its varying intensities unique and indescribable; but this does not prevent our examining objectively the conditions of its activation and its relation to other aspects of our total being. There are two obvious modes of approach to this inquiry. On the one hand, we might investigate the notions of right and wrong of various peoples and epochs, to learn whether conscience always approves or disapproves the same kinds of behavior. We have already at our disposal a vast bulk of materials, collected by historians, ethnologists, and sociologists, which proves that notions of right and wrong have varied immensely in the several branches of humanity, or even in the same people at successive epochs of its history. Acts the most highly praised by one people are the most vehemently condemned by others. We must conclude from these well-attested facts either that the manifestations of conscience are different in people of other cultures than in ourselves, or that the same feeling may attach itself to acts the most diverse.

If we make the not improbable assumption that the conscientious feelings of all normal people are approximately the same, we must look for their common ground not in what conscience approves or disapproves, but in what determines its approval or disapproval. If people of one society regard theft as criminal while those of another society hold it to be laudable, then obviously, granting that there is a similar arbiter of conduct in all of them, it must respond in diverse ways to the same sort of behavior. But it is possible that if we consider the act of stealing not in isolation but in relation to the whole body of customs and beliefs of each culture, we shall find a fundamental similarity in the relation, which the approved act bears to the pattern of culture as a whole. This is a point to which we shall return in Chapter XI.

On the whole, however, I believe that we shall be on safer ground if we use the introspective method in our analysis of conscience, for only in our individual selves can we survey in their fullness all the varying shades of feeling which we unite under this term. We shall also detect feelings which verge on those of conscience but do not properly appertain to it. When we have mapped the range of occurrence of conscientious feelings in ourselves, we shall be in a better position to consider in broad terms its relation to other aspects of our being, and its function in the conduct of life.

2. Two Conditions of a Quiet Conscience

The first fact that personal experience tells us about conscience is that it is, on the whole, a source of pain or unrest rather than of positive enjoyment. It is a goad to stimulate us when we are lax or remiss rather than a lure to tempt us forward. We suffer more or less acutely from its disturbed states, yet find no corresponding pleasure when its equilibrium has been restored. But pleasures and pains are relative and after an acute discomfort, a milder one may seem almost pleasant. Yet in its "best" or most satisfied states, conscience is more than mere surcease of distress. When we have corrected conditions which have been causing our conscience to trouble us, we experience, for a shorter or longer interval, a feeling of contentment, peace, and inner wholeness, which is not only gratifying in itself, but the firmest foundation for all the quiet and enduring happiness that calm affections or constructive occupations can bring us.

It is almost superfluous to describe here the typical or standard conditions in which we become aware of conscience. Twinges or pangs of conscience arise when we have disobeyed some rule of conduct prescribed by the society in which we live or one which we have set up for ourselves as a result of mature reflection, when we have procrastinated or neglected to perform some recognized obligation, or when we have inadvertently hurt or caused great inconvenience to those about us. The actual feeling may vary from mild but persistent nagging, as when we are tardy in fulfilling an obligation or keeping a promise, to acute and lingering distress, as when we have done some misdeed whose consequences are irreparable. These extreme states of an unquiet conscience are greatly dissimilar, but because of a fundamental likeness and the innumerable intermediate shades of feeling which unite them, we seem justified in designating them all by the same name.

If we analyze more carefully the conditions which must be fulfilled to satisfy the conscience and prevent its troubling us, we find at least two, which may coincide or be irreconcilable. To enjoy a quiet conscience, I believe that most of us find it necessary that our conduct conform not only to our standard of moral rectitude but also to the norms of the society in which we dwell. If our notions of right and wrong are wholly conventional, no discrepancy will arise between these two conditions, and by following the rules approved by our friends and neighbors we shall preserve a tolerably calm conscience. But if our moral sensitivity is unusually acute, or we have thought deeply about ethical problems, we may develop standards of rectitude at variance with those of our contemporaries. Then if we feel constrained to follow conventional usage in despite of our convictions, we shall be troubled in conscience; and if our conduct departs too conspicuously from that of our neighbors we may also feel uneasy.

If we are weak, we shall allow ourselves to be governed by external pressure, and perhaps by degrees forget that we once cherished ideals which seemed to us higher than those of our society, until at last we feel at ease when our behavior is conventionally correct. If we are stronger, we shall do what seems right to us, even if it sets us apart from our compeers; but perhaps at first we follow our own rules as quietly and unobtrusively as possible, striving to be true to ourselves on the one hand and conformable to our companions on the other—struggling perhaps vainly to preserve the inner comfort that comes from harmony in all its aspects. Only as we grow stronger can we follow our inner light in defiance of the prejudices of those around us and without feeling conscientious scruples or something very like them. Hence to have an easy conscience, two forms of harmony seem necessary: (1) that our deeds should be consistent with our convictions, and (2) that our conduct should conform to socially recognized standards. Strong, self-reliant persons who find their notions of right and wrong at variance with those of the crowd may at length be approximately satisfied if their life fulfills the first condition; weak and vacillating persons in the same circumstances will come to rest in the second condition;

but for many people it seems necessary to make a fair adjustment on both the inner and the outer side in order to enjoy peace of conscience.

Hence a curious phenomenon, which those capable of moral growth and independent judgment, or whose circumstances have varied sharply with the passing years, must have noticed in themselves. We find that it is not easy to deviate from a habitual standard of moral rectitude, even when the most disinterested reason persuades us that it is not applicable in some special contingency. Many of us, I believe, would experience certain conscientious scruples when telling a lie to shield an innocent person from ruffians who wield arbitrary power, or to conceal upsetting information from a parent hovering between life and death. Similarly, when through a change in criteria we become convinced of the rightness or the moral indifference of some act which from earliest childhood we had been taught was wrong, we at first perform this act with a certain moral hesitancy, a slight repugnance against violating our earlier rule of conduct—a feeling still far weaker than that which would weigh against an act which we knew to be unconditionally wrong.

This "quasi-moral" sentiment, to use Sidgwick's term, has been adduced in support of the view that the feeling of rightness is primary rather than derived from instruction or reflection. But the principle of association readily accounts for our sentiments in such cases. If through long years we have been taught that it is wicked to work on the sabbath, we shall for a while experience this sense of wrongness when we labor on this day, even after we have convinced ourselves that our earlier instruction had been mistaken on this point. An exactly similar aura of feeling hovers about the superstitions amidst which we grew up. We must indeed school our most intimate and spontaneous sentiments to perfect rationality if we would lose all lingering traces of the associations of childhood. We may no longer believe that to walk beneath a ladder brings bad luck, yet the ghost of our dead belief may retain sufficient influence to make us take two extra steps to go around rather than beneath the ladder. There is always a lag between our feelings and our new situation.

3. Our Vital Need of Harmony in All Its Aspects

In addition to the pricks, pangs, and twinges of conscience that spring from crimes, sins, and other deviations from moral standards in the narrow sense of the term, we observe in ourselves similar feelings which throw a flood of light on the nature of the conscience and its place in our whole psychic constitution. In viewing our past lives, I suppose that most of us discover certain vacillations, inconsistencies, and blunders, which were neither sinful nor disgraceful and perhaps inconvenienced no one so much as ourselves, yet which remain as sore places in memory, and in retrospect pain us as much, or almost as much, as deeds which were morally reprehensible. This feeling persists even when with advancing years we come to recognize that these youthful derangements were the almost inevitable phases of our intellectual or spiritual development, and we might have avoided them only by such close compliance to narrow conventional ways as would most probably have stunted our inner growth. In the retrospect of our lives these false steps and inconsistencies often stand out beyond other events that were far more important, precisely because they do not blend harmoniously with the whole picture; as a slight unevenness beneath the paper on which we write distracts our attention from the smoothness of all the remaining surface. Ideally, our development should be harmonious like that of a plant growing in rich, sheltered earth; and these intervals of confusion oppress memory like a troubled conscience.

In a somewhat similar way, we are made uneasy by our acceptance of any belief or opinion which clashes, or seems incompatible with, the whole structure of our acknowledged beliefs. Until we can either reconcile the discordant belief with our guiding principles or reject it as false, it nags and distracts us like a neglected duty. But it is in creative work of all kinds that we most frequently experience feelings hardly to be distinguished from scruples of conscience, and this fact is widely recognized in the expression "a conscientious worker." To a careful writer, a clumsy or ambiguous sentence annoys like a broken promise. A carpenter who takes pride in work feels, on making a loose joint, an uneasiness similar to that which assails an upright person who has broken a rule of moral conduct. An error in a computation or an account calls us back again and again, until we finally ferret it out and make the figures tally. In general, a mistake in our work, even when it is improbable that others will learn about it or that it will cause loss or harm to anybody, troubles us in much the same way as a moral fault.

These facts, which I suppose are familiar to nearly everyone, seem to prove that the conscience is not a special department of the mind concerned solely with questions of moral right and wrong, but a mode of feeling closely associated with all our endeavors. It functions in cognitive and esthetic contexts, and indeed in every activity which demands coordination and articulation and the adjustment of parts to the whole, no less than in moral situations. Whence we may conclude that we have no more a special moral sense than we have a special esthetic or social sense (using these terms to designate particular faculties of the mind); but that the term "moral sense" refers merely to the single integrative function of the mind when applied to moral relations, just as the term "esthetic sense" refers to this same mental activity when applied to situations of the sort that we designate as esthetic.

What, then, is conscience? *It is our direct awareness of our vital need of wholeness and harmony in all that concerns us.* In each living thing there is a constructive activity, its enharmonization, which orders all its constituents into the most coherent and harmonious pattern that they can form in the given conditions. This constitutive process makes itself felt in the mind as its conscience, whose function is to promote the harmonious integration of aspects of our lives which are controlled by volition and may be regulated by deliberate choice. Conscience is the immediate pressure upon consciousness of the creative energy which, silent and unseen, pervades our whole being. It manifests itself chiefly as an uneasiness, a nagging, a pain more or less acute, which arises whenever a disharmony is perceived by the mind; and it persists until this disharmony is corrected, or in more sensitive minds, it may linger long after the correction has been made. It inevitably influences all that we do, for harmony and wholeness are necessary to us not only in our moral relations with our fellows, but in every other department of our lives.

We can hardly avoid postulating the presence of conscience or something quite similar in animals whose activities follow innate patterns or are, as we say, instinctive. We may, if we insist, call it a "protoconscience" or an "instinctive conscience" to distinguish it from our own, which we imagine to be more acutely sensitive. But whatever its subjective aspect, which is beyond reach of our curiosity its function in these animals is the same as in ourselves: to coordinate and blend into a coherent pattern all those activities which are influenced by consciousness, and to prevent deviations from the ruling pattern.

4. Why Awareness of Moral Lapses Brings More Acute Distress Than Disharmonies of Other Sorts

In opposition to the view presented in the last section, it might be urged that the pangs of conscience which we experience when we have sinned, committed a crime, or otherwise transgressed a moral rule of conduct, differ in intensity, and even in kind, from the uneasiness that we feel when we have discovered a mistake in our work or a blunder in our speech. But I hold that the primary or fundamental feeling is the same, and its internal source the same, in all those cases which trouble a "conscientious" worker or performer, as in moral faults. The greater and more prolonged distress that we often feel when we have become aware of a moral lapse resides not in the primary feeling itself, but comes from a variety of subsidiary feelings, stirred up by a number of attendant circumstances, that cluster around and fuse with it. In the first place, we can often correct the flaws in our work; and while our mind is occupied with planning or carrying out the improvement, it is diverted from the twinges of conscience. Frequently, we can remedy such mistakes before they are noticed by others; or, if they come to the attention of others, will cause them little harm; and, in any case, they are more likely to be pardoned than moral faults. Yet our inward uneasiness is apt to persist until we have corrected the mistake in our work or, if it be minor, until it has been displaced from our mind by matters of more importance.

Moral lapses are less likely to be overlooked by other people than mistakes in work, because everyone is expected to know the basic rules of conduct of society, whereas the techniques of any occupation are learned only by the relatively few who engage in it; hence nearly everyone whose attention is drawn to our wrong conduct will recognize it for what it is, whereas only members of the same profession are likely to become aware of the professional blunder. Wrong conduct usually affects other people adversely, and may bring them great inconvenience, loss, or suffering—it is usually for this very reason that it is considered wrong. When one has been made aware of fault and the mischief it has wrought, the sensitive person may be assailed by acute sympathetic pains. Add to this the shame of being known as unjust or evil, the censure and slights to which one is exposed, the avoidance by former companions, the fear of punishment if one's misconduct was legally a crime, the remorse and the self-condemnation, and we can readily understand how the person who breaks a moral rule suffers inner pangs so much more intense than those which assail the blundering artist or craftsman, that they often seem to spring from a separate source. More than blunders of other kinds, moral lapses undermine the foundations of our life; and the self-reproaches that they arouse in us when recognized are correspondingly acute.

But the single fact of being put to shame before one's fellows is sufficient to account for a large share of the differences in feeling in the two cases. The schoolchild who falters or makes a mistake in a public recitation may suffer an agony of embarrassment and confusion hardly inferior in intensity, if shorter in duration, than the remorse which follows the commission of a crime; and even an orator as experienced as Cicero confessed in his maturity that he never arose to address an audience without turning pale and trembling in every limb. I believe that we may fairly conclude that the primary feeling of a disturbed conscience is fundamentally the same, whether it arises from a publicly recognized moral fault, a departure from our habitual standard of conduct known only to ourself, a flaw in our work, or any other disharmony for which we know ourself to be responsible. The intensity of the feeling will depend largely on the magnitude of the disturbance. The peculiar character of the conscientious pangs which may follow the commission of a crime or serious moral lapse stems from other feelings, such as shame, fear, remorse, and at times sympathetic suffering which stirred up by the same event as the conscientious twinges, fuse with them into one massive feeling whose components are difficult to analyze.

Nietzsche, who had some true insights into moral questions, but caused great confusion by publishing before he had thought them out to their logical conclusions, believed that conscience is simply the work of humanity's cruel, predatory instincts, which, when thwarted in expressing themselves by external action, turn inward and find satisfaction in savagely torturing the very mind in which they arise.[1] Freud had somewhat similar views, and saw in conscience the turning against oneself of the "death instinct," which at one time prompted the murder of the patriarchal father. A grain of truth may lurk in these views as applied to certain exaggerated or morbid states of conscience. But before an instinct or an innate mode of feeling can become hypertrophied or diseased it must exist, and it is not likely to have arisen and become widespread in a species unless it had some vital and necessary part to play. This normal role of conscience is the restitution of harmony in situations which have been infected with discord. In healthy minds, it incites active endeavor to correct the distorted relationships, to rectify the flaws in our work, excogitate the inconsistencies in our opinions, smooth out the strained relations with our companions, right the wrongs we have done. While we are engaged in these restorative efforts, conscience may be a goad but is rarely a torturing monster. But in cases where reconstruction seems intrinsically impossible, as when the injury we have done is irreparable or our social disgrace is too flagrant to be outlived, then indeed conscience, thwarted in its usual salutary function, may turn against oneself and become a merciless persecutor.

5. The Innate Preference for Harmony as the Intuitive Foundation of Morality

Locke's analysis of the human mind, no less than a great mass of data gathered from all parts of the Earth by travelers and ethnologists, make it certain that humans do not possess moral intuitions in the form of innate dispositions to perform certain acts as right and avoid others as wrong.[2] We possess no moral maxims inscribed on our minds or hearts at birth. Yet of all the numerous schools of ethical theorists, the Intuitionists reveal the most profound understanding of the foundations of morality in human nature, although they seemed to have failed sufficiently to analyze their true insights. Everything that we are and do and think must have its ultimate foundation in our innate constitution, which is the primary datum in all our attempts to understand ourselves, and beyond which direct analysis cannot go, although the study of evolution may suggest explanations of what we find within us.

Just as whatever is poured into our minds through the senses takes a form determined by our whole psycho-physical nature, so whatever we do is ultimately traceable to innate motives, for which we can assign no reason except the fact that we happen to be made that way. All moral exhortations must touch one of these innate springs of action in order to be effective; and all moral rules must be grounded on our primitive intuitions, else fail to secure obedience. This truth was nowhere more clearly recognized than by some of the great Intuitionists of the nineteenth century, like Lecky and Martineau, who, while freely admitting that humans possess no innate rules or maxims of conduct, yet insisted that we are so constituted that, as through our daily interactions with the world we become aware of moral predicaments and problems, we are constrained by our own nature to recognize certain modes of behavior as nobler, more worthy of ourselves, or more righteous than other conflicting modes of behavior, and to give tacit approval to these higher modes, even when passion or weakness interferes with our following them.[3]

In considering conscience, we have approached very close to the fountainhead of our moral nature. In simplest terms, conscience is just that sense of strain or uneasiness caused within us by any disharmony in our conduct or thought which we explicitly recognize or vaguely feel. This in turn may be traced to that striving to create and to preserve a coherent unity among all the constituents of an organism, which is the primary fact of life and makes it possible. The least disturbance of the harmonious equilibrium of its smallest parts leads in every healthy organism to efforts, vigorous even if unfelt and unseen, to restore the balance. More violent or pronounced disturbances cause, at least in the higher animals, pain, which usually incites energetic movements to achieve a more harmonious adjustment. When the disharmony is not in the body itself, but in consciously controlled attitudes and activities which adjust the animal to its surroundings, especially to social companions whose cooperation is so necessary to its welfare, a corresponding discomfort is felt, a subtle uneasiness in the mind which spurs the animal to make efforts to remove the cause of discord, just as a physical pain leads to an attempt to assuage it. With an increasingly sensitive mind, a similar distress is caused by any perceived disharmony, in one's work, in one's conduct, even in one's inmost thoughts. But the pain or distress caused by all these disturbances of equilibrium, within the body, in its external relations, or in the mind, arises from the primary need of every living thing to preserve harmony in all that concerns it.

Our basic moral intuition, if we may call it this, is that harmony is preferable to discord; and this is rooted in that organization of our bodies and minds which causes us to experience pain or uneasiness when equilibrium is disturbed, ease and peace of mind when it has been restored. In this all humans, as indeed all sentient beings, appear to be essentially the same; so that we may regard it as a universal feature of animal nature. And when we have recognized this fact, we can survey all the bewildering varieties of human culture, all the fluctuating notions of right and wrong, without impugning the one great truth on which Intuitive Ethics rests.

All the cruel and revolting practices of the rudest tribes, and of many people more advanced in civilization, have sprung from the effort to preserve life in a perilous environment, with a mind bewildered by the first groping steps of a free intelligence, and in the midst of hostile peoples whose thinking was similarly confused. But take the rudest savages who until a few generations ago might have been found in the islands of the Pacific, the interior of Africa, Australia, or the remotest reaches of the vast Amazonian forest, savages who adorn their huts with the gruesome heads of slaughtered enemies, eat their flesh, kill their aged parents, possibly burying them alive, and get rid of their wife when tired of her. Have these benighted people a sense of right and wrong, or have they not? If they have not, then, given the unruly desires coupled with the restless imagination of even the least advanced humans, their life and conduct will follow no definite, predictable pattern; for unconventional modes of behavior must certainly from time to time occur to them, and without some restraining influence they will follow them. But the most striking feature of savage society is its conservatism, the persistence of the same customs from generation to generation; and this implies that its members as a whole, and in spite of more or less frequent aberrations, conform to the ancestral ways. Hence it appears that certain modes of conduct are held to be right by these savages, and others as wrong.

What induces savages to conform to these, in our view, so outrageous codes of behavior, save the wish to avoid the uneasy feelings which assail them when their conduct clashes with the ways of their fellow tribesmen or violates the usages which from childhood they have been taught to regard as the immemorial customs of their people? To be sure, this same conformity to tribal habits brings the savage into continual conflict with neighboring groups. In the interpretation of behavior, it is necessary to bear constantly in mind that not all disharmonies distress us, but only those of which we become aware, and above all those for which we seem to be responsible. Just as errors in diction fail to perturb the person who has heard nothing of the unities of grammar, so incoherencies in our lives may disturb us little until our attention has been focused on them, either by other people or by their painful consequences to ourselves.

Discord with fellow clans members among whom they live, with an intimacy that we might find scarcely tolerable, is felt acutely by savages, and so is the imagined displeasure of the supernatural guardians of the tribal mores. Conflict with neighboring tribes is less strongly felt, and it might never have occurred to the primitive mind that more harmonious relations with them are within the realm of possibility; for the state of enmity with surrounding peoples has persisted without interruption as long as the tribal memory reaches. But some day, with increasing foresight and intelligence, the tribes member will find that this constant friction with neighboring groups is irksome, the source of much apprehension and great material loss. Once the disharmony has been felt and a more peaceful state has been conceived, measures will be taken to remedy the situation; and tribes will amalgamate into peaceful unions, as happened with the Five Nations of the Iroquois. Little by little, the very thought of internecine strife grows intolerable to people of high moral sensitivity, to whom the establishment of universal peace becomes the chief desideratum of civilization.

The disharmonies which first affect animals are within the body and lead to unconscious and then to conscious efforts to correct them. Next, animals become aware of lack of harmony with their immediate environment, lifeless and living, and strive to improve their relations on this side. Finally, the animals become reflective humans, takeing notice of their discord with beings more remote from themselves, beings which affect their life less intimately, and even of disharmonies among the contents of their mind, and they similarly strive to remedy the situation. It is not the disharmonies that we perceive in the life of some other creature, but those of which this creature itself becomes aware, that stir it to remedial action; and this awareness depends on its nervous sensitivity and the fineness of its perceptions. But at whatever level the disharmony is felt, the results are similar: it stirs up in the sentient being a pain or uneasiness, which persists until the discord is overcome; and this inner stress, when caused by situations which can be altered by our volitions, we attribute to conscience.

If anyone doubts that a constitutional preference for harmony is the foundation of morality, let him or her reflect on the consequences of that craving for strife which overcomes us whenever certain passions, forced upon animal life by the struggle for existence, such as hatred, rage, malice, and envy, temporarily gain control of our minds. Then imagine what the effect would be if these disruptive passions, instead of being secondary developments, were an expression of our true and primary nature, so that we had a permanent appetite for discord of all sorts, feeling more satisfied when torn between conflicting motives than when our spirits are calm, when our thoughts are disordered than when our mind is clear, when we hate and quarrel with our neighbors than when we dwell in amity with them, when at war than when at peace. If that preference for strife, which at times surges up in us, as a transitory and one might say a pathological state, were to become constitutional and permanent, we would doubtless cultivate discord not only until all moral order vanished, but until we ourselves dissolved into the elements of which we are composed.

6. Consequent Preference for the Wider and More Perfect Harmony

The same organization of the mind which impels us to prefer harmony to discord causes us also to prefer the wider, more inclusive, and more enduring harmony to the narrow, imperfect, and transient harmony. For we can hardly conceive the extension of a system of harmonious relations beyond its present confines without first becoming aware of the disharmonies which surround it; and when our minds have become accustomed to the wider view, the more distant disharmonies affect us in essentially the same manner, if more faintly, as those which touch us more intimately. Thus, conscience is not only an instrument of moral stability, but also of moral growth; not only does it operate to preserve the integrity of an ancestral code of morals, but likewise to create an ampler vision for our descendants. In this task of amplification, it is impeded chiefly by the ingrained conservatism of humans, which makes it hard for us to conceive a wider harmony and still more difficult to take active measures to bring about its realization, and by those disruptive passions which inevitably grew out of the struggle to survive in a competitive world.

In the view of James Martineau, moral intuitions take the form, not of an innate recognition that certain specific acts are right and incumbent on us and certain others wrong, but of an intuitive awareness that certain motives or springs of action are higher, nobler, or more worthy of ourselves, than other competing motives. It is not our acts themselves so much as the inner determinants of these acts which we intuitively assess. We have no moral maxims impressed on our minds prior to all experience; but we are provided with a scale of values which, although it undeniably develops through experience, does so in a manner determined by our inherited mental constitution, hence may properly be called intuitive.

In *Types of Ethical Theory* (part II, book I, chapter VI), we need not assume that the primary moral intuition is present in the human mind as a verbally formulated proposition that harmony is preferable to discord. So far is this from being the case, that I am not aware that any philosopher has ever stated this important truth. All that it was necessary to demonstrate is that this innate preference is the foundation of our moral choices; that our judgments, when they escape the domination of greed, passion, and bigotry, are made as though we were guided by some such maxim. And if we carefully examine those abiding preferences which are the foundation of morality, we see that they conform to this principle. In our homes and the arrangement of our possessions, we prefer order to disorder. In our surroundings, we prefer beauty, which is the harmonious blending of lines, masses, and colors. In our relations with our associates, we prefer friendship to enmity. In our minds, we prefer truth, whose warrant is the coherence of facts and interpretations. In our bodies, we prefer health, which is the harmonious cooperation of all the parts and functions of an organism. We prefer happiness, whose foundation is harmony in every aspect of our existence, to the sorrow or spiritual distress which overcomes us when our lives are infected by discord. Finally, we prefer life, which rests upon many harmonious adjustments within ourselves and with the environment that supports us, to death, which ensues when these harmonies are destroyed. In the measure that these intuitive preferences are weak, our morality becomes hard and narrow. If all were absent or reversed, we could not be moral beings.

The recognition that moral endeavor is primarily a striving to attain a more perfect, inclusive, and enduring harmony helps us to understand why conscience is so difficult to satisfy, and why this difficulty increases as we grow in intelligence and sensitivity. Our deeds, as we trace them outward from their source, affect an ever-increasing number of beings, until we lose sight of their consequences in the intricate maze of the living world. In order to reach, in the time available to us, a moral judgment which will provide guidance for action, we must in many instances arbitrarily narrow our frame of reference, excluding from consideration beings which have less claim on us, or those which will be less directly affected by what we do. To the best of our ability, with calmness and fairness, we choose the course, which promises the greatest good within this rather artificially delimited field; and this is all that practical morality can demand of us. But unless we are stupid or insensitive, we are aware that beyond these limits are beings which will be adversely affected, perhaps suffer severely, as a consequence of our decision. Conscience, which is the voice of our inmost self's demand for perfect and comprehensive harmony, is troubled by these discords, however remote from ourselves, which we cannot avoid. The sophistries and evasions by which we sometimes strive to sooth it are, as is often said, the devil's counsel, for they quench that divine dissatisfaction with our limitations which is at once the tragedy and glory of our human state, the stimulus of all moral and spiritual growth.

Chapter Eight
Pleasures and Happiness

1. Primary Bodily Pleasures and Pains

A LARGE SHARE OF our spontaneous activity is directed toward the enjoyment of pleasures and the attainment of happiness. Many thinkers have found in one or the other, or both together, the supreme goal of human effort, or attempted to interpret moral sentiments and endeavors in terms of these eagerly sought ends. Moreover, it seems true that people commonly believe that there is some connection between pleasures and happiness, yet they might find it difficult to tell just how they are related. Hence, before proceeding further with our inquiry, we must examine the circumstances in which these affections are experienced, and attempt to understand their vital and spiritual significance.

We would probably try in vain to convey to an intelligent being who lacked all affections just what we mean by either "pleasure" or "happiness," but we might make him or her understand the conditions of their occurrence. And it would certainly be easier to explain the circumstances in which we experience pleasure than to give him or her some notion of happiness. Since pleasures, although often more intense, are of briefer duration than happiness, more easily won and more readily lost, and they appear to require a less elaborate psychic organization, we shall first examine them and then pass on to happiness. It will also be necessary to pay attention to the correlative of pleasure, pain; for it is difficult to understand the significance of one without that of the other.

An animal body is a sort of society or club, whose members are all the varied substances of which it is composed. Since it is constantly losing some of its members by the wastage of materials and energy in its daily activities, it must admit new ones to replace its losses; and, while it is young, admissions must be made to provide for its growth. Moreover, it is surrounded by hostile organisms, such as parasites, which try to force themselves into this club for their own selfish ends; while deleterious materials like poisons and thorns may accidentally slip through the doors and upset its delicately balanced organization. Thus the animal faces the problem of admitting certain things into the assemblage of materials which is its body and holding others aloof. But it does not understand why some substances should be welcomed and others turned away; even we, for all our chemistry and physiology, do not know just what peculiar feature of their molecular organization makes some vegetable substances wholesome food and others deadly poisons. The animal can tell what to welcome and what to turn away only by means of the credentials each presents as it applies for admission to the body; and these credentials are the agreeable or disagreeable sensations experienced by smelling, tasting, or touching them. A pleasant sensation is a card of admission or letter of introduction to that clubhouse of materials which is an animal body; an unpleasant sensation causes the door to be slammed in its face. This is the biological significance of the most elementary pleasures and pains.

Let us now view the same matter from a broader philosophical viewpoint. A harmoniously integrated pattern like a healthy living body is built up of elements which in most cases have been accumulated little by little from varied sources. At the moment of entering, or trying to enter, such a system, each external substance or body is a crude novelty. Some of these novelties are capable of becoming harmoniously adjusted components of the pattern and thereby increasing its amplitude, coherence or perfection, while others are not. Those of the former class, especially when they must be acquired or ingested by the animal's voluntary activity, are as a rule sources of pleasure; those which would be deleterious usually produce unpleasant or painful sensations. Typical examples of novelties which can be harmonized are wholesome food, and water when one is thirsty. Examples of novelties which must be resisted because they cannot be assimilated are injurious foods or chemicals, foreign bodies such as thorns, splinters, and burrowing parasites, and excessive energy in the form of heat.

It seems probable that an animal which has lived for countless generations in a stable environment will give the biologically appropriate response to all the materials widespread in its habitat, eating wholesome foods because they are a source of pleasure, avoiding poisonous substances because they arouse disagreeable sensations. Since an animal in strange surroundings will frequently eat poisonous things, and people are often violently upset by foods that taste good, it is evident that there is originally slight correlation between the physiological effects of a substance and the sensations it produces when tasted or smelled. The sense organs of animals are not so constructed that every useful or wholesome substance with which they could possibly be brought into contact automatically stirs up agreeable sensations and every deleterious stuff produces feelings of pain or disgust. If they were, not only would animals lead safer lives in changing environments, but some of the difficult problems in controlling human behavior could never have arisen. The nice adjustment of animals to their hereditary environment seems to be the result of a long course of variation and selection, of trial and error, by means of which individuals which were led by their sensations to make inappropriate responses to surrounding substances were eliminated, and thus was produced a line of creatures that found pleasure in what was good for them, pain in what injured them.

Not only must an animal acquire what it needs and repel what would injure it, it must preserve what it has and sometimes expel from its body things that have entered by accident or accumulated by its own vital processes. Since it might not understand just how the removal of contents or parts of its body would affect its welfare, it must be led by appropriate sensations to make the proper responses. Nothing so jeopardizes its life as the loss of a limb, sense organ, skin, or blood, and accordingly the tearing or cutting of its flesh causes violent pain. Likewise, the loss of too much energy in the form of heat is fatal to any warm-blooded animal; hence cold, which is the sensation that it experiences when heat is flowing too rapidly from the body, is an unpleasant feeling, which it strives to avoid; just as the influx of too much heat, as through contact with flames or boiling water, is an exceedingly painful experience, which it violently resists. But since in metabolism and muscular activity an animal often produces heat in excess of its needs, the removal of this heat is necessary; and a mild coolness is a gratifying sensation. Likewise, the elimination from the body of waste products and secretions, especially when they have accumulated in excessive amounts, produces a more or less agreeable sensation. And the removal of a thorn or splinter, or even an aching tooth, although in itself usually a painful operation, yields a feeling of relief akin to pleasure.

Another category of pains consists of those caused not by gains and losses but by the continuing lack of things necessary to preserve life or the continued presence of injurious materials. Of the former, hunger and thirst are well-known examples. Tiredness, which when acute is painful, seems to be caused by the accumulation of waste products of muscular activity that the body is slow to eliminate. Likewise a splinter or other foreign object that remains in the flesh may be a continuing source of pain.

We may summarize the foregoing paragraphs by saying that in a healthy animal well-adjusted to its ambience the acquisition of novelties which can be harmoniously incorporated into the body is commonly a source of pleasure; while the removal of things that have accumulated in excess, or that have been forced into the body, is associated with agreeable sensations or at least a feeling of relief akin to pleasure. The entry into the body of disruptive elements, as likewise the removal of organs or harmoniously adjusted elements, is the source of pains, which are often excruciatingly violent. Other pains are caused by the prolonged lack of necessary stuffs or the continued presence of deleterious substances. In a healthy animal, bodily pleasures and pains are associated largely with losses and gains, shortages and excesses. Gains and losses which increase the body's harmony or completeness are in general sources of pleasure; losses and shortages, gains and excesses which decrease its harmony or completeness are sources of pain. Can these correlations, which are shown schematically in the diagram below, be extended beyond the purely corporeal sensations?

SOURCES OF PLEASURES AND PAINS

Harmonious Elements

Acquisition
(or continued presence)   (or continued lack)
Loss

↙   ↘

Pleasures   Pains

↖   ↗

Loss   Acquisition
(or continued lack)   (or continued presence)

Inharmonious Elements

2. Primary Mental Pleasures and Pains

In order to stabilize their lives and increase their security, animals of some kinds acquire external possessions, as by building nests and storing food. Even primitive human societies need an impressive array of artifacts to carry on their daily activities; while civilized people accumulate a vast variety of possessions, including land, buildings, money, household furnishings, clothing, and objects of art. In general, the acquisition of anything useful or beautiful, or of the means of procuring useful or beautiful articles, yields pleasure; whereas the loss of these things is a painful experience. Although of a character quite different from those associated with bodily changes, these mental pleasures and pains are in some instances so intense that we prefer the former to sensuous enjoyments, and would suffer severe physical pangs to avoid the latter. The acquisition or loss of inharmonious elements, however, has psychic effects much less pronounced in the case of external possessions than in that of things which enter into the body itself. We are sometimes annoyed but seldom pained when somebody gives or thrusts upon us some article which will not fit into our household or manner of living; and we may experience a mild sense of relief when we finally disburden ourselves of some cumbersome or ugly chattel. Apparently the reason why the feelings associated with incongruous external possessions are so much less intense than those occasioned by inharmonious intrusions into the body is that the former are easier to cast off and rarely leave permanent lesions. In general, however, the pleasures and pains associated with the acquisition and loss of external possessions closely parallel those caused by quantitative changes in the body itself.

Most animals associate at least briefly with others of their kind for reproducing their species, and some live in family groups or even populous societies. Nearly all social animals find life easier and more pleasant in the company of others of their kind than in solitude, and some cannot long survive when separated from their communities. Accordingly, social animals experience pleasure when united with their companions and pain when separated from them, just as they feel pleasure when they acquire a wholesome food and pain when part of their body is torn from them. Often it is not the first meeting with one who will prove to be an agreeable companion that causes pleasure, for we are uncertain whether he or she will meet our needs or satisfy our aspirations; just as, when offered some strange fruit, we are not sure at the first taste whether we like it or not.

The most typical of the pleasures and pains to which we now refer are those experienced when friends or lovers meet after a separation, or when they part for a long and indefinite period. Death, the most final separation of all, causes that acute mental pain called grief. The contrary pains and pleasures are also prominent in social relations: we are distressed by the arrival of one whom we dislike and gratified when we are at last relieved of the person's presence. Moreover, the continued absence of all companions causes oppressive loneliness, which is a sort of spiritual hunger; whereas the prolonged presence of a disagreeable person can be an exceedingly unpleasant experience. There is thus an almost perfect correspondence between the circumstances which give rise to bodily pains and pleasures and social situations which produce mental pains and pleasures.

Like the body, the mind has appetites and grows by gathering things from its environment; and, as with the body, the acquisition of the materials which nourish it is a source of pleasure. To every healthy intelligence, new sights, new sounds, new information that is significant and can be assimilated, give more or less intense gratification; and it is not so soon satiated with these things as the body with food. Similarly, the loss of information distresses us like the loss of some external possession. Obviously, we are not pained at the time when some cherished recollection or hard-won fact slips from memory; for it will not disappear while we are actually conscious of it. But when at last we try to recall the word or fact or incident and cannot, we are grieved; and our distress would be greater if we did not invariably hope that the lapse of memory is only temporary and the forgotten idea will sooner or later return to us.

But just as not every food that enters the mouth gives pleasure, but as a rule only those which the body can assimilate, so not every fact that pours into the mind is gratifying. If we see at once that it threatens a cherished belief or is incompatible with a favorite theory, it gives us pain almost as when a thorn enters the flesh. Sometimes the distress is not immediate but develops slowly as we ponder the new information and try to discover its significance, just as a delicious but unwholesome viand may later produce a painful indigestion. In this case, the removal of the supposed fact, as by conveniently forgetting it or proving its falsity, affords us a pleasurable sense of relief, akin to that which follows the elimination of some noxious substance from the body.

When we turn from the mind's cognitive functions to its esthetic enjoyments, we find closely similar facts. To one sensitive to beauty, the first sight of a beautiful object brings intense delight; whereas the removal from one's surroundings of an object cherished for its loveliness, as a painting or household ornament which must be sold to raise money, a tree or flowering plant which dies, causes us pain. Likewise, the first sight of something ugly pains us, and our distress is intensified when we are aware that we must see it daily. But the removal of such an offending object is highly gratifying. These feelings stirred up by the first encounter with a beautiful or ugly object are different in quality and usually more intense than those which prevail in the course of long association with it; just as those produced by the arrival of a friend, or the acquisition of new information, or even the eating of delicious food, differ from the feelings we experience while living with the friend, contemplating the information, or digesting the food. The long-continued satisfactions seem more closely allied to happiness than to pleasures, and are at least transitional between these two modes of feeling.

The conclusions we reached by the consideration of bodily sensations have been confirmed by the examination of social, intellectual and esthetic experiences, and we may summarize the results of our inquiry as follows: Pleasures and pains, whether sensuous or of a more intellectual character, are typically intense and relatively brief. They are chiefly associated with gains and losses, or with deficiencies and excesses. Pleasures are produced by the acquisition or arrival of things which can be harmoniously incorporated into any aspect of the whole pattern of our lives, or, in a usually less intense and rapidly developing form, with the removal of elements which prove to be or have become incompatible with the integrity of this pattern. Pains in varying degrees are caused by the intrusion of something incompatible, or the removal of some harmoniously adjusted constituent of the pattern, or the absence of something necessary to our welfare, or the continuing presence of some inharmonious element. These typical reactions are most consistently exhibited by an animal well-adjusted to a hereditary environment and well acquainted with its living and lifeless components. In strange surroundings, or those which are rapidly changing, they no longer consistently hold; for things which will prove incompatible or injurious are sometimes greeted with pleasure, while those which might be beneficial are rejected as unpleasant.

It would be an immense advantage if we could always trust our feelings of pleasure or pain to prompt us to make the right responses to the situations in which we find ourselves; for thereby we would be spared many perplexing decisions; and because we acted spontaneously we would act with less effort and strain, saving our precious energy for higher pursuits. Although it is probable that many animals in a state of nature can trust their spontaneous inclination to pursue the pleasant and avoid the painful to guide them safely through life, humans have for many generations been changing their circumstances so rapidly that they can no longer place much trust in these spontaneous responses. The most we can say, in view of the biological significance and probable mode of origin of pleasures and pains, is that activities from which we derive pleasure bear a *prima facie* presumption of vital soundness and rightness, whereas those which cause pain to self or others are likely to be injurious and wrong. But in the case of humans, this presumption must be subjected to a searching examination before we can accept it.

In discussing pleasures and pains, we have been dealing with an immense variety of states of consciousness which we divide into two great categories. What is the basis of this division? Unless we and everyone else who talk about pleasures and pains classify our experiences in a manner that has no foundation in fact, there must be some property common to all members of each of these two great groups; but when we analyze them, we find it most difficult to discover what this property is. For my part, I can find no single quality present in all the experiences that I regard as pleasant, and none in all of those which are painful. It is not something inherent in the experiences themselves, but rather my reaction to these experiences, which determines their classification as pleasant or painful. The sensations and affections which I call pleasures are those which I seek when they are absent and strive to prolong when I have them; those which I call pains I try to avoid when absent and to remove when present. I do not desire certain sensations because they are pleasant, but rather they are pleasant because I desire them; I do not shrink from certain feelings because they are distressing, but rather they are distressing because I shrink from them. The root of the distinction between pleasures and pains is not in the quality of the excitations themselves, but in something more central to myself, which gives to each its affective color.

That this is the true foundation of the classification into pleasures and pains seems to me obvious from the fact that the same sensation, as, for example, the taste of a food, may be pleasant, indifferent, or even somewhat disagreeable, according to my internal state at the moment. If a sensation had some intrinsic quality, which made it pleasant, it would necessarily be pleasant whenever we experience it. Hence we must conclude that pleasantness or painfulness is not an intrinsic quality but a relational quality of an experience. And if we admit that pleasures are so-called because of our desire to get or retain them, it does not seem absurd to attempt to compare the most diverse of them, and even to assign a numerical value to each, on the basis of the strength of this desire; while similarly pains might be measured by the intensity of our desire to avoid or remove them. Thus a hedonistic calculation, such as the Utilitarians were fond of talking about, does not appear to be a ridiculous notion, although in practice such a calculation encounters apparently insuperable difficulties. But even if we could compute the net pleasure of a life by assigning to each experience a numerical value with a positive sign if pleasant and a negative sign if painful, such a summation would tell us nothing about the happiness of this life; for, as we shall see, happiness is something quite different from an aggregate of pleasures.

3. Transition from Pleasure and Happiness

Although pleasures are associated with the acquisition of the elements, material and mental or spiritual, necessary for a prosperous and happy life, such a life is more than a sum of pleasures. Something else is requisite for the kind of existence that we call happy. But we must defer the consideration of this additional principle until we have examined certain experiences which appear to be intermediate between the pleasures that we have already discussed and happiness, between pains and unhappiness. The pleasures we have considered, which I take to be the most elementary sort, are generally intense but brief. The bodily pleasures are chiefly of local origin, caused by the stimulation of a single sensory organ or possibly of two cooperating organs, as when the tongue and the olfactory system work together in producing the complex sensation that we call a taste. Since the senses are the doorways of the mind, we owe even the pleasure that we derive from learning to our sensory organs, principally to the eyes and ears, or to the two working in conjunction, as when we attend a visual demonstration accompanied by a verbal explanation. That our esthetic delights would be impossible without the senses is too obvious to deserve mention. Our physical pains, especially those caused by the laceration or loss of some part of the body, are also of local origin. They differ from the corresponding pleasures not only in their usually far greater intensity but also in their longer duration, which is to be attributed to the persistence of the lesions responsible for them.

The experiences we have now to examine, transitional between pleasure and happiness, or between pain and unhappiness, differ from primary pleasures and pains in being, when of the sort that we call physical, on the whole less local in origin and usually of longer duration. This distinction holds good more consistently in the case of the pleasures than in that of the pains, which in any case tend to be lasting. When the pleasures are mental rather than physical, they are also more diffused in the sense that they are not, as those already considered, associated with a single fact or event so much as with a group of facts or events. Thus, in either case, a larger mass of feelings or thoughts is involved in these transitional satisfactions than in the pleasures of the first class.

Among the gratifying feelings which we are in doubt whether to include under the heading of pleasures or of happiness are those for which a fine climate is responsible. The beneficent effects of a salubrious and invigorating atmosphere are felt not in any particular organ so much as in the organism as a whole; yet an important part of this total effect is certainly to be attributed to the mild temperature of the air in contact with the skin and the brilliance of the sky which constantly greets our vision. Although perhaps less intense, the pleasure we derive from an excellent climate is more enduring than any of those associated with bodily acquisitions, like those of eating and drinking; and if not in itself a sufficient foundation for happiness, such an ambience can be a most important component of felicity. Conversely, a climate which for days together is damp and gloomy, either too hot or too cold, can cause an organic depression which is almost a continuing pain; and if not in itself capable of producing unhappiness, depressing weather undoubtedly makes it easier for one to fall into a gloomy mood.

Among the transitional experiences are agreeable activities, physical, intellectual, and social. The gratification we derive from an active game or physical exercise, like tennis or swimming, can hardly be traced to the stimulation of any particular sense or organ but is due to the harmonious cooperation in heightened activity of many muscles and organs, in the coordination of eye and mind and limb to produce a desired result. Similar effects are to be observed in pursuing crafts that require judgment along with the exercise of manual skills. It is not pushing the saw up and down so much as keeping to the line when we cut a board, and seeing that all our joints fit snugly, that makes carpentry a satisfying occupation. Intellectual pleasures are derived not only from the acquisition of fresh information but in sorting over the facts already in our possession, extracting their meaning, and drawing conclusions from them. Although the discovery of a fresh fact that has been long and stubbornly sought may yield the more intense excitement, the excogitation of data already in our possession affords a quieter and more enduring pleasure, more closely akin to happiness. The delights of social intercourse are due to many and complex factors, including the charm and grace of one's companions, their compatibility with oneself, and the stimulating flow of ideas.

Sometimes when engrossed in these agreeable activities, or enjoying pleasures of other sorts, we would find it difficult to say whether we are happy or not. But whenever we are doubtful whether we are happy or merely diverted from our misery by transient pleasures, there is one infallible test that we can apply. True felicity will always withstand self-examination; but when we try to conceal a persisting cause of unhappiness beneath a round of miscellaneous pleasures, we need only to pause in the midst of our most intense enjoyment and look into our own spirit, to discover how wretched we are.

None of these pleasant activities, physical, intellectual, or social, is in itself sufficient for a happy life. But even when oppressed by persisting causes of unhappiness, we can often forget our troubles and enjoy a blissful hour when engaged in such activities; and they are, on the whole, more effective in helping us to regain a more cheerful mood than any sensual gratification and even than any of the pleasures of acquisition. Although not yet an adequate foundation for felicity, these experiences that lie between the primary pleasures and happiness show us clearly in what direction we must move in order to attain enduring felicity: we must organize the experiences and activities of which a life is compounded into a coherent, harmonious whole.

4. Instinctive Happiness and Its Vulnerability

Of happiness we may distinguish two contrasting kinds, which for brevity may be called instinctive happiness and rational or Stoic happiness. The reason for this last designation will become clear in the course of our discussion. Instinctive happiness is the sort which we suppose to be enjoyed by animals living prosperously in their hereditary environment, and by people in an old, homogeneous and stable culture. Unfortunately, no one can fathom the minds of animals, and few humans in our restless, rapidly changing modern world live in a society which still basks in the light of a mellowed tradition; but from time to time some of us come close enough to instinctive happiness to learn its conditions and to imagine what it would be like in its perfection.

In the first place, we need a solid foundation in robust health, without which this sort of felicity is certainly difficult and perhaps impossible to attain. And this, of course, implies an adequate supply of wholesome food and a shelter which allows restful repose, although it need not be elaborate nor even comfortable to one whose body has been softened by modern luxury. There must also, in the case of a social animal, be companions who yield a sense of intimacy and security, with mating and the begetting and rearing of offspring at the proper period of life; for this kind of happiness is hardly possible if any of the natural instincts is thwarted. The life-preserving activities—whether they be food gathering or agriculture with associated crafts—although strenuous, must not cause excessive fatigue or strain, so that each one sets about his or her daily occupation eagerly or at least contentedly, and not as though driven by a slaveholder's whip or the equally stern lash of economic necessity. In a society of simple people, there would perhaps be periodic gatherings with singing, dancing, and games, to satisfy social impulses. Above all, these happy people would not be perplexed by foreign or revolutionary ideas, which make them doubt whether their traditional way of living is after all the best, whether their government is as it should be, whether their gods approve the rites held in their honor, or even whether the gods exist. Moreover, each individual would be careful to obey the laws or customs of his community, and even to honor the prejudices of his neighbors, so as not to antagonize them and perhaps draw severe punishments upon himself.

In a life which yields instinctive happiness, all the important components are blended in a coherent, smoothly running system. To begin with, there is that harmony of all the parts and functions of the body which we know as health; and this in turn implies an adequate adjustment of the organism to its physical environment. Individuals must be compatible with those others with whom they are closely associated, so that a fair measure of concord pervades the family and the community. The various activities of life, as work and recreation, production and consumption, must be adjusted to each other with measure and proportion. Such a life will not be lacking in pleasures, for the most part such as are associated with the acquisition of its necessities and the rearing of offspring; but these will be on the whole few and simple in comparison with those which the more prosperous citizens of industrial societies manage to crowd into their days. If the members of an old and stable culture are happier than restless moderns, it is not because their lives contain more comforts and excitements, but because its elements are fused into a more harmonious whole.

Instinctive happiness is the kind that has attracted the majority of humanity. Relatively few of those who have striven to cultivate this sort of happiness have enhanced their lives by building upon a broad foundation of animal satisfactions a substantial superstructure of esthetic delights or intellectual gratifications. At its best, a life that satisfies the deep vital appetites and affections has much to recommend it; and if to these natural joys one can add a measure of spiritual fulfillment, it would appear to be ungrateful to expect our few score years to yield us more.

The chief objection which the prudent individual will raise against instinctive happiness is its tragic instability. Founded as it is on health, family ties, a home, friendships, the respect of neighbors, participation in communal activities, a satisfying religion, and at least sufficient wealth to support these varied features, it is at the mercy of a thousand mischances, including disease, the death of loved ones, loss of property, the slander of malicious neighbors, the hazards of war, natural catastrophes, and all the other accidents of an active life. Cautious people use all their ingenuity to guard against such hazards, but in vain; and few pass through life unscathed by some of these calamities so blighting to instinctive happiness. Hence nearly everyone acquires a few comforting maxims and scraps of ancient wisdom to repeat for his or her own consolation when smitten by these recurrent blows; and the tenor of all these wry sayings is that such misfortunes are the common lot of humanity.

From ancient times, a small minority of people have felt that to live at the mercy of all sorts of cruel and ridiculous accidents is intolerable. Like everybody else, they wished to be happy, but only a felicity that was proof against all mischances could satisfy them. So they invented a new sort of happiness, whose cultivation required the exercise of reason fortified by an unusual measure of pertinacity and self-control. Although in ancient times each of the more thoughtful cultures, as those of India, Greece, and China, developed methods for the attainment of rational happiness, in the West no school of philosophy carried the enterprise as far as the Stoics; hence we may designate this particular kind of felicity as "Stoic happiness."

5. The Foundations of Stoic Happiness

A happy life differs from a mere succession of fugitive pleasures in the structure which binds all its components into a coherent whole. For a creature so complex as humanity, instinctive happiness depends on a rather extensive pattern of relations. Consider how many delicate physiological adjustments must be preserved to safeguard the health of each of the several individuals who make up a family; how many psychic adjustments to preserve the cheerfulness of each and their harmonious association; how many economic adjustments to maintain the family's position in the state; what feats of diplomatic jugglery to preserve their country's peace in an unstable community of nations. The failure of harmony at any point in this vastly extended fabric of relations can spell disaster to instinctive happiness.

In the measure that we can contract the network of relations on which our felicity depends, it is at the mercy of fewer hazards, hence more firmly established. If one's welfare depended only on what happened in one's own country, it would be more secure than in our modern world, where events in any nation may have far-reaching international repercussions. If it depended only on what occurred in one's own household, it would no longer be jeopardized by the political and economic upheavals of the state. If one's happiness could not be shaken by what befalls the members of one's family but only by what happens directly to oneself, it would be still more secure. If the mishaps which afflict the body could not upset peace of mind, one's position would be even more firmly established. And if one's happiness were proof against the mind's irrational vagaries but depended on reason and volition alone, it would be well nigh impregnable. With each contraction of the network of relations by which our felicity can be affected, its vulnerability is correspondingly decreased.

Once our attention has been called to this fact, it is so clearly evident that no demonstration is necessary; but it required philosophic genius to discover it in the first place. In the West, Socrates, Antisthenes, and Diogenes came successively closer to this discovery; but Zeno, founder of the Stoic school, and his successors worked out the method in the greatest detail. They promised people that their happiness would be unshakable if they could establish it on a relationship of a single sort, that between one's moral purpose and his conduct. Since happiness is always more than a single sensation and depends on harmonious relations of some sort, no further contraction of its foundation seems possible. This is the meaning of the doctrine that happiness depends on virtue and virtue alone, widely held by the ancient philosophers, but most distinctive of the Stoics.

In establishing their admirable system, the Stoics gave no strained interpretation to the word virtue. For them, the moral virtues were those generally recognized in Classical civilization, wisdom, courage, temperance, justice, veracity, generosity, gratitude, and benevolence. To this last they gave a wider scope than it previously had; for they regarded as their brothers, to be treated with justice and clemency, every human being, not merely other members of their own city or society. In their view, to establish one's mind in virtue, then to make every voluntary act a perfect expression of this virtue, was the single condition necessary for the most complete happiness. This led them to affirm that only what is honorable or righteous is good, and all other so-called goods are delusory.

In conformity with this view, the Stoics assigned an almost negligible value to all the usual objects of human desire. If happiness is the supreme good or end, everything indispensably necessary for its attainment must be counted good as means; but things indifferent to this end are not even good as means; the most that can be said in their favor is that people commonly prefer them. Among these "things preferred" were health, personal beauty, wealth, fame, social position, spouse and family, friends, wholesome pleasures of all sorts. Stoics, sharing the tastes of others, might seek and possess these things, or some of them, if they could do so with no compromise of virtue, and so long as they kept constantly before themselves the fact that no one of them, nor all of them together, was an essential constituent of happiness, which would be nowise diminished by the loss of every material possession, every human tie, every bodily perfection. In the utmost extremity of pain and destitution, so long as a person's honor is unstained and he or she harbors no delusions as to the value of what has been lost, felicity is complete.

Viewing the Stoics' uncompromising disdain of pleasures, pain and all worldly advantages, we often carelessly assume that they did not really care about happiness, or that they defined the word in such a way that it meant something quite different from what we ordinarily understand by it. But this is a misconception; I doubt if the world has ever seen another group of people so doggedly determined to win true happiness, and the most exalted joy. The immortal gods were for the Classical world the archetypes of beatitude; but the Stoics, although they had no fixed doctrine of immortality, would not concede that even a god could be happier than their ideal Wise Person.

Common sense would say that the quantity of happiness that any being enjoys is given by the product of the degree or intensity of this felicity and its duration; so that of two people whose happiness is equal in intensity, one who lives twice as long experiences twice as much happiness; whereas an immortal god, whose joy endures forever, is blessed with infinitely more happiness than any mortal could possibly know. The Stoics denied all this, asserting that in assessing happiness the only point to be considered is its perfection. Even if we die young, the individual who achieves perfect virtue is no less happy than another who lives many years; indeed, no whit inferior in beatitude to a god. For, as Seneca said, in an instant of time virtue completes an eternity of good.[1] He wrote eloquently of that wonderful dispensation of nature which makes it possible for a person, for all the briefness of his mortal span and all the accidents to which he is liable, to equal an immortal god in joy. The Wise Person might even be held to have the advantage over the gods, for he wins this serenity by his own strenuous endeavor; whereas the gods possess it from the beginning. Far from being indifferent to happiness, the Stoics were so determined to win and keep it that they would admit among the factors which might influence it nothing not wholly within their control. If there is anything which may be said to be completely within an individual's power, it is the determination of his own voluntary acts. Hence the Stoics maintained that to make every act, and every opinion, the perfect expression of a virtuous mind, is all that happiness requires.

At this point we may pause to notice one peculiar feature of the Stoic doctrine. Although their "things preferred" are of negligible value when compared with the exercise of the moral virtues, these things determine the nature of virtue. It is because people wish to keep their property that they set store by justice, because they enjoy receiving gifts and favors that they praise generosity, because they prefer pleasure to pain that they esteem kindness and gentleness. If we were so constituted that we preferred sickness to health, a mutilated body to a whole one, penury to plenty, the contempt rather than the praise of our compeers, it is conceivable that we should still discover a distinction between virtue and vice; but our virtues and vices would be far different from those which we at present recognize. As has been often demonstrated, the commonly acknowledged virtues are those attitudes and behaviors which best conduce to the material prosperity and instinctive happiness of people in societies. Hence, to say that although justice and veracity are true goods health and wealth are not, seems to be turning things upside down and confusing means with ends.

We can avoid this difficulty by agreeing that the true end of life is to perfect one's character, and that the noblest or most virtuous person is the one whose activities most promote the formation by other individuals of the sort of character we desire for ourselves. In this case, the commonly recognized goods, the "things preferred" of Stoicism, are such because they are the foundations of a healthy society, wherein the greatest number of individuals can attain spiritual perfection. But it is only insofar as they promote this highest end that they can be preferred or called good.

6. Psychological Truths Underlying Stoicism

The Stoics did not deceive themselves that their kind of happiness could be easily achieved. They sometimes admitted that their ideal Wise Person, who alone could enjoy perfect felicity established solely upon virtue, might appear once in five hundred years. What is to be said of their doctrine: is it a fantastic delusion or founded upon a true understanding of human nature? The Stoics were notorious in antiquity for their exaggerations, the famous paradoxes, which philosophers of rival schools repeatedly undertook to ridicule. Yet when due allowance is made for a somewhat hyperbolic habit of speech, I believe we must admit that their teaching contains great and important truths, which our pleasure-loving modern world too frequently overlooks.

If we examine our own experiences, it is not difficult to discover some of the psychological truths on which the Stoic doctrine of happiness firmly rests. After early childhood has passed, we no longer live wholly in the present, and the character of our memories has a profound effect on our felicity. Some of our experiences are more adequately preserved in memory than others. I believe it generally true that we find it easier to recall our acts and the motives which determined them, what we did and said on any outstanding occasion, than our pleasures and pains. Sensuous pleasures and pains in particular seem difficult adequately to represent in consciousness when their exciting causes are absent. Hence when we pursue some pleasure in a shameful manner, the vivid recollection of our dishonorable motives and actions continues to distress our memory long after the gratification has been forgotten, and in the course of years we pay for our brief pleasure with an incomparably greater sum of pain.

None of life's many sorrows is harder to bear than the loss of a loved one. To recall the kind deeds he or she did for us merely intensifies our sense of loss and desolation; and to know that we were neglectful, repaying kindness with ingratitude and neglect, adds remorse to grief and immeasurably increases our woe. But to remember that we were always generous and dutiful, neglecting no measure for his or her welfare, greatly assuages our sorrow. We reflect that, so far as lay in our power, our association with the deceased was beautiful and harmonious, and it was through no voluntary negligence or guilt of ours that he or she was taken from us. The memory of such a friendship becomes more sacred and consoling with the passing years. Here, again, by paying attention to our active rather than our passive states, we diminish our pain and even increase our happiness.

We are so constituted that any experienced harmony is pleasant to us, and the more intimately it touches us, the more it contributes to our felicity. What we do is closer to our inmost selves than what is done to us; how we act upon the world is a more faithful revelation of our nature than how it deals with us. To make our deeds conform to our guiding principles is a most important constituent of felicity, and conscientious persons would not deem themselves happy if they were obliged continually to violate their self-imposed rules of conduct to conciliate a hostile world. But again and again we must choose whether we will remain true to our principles at the price of hardship and pain, or whether we will win ease and wealth by betraying them. Although a dull and sensual nature may perhaps gain greater satisfaction by electing the latter course, it is doubtful whether a finely organized mind does not lose rather than gain in felicity whenever it sells its principles for material advantages. The Stoics were sure that such betrayal of one's honor is fatal to happiness.

Perhaps what seems at the first glimpse the most flagrant exaggeration in the Stoic doctrine of felicity is that pain is inconsequential to happiness. It happened to be not a Stoic but Epicurus himself who declared that even on the rack an individual might be happy, but the Stoics assented heartily to this opinion of a philosopher whose teachings were on the whole repugnant to them. To moderns with an almost pathologic hypersensitivity to pain, this seems an outrageous prevarication. But if it could be demonstrated that in certain circumstances sensations commonly accounted pains are not only compatible with contentment or peace of mind but actually increase it, this tenet would lose much of its incredibility. And this appears to happen whenever the pain is part of a whole which seems to require it for its completion. When we are engaged in some enterprise to which we believe it our duty to dedicate our last ounce of strength, the feeling of fatigue, which when extreme can be very painful, enhances our satisfaction with what we have accomplished; for it is an insistent proof that we have not fallen short of what we demanded of ourselves or what others expected of us.

Religious enthusiasts, who believe that their innate sinfulness or early transgressions can be expiated only by pain, are apparently happier when suffering self-inflicted tortures than they could be without them; for in their life they are necessary for the accomplishment of their purposes. One who reads the lives of the medieval Christian ascetics, such as the blessed Henry Suso, can hardly avoid the conclusion that the horrible tortures they inflicted on themselves were actually a source of pleasure; for thereby the devotee felt drawn more closely to the beloved Savior who had suffered for his or her sake and who should be imitated.

Among barbarous peoples in many parts of the earth, it was once the custom to wail aloud, tear out the hair, gash the flesh, and otherwise mutilate the body, when mourning the death of a kinsman or a ruler. In the actual situation, these self-inflicted injuries were probably not nearly so painful as they seem to us when we read about them in a calm mood. In the heightened emotional state of the mourners, these lesions might have been actually gratifying. To the primitive mind, the feeling of pain and loss occasioned by the death seemed to call for some further violent sensations to complement it; and to achieve what the situation demands is always satisfying. It is significant that such extravagant rites of mourning appear not to have died away spontaneously, because people found them unbearably painful, but to have been suppressed by ancient lawgivers, among whom were Solon of Athens and Numa Pompilius of Rome, and in Israel whomever promulgated the rule given in Deuteronomy 14:1.

Hence it is no extravagant paradox to hold that pain is compatible with happiness, at times even an essential constituent. The question is whether pains that are actually sought can be accounted pains at all. As pointed out in section 2 of this chapter, when we examine all the immense variety of sensations which we classify as pleasures, we find that the only psychic feature they possess in common is the response they arouse in us: we seek them when absent and strive to prolong them when present. Similarly, we try to avoid pains when absent and to rid ourselves of them when present; and believe it impossible to discover any other basis for the separation of all our vast variety of qualitatively different sensations and feelings into the two great categories of pleasures and pains. Hence, when we seek some experience that is normally accounted a pain, that pain has become for us a pleasure. Such a transmutation of our spontaneous response to a given stimulus is not so rare as one might suppose; everyone who, disgusted or nauseated by a first experience of tobacco or strong liquor, persists in using it until he or she becomes a habitual smoker or drinker, has accomplished this transformation. When for such trivial ends weak-willed persons can change pains into pleasures, it is not absurd to suppose that a strong-willed person, who has resolved to bear suffering or torture because he or she cannot otherwise remain true to a moral purpose, comes at last to feel that these discomforts, which bear testimony to strength of character, are actually a component of happiness. Even a toothache that we have necessarily borne for many days becomes at last so much part of ourselves that we almost regret the removal of the aching molar!

When we read in Aristotle or other ancient philosophers that children and animals cannot be happy, we are at first amazed by this so paradoxical assertion. We may look back on childhood as the happiest period of our life; and although we cannot examine the feelings of the birds and squirrels that gambol in our trees, we often suspect that their lives are more joyous than our own. But when we recall that this statement refers to rational or Stoic happiness and not to spontaneous or instinctive happiness, we are constrained to recognize its truth. Obviously, only a rational being can cultivate a form of felicity which involves the transmutation, under the guidance of reason, of a large share of spontaneous reactions to life's varied predicaments. But I suspect, from my observation of animals, that they come closer to fulfilling the conditions of Stoic happiness than philosophers, who have been on the whole most ungenerous in their judgments of them, they admit. The prime requisite of Stoic happiness is to make one's acts conform to one's guiding principles, even when this cannot be done without suffering many discomforts and losses, which most people would regard as fatal to happiness. Now the innate pattern of behavior of an animal is the counterpart of the moral purpose of a rational human; and we frequently behold them remaining faithful to this pattern, as in attending their eggs or young in adverse circumstances, when if they consulted merely their physical ease they would doubtless follow some other course. They are better Stoics than the philosophers will admit!

7. Proposed Solutions of the Problem of Proportioning Happiness to Virtue

In childhood, we learn to associate good behavior with happiness, transgressions with pain, by means of the rewards and punishments which our elders mete out to us. This early association is strengthened in later life by the treatment we receive from other members of the community, according to whether they conform to its ways or depart from them. It is not strange that from an early period humans have suspected that there must somehow be a close relationship between the moral quality of their conduct and their eventual felicity. But although nearly all somewhat thoughtful peoples seem to have believed that virtue somehow yields happiness and wickedness misery, they have differed greatly in their notions of the form this felicity or suffering would take and the methods by which it would be brought about.

The earliest form of this belief seems to have been that the tribal god, who by his decrees determined what is right and wrong, would himself reward the virtuous and chastise the wayward. His recompense to the righteous usually took the form of abundant harvests, wealth, success in war, teeming offspring, health, and longevity; whereas his wrath was poured forth as famine, pestilence, defeat, sterility, and death. The concept of individual responsibility dawned slowly in the human mind, and at first the whole community was held accountable for the faults of some of its members and suffered accordingly; or the sins of the parents were visited upon the children: for humanity had not yet invented a hell where each erring individual received punishment according to his desert. This is the view of the earlier portions of the *Old Testament*. But, at about the time of the Exile, a heightened sense of personal responsibility was developing in Israel, and the prophets declared that each individual would be punished by God for his own transgressions.[2]

The *Book of Job* pointed out what is all too evident to every thoughtful observer, that in this life the righteous often receive much unmerited suffering, whereas the wicked may prosper greatly, at least in material things. In order to maintain that virtue always brings happiness while sin begets suffering, it became necessary to suppose that rewards and punishments were apportioned after death rather than in this world. Although the most primitive religions know little or nothing about this, each of the more advanced religions developed its own elaborate eschatological scheme, whereby the residual injustices of earthly life would be corrected and happiness be proportioned to virtue. Zoroastrianism, Christianity, and Islam, like the ancient Egyptians, assigned to each human soul a single incarnation, after which it would be judged according to how it behaved while in the flesh and assigned everlasting torments or endless bliss, the latter perhaps to be enjoyed after a finite period of purgation. Jainism, Buddhism, and Hinduism supposed that each soul or character passes successively through many human, animal and even vegetable bodies, after each incarnation proceeding to a temporary heaven or hell to receive the delights or tortures which are its due according to the Karmic law, then returning for another period in the flesh, with the possibility of final release from the round of incarnations if the aspirant make strenuous efforts to achieve this. Modified versions of metempsychosis, sometimes involving a limited number of incarnations, were adopted by Pythagoras, Plato, some schools of Gnosticism, and in medieval times, by the Kabbala.

In early modern times, rationalists, such as Locke, thought that the state should by legislation arrange that virtue receives happiness and vice is penalized.[3] Although modern states do undertake to punish the transgression of their laws, there are forms of vice, even more revolting than some of those for which people go to prison, which the state does not find it feasible to castigate. And no modern state has ever, to my knowledge, pretended to recognize, honor, and reward outstanding moral qualities in its citizens. Obviously, instinctive happiness depends on many factors, including health, human associates, success in business, which it would be ridiculous for a government to undertake to guarantee even to the most meritorious members of the community.

Of all the proposed solutions to that insistent question

of the human spirit, how righteous conduct could receive the happiness it seems to deserve, the ancient philosophers, above all the Stoics, gave the most credible answer. In demonstrating that virtue itself is an adequate foundation for happiness, they made the recompense of righteousness immediate and certain, without the need of the intervention of a legislator and judge, human or divine, nor all the mysterious machinery of Karmic retribution. In this, Stoicism seems to me to have risen to greater heights even than those Indian religious philosophies which in certain ways resemble it. The Jaina or Buddhist ascetic, who has extinguished desire and cleared his or her spiritual vision of all obscuring fog, is held to enjoy, while still incarnated in the flesh, nirvanic bliss unshakable by anything that might befall in the course of nature. In this, he or she resembles the Stoic Wise Person; but nearly always his liberation was attained by a degree of withdrawal from the world and its concerns which Stoicism, with its insistence on civic duties and social virtues, would hardly approve. But before winning that spiritual enlightenment which would ensure, when one had escaped from one's present and last fleshly abode, one's final release from the round of incarnations, the ascetic's spirit had passed through temporary heavens and hells, in each receiving joys or torments earned in its preceding sojourn in a body, just like any other soul. The bliss of final release is superimposed upon rewards and punishments of another sort.

Stoicism avoided this complication. For it, virtue required no external support of any kind to gain the happiness it merited. Even Kant, perhaps the sternest moralist among the major philosophers of modern times, could not follow it into the rarefied atmosphere of this cold alpine height. He taught that, although a good deed performed for the sake of one's own happiness lost in moral worth, the righteous person deserved to be happy; and because he did not discover any other means whereby virtue would finally receive the happiness due to it, he was led to postulate a Divine Ruler, who would give to each the felicity merited.

8. Final Assessment of Stoic Happiness

How shall we finally assess the Stoics' claim that virtue alone is sufficient to ensure the most perfect happiness? Although Stoicism, with all its outstanding merits and amusing hyperboles, has long ceased to be a way of life that is actually followed, having given way to creeds adapted to a weaker, less self-reliant society, the point is of sufficient importance to merit our serious consideration; for our whole understanding of happiness is bound up in it. Can we admit, what follows clearly from the Stoic teaching, that the individual without friends or possessions, alone and in pain, with the certainty of a cruel death held before his or her eyes, is if perfectly virtuous no less happy not only than the most prosperous of his or her fellows, but than an immortal god?

In examining this contention, it will pay us to examine the practice of the Stoics themselves. Unlike the Hindu *sannyasin* or the Buddhist *bikkhu*, unlike their contemporaries and philosophical kinsmen the Cynics, the Stoics did not relinquish all possessions and attachments to live as homeless, wandering ascetics. On the contrary, they married, established homes, reared families, cultivated earnest friendships, engaged in lucrative occupations, were administrators and not infrequently kings. All the advantages which thereby accrued to them were, according to the doctrines of their school, permissible as "things preferred," although they did not rank as goods; and they must keep constantly in mind that the deprivation of any or all of them would not reduce their true happiness in the least degree, so long as they maintained the right attitude toward them. Thus it behoved Stoics not to become blindly and passionately attached to spouse, children, friends, or possessions; for in this case they could hardly avoid feeling that they suffered a great loss if they were taken from them; and then their felicity would be at the mercy of events not wholly controlled by their will, and most insecurely established.

In marrying and begetting children, forming friendships, and acquiring property, the Stoics played a difficult and perilous game. They were constantly in danger of becoming so warmly attached to spouse or offspring, or else so fond of possessions, that the death of one or the loss of the other would seem a real evil to them; and this is what they were concerned to avoid. To enjoy things while we have them, yet serenely accept their loss, demands the perfect discipline of the sentiments by the will and an equanimity most difficult to achieve. Why did the Stoics incur the risk of forming attachments which, despite their most strenuous efforts, might become the occasion of upsetting their philosophic calm, if they did not feel that a life which had a place for some of the spontaneous affections and instinctive satisfactions was somehow superior to one whose happiness is founded on virtue alone?

We might call Stoics living prosperously and virtuously in the midst of family and friends as in the "expanded state," and those who had lost everything except their virtue as in the "contracted state." Their philosophy taught that their happiness in these two states was equal; for even in the second state they could preserve the most perfect felicity, and that which is perfect cannot be improved. Their actual conduct seemed to belie this doctrine. Since harmony is the foundation of happiness, it follows that the broader and more inclusive this harmony, the greater one's felicity must be; and that health, friendships, agreeable surroundings, and other modes of harmony cannot be indifferent to it. The most we can admit is that even in the contracted state they enjoyed the greater and more important part of happiness, its massive trunk and branches, from which all foliage and flowers had fallen. This much, I am convinced, we must concede to Stoicism, and it is a most important concession. From Plato onward, a large share of the Classical philosophers either implicitly or explicitly allowed this much of their claims; most moderns would refuse to follow them so far. Yet certainly those who make the motive of every act a perfect expression of their inmost nature cannot be quite unhappy.

9. The Relation of Pleasures to Happiness

Instinctive and Stoic happiness are not the only kinds which people have contemplated and hopefully pursued. The Epicureans sought to build happiness with quiet pleasures; virtue, they taught, was desirable as a source of pleasure. In order to avoid disturbing intrusions into this garden of ease, Epicurus refrained from matrimony, recommended abstention from all civic interests, and relegated the gods to a serene and isolated heaven, whence they could no longer influence the course of mundane events. In view of his mistrust of all other attachments, whether to the gods above or to the human community, his craving for friendship is almost pathetic; for thereby he revealed, despite his philosophy, that human happiness cannot be founded on pleasures alone, with the denial and suppression of the spirit's inherent tendency to reach out and identify itself with a larger whole. Other people have sought to establish happiness on esthetic enjoyments or quiet intellectual pursuits, with a similar suppression of other demands of their nature. But instinctive and Stoic happiness are the two varieties of felicity which have had the most convincing advocates. In many respects, they stand at opposite poles; so that if we can understand the role of pleasures in each we shall know the true relation of pleasures to happiness, which is the chief concern of the present chapter.

In the first place, it has become evident that pleasures and happiness are related as means and end. The most elementary pleasures, as those we experience in eating and drinking, winning possessions, seeing new sights and hearing new sounds, are associated with the acquisitions that we need for a prosperous and satisfying life. But we do not call such a life a "life of pleasures;" we use a different word and refer to it as a "happy life." Although we commonly use "pleasures" in the plural, we scarcely ever speak of "happinesses;" if we do, it is to compare the felicity of different persons rather than to designate successive experiences of the same individual. The way we commonly employ these words seems to reveal that one's happiness has a sort of unity, like his character or his wisdom; whereas his pleasures form a plurality, like his chattels. And in this, language, which has grown out of and epitomizes the collective experiences of great numbers of people, reveals a profound comprehension that eminent philosophers have sometimes lacked.

The Utilitarians, for example, were constantly talking about pleasures and how their number and intensity could be increased to the maximum. But when they needed a term to designate the total quantity of gratifications enjoyed by a person or a nation they used the word "happiness;" and we rarely find in their writings any suggestion that they were aware that an individual's happiness is more than the algebraic sum of the pleasures and pains which had fallen his or her share. But we have already seen that in certain situations, as in heroic dedication to some great endeavor, the inclusion of certain pains increases the value of the whole and the satisfaction we derive from it. If we were to attempt by means of a hedonic summation to assess the happiness of a day or a life by adding together the values of its pleasures and pains, the former with a positive and the latter with a negative sign, and we assigned to these heroic pains the negative values they would have if they occurred in some other context, we would come very far from arriving at the correct figure.

This single example is sufficient proof that happiness is more than an aggregate of pleasures and depends largely on the way they are combined. Some scheme of arrangement is necessary to make pleasures produce felicity. Pleasures are to a happy life as bright colors to a beautiful painting. A life crowded with the most exquisite delights but lacking in coherence is just as far from being happy as a canvas daubed all over with lovely hues by a bungler is far from being a work of art. A connoisseur prefers a sketch made in pencil or charcoal by a master hand to the brightest picture executed by one ignorant of draughtsmanship. Such a drawing devoid of color corresponds to Stoic happiness in its contracted form; and the fact that the ancient philosophers preferred such a life, established in virtue but unadorned by the gay hues of pleasures, proves that they were connoisseurs in the art of living. They at least possessed the outline of happiness, and it would not be difficult for them to fill in the colors if circumstances favored. But when a canvas is covered with bright pigments applied at random, it is irremediably ruined.

It is evident that happiness can be established upon a very slight material and intellectual foundation, if its elements are skillfully combined according to a guiding principle, and perhaps it could be maintained without further pleasures. But since pleasures are so closely associated with the acquisition of the stuffs with which a pattern of life is built and expanded, it would seem that happiness devoid of pleasure would be at best a static harmony, unable to satisfy a being with a principle of growth within it. The chief contribution of pleasures to happiness may reside in the spiritual or intellectual growth which is hardly possible in the absence of the fresh experiences of which they are the usual accompaniment. Painful experiences may also contribute to our wisdom and insight; but insofar as they promote spiritual growth, in retrospect we find something pleasant in them and are grateful for them.

But that neither a surfeit of pleasures, nor the growth-promoting experiences which many of them accompany, are in themselves sufficient to produce the greatest felicity is evident when we compare youth with maturity. If happiness resulted from the mere summation of pleasures with absence of positive pains, youth should be by far the happiest period of life. Then fresh experiences, each delightful in itself, press in crowds upon senses still alert and keenly receptive. Each day we add to our store of knowledge, constantly tasting the pleasure of new intellectual acquisitions. Health and vigor are at their apogee; we have few bodily pains and scarcely any worrying responsibilities; the future beckons with endless flattering prospects. Yet in spite of so many reasons to be glad, youth is often perplexed and ill at ease, if not positively unhappy. The very number and variety of experiences, often delightful in themselves, confuse and disturb. The poor youth feels himself or herself pulled simultaneously in many directions, for the multitudinous pleasures which life offers have not yet shaken down into a coherent pattern. Age, which has fewer sources of delight and more pains, is often the happier period, especially for the person who by the long exercise of thought and self-control, has succeeded in giving life consistency, defining its purposes, regulating its pleasures by needs and capacity to enjoy. The philosopher Hume declared that his last years were his happiest, although he was then in his sixties and dying slowly of "an inflammation of the bowels." Seneca,

Samuel Butler, Robert Browning, and other writers have likewise borne testimony to the superior happiness of the serene evening of life.

10. Is a Narrow Egoism Compatible with Happiness?

Some people go through life engrossed in the purely selfish pursuit of pleasures. Many of these pleasures would not be approved by an intelligent egoistic hedonist, because they will later be paid for by pains which outweigh them; but even the farsighted hedonist might lead a disgustingly selfish life. Since so large a share of our pleasures are derived from material acquisitions, they are necessarily selfish; because what one consumes is no longer available to others, and in this world most material goods are in short supply, inadequate to fill the demands which teeming life makes upon them. One's *motive* for seeking intellectual possessions may be just as egoistic as that which leads to the pursuit of material things. Yet the beneficial *effect* of acquiring knowledge is less concentrated in the self; for intellectual and spiritual goods may be shared among an indefinite number of minds with no diminution of the amount that each receives, whereas in general the material things that one person uses become unavailable to another.

Although it seems obvious that there may be a wholly egoistic pursuit of pleasures, it is not so certain that there can be a wholly selfish happiness. At least, it is clear that neither of the forms of felicity that we have analyzed, instinctive happiness and Stoic happiness, is compatible with a selfish life. Instinctive happiness requires, among other things, the satisfaction of our deep vital impulses. As we learned in Chapter VI, some of these impulses serve for the preservation of the individual while other's are directed outward toward the multiplication of the species and, in social animals, the welfare of the group. For many men and women in the prime of life, instinctive happiness seems scarcely possible without marriage, parenthood, the tender nurture of children, and perhaps also a recognized if humble position in the community, such as can be won only by some regard for its wider interests.

It seems futile to argue whether one does all these things merely to increase one's own felicity. If we are so constituted by nature that it is impossible for us to be moderately happy without dedicating a portion of our strength to the service of others, we cannot be egoistic without being altruistic, and we cannot be altruistic without being egoistic. Although there is undoubtedly much unmitigated egoism in our nature, in a wide segment of human endeavor the distinction between the two is largely artificial; and we would be justified in calling the same motive either egoistic or altruistic according to the side from which we view it. Since in many animals the welfare of the individual and that of the species are not antithetic but complementary, it is illogical to suppose that there could have arisen a wide chasm between egoism and altruism. A social animal appears to be so made that it cannot be happy without performing certain services for its kind, and it cannot perform these services to its kind without increasing its happiness; and this is about all that can be said about the matter. What seems certain is that it cannot augment its felicity by turning back upon itself impulses which life has directed outward; and the belief that this can be done is the tragic fallacy of egoism.

Moreover, it is doubtful whether we can draw a valid boundary between egoism and altruism except in minds capable of clearly distinguishing private from public gains. Until one analyzes one's act and tries to separate the advantages that it will yield to self and those that it will bring to others, it can hardly be called either selfish or altruistic. Since much instinctive happiness seems to be enjoyed by animals and even people who mate, beget offspring, and faithfully attend them without having calculated how much their course will increase their own pleasures and how much it will promote the welfare of their kind, it is useless to try to separate its egoistic and altruistic components. Much so-called selfishness is merely narrowness of vision. At most we might say that instinctive happiness is based upon specific rather than individual selfishness, by which we mean that it depends upon the satisfaction of impulses which serve the species rather than of the individual. It is selfish, then, as compared with an altruism which looks beyond the welfare of a single biologic species to that of all sentient creatures or all living things.

When we turn from instinctive to Stoic happiness, we find that this, too, is incompatible with a narrow egoism. Stoic happiness has for its sole foundation integral virtue, which includes not only fortitude and temperance but such social virtues as justice, generosity, and magnanimity. Were this kind of happiness founded upon the self-regarding virtues alone, it would never permit the individual who cultivated it to sacrifice self for a principle; for prudence would then be the highest principle; and unless one expects recompense in heaven, the sacrifice of one's life is incompatible with prudence. But it was a tenet of the Stoics that an individual should suffer torture rather than become the accomplice of an act of injustice, and that so long as one did what was honorable no pain could destroy one's felicity. Since Stoic happiness is impossible without the cultivation of social virtues, it cannot be a selfish happiness. It is worthy of notice that the ancient philosophers who held that virtue is sufficient for happiness seem rarely to have been troubled by the conflict between egoism and altruism which bedevils recent ethics; and this was because, unlike many moderns, they knew how to distinguish between happiness and pleasures. Much of our latter day confusion arises from the failure to make this distinction clear. If we believe that the happiest life is that which contains the most intense pleasures in the greatest number, we inevitably raise the conflict between egoism and altruism.

For a mind not wholly insensitive to everything beyond the sensations of its own body, an essential component of happiness is harmony with surrounding beings. But a harmonious relationship is always reciprocal: A cannot live in concord with B unless B dwells in concord with A. Both will benefit by this harmony, and their happiness will be increased thereby. This consideration alone makes it clear that for a being endowed with fine perceptions and sympathy, a purely selfish happiness is an impossibility.

11.We Can Deny Ourselves Pleasures but Not Happiness

The final contrast to be noticed between pleasures and happiness is that we may deny ourselves a pleasure and possibly even most pleasures, but nobody can repudiate the quest of happiness, or make any voluntary decision, which he or she believes will diminish ultimate felicity. That we can deny ourselves a pleasure is a fact so well attested by the daily experience of every normal person that it seems superfluous to labor the point. It might be argued that we can deny ourselves an immediate gratification only when we foresee that it will interfere with our enjoyment of some greater but more remote pleasure, or that it entails pains which outweigh it. But to prove that it is possible for humans voluntarily to relinquish most or nearly all the experiences that are commonly accounted pleasures, one need only point to the scholars or the saints who, having it in their power to enjoy many of the delights which their neighbors so eagerly seek, renounce them in order to increase knowledge or win spiritual release. But whether it is psychologically possible for human beings to elect any course which, on the most careful consideration promises to destroy or diminish their own ultimate felicity is a question we must ponder carefully, because some individuals have professed to abandon the quest of happiness.

In the intimate diary of Henri Frederic Amiel, the Swiss professor of esthetics and moral philosophy, we find, under date of January 29, 1866, the following passage: "Since we cannot be happy, why give ourselves so much trouble? It is best to limit oneself to what is strictly necessary, to live austerely and by rule, to content oneself with a little, and to attach no value to anything but peace of conscience and a sense of duty done." Notice the phrases "content oneself," "peace of conscience," and "sense of duty done."[4] Now, whether we call these states pleasurable or not, they are undeniably agreeable modes of consciousness. Amiel was striving, as by the psychic laws of its existence every thoughtful creature inevitably strives, to attain the most satisfying state of consciousness which his own somewhat melancholy nature and the circumstances of his life would permit. In common language, he was yearning for happiness, at the very moment when he professed to renounce his effort to win it.

The more austere moralists have sometimes shied away from the word "happiness" because of its hedonistic implications, yet they have recognized the need and the inevitability of striving to cultivate a satisfying state of mind in addition to, or by means of, virtuous conduct. This was Kant's procedure: he applied the phrase "intellectual contentment" to that satisfaction with one's existence, analogous to happiness, which necessarily accompanies the consciousness of virtue; and he held it to be "at least indirectly a duty" to cultivate felicity of this sort.[5] That the happiness of a thoughtful person is built up of elements very different from that of a child or an animal no one will deny; but it seems misleading to insist on having a different term for it; for every kind of happiness arises from the harmonious integration of all the components of a life. Kant did not, in this passage, deny the psychological necessity to seek one's own happiness; he affirmed the moral obligation to do so.

It is useless to seek some moral authority so high and overpowering that we freely choose to obey its august commands at the price of renouncing some other course which, in all its details, and all its foreseen consequences, we contemplate with greater satisfaction, as more conducive to our ultimate well-being or happiness. Even if we are convinced that Nature, or Reason, or God himself has determined what conduct is righteous, whether we act in conformity with this standard or disregard it will depend on the happiness we expect to win.

Let us suppose that one is convinced that virtue is conformity to the will of God, and one believes that one can ascertain beyond all doubt what God wills. One will still follow or ignore this divinely established rule of conduct according to whether this or some other course promises greater ultimate happiness. If we make a deliberate choice, we will weigh the sense of peace and wholeness, which comes from submitting to the divine will, and doubtless also the promised bliss of heaven, against the satisfaction promised by some forbidden course along with the pains that may accrue to us from inciting the divine wrath. The stress laid by popular religions upon the joys of heaven and the torments of hell, the infinite elaboration of delightful or gruesome details, is the strongest proof that we could possibly have that, even when people believe that certain courses of action are commanded by the author of their being, they will not or cannot neglect the pursuit of happiness in order to follow them. The pity is, not that we are so constituted that they cannot renounce happiness for virtue's sake, but that they so often suppose that there is a rift between them, as they do whenever they believe that righteousness can receive its need in felicity only by means of the arrangements made by some lawgiver, human or divine. The ancient philosophers knew better.

Even suicide is an affirmation of the persistent demand for happiness; for when none of the courses open to us promises surcease of pain and at least a modicum of felicity, death is the choice most compatible with this demand. Self-destruction would be more common if it did not require so much courage, and if hope were not so indomitable.

We can deny ourselves pleasures because they are only means; and when means are not essential to the end, or when in certain circumstances the usual means would interfere with the attainment of the end, the rational person readily dispenses with them. But we cannot relinquish the pursuit of happiness because it is the end of life. We are formed by a process which constantly tends to order all the elements of body and mind into a harmonious pattern, and the subjective aspect of this harmony is happiness. To abandon the quest of happiness is to resist the movement toward harmony, and this is to set ourselves in opposition to the process which made us and to repudiate the source of our being. No sane person can do this.

Chapter Nine
The Determination of Choice

1. Contrasts Between Choice and Other Modes of Determination

THAT WHICH CHIEFLY distinguishes intelligence from other attributes of mind is its capacity to foresee or anticipate the future. Sensations and emotions are always experienced as immediately present; appetite is felt as a tension toward some still unrealized objective, yet without other mental faculties it fails to foresee its own satisfaction; memory obviously deals with the past. But the true province of constructive intelligence is the future; and from the point of view of an animal struggling to survive in a perilous world, the only value of knowing the past is that it provides a baseline for taking a sight into the future. At an advanced stage of development, intelligence may find its highest satisfaction in reconstructing the past, in the manner of the historian or the geologist, or in discovering the timeless laws of nature or of thought, without regard for practical consequences. But applied science measures its success by its ability to predict and control coming events; and even those to whom knowledge of nature is precious for its own sake do not fail to recognize that successful prediction is one of the strongest proofs of the validity of their interpretations; for without understanding, accurate prediction is impossible.

This conscious inclination toward the future, this awareness of coming events, is one of the most momentous novelties that life brought into the world. We have no reason to believe that inorganic bodies, as rocks and minerals, or vegetables, or even the simpler animal, are at all concerned with the future; so that their movements and other activities are determined solely by the past and present. But intelligence gave birth to a new mode of determination by which the future acquired a voice in its own creation. Now, at last, the phenomenon of choice appeared upon Earth. We need not say "free choice," for there is a certain redundancy in this expression. So long as we can choose, we are free in the everyday meaning of the word. When analyzed, the concept of freedom leads us into some of the most perplexing of metaphysical questions, which are most profitably discussed in other connections. By choice we mean the ability to select between two or more alternatives, present or imagined, on their own intrinsic merits, and without reference to the problem of indeterminism or freedom of the will.

It is not difficult to establish a criterion for choice. If we subject any unattached lifeless body to two attractive forces of equal strength, as a scrap of iron exposed to the poles of the same sign of two similar magnets, it will move forward in a line which bisects the angle formed by their directions. If one of the forces is stronger than the other, the body will advance in a line which takes it closer to the greater attraction, in a manner which can be determined by constructing a parallelogram of forces; but it will not move directly toward the more powerful attraction as though the other were wholly absent. Thomas Knight long ago demonstrated that gravitation and centrifugal force have similar effects upon sensitive growing shoots and roots. When the positively geotropic roots of seedlings were attached to a revolving wheel, in such a manner as to expose them simultaneously to these two forces, they grew in a direction determined by their physical resultant. A green shoot which receives light from two sources, separated by an angle of something less than a hundred and eighty degrees, will bend in a direction which bisects this angle if the intensities are equal; but if they are unequal it inclines toward the stronger light in the measure in which its intensity exceeds that of the second source. Under corresponding conditions, a free-swimming, positively phototropic protozoan or tiny crustacean will take a course intermediate between the two sources of illumination. Organisms which behave in this fashion, try to orient themselves so that both sides of the body receive equal intensities of light, or heat, or whatever directs their movements.

But animals equipped with more perfect organs of sense, which provide clear images of the objects toward which they

strive, do not make such compromises between competing solicitations. They may at first vacillate between them,
but as a rule they finally go straight for one or the other, a
phenomenon which students of behavior call "telotaxis."
Philosophers, puzzling over the problem of free will, used
to wonder whether Buridan's ass, placed precisely midway
between two bundles of hay exactly equal in size and fragrance, would not starve where he stood, like a dead weight
pulled by two stretched springs of equal tension, because
of the impossibility of preferring one tempting bundle to
the other. Theoretically, such an unhappy fate might await
some humbler creature, governed by tropisms, which fell
into a similar predicament; although even in this case oscil-
lations or random movements would before long carry
it so far out of the position of perfect equilibrium that
it would be more strongly drawn to one attraction than
the other, and so escape the impasse. But can anyone who
knows donkeys doubt that Buridan's ass would promptly
go to one bundle of grass, devour it, then if still hungry
turn his attention to the second?

The possibility of selecting one of several competing
attractions implies the capacity of releasing oneself from
the immediate influence of the others. Thus, every choice
involves a decision, or cutting off of alternative responses.
When we review our own deliberate choices, it is often
difficult to tell whether the acceptance of one alternative
or the denial of the others was the salient feature of the
act. We follow the second method whenever we arrive
at a choice by a process of elimination. But by whatever
route a choice is reached, this capacity of responding to
one of two nearly equal attractions, almost as though the

other did not exist, distinguishes choice from all purely mechanical modes of reaction, and even from the tropisms of the simpler organisms. From the neurologist's point of view, deliberation and choice are made possible by the interposition between the afferent and efferent nerves of a labyrinth of channels, which permit a nervous discharge to follow alternative routes, and of some arrangement to allow delayed rather than immediate response to an external stimulus. Such an arrangement is present in animals whose behavior is largely instinctive, but is not functional in the case of pure tropisms.

In the face of three or more competing attractions, choice differs even more strikingly from mechanical response than when only two alternatives are offered. Suppose that I am called upon to select between A, B, C, and D, all of which entice me strongly, but only one of which I can have. If I select A, it is because it attracts me more powerfully than B, C, or D singly. But their combined forces of attraction, we shall suppose, far exceeds that of A; so that if I could have these three together, I would not hesitate to take them in preference to A. At the moment when I make the decision, the rejected alternatives are all in the same category and seem to act together, pulling against the preferred object, almost as though they lay all together on my left side with A alone on my right. In any system of purely mechanical determination, it is impossible for a body to move toward a single attractive force which is opposed by the greater sum of a number of separately weaker forces. To learn how difficult it may be to choose between multiple attractions, one need only watch women trying to select a dress or a length of printed fabric in a well-stocked shop.

It is necessary to distinguish choice not only from the tropisms of the simpler organisms and the modes of response of mechanical systems, but from other methods of determining activity in intelligent beings like ourselves. For by no means all of our actions, even those potentially under the control of the will, are preceded by an act of choice. We are often moved by impulse, by habit, by the dominating force of some masterful personality, or by the impact of some compelling situation. In all such instances we act irreflectively, as though impelled by the past instead of attracted by the future. So long as we act in any of these ways, we do not feel that we are freely constructing our future. An exception might be made in the case of habits, which are often developed deliberately as a result of some past choice; yet, so long as we follow them unreflectingly, our action is determined by the momentum of the past rather than by the attraction of the future.

2. Mental Faculties Involved in Choosing

Even when we choose between objects or situations immediately present, we are drawn forward by the promise of the future, although perhaps of a future distant by only a moment or two. For if we were perfectly satisfied by the actual relation of these objects to ourselves, we would feel no inclination to make a choice. If Buridan's ass could have satisfied his hunger by the contemplation of the two bundles of hay from a point midway between them, he would have had no incentive to choose one or the other. But this choice was vitally necessary to him, and in making it he determined a new relation between himself and the piles of grass; instead of gazing upon both he took possession of one, leaving the other, possibly, to be devoured by his master's cow. So, too, the woman in a shop must make a decision, which changes her relation to the merchandise offered for her choice. Although free to enjoy the sight of all the enticing dry goods before her, she can become the possessor of only one or two pieces, and to effect this change she must look to the future, trying to decide which purchase will best satisfy her needs. The difference between present enjoyment and choice can be appreciated by comparing one's feelings in a public art gallery, where the relation to all the paintings on display is essentially the same, and in an art dealer's shop, where present enjoyment is modified by the necessity to make a decision that will give possession of some particular object.

We often choose so rapidly that it is scarcely possible to distinguish all the elements involved in the act. When we weigh the respective advantages of alternative objects or courses of action distant from us in time or space or both, we are more likely to become aware of all the factors that enter into a choice. In the first place, we try to foresee the future, and in particular how each contemplated act will affect us. In this effort, we depend largely upon memory of past experiences in similar situations, because without knowledge of the past and faith in the uniformity of nature we would be at a loss to anticipate the future. In projecting ourselves into the contemplated situation, we are above all interested in how it will affect our feelings, whether it will bring us pleasure or pain, joy or sorrow, satisfaction or disgust. And of course, in this phase of our deliberation, too, we are guided by recollections of similar affections. Thus the affective no less than the rational functions of the mind play important roles in each important choice we make.

Consideration of the conditions in which mind evolved makes it seem likely that it acquired all these so varied capacities solely to enable us to guide our future life. Without intelligence, we could not plan our activities; without emotions, feelings of pleasure or pain, it would be indifferent to us what the future might bring; without memory, we would lack both that knowledge of the past without which we could not forecast the future and that experience of our capacity to enjoy and suffer which makes the future momentous to us.

3. Choice a Unique Mode of Determination

But how can the future determine the present, as it seems to do when we make a deliberate choice? The future does not yet exist, and the nonexistent can have no real influence upon contemporary events. Or one might argue that our only criterion of existence is the ability to effect changes in other existents and ultimately in ourselves; and since the future seems to have this effect upon a being capable of choice, it must in a manner already exist. The difficulty with this interpretation is that it destroys its own validity. The purpose of choice is to determine the future. That which exists has already taken shape; insofar as it is itself a determining factor, it is no longer open to determination. Accordingly, if the future determines our choice, that choice is useless; it is not needed to create what already exists.

Deliberation, then, must consist in forming conjectures about the future, and weighing them one against another. These thoughts are actually present, although their importance lies in their inclination or tension toward the future. But our surmises about the future are, for serious thinkers, too flimsy to merit prolonged consideration unless founded solidly upon knowledge of the past. And even those who conjecture wildly, without due regard for probabilities, do so by throwing together the elements of past experience in haphazard fashion. So that it is certain that our notions of the future are based upon recollections of the past, even when these are arranged in novel combinations. And the mind that chooses between the several views of the future which solicit its assent is also a product of the past, as represented in heredity and individual experience. Hence a choice seems to be wholly a product of the past. Whether or not an element of indeterminacy enters into it, seems irrelevant to our present discussion.

Yet even if we are constrained to conclude that a choice, like a mechanical effect, is a product of the past, it does not follow that there is no important difference between these two modes of determination. The possibility of influencing activity by notions or anticipations of the future, even if these are themselves products of the past, is a unique mode of determination, unlike, so far as we know, anything to be found in the non-living world, and it has had momentous effects on the course of history. Choice involves indirectness in the causal sequence, which distinguishes it sharply from mechanical causation, no less than from all the instinctive and impulsive activities of living things. In deliberation the mind creates, by the exercise of its synthetic faculty, those images or anticipations of the future which will determine its choice. In trying to foresee how the future will affect us, we generate the determinants of our own activity.

4. The Common Measure of All Motives

We are now prepared to consider the determination of choice, or how we decide between alternative courses of action. It is generally admitted that as between a pain and a pleasure, neither of which has foreseen consequences of much importance, all normal animals choose the pleasure; of two pleasures, they choose the greater; and of two pains, the less. But it is only in the very simplest cases, those so plain and straightforward that we make a decision with scarcely a pause for deliberation, that we choose in this easy, direct fashion. For a large proportion of our acts have more or less remote effects upon ourselves or others, which it is the business of intelligence to consider. The food we like best may injure our health, and we are constrained to weigh present transitory pleasure against future prolonged discomfort. Or a painful operation, like the extraction of a tooth, promises release from suffering; and we balance present acute agony against future, continued freedom from ache. Or we must decide whether we would be justified in neglecting an important task, upon which we have been engaged, for the sake of an excursion we would greatly enjoy. Or a clerk, severely tempted to slip a few of an employer's bank notes into his or her pocket, weighs the pleasures they could buy against the prickings of an outraged conscience and the disgrace and punishment that would follow the detection of the theft. The combinations which enter into choices are practically endless; but fortunately, one writing on this subject, unlike the expositor of some scientific theme, may suppose that readers are already familiar with a fair sample of them, and proceed to analyze them.

Before doing this, it will be well to devote some attention to the terms we shall use. The pursuit of pleasures and avoidance of pains are often said to be the chief if not the sole motives of human conduct. But do we always pursue pleasures in any spontaneous meaning of the word, and are pains, as commonly understood, what we invariably most wish to avoid? Not only the impulsive, unquestioning acts of animals, but many of the activities we undertake after a good deal of careful deliberation, seem to be done in response to some inner necessity rather than in view of the pleasures they promise to yield us. Is it for the sake of pleasures that we perform some task with painstaking care, when a more slipshod performance might bring us the same material gain? Is it for pleasures that humans undertake to alleviate the suffering of strange people or of animals, an occupation that exposes them to sights, odors, and situations painful to a sensitive nature? Are pleasures the sole motive for embarking on some great creative endeavor in art or science or literature, which for years will tax to their limits one's strength, patience, and ingenuity? Would a person who had carefully weighed all the toils and hazards marry and rear a family merely for the pleasures it will bring him? A considerable share of our activities seems to flow from some urge deeper and more central to our being than this superficial incentive. The fulfillment of our nature, and the happiness that springs therefrom, rather than pleasures, is the end of much of our effort.

To understand how choices are made, it is necessary to discover the common measure of all actual motives. Since in the endless mutability of circumstances any possible motive may be brought into competition with any other, obviously they must be somehow commensurate; for between two things which possess no single quality in common, no comparison is possible. We are sometimes called upon to decide whether we shall pursue pleasures or work for money, although between an affection of the mind and a coin in the pocket there seems to be no common measure. But, in this instance, we avoid the difficulty by considering the satisfactions that the possession or the spending of money will bring us, and balancing them against those we expect to derive directly from the alternative course of action.

We are often torn between pleasure and duty, or between the satisfaction of appetites and the dictates of conscience. Since such dilemmas arise and can be solved, it follows that, despite the qualitative differences they undoubtedly possess, pleasure and conscience have something in common. To compare pleasure with feelings which we attribute to conscience may be distasteful to those who regard the latter as a divinely implanted faculty, unlike anything else in our nature; but, before they indignantly reject the comparison, let them carefully ponder the consequences. If pleasure and conscientious feelings share no common property which makes it possible to weigh them against each other, then, when in obedience to conscience we deny ourselves some pleasure, this cannot be the outcome of a true choice. Consequently, we have not reached a decision by weighing alternative courses of action and selecting that which is most attractive to us in its promised effects. On the contrary, in obeying conscience we have acted in response to some irresistible inner compulsion, which drives us forward almost as though we had been sent staggering by a push on the back too powerful to be withstood. Accordingly, our act is determined by the past, without reference to the future, like the movement of a stone thrown from the hand or of a bullet shot from a rifle; and it would seem as proper to discuss the morality of a stone or a bullet as of a person. This conclusion, to which most students of ethics would no doubt vehemently dissent, seems the inevitable result of denying that there can be anything commensurate in pleasure and conscience.

It is equally imperative to forestall the opposite conclusion, that the conscience is primarily a source of delight. The more we cultivate our esthetic sense, the more joy we find in nature and the arts; the more we train our intellect, the more satisfaction we derive from thinking. But the more we cultivate the conscience and the more sensitive it becomes, the more difficult it is to satisfy and the less peace it allows us. I suspect that a perfectly tranquil conscience is one that has never awaked. Probably most people would agree that conscience is, on the whole, a source of more distress and even pain than of gratification. And this is understandable, for it agitates us whenever our conduct deviates from our principles or ideals; and while it is easy to fall short of our ideals, it is difficult if not impossible to exceed them. We cannot deliberately be better than we aim to be; and if, because our principles are low, we accidentally rise above them in action, there is slight merit in this and little cause for self-congratulation.

Yet if conscience is more often a source of distress than of complacency, we need only to live with its sharper moods to become convinced that the peace and inward calm which we experience when it is approximately satisfied is, by comparison, a most gratifying state of mind. It is to avoid the bitter rebukes of an outraged conscience and enjoy the sweet content of its less agitated states that we consider it in making a choice, weighing this feeling against the pleasures anticipated in some course of action on which it frowns. A good conscience is to the mind what good health is to the body. Each, in its own sphere, is an expression of that organic wholeness and vital integrity which it is the chief business of every living thing to preserve. Not only is such wholeness pleasant in itself, it is the indispensable foundation of all enduring happiness.

It appears, then, that the motives which influence choice are always expected states of feeling, but these range all the way from the grossest sensual pleasure to the fulfillment of our most central impulses, the calm of a satisfied conscience, or the exultation of some moral or intellectual achievement. As feeling, all these so diverse states have something in common; and it will be useful to have a single term to designate the whole range of them. Pleasure has been defined as a state of mind which we strive to produce and to preserve. By an easy inversion, we might say that every feeling which we try to bring into the mind and keep there is a pleasure. And certainly when we act from choice, we elect that course which, as far as we can foresee, will produce a feeling which we want to have and to preserve. What sane person would prefer a course whose only foreseen result, on the affective plane, would be a state of mind one wished to avoid? But when we use "pleasure" in this sense, the word covers a vast range of mental states—virtually the whole of those not positively disagreeable or so faint as to be practically neutral.

It is, as J. S. Mill decided when he broke away from the Utilitarianism of Bentham, a hedonist fallacy to suppose that between "pleasures" the differences are merely in intensity and duration, so that all are accurately measurable on a single scale.[1] Henri Bergson went farther than this, pointing out that distinguishable mental states are in general qualitatively distinct. Thus the felt difference between two degrees of whiteness, or between two weights held in the hands, is not a mere intensive quantity but of a qualitative order; as anyone can prove for himself or herself by observing the distinct quality of sensation caused by holding a lighter or a heavier stone, or looking at the same paper in a brighter or a dimmer light. Through experience, we learn to associate with these qualitative differences quantitative differences in the external stimulant; so that, without the use of instruments, we can usually tell which of two weights is heavier and which of two lights brighter, in such a manner that a balance or a photometer, which can detect only quantitative differences, will confirm our conclusion.[2]

If physical differences, in themselves purely quantitative, cause qualitative differences in sensation, we must surely expect qualitative differences between the several states of consciousness which we find agreeable and wish to preserve. To cover them all by the word "pleasure" is surely stretching this term almost to the breaking point, or so divesting it of its usual connotations that it becomes a mere technical term of psychology. Perhaps it would be preferable to restrict the philosophical use of the word "pleasure" to the ends sought by the Cyreniac School, which seems to have been the first in the West to develop hedonism as a formal doctrine. We might simply say that states of consciousness which we strive to arouse and to preserve have positive value, while those which we try to exclude possess negative value. Among the former are happiness, contentment, satisfaction, peace of mind, good conscience, joy, calmness, no less than sensual pleasures. Perhaps "satisfaction," the most neutral in tone, is the word that best represents the whole group.

Despite the immense variety of qualitative differences that we discover in material objects, all possess in mass a common property; so that objects as diverse as air and stones, flowers and scrap iron, can be compared quantitatively by mass. Similarly, all the innumerable experiences of life possess in their satisfactoriness or value a common property which permits their direct comparison. Thus satisfaction provides a basis of comparison between all mental states, as mass between all material objects, and it might be termed the gravitational force of the mind. Sensual pleasures do not seem to be the typical sort of satisfactory experiences, but rather a special group of them. The feeling or realization of growth or accomplishment is, to a refined mind, more representative of a satisfying experience. The pleasure we derive from any sensuous experience depends primarily on the constitution of the nervous system; its value, on the organization of our thoughts and our ideals. The first is immediate, the second emerges on reflection.

But before accepting the conclusion that we always choose the course which promises to yield us the greatest ultimate satisfaction or value, it will be necessary to decide whether it is possible to act wholly for the benefit of others, completely regardless of self. This matter was considered briefly in Chapter VI, but it is of such great consequence to our present discussion that we must pursue it farther here.

5. The Ultimate Ground of Choice

Chapter VI demonstrated that we are innately endowed with altruistic no less than self-regarding motives. We can hardly doubt that impulses of the first sort sometimes issue in spontaneous, uncalculated action, as when we share some sudden good fortune with those about us, or as when a mother unreflectingly rushes into danger to save her child. But the unpremeditated sharing of pleasures or of danger obviously does not involve forethought; it is more like an instinctive act. What interests us now is the more deliberate action which is planned in advance, with a weighing of alternative courses, as when we decide which of two suggested procedures we shall follow. In cases of this sort, whenever we think of acting for others, we can nearly always imagine some alternative course directed solely to our own advantage. Should I give this money to charity, or use it to buy new clothes? Should I devote the evening to helping some civic cause, or spend it more enjoyably at the theatre? Should I permit my assistants to share the honors that our work has won, or take it all for myself? Should I devote my declining years to some generous cause, or enjoy a well-earned rest? It is questions of this kind that concern us here.

In all deliberate activity for the benefit of others, we first imagine some change that we wish to produce in the condition. They are sick, and we would have them well; starving, and we would see them adequately nourished; ragged, and we would behold them decently clad; homeless, and we would see them housed; ignorant, and we would have them enlightened; miserable, and we would make them happy. The envisaged state of those whom we will serve seems to be the proximate cause of our effort in their behalf. But not only are these intended beneficiaries external to us; their contemplated state is still in the future; and as became clear in section 3 of this chapter, we cannot admit that what does not yet exist can be the effective cause of present action.

When I decide to work for some other person's benefit, what actually determines my activity is my present notion of the change that I intend to bring about in or for that person. The idea, although pointed toward the future, is actually existent in my mind. It is surrounded by an overtone of pleasure, satisfaction, or sense of fulfillment, which often contrasts sharply with the feeling of sadness, repugnance, or discomfort that hovers about my notion of the present misery or distress of the one whom I have resolved to benefit. However, the mere thought of the improved condition of some other being is not adequate to incite me to exert myself in his or her behalf. Could I feel as much satisfaction in simply imagining the other person in a happier state as I feel in picturing myself actually striving to create this state, I would rest in my generous dreams, never bothering to bestir myself. In addition to the change from the sadness which accompanies my idea of some other being's present state to the gladness that plays about my notion of the condition in which I propose to place the other being, something else appears to be necessary to move me to action, and this is the satisfaction with which I contemplate my proposed activity directed toward this end. Moreover, in order that the happiness that I feel in imagining this effort for the benefit of another being may issue in action, it must be greater than that associated with any alternative course presented for my consideration at the same time.

What save anticipation of one's own future enjoyments, or avoidance of one's own impending pains, could make one's thoughts hurry into the future? It might be urged that anticipation of the felicity of some other being could have the same effect. But one can have no notion of the satisfactions of others except as a consequence of experiencing one's own. Before we can use foresight to procure enjoyments for others, we must already have formed the habit of doing so for ourselves; and like all habits, this will be difficult to overcome. The best that most of us can do is to share our satisfactions with others.

There is yet another manner of viewing this question. Suppose that I wish to wash and clothe and feed a dirty, ragged, hungry urchin. This benevolent desire is in me, not in the child, who may resent the bath and fresh clothes, because ignorant of the advantages of cleanliness. Whether my desire has reference to a future state of myself or of someone else, it is equally my own desire, and if realized the satisfaction must be mine; for it is obvious that a desire cannot exist in one person and its satisfaction in another. In addition to any happiness that I may bring to the child, I can by no means avoid the contentment which comes from the fulfillment of my wish, which may or may not be augmented by a sympathetic glow of pleasure as I view the child's happy face. But possibly the child is so incorrigibly dirty, rebellious, and ungrateful that the satisfaction I feel in fulfilling my desire to see him or her clean and well-fed is evanescent, quickly followed by a sense of futility when I realize that, within my means, I can do little to improve his or her wretched plight.

Although it is evident that we often feel a wholly unself-ish desire to help others, it is equally clear that we experience within ourselves some happiness or satisfaction in so doing, or at least in contemplating such action of its results, and that without this we could not deliberately (although we might impulsively) advance the welfare of other beings. This is the one question that remained to be settled before we could accept the conclusion that when acting deliberately we always choose the course that prom-ises to yield us the greatest ultimate satisfaction.

Such a promise, as we all know to our sorrow, often fails of fulfillment; a truth confessed in the common say-ing that "anticipation is better than realization." In order to avoid all suggestion that the uncertain and still non-existent future is an effective cause of present action, we may more accurately phrase our conclusion by saying that when acting deliberately we always choose that one of two or more alternative courses in the contemplation of which we experience the greatest satisfaction. And since two courses cannot be contemplated simultaneously but only in quick succession, it is probably the feeling we experience as our thought passes from one to the other that finally determines our selection. Often we make such a transition repeatedly in the course of an extended deliberation. If, in contemplating two alternatives A and B, we feel an enhancement of value in turning our thoughts from A to B and a decline in value in passing from B to A, and we experience these results consistently, we finally decide in favor of B.

This truth about the grounds of human choice was clearly and repeatedly enunciated in the later writings of Plato, who certainly was not deficient in moral idealism.[3] It is sometimes called the law of "psychological hedonism," and it has had a chequered history in modern ethical thought. Combated by Butler and Hume, it was, in the opinion of some philosophers, finally demolished by them; although it seems to me that Butler proved that we can act unselfishly, not that we can choose a course which fails to satisfy us. In the long and involved discussions of this doctrine, we tend to lose sight of its precise meaning. If it means that people cannot perform generous *impulsive* acts, for their children or even for strangers, as jumping into deep water to save a drowning person, it is belied by an overwhelming mass of evidence. If it is taken to mean that we do not have wholly unselfish wishes for the welfare of other sentient beings, it appears to me to be equally false. The rule of psychological hedonism comes into force only when we are deliberately choosing between alternative courses in which the future well-being or happiness of others is at stake along with our own, and in such cases I maintain that we always elect the course in the contemplation of which we experience the greatest satisfaction or happiness, even if this course turns out to be one which gives many solid advantages to others, but to oneself no more than the joy of having done a generous deed.

The preceding analysis reveals not an innate selfishness but a fundamental altruism of the human mind. If our primary motive were invariably to assure our own felicity and that alone, and we happened to discover empirically that it is often possible to increase our happiness by benefiting others, we would be constrained to recognize a radical selfishness in our nature. But the true situation is precisely the contrary. As we learned in Chapter VI, life implanted in all social animals certain impulses which operate for the benefit of their dependent young and social companions; and as humans became reflective they discovered that by giving play to these impulses they increased their own satisfaction, which of course furnished an additional incentive for undertaking such activities. If I could do outstanding services for other beings without feeling a gratifying spiritual elation, I would deem my nature far poorer and more pitiful than it is; and I believe that a person might experience such great happiness in performing an act that would materially improve the condition of all sentient beings, that he or she would submit to cruel torture for this end, yet feel that a gain rather than a loss in meeting death in this fashion.

It is the sympathetic glow that we experience when contemplating action for the welfare of others that often permits us to prefer such a course to a competing course which promises purely selfish gains, and this is the truth which reconciles altruism with psychological hedonism. This law is a mere statement of fact, not to be confused with ethical hedonism, the doctrine which holds that to procure the maximum of pleasure, for self or others, is the right and proper goal of moral endeavor. Still, the word "hedonism" perhaps smacks too strongly of the pursuit of sensual pleasure, and in the eyes of many throws upon the doctrine of psychological hedonism an opprobrium which it by no means deserves. We have already contended that people can and do frequently deny themselves pleasures of all sorts, but cannot cease to strive for their own ultimate happiness. Hence it might be better to substitute the expression "psychological eudaemonism" for the view that we have been defending. Or, perhaps best of all, we can call it simply the "Law of Choice."

A corollary of this law is that we cannot spread benefits with an Olympian disdain of the happiness we engender, but must always in some measure participate in the blessings that we bestow; that we cannot perform good deeds with proud aloofness, but must ever be reminded by a sympathetic glow that we have much in common with the least of the creatures that we benefit.

Another corollary is that the good people do not differ from the wicked in that the latter seek only personal satisfactions, while the former strive only to do what is right, but they differ in the kinds of activities which please them. Both, by a law of nature, follow the course which they find most satisfaction in contemplating, which they believe will yield them the greatest ultimate happiness;

but they differ profoundly in the kinds of behavior that fulfill this condition for each of them. Wicked people are perhaps more often mistaken in their estimate than good people, so that what they anticipate with pleasure they often experience with sorrow. This appears to be largely a result of faulty early training and education, of not knowing what is good, if not of innate psychic defects. But this fundamental similarity in the determination of choice in the good and wicked alike is the best hope for the regeneration of the latter.

I believe that anyone who will give careful attention to what happens in his or her own mind when deliberately selecting a course of action will discover that the Law of Choice holds good. Of two alternative courses, we cannot avoid electing that which, on the whole, promises the greater satisfaction to ourselves. When a conscious being chooses, he or she must inevitably prefer that which is most agreeable to consciousness—for what other measure of value do we possess? The ultimate determinant of choice must ever be some feeling in the mind. Call it happiness, call it satisfaction, call it inner peace, call it a sense of fulfillment—these are names for the same subjective state viewed under varying aspects. Whatever compelling reasons our religion or philosophy may adduce for preferring a certain manner of life, we shall not freely adopt it unless it somehow satisfies us. But hedonism, or even eudaemonism, seems to some people to be inadequate. The doctrine itself does not bring us that sense of completeness for which we yearn. We suspect that rightness must have some authority or sanction higher than our personal feelings; that there must be in the cosmos, or beyond it, some standard to which we should conform. The only way of overcoming this difficulty is to recognize that the same creative process, which determines ultimate rightness has so made us that in this rightness, we find our truest happiness and peace. But we must be careful lest false pleasures deceive and lead us away from this perfect fulfillment, which alone can finally satisfy us.

6. The Compelling Power of the More Harmonious Pattern

Human nature is so complex, motives of action so subtle and intricately compounded, that the most painstaking attempt at clarification generally results in oversimplification. In inquiries of this sort we at best approach the truth asymptotically. Although it is evident that we choose the course in contemplation of which we experience the greatest satisfaction, it would be wrong to infer from this that we are able accurately to assess all the positive and negative elements in such a course, and strike the balance between them with mathematical precision. One reason for this failure is the fact that certain modes of experience are intrinsically more representable than others, so that we can anticipate them more vividly and recall them more adequately.

Moreover, our capacity to represent one aspect of experience may vary independently of our ability to imagine another. Thus, as we grow in intellectual power, we experience an increase in our capacity for thinking or imagining relations, but little or no corresponding increase in the intensity of sensations or emotions. As we cultivate our minds, we find it easier to represent to ourselves, let us say, the relation between diligence and success; but we do not, I believe, anticipate or remember a feast more vividly than when we were children. On the contrary, as the range and depth of thought increase, our representation of sensual delights appears to lose sharpness. In addition to this slow but permanent change in our ability to represent past or future experiences, this capacity fluctuates more rapidly from day to day and even from hour to hour. In our joyous moods, it is easy to anticipate happiness but more difficult to imagine ourselves sad; when downcast or discouraged, we can forebode ills with a peculiar vividness, while joyous occasions are at best vaguely pictured. Our present mood inevitably tinges with its own color all our present thoughts.

Even a highly cultivated mind finds it difficult to imagine pains or pleasures never experienced, although it may adequately conceive relational situations known only by description or inference. In contemplating any course of action, the mind dwells longest on those aspects of the total situation which can be most fully and vividly imagined. Hence our estimate of the satisfaction to be derived from a given course of action varies not only with the intrinsic representability of its components but with our period of life and the circumstances and mood in which we consider it. But the state of mind in which we contemplate a situation and that in which we finally enter upon it may be wholly different, thereby deceiving all our expectations. With so many uncontrollable variables and sources of error, one wonders that moralists could ever have seriously entertained the notion of guiding human life by a "hedonistic calculus."

Our appraisal of a contemplated course of action will be strongly weighted by aspects which detain the mind, while those difficult to imagine will be slurred over and fail to receive the consideration they merit as sources of pleasure or pain. Where there is pleasant variety of detail, a multitude of harmonious relations, the cultivated intelligence will affectionately linger; but where there is high intensity with slight diversity, as in many bodily pains and pleasures, it will but briefly pause. The pursuit of one's hobby, animated conversation, a journey through picturesque country, an absorbing study, all sorts of intellectual, esthetic and social experiences—whether in prospect or retrospect, these possess sufficient wealth of detail pleasantly to engage our thought for long intervals. Extreme heat or cold, hunger, a wound, a painful illness, the stings of insects, a toothache—these things make us acutely miserable while we endure them, yet can hardly be represented in their full intensity when not actually present to us; and the healthy mind passes lightly over them because they contain few distinguishable features. Hunger or fatigue, for example, remain much the same from minute to minute despite slowly increasing intensity, difficult to imagine when not immediately experienced; but the details of a diversified landscape through which we walk are constantly changing, bringing ever fresh delight to counteract our hunger or weariness. The residual effect of our contemplation of a proposed course of action determines whether we accept or reject it. Where the mind dwells with delight, it will lead the body if it is able.

Thus, when a traveler recalls a journey, the exhilarating sights and exciting adventures will claim a far larger share

of memory than the discomforts, which are often dispro-
portionately diminished in recollection. Add to this the
happiness of pursuing a favorite study, the fascination of
the unknown, the satisfaction of advancing human knowledge, the fame which follows an important discovery, and
one can understand why the seasoned explorer again and
again sets eagerly forth on journeys which he knows from
past experience will be attended by more perils, suffering,
and hardships than the average could well endure. Similar
considerations make it clear why the satisfaction of viewing great masses of facts in ordered relations can induce
the scholar and the investigator to "scorn delights and
live laborious days;" how the vision of a new and more
equitable social order can spur the reformer to undertake
the most arduous labors, attended by scorn, penury, and
danger; and how an ideal of perfect harmony between
what is best and most enduring in oneself and the ineffable source of one's being, can lead the saint to carry out
vigils, sacrifices, and penances which would exhaust a person of weaker fiber.

Given the qualitative differences between the many
varieties of satisfying states of consciousness that we earlier
noticed, and which would complicate all attempts to assess
them on a purely quantitative basis, it seems inevitable that
the *time* any contemplated experience can induce the mind
to linger agreeably upon it must be a most important factor
in determining a choice. But the mind will dwell longer
upon an experience the more representable it is, and this
in turn will be a function of the number of distinguishable
details that it includes. Moreover, the greater the number
of details, the greater the number of relations between

them; and if these relations are harmonious, the mind will be strongly attracted to them. Since a large share of moral endeavor consists in establishing harmonious relations between distinct entities, this peculiarity of thought fortifies moral effort and encourages us to strive for the fulfillment of our ideals.

No doubt an excruciating pain may leave so deep an impression on a sensitive mind that no imaginable advantages can tempt the person to risk its repetition; and some pleasures are so intense that no resultant pains or penalties can deter a coarse, undisciplined nature from pursuing them. But leaving aside these extreme and somewhat exceptional cases, it seems to be a rule of the cultivated human mind that the experience which promises amplitude and variety tends to be preferred above that which is marked by simple intensity, in a manner which in no way reflects the algebraic sum of the pleasures and pains involved in it—admitting that such a summation can be at least roughly made. Of two complex patterns of conduct of equal breadth presented to our consideration, the one which is more coherent and harmonious will in general claim our allegiance; while if the patterns are of approximately equal coherence, the more ample will as a rule be preferred. The importance of this principle of choice can hardly be overestimated. To it we owe every important advance in morality, in politics, in science, and in art. In Chapter VII, I maintained that the solid kernel of truth in Intuitive Ethics is derived from this principle.

Our evaluation of a course of action is rarely final, but subject to constant revision as the action develops; and long after a decision has been made and carried out, we pass judgment on it in the light of its effects on our sub-sequent life. This, then, is the method we employ to check the wisdom of each separate choice; but how shall we assess the value of our life as a whole? By what process do we elect one course of life in preference to another? Since the same mind, which makes a choice in some small mat-ter does so in this, to us, most momentous of matters, it necessarily follows the same method, working now on a larger scale. As we appraise a single act by considering its effect on the course of a life, so we may examine the value of a life by viewing it in relation to some larger whole, some system in which an individual life is only a detail. Thus we might assess the worth of a life by scrutinizing it against the background of a family, a nation, a religion, or an ideal of conduct. Such an examination may profoundly modify the satisfaction which the contemplation of one's life affords. A critical survey of existence in all its impli-cations can hardly fail to affect the contentment of any rational being who, in addition to a developed conscience, has wide sympathies and a pinch of imagination. The very capacity to undertake a survey of one's life in its broad relations implies a moral sensitivity, which will be deeply stirred by the conclusions to which this survey leads. For such a person, happiness depends not only on the coher-ence of all the details of a private life, but likewise on its felicitous articulation with surrounding lives, its harmo-nious blending with an encompassing whole.

Beyond this satisfaction with one's whole life when so viewed, there is no court to which a person of inde-pendent thought can appeal for a judgment of its worth. It seems, then, that the happiness or satisfaction, which one feels when viewing one's life as a whole, in all its relations, ultimately determines whether one will persist in one's present course or choose some different way of life. Those who are insensitive to the wider relations of their manner of life will perforce judge it by its internal texture alone. They may be influenced by the comments and criticisms offered by others, or even by threats of punishment in the hereafter; but they will alter their way of living in response to these external influences only when such a change promises to make it on the whole more satisfying to them, by increasing their felicity or at least diminishing their discontent.

If we ask why we choose in this manner, why the more ample and the more harmonious patterns of relations almost invariably wins the allegiance of one who is capable of conceiving and appreciating them and is not turned away by ingrained prejudices, the answer is that this is in accord with the whole movement which made us what we are. We are formed by the aggregation of atoms into ever larger and more complex molecules, of molecules into cells, of an increasing number of cells into tissues, of tissues into organs, and of organs into an organism which with the passing generations, became not only larger and more complex but also more perfectly coordinated. Our mind develops by uniting simple excitations into meaningful patterns, by combining images to form concepts, and organizing these into those coherent patterns by which alone truth may be known. Each of us is a product of an aeonian process of pattern formation, of organization, of growth in body and mind; and this impulsion that permeates our being obliges us to prefer the wide to the narrow, the harmoniously coordinated to the loosely articulated and jarring pattern, and to choose this greater breadth and perfection in a manner which disdains mere sensual excitations. By building up a variety of comprehensive visions of the future and always choosing the widest and most coherent, we give a more harmonious future a voice in its own creation.

7. Congruence of the Psychological Fact and the Moral Obligation

The psychological fact that we cannot avoid choosing the alternative in the contemplation of which we experience greatest satisfaction or value is obviously distinct from the ethical doctrine that we ought always to choose the course which promises to yield us greatest satisfaction or happiness. Yet it is futile to command one to do what one's whole organization makes it impossible to do. The Law of Choice is a condition to which moral teaching must adapt itself on pain of becoming ineffectual. Even within this limitation, ethics can exert a powerful influence by calling attention to near and remote consequences of our acts which we might have overlooked, by purifying our motives and refining our values, so that in surveying a course of action we see it in a fresh light and are differently affected by the prospect it presents to us. We still inevitably choose the course in contemplation of which we experience greatest satisfaction, yet this satisfaction has itself been altered by our changed point of view; so that it is indubitable that moral considerations have influenced our conduct. Beyond this, moral training cannot go. Are we to regard this limitation as a fact to be reluctantly accepted, to which morality must somehow resign itself, or one which can be cheerfully admitted, with no feeling of restriction or loss?

The Law of Choice is compatible with the highest moral aspirations, when we understand it truly. Because I must always make the choice which most completely satisfies me, it does not follow that every choice that I make is the most satisfying that I could have made in view of the possible alternatives. That which satisfies me today may leave me dissatisfied tomorrow. To avoid such painful disillusion, I must learn to separate those internal grounds of choice which are variable from those which are constant; I must clearly distinguish the primary, central determinants of my being from the shifting secondary springs of action. I am assailed by appetites and passions which wane as swiftly as they waxed, and it is futile to try to win lasting satisfaction and happiness by subservience to that which is itself variable and transitory. But at the core of my being is a creative activity, my enharmonization, which is ever the same, remaining unchanged beneath shifting passions necessary for the survival of an animal in a mutable and often hostile environment. If I can satisfy this steadfast central energy, I shall achieve a peace so deep and lasting that I shall not readily be tempted to give preference to some appetite or whim which cannot be permanently satisfied, for the simple reason that it is itself evanescent.

But this central self is the presence within me of that very activity which has brought all harmony into the world and is the primary source of all moral effort. In satisfying this self, I am true to the fountainhead of all goodness and all morality. And this inmost determinant of my being can be satisfied only by that course which, of all recognized courses, brings the greatest amount of harmony into the world; for its whole effort is directed toward the increase of harmony. Only when I act in conformity with this primary source of life can I experience lasting contentment. We may pass, then, from the psychological law to the moral imperative, deducing from the fact that, when we act after due deliberation, we always choose the course which most completely satisfies us the moral rule that we *ought to* follow the course which most completely satisfies us. But we must be exceedingly careful that the self which we strive to satisfy is the permanent, constant self rather than some transitory modification. To mistake what is secondary and shifting in ourselves for what is primary and abiding, and to try to satisfy the former to the detriment of the latter, may be as disastrous to oneself as to others. Only by choosing the course which will bring enduring satisfaction to ourself can we reconcile the psychological necessity with the moral obligation. Then we may agree with Locke that "the highest perfection of intellectual nature lies in a careful and constant pursuit of true and solid happiness; so the care of ourselves, that we mistake not imaginary for real happiness, is the necessary foundation of our liberty."[4]

Far from weakening morality, this assimilation of moral obligation to psychological necessity, of the ethical "ought" to the "must" of natural law, lends it a strength and authority it has hitherto lacked. The certainty that all humans contain within themselves a moral force impelling them to prefer the kind of conduct that ethics recognizes as right, gives us fresh confidence; for we know that when certain conditions have been satisfied, the desired results must ensue. These conditions are, first, a correct understanding of our own nature; second, a vivid apprehension of the effects, immediate and remote, of any contemplated act; and third, the ability to control the disruptive passions that make people act against their better judgment. But just as in science or technology many results which, we are sure from the known laws of nature, will follow if certain conditions are fulfilled are exceedingly hard to achieve, because of the great practical difficulties in creating these conditions, or because of the scarcity or the refractoriness of the materials that must be employed; so, in the field of human conduct, effects which we are confident will follow if certain conditions are realized may be hard to accomplish, because of the difficulty of fulfilling these conditions. And since living organisms, and especially humans, are systems of far greater complexity than the chemist or the technologist ever deals with, the practical obstacles to be overcome may be tremendous. Nevertheless, to be certain that both righteousness and happiness will follow when certain definable conditions are fulfilled gives us a new hope and a fresh inspiration.

Chapter Ten
Moral Freedom

1. Meanings of "Freedom"

WE NOW APPROACH a difficult and warmly debated question, whose importance for ethics has, in my opinion, been greatly exaggerated. I believe that neither our conception of what constitutes the proper end of moral endeavor, nor our judgment of the means to be employed in reaching this end, will be affected by the answer we give to the problem of free will. At most, our estimate of the probability of attaining our goal might be somewhat altered by our view; but no morally mature person would relax an effort to reach the goal merely because of a conclusion that the probability of ultimately winning it was a little less than at first suspected.

As one aspect of the general problem of determinism and its effect on the whole course of cosmic history, the question of free will seems more pertinent to general philosophy than to ethics; and in this connection I have already treated it in *Life Ascending*.[1] If it has much significance for ethics, this is chiefly in connection with such matters as merit, praise and blame, reward and punishment, especially retributive punishment, if one insists on inflicting such penalties in disregard of all the most enlightened teaching since Plato's day. The relation of moral freedom to vindictive punishment requires further examination; for I believe that a better understanding of the implications of free will would cause a reversal of the common opinion as to how it should affect our procedure. The relevance of moral freedom to this rather restricted field of human opinion and activity, no less than the great importance that some writers have attached to it, make it advisable to consider a subject so controversial that I would gladly avoid it, and to try to clarify our thinking about it.

I can discover only two fundamentally distinct meanings of the word "freedom" when used in contexts pertinent to ethics: (1) freedom from prior determination, and (2) freedom to express one's own nature. (1) Freedom from prior determination appears to be synonymous with indeterminacy, so that in our present connection it means simply indeterminacy in the act of willing, which is what is commonly meant by "free will." (2) Freedom to express one's own nature may have two meanings, according to how we interpret the phrase "one's own nature." (2a) If we mean our total nature, ourselves just as we are with all our various and at times conflicting impulses and passions, then freedom will signify the absence of external obstacles to the satisfaction of that particular impulse or desire, however fugacious, which seems at any particular moment best to express this nature. Since a large share of the barriers which separate us from the fulfillment of our desires are erected by law and custom, freedom in this sense includes political freedom; but actually it is more than this, since nature also places many obstacles in our path. Thus complete freedom would mean lack of all restraint by law or nature—an unattainable condition. (2b) If we accept the view that animal, including human, nature is compound, consisting of a primary determinant or inmost self plus an array of passions and attitudes (conveniently referred to as one's "secondary nature") which it has gradually acquired in the long course of evolution, then freedom may mean the ability of this primary determinant or true self to express itself fully, without hindrance by contrary elements in our secondary nature. In this case, it is not the absence of external obstacles, such as those created by society or the natural world, but of those within our total selves, which is the essence of freedom. Perhaps we shall also have to overcome external resistance in order to make our freedom perfect, but this does not seem so urgent as the removal of the internal barriers that often make it impossible for the primary determinant to control even our volitions. It may be that we shall find that freedom in the first sense (1) is indispensable to freedom in the last sense (2b); but it may also turn out that these two sorts of freedom are antithetic. This is a question to which we must give serious attention.

"Freedom," as commonly used, is largely an honorific term, implying absence of ignoble bondage or degrading restraints. In sense (1) the bondage implied is that to the past in any form; in sense (2a), to things which impede the expression of one's total personality; in sense (2b), bondage to the baser elements of one's own nature. Thus, in addition to the scientific (or perhaps metaphysical) problem of deciding in what sense, or to what degree, we can be exempt from any of these forms of dependence, the moral philosopher is confronted with the problem of deciding which of these exemptions is nobler, more desirable, or morally preferable. And here, of course, we are dealing with a question of values rather than of facts.

Freedom in sense (1) can be had only as a gift of nature; or, on Kant's view, we owe it to something beyond nature, the transcendent realm of things-in-themselves. Freedom in sense (2) must be won by our exertions. In sense (2a), by struggling against all the obstacles which the state, society, and nature oppose to our will; in (2b), primarily by struggling against the baser elements of our own nature, only secondarily by overcoming external obstacles.

The differences between these several kinds of freedom will become clearer when we look at some of the historic views on the subject. The Stoics were strict determinists, hence for them freedom in sense (1) was an illusion; yet they distinguished between freedom and its absence. A human is a rational being, having within a portion of the same Reason (Logos) which, as Providence, governs the whole Universe. When human reason is clear and unobscured by passion, one recognizes this correspondence, or rather identity, between the primary determinant of one's own nature and the Providence that governs the Cosmos, and one gladly accepts what necessarily is, thereby becoming free. The foolish person, whose reason is clouded by passion, strives to resist the cosmic Reason, but in vain; is dragged along resistingly, like a little dog on a leash, and so is enthralled to necessity.

In Modern times Spinoza, who owed much to Stoicism, was likewise a strict determinist; and for him, too, freedom was to be won by gaining that deep understanding of humanity and nature which made one accept gladly everything that befell him, because he knew that it could not have been otherwise. In the very different system of Gottfried Leibniz, the monads had the maximum freedom to express their total nature; since they could not be affected by anything external to themselves, nothing could interfere with the self-development of each. On the other hand, the maintenance of the pre-established harmony demanded the absence of all indeterminate effects. The activity of each monad was strictly determined by its own past, and its own past alone, so that it was free in the wider meaning of sense (2).

Kant's doctrine of freedom is more complex and somewhat obscure, so that it is difficult to present in a few words. He distinguished between an empirical self, strictly subject to natural causation, and a noumenal or true self, which stood beyond or above nature but expressed itself through the empirical self. If the noumenal self had a perfectly definite character, so that it could make only moral choices in accordance with the Categorical Imperative, Kant's concept of freedom would conform to (2b) in our scheme. But apparently the noumenal self could will to manifest itself either as a righteous empirical self or as one capable of evil. Hence it was free from all prior determination, so that Kant defended freedom of the first sort (1).

Bergson thought it important to assert life's freedom from prior determination; but I suspect that the maximum degree of indeterminacy toward which his *elan vital* moved would, if realized, involve the world in hopeless confusion. Of more recent ethical philosophers, none has so stoutly maintained the reality of free will, and its fundamental importance for all moral endeavors as Nicolai Hartmann; but he seems to be uncertain how frequently a free volition occurs, and how we can recognize it when it does happen.

2. Confusions Which Support the Notion that Volitions are Indeterminate

Everyone who has made a difficult choice is familiar with the mental processes, which support the notion that the will is not subject to causality. The mind oscillates between two or more alternatives which are almost equally attractive, or between a course of action which it views with delight and a distasteful duty that competes with this. Turning our attention repeatedly from one to the other, we view all the advantages which each course offers and weigh them against the deprivations or penalties which it entails. Again and again, we are on the point of electing one of the alternatives, when the thought of certain disagreeable consequences, or a surging vivid apprehension of what we shall lose by not choosing the competing attraction, further delays our decision. Finally, we settle on one of the alternatives, and say that we have made up our mind; but probably we shall not feel that our decision is final until we have taken some overt step, such as declaring our intention to another, which seems to set the seal upon it.

At the moment when we make the decision, both of the competing courses seem so equally available to us, that we believe it in our power to have chosen the other, even if every event in the past history of the Universe which somehow affected us had been exactly the same as it was. We choose A, saying that we could have chosen B. Where the choice involves moral guilt or merit, this "could" assume great importance. If it was impossible for us to avoid the volition which flung us into crime, our guilt seems to vanish, or at least to be greatly diminished, because then we can look upon ourselves as the innocent victim of an inexorable causal nexus, and ask others to view us in the same way.

But I believe that the notion that we could have followed the rejected course arises from the confusion of two distinct possibilities. The first is the physical possibility of performing either A or B if we should choose it. Obviously, we detect no insuperable impediment to pursuing either of these two courses; if we did, we would not have given them serious consideration as alternatives. Quite distinct from this is the possibility of willing to pursue either A or B, in the face of competition by the other. Since what engages our attention while we deliberate is the consequences of the two alternatives rather than the psychic processes involved in our choice, we confuse the objective possibility of carrying them out with the subjective possibility of willing to follow them. And this confusion has given rise to the illusion that we could, in the conditions actually prevailing, have chosen the alternative that we rejected.

To contend that we could have chosen otherwise than we did seems to make deliberation, to which we devote so much time and mental energy, an unprofitable procedure. We are faced with two or more alternative courses of action, and our task is to discover which will best meet our needs or accord with our nature. We test these contemplated courses in relation to some fairly constant factors in ourselves; and our method is to carry out a mental experiment, imagining that we actually perform the action in question and noting our response to its several phases as well as its more remote effects, as far as they can be foreseen. If our nature is so plastic that we can adapt ourselves equally well to either course and be equally satisfied with all its foreseeable consequences, we are wasting our time in pondering them so carefully. We might as well decide by tossing a coin or throwing dice, as people sometimes do when they cannot otherwise extract themselves from a difficult dilemma. If volitions are not always, or at least usually, strictly determinate, it would seem to make little difference whether we reach our decisions by calling "heads" or "tails" or by careful excogitation. The impossibility of electing the alternative which least conforms to our nature is the best safeguard of our freedom. It is aside from the point to say that, if either *A* or *B* had been presented to us alone, we would certainly have accepted it; for the problem we face is to will *A* or *B* when both confront us; and this greatly alters the situation.

While we choose between alternative courses, we seem to be in a room with several open doorways, each giving access to a path or hallway that reveals no insuperable obstacle to our progress. But if we tried to pass through some of these doorways, we would find that they are closed by transparent glass that effectively blocks our exit. Only one is open to us. The invisibility of the barriers that block our advance in certain directions gives rise to the illusion that we might have passed through them. An intimate friend can sometimes predict what a person will do in given circumstances better than himself or herself. He does not see the delusive openings that beckon the other in diverse directions, but forms a prediction by considering the known constants of the person's character.

The belief that our volitions always or sometimes escape causal determination seems to be strengthened by the common view that the will is a particular part or faculty of the mind, occupying a privileged position and exercising command over all those activities of the sort that we describe as voluntary. We tend to think of it as someone seated in a chariot holding the reins which control the horses, to use Plato's simile, or in modern terms, as the driver of an automobile with his hands on the steering wheel. But we shall have a much clearer understanding of the situation if we recall Hobbe's statement that the will is merely "the last appetite in deliberating"—that impulse or desire which finally gathers enough strength to produce action.[2] A person's will, then, is each of his dominant impulses by turns or perhaps it would be more correct to say, in the manner of John Dewey, that there is no will, but only willing.

But before any motive can make us act or commit ourselves in any way, it must overcome a resistance. On one side we have the motive inciting us to action of some sort, on the other the whole mass of innate and acquired dispositions—of habits, inclinations, memories, ideals, desires, and aversions—which constitute our personality. The motive usually emerges from this psychic mass, but in clamoring for action it distinguishes itself from the whole and must overcome its inertia; for without the cooperation of the whole the motive cannot accomplish its aim. If it is some habitual activity that the impulse seeks, the mind is easily moved to it. But if the demand is unusual, the whole psychic mass is aroused and tests the strength of the claim made upon it. Perhaps there will be memories of pains or losses incurred in some similar adventure in the past, and these will oppose a strong resistance to the present impulse. The immediately active motive must possess a certain congruity or solidarity with the whole mind in order to win its assent to the indicated course. Whether this motive is some bodily appetite, some moral claim, or some personal aspiration, the same process ensues. A categorical imperative or a value stands in just the same relation to the whole psychic mass as the basest temptation.

This structure of the mind, which makes it necessary for the whole mass to be stirred and its inertia overcome before it can assent to any course of action, is the guardian of our freedom (in sense 2a of 2b). At least, this safeguard is effective whenever willing is preceded by careful deliberation; although when we act impulsively our motive seems to escape its control. Thus a reflex act cannot be called free, for the determining factors are physiological rather than psychic; it escapes the influence of that central psychic mass which we call ourself and is not subjected to its selective action. But a deed which we perform after careful reflection is free because it carries the whole self along with it. The more we cultivate the habit of resisting sudden whims until every aspect of our personality can, by deliberation, be aroused to assert its just claims, the freer we become. But if indeterminate effects in the mind should short circuit or annul this procedure, the volition would seem to be no longer our own, and we would be the victim of accident rather than a free agent. Freedom in the sense of expressing our personality in our actions would be curtailed or destroyed if each volition were not the necessary result of antecedent conditions.

3. Freedom as the Perfect Expression of Our Original Nature

Our total personality contains many attitudes and modes of behavior forced upon our stock in the course of a long evolution, some of them antithetic to the primary determinant of our being. If current views on the method of evolution are correct, these discordant elements owe their origin to those uncontrolled genetic changes known as mutations, and they persisted because they promoted survival in the fierce competition of an overcrowded world. Although a volition determined by the relative intensities of all the actual components of our complex nature is certainly freer than one into which indeterminacy enters, it does not seem to conform to our conception of the highest freedom; for the mind that wills has had many things impressed upon it by natural necessity, early associations, and perhaps also a defective education.

Perfect freedom is to be found only in action which conforms to the process which made us what we are; for we are then no longer held in thrall to modifications forced upon us in the course of evolution but act in obedience to our primary determinant alone. But this determinant, our enharmonization, is a segment of the harmonization which pervades the Universe and has produced all its order and beauty. It is the source of all moral endeavor, and no volition which conforms to it can obey a base or wicked motive. Freedom in this highest sense cannot be the capacity to will either to assist or oppose harmonization, to choose either good or evil. Our enharmonization cannot impel us toward discord, for this would contradict its own essence; whence it is evident that when we choose something else in preference to harmony we reveal our dependence on some secondary mode of determination.

For us, perfect freedom can consist only in participation in that single act of freedom which appears to be possible in a Universe, the act which determined in grand outlines, although not in all details, the whole course of its history. Only when we elect that course which of all the courses apparent to us, promises most to advance harmonization are we free. Every other choice reveals either ignorance of the good, or bondage to attitudes forced upon our stock in the course of evolution, or else to irrational chance. From this it follows that only insofar as our nature is fundamentally and originally moral can we be both moral and free. Were we otherwise constituted, to be moral would imply subjection to external factors and a form of bondage.

This view differs from that of some of the advocates of moral freedom. Kant taught that the true or noumenal self may choose to manifest itself in the phenomenal world of space and time in some evil or imperfect form, although it always has the power to obey the moral law. It seems to follow from this that the noumenal self is not wholly good but has a mixed or indeterminate nature, and sometimes evil traits predominate in it; or if wholly good, it elects evil because it is infected by indeterminacy and its volitions are not its own. Thus the case for moral freedom is upheld by asserting either that no part of ourselves is intrinsically good or that our inmost self lacks the power to control its decisions. Similarly, Nicolai Hartmann made the self independent of the moral law, assigning to it freedom to choose value or disvalue; and thereby he also left our inmost nature vague and indeterminate. All these attempts to assert our freedom, even in the face of moral imperatives, do so at the price of denying that we have within us anything which is wholly good or even quite definite in character. For it is absurd to suppose that any being can demonstrate its freedom by repudiating its own nature, when the highest conception of freedom is perfect conformity with the primary determinant of one's being.

If we accept the view that freedom is not the absence of causation, but action that conforms to the process that made us rather than to secondary modifications of our nature, we shall no longer be troubled by the difficulty which distressed Boethius, how our free will could be reconciled with God's foreknowledge of everything that would happen in the world. If freedom means indeterminacy in willing, then the skillful argument which in the fifth book of *The Consolation of Philosophy* is placed in the mouth of Philosophy seems inconclusive; for if indeterminate events could be foreseen, even by an omniscient intelligence which views the whole pageant of temporal events as one eternal and changeless present, they would seem to be in some sense already determined and no longer what they profess to be.[3] But if we understand by freedom the perfect expression of one's nature, then the antithesis between freedom and the reign of law vanishes, and an individual's actions can be free yet fully predictable by an omniscient intelligence. Even if our primary nature must contend for supremacy with our secondary nature, each of these contrary components of our total personality has at a given moment a definite intensity, and the stronger will prevail; and this could be foreseen by an Intelligence such as Boethius postulated. And this omniscient being might also foretell when, by the exercise of appropriate disciplines, individuals would have so subdued their passions that their primary nature rules supreme, and what course the free person would then pursue in a given situation.

The notion that freedom and necessity are antithetic seems to have arisen from the hypostatization of Necessity, making of it an external force or a goddess, who rules over all the acts of humans and even of gods. Such a personified Necessity was widely worshipped in Hellenistic and later Roman times as Fate, who, significantly enough, was often confused with Fortune or Chance, an implicit admission that an iron external law and the absence of all law are equally inimical to human autonomy. Nobody who obeyed some external Necessity could deem himself or herself free. But there is no evidence that a Fate of this sort exists. Even physical objects whose movements conform minutely to natural law do not obey external necessity so much as the necessity of their own nature. In a gravitational field of a certain strength, a pendulum swings with a definite period, because that is just the period to which its nature is attuned. If some external force interferes, it will change this rhythm; but the pendulum will return to it as soon as it is at liberty to do so. The orbit which the Earth follows in its annual revolution about the Sun is an expression of its own nature, and its unopposed yet orderly progress is the very symbol of freedom, yet minutely predictable by the astronomer. Although causal sequences follow very different routes in a human mind and in lifeless systems, it is not intrinsically impossible that our volitions should be predictable, with no impairment of their freedom.

4. Discussion of Certain Misunderstandings

Although the question of indeterminacy is of the greatest importance for the interpretation of cosmic evolution, indeterminate effects, if they do in fact occur, need not enter into the act of willing more than into events of other kinds, in living or even lifeless systems. Indeed, of all the points where it might occur, indeterminacy in our volitions would seem to be the most dangerous sort; for if it arose here our deeds might cease to be the faithful expression of our constant purposes, and nothing could be more disastrous to us. If the processes which lead to our choices and volitions are not subject to strict causality, our freedom is jeopardized, for we become the victims of irrational chance. Yet, as was demonstrated in the preceding chapter, the causal sequences which reign in the mind, especially in serious deliberation, follow courses which seem to be without parallel in physical systems, so that mental causality differs greatly from mechanical causality.

In view of the great perils which would constantly menace us if our volitions were not subject to some sort of causation, to believe that our volitions are "uncaused causes" we should require evidence stronger than has ever been brought to the support of this hypothesis. But to accept an unpalatable view merely because there is strong evidence in its favor, or to reject a cherished opinion merely because it rests on inadequate proofs, requires a devotion to truth and a mental discipline which most people lack. It is not because the doctrine of free will can present irrefutable evidence, but because it flatters human vanity and seems to hold out to us a certain hope, which the opposing view fails to give, that it has been so fiercely defended. Perhaps no attack on this cherished dogma will be successful if it does not, in addition to questioning the evidence on which it rests, correct misunderstandings which make it attractive. Would we hold a higher opinion of ourselves if our volitions are indeterminate than if they are determinate? Would our moral endeavor be futile in a world ruled throughout by strict causality? Would the moral worth of a generous deed be diminished or destroyed if it could be demonstrated that the doer could not have done otherwise than he or she did? Our answers to these questions will not, of course, settle one way or the other the problem of moral freedom. But if by examining them we can remove certain prejudices, so that it will be possible to approach the matter with a more open mind, we shall have paved the way for more profitable discussions in the future.

In the first place, the doctrine of free will has been attractive because it seems to assert human superiority over nature, and especially over the other animals. Although popular zoology has long been the handmaiden of popular ethics, the source of countless edifying examples which the humbler creatures furnish to erring, headstrong humanity, this appeal to the animal kingdom for moral guidance has, on the whole, been as disturbing to moral philosophers as to scientific zoologists. The philosophic moralists have, on the contrary, been at pains to assert the distinctness of human morality from anything to be observed in nonhuman creatures. To believe that our volitions are, at least occasionally, exempt from causality, whereas their actions are always strictly subject to it, seems to separate us from them by a vast gulf, making us beings of a distinct and higher order. Hence this doctrine supports the contention that it is right for humanity to exploit other forms of life in whatever way redounds to our supposedly greatest advantage.

But this is an ungenerous attitude, for which we pay in subtle ways. Far from being reluctant to see moral worth in the acts of animals, we should look diligently for it, and welcome gladly whatever indications of it we can find. We hear much today about humanity's loneliness in a hostile universe, a view which seems to cast a blight upon our most cherished aspirations. But if we are to feel less alone, it must be by discovering in the nonhuman world that which is similar to ourselves, and especially to that aspect of ourselves which we take to be highest and most unique, our moral nature. And where could we search for this with greater prospect of success than in creatures which science asserts to have sprung from the same stem as ourselves? Every indication of their affinity to us, not merely in anatomical structure and physiological processes but in spiritual and moral qualities, should be acclaimed as a bond that links us to a larger whole, and makes us feel less alone in a world of which space and matter are the most obvious components.

It seems inconsistent to see moral worth in a human parent's sacrifices for his or her children but not in a bird's, a quadruped's, or even an insect's devoted services to off-spring. But however we might view this matter, it is evident that our moral superiority to other animals does not depend on how our volitions are determined but upon the breadth of our sympathies and the quality of our foresight. We are morally superior to some other being exactly in the measure that we can conceive an ampler society, embracing a wider range of creatures in a more harmonious synthesis, and work devotedly to make this vision real. And just as in any other enterprise, we are more likely to be successful in this supreme endeavor if the materials with which we work, including ourselves, conform strictly to certain causal laws that can be understood by us, than if they exhibit indeterminate, hence unpredictable, behavior.

In the second place, it has appeared to some that without free will true creation would be impossible and our moral conflicts, with all the suffering they at times bring to us, without significance. This view certainly does greater credit to our nature than the one we have just considered, but it is founded on a misunderstanding. Let us for a moment admit that we are mere machines, subject in every thought and feeling to strict causality and even (which I believe to be false) to just the same kind of causal sequences that prevail in some machine that we construct of rods and wheels. But everyone recognizes that certain machines, such as airplanes and calculating machines, produce results which could not otherwise be achieved. And it might be that the world's advance toward an ampler harmony depends on the presence of machines as complicated as ourselves, with our sensitive conscience, our ability to compare, to reason and foresee, to hope and doubt, to love and hate, to enjoy and suffer. Such a machine, it appears, can accomplish things beyond the range of any simpler machine; just as an electronic computer can give answers which cannot be found with an abacus. We cannot pass from the premise that our moral struggles are subject to strict mechanical causality to the conclusion that they are futile or without significance. Harmonization required just such machines to raise creation to higher levels.

If one continues to believe that the unique contributions which our moral efforts make to the progress of harmonization would lose their value if it could be proved that they are the necessary results of antecedent conditions, one need only compare morality with mathematics. With certain exceptions, each mathematical problem has a single answer, so that when its terms are given, its solution is already predetermined, and would be foreseen immediately by a supreme intelligence. Is it, then, quite futile for a person to spend years learning mathematics, then to devote many days of strenuous concentration to a problem, only to obtain a result which could not have been different? Everyone will reply that, although the answer was predetermined, the mathematician's labors were necessary to make it known, and without them it could never have entered the minds of human beings and been of use to them. Similarly, even in a world governed throughout by strict causality, our moral endeavors would accomplish results which could have been achieved only by first creating beings capable of benevolence, foresight, and choice; for such beings can settle conflicts, reconcile opposing aims, and expand harmony in a manner which would be otherwise impossible.

Thirdly, there are the questions of moral worth, merit and demerit, responsibility and guilt, rewards and punishments, whether by humans or God. It is because of its supposed relevance to these matters that the problem of free will has been so persistently and warmly debated; and the proof of this is that, just in the degree that people have looked for external rewards and punishments, they have been concerned with this perplexing dilemma. The Stoics, who had a concept of virtue and duty which has rarely been surpassed, were not troubled by the question of free will, because they did not look for any external reward for virtuous conduct. When right conduct is itself the foundation of happiness and vice itself misery, it becomes superfluous to examine the causes and the quality of a person's deeds with a view to assigning appropriate reward or punishment. Plato was not much concerned with free will, because he advocated cathartic but never vindictive punishment; and remedial punishment justifies itself by the end toward which it is directed, without becoming involved in problems of radical responsibility. It was not until Christianity made the ancient world familiar with the concept of a jealous and vengeful God, who inflicted punishments which could not possibly be purgative because they were eternal, that the problem of free will became acute; and it is highly significant that perhaps the most earnest discussion of the question to be found in the extant writings of the Classical philosophers is from the pen of the last of them, Boethius, who served a Christian emperor, and possibly had embraced the faith himself.

The difficulties and confusions which surround this problem will become evident when we consider how the knowledge that the will is free or not free should affect God and humans in assigning retributive punishment to erring mortals. An omnipotent God who had created humanity as a system governed by strict causality in a wholly determinate world could not, without offending our human notions of justice, punish us vindictively when we sin; for the creator of a system ruled by inexorable necessity is personally responsible for everything that occurs in it, hence God would be the cause of our transgressions. But if our will is not subject to causality, then our volitions are the expression of some element in the world for which this God is not ultimately responsible; and God might without inconsistency pour out wrath upon the unfortunate possessor of this will. God would then be repressing or stamping out a component of the world alien to self, and it would seem that this could be done without considering whether the offender could have behaved differently. God might say to the victim of his anger: "It is not because *you* are or are not responsible for what you did that you must suffer, but because *I* am not responsible for it." A theology which maintains that a just God punishes vindictively must, to uphold the credit of this God, defend the doctrine of free will.

But when a society punishes its erring members, it is at liberty to approach the matter from another side; for, although it is in large measure responsible for the character of the people who compose it, it does not claim to have created them or to control them in every respect. If felons' misdeeds are the necessary and inevitable consequence of their nature, it reveals some radical flaw in it; hence it would not be irrational to destroy such a person as intrinsically bad. But if their will is free and their volitions are not determined by fairly constant factors within them, it would be unjust to punish them except as a remedial measure or for the protection of the community. A person might not have been able to control this internal hazard which drove him or her into acts that had no foundation in character. If placed a second time in exactly similar circumstances, he or she might behave quite differently; just as when we toss the same coin it sometimes falls with one side up and sometimes the other. Even more, if one's acts do not spring necessarily from one's constitution, it would be foolish to incarcerate anyone for the protection of society; for the person who has hitherto behaved in the most exemplary manner might tomorrow commit some hideous crime, while the convicted criminal might perform some notable civic service.

For a society which bases its right to punish upon the doctrine of free will, it is most inconsistent to exempt criminals from punishment when they can prove that they are insane, yet to punish for the same crime individuals called sane. Insanity in all its forms is a conspicuous failure of mental integration, a loss of coherence in personality and character. The reason for pardoning the insane is that their acts are not controlled by their total personality, as seems usually to be true of normal people. But if it happens that volitions are not always causally determined, then it might be that somebody's misdeed was done because his or her willing had escaped control by character; and every criminal would appear to be in much the same plight as the insane offender. When we become aware of the perils in which "free will" would involve us, far from hailing it as a divine gift we shall fear it like a deadly poison.

But if we take the view that volitions are subject to certain rules of causation which are not yet sufficiently understood, then we must recognize that a society cannot disclaim responsibility for at least a large share of the misdeeds of its members. For if its older members had set a better example and provided more adequate training for the children, they would be less likely to go astray. In any case, if the perplexities surrounding the problem of free will make us more cautious in assigning guilt, this is a great gain. To attribute freedom in a radical sense to a depraved criminal in order that we may apply punishment, is to ascribe godlike originality to a creature that is something less than human.

5. Free Will and Moral Worth

There is a rather widespread view that the moral worth of one's deed depends on the possibility of having done otherwise; whence it follows that the perfected or holy will, which cannot choose evil, pertains to a being that is no longer moral. Among philosophers, this view was held by Kant and Hartmann; and mystics likewise have believed that the liberated spirit rises above morality. Let us concede that the peculiar features of human morality reveal it to be the endeavor of beings who are striving toward, but have not yet achieved, perfect goodness. But can we seriously contend that some deed of outstanding nobility, which has served as an inspiring example to generations of people, would lose all moral worth if it could be proved that the actor could not have done otherwise in the given circumstances?

The return of Regulus to Carthage, in obedience to his plighted word that he would come back to die if he could not persuade the Roman Senate to make peace, is the classic example of patriotic devotion combined with faithfulness to a promise. Would our admiration for Regulus be destroyed if it could be demonstrated that a person of such a character, placed in such circumstances, could not have chosen otherwise? But if his decision was not strictly determined by antecedent conditions, then it would appear to follow that it was a matter of chance; so that, if he faced exactly the same alternatives a second time, he might have done differently. Far from increasing our respect for Regulus, the suspicion that his historic decision owed more to the hour and the day when it was made than to permanent traits of character, would destroy it.

What would appear to remove a decision from the category of moral choices would be, not the certainty that it was determinate, but the knowledge that in making it the person had not to contend against contrary inclinations, to overcome fears and opposing desires—so that no real choice was involved in it. If Regulus had been so constituted that the prospect of leaving forever his city and friends caused no pang of regret, if no quiver ran through his flesh as he contemplated the cruel tortures the Carthaginians were wont to inflict on their captive enemies, then we would be constrained to conclude that he was either a god or an automaton, and his decision involved none of the elements which enter into our moral choices. It is not the fact that a choice was the necessary outcome of prior conditions, but that it was made without the necessity to contend against opposing inclinations, which would appear to divest it of moral qualities; for it would then lack the distinctive features which give their peculiar flavor to our own moral determinations. In this case, the deed might be formally correct without furnishing a moral example for us; for we would realize that it was reached by a route that we could not follow. But if by long and strenuous self-discipline a person should train himself or herself to choose always the right course with scarcely any inclination to follow contrary courses, no matter how much pain or sorrow they might bring, he or she would seem not to lose but to gain in moral stature. If the moral struggle has ceased, it is only because he or she has won a moral victory.

One who chooses the right way with scarcely any effort or struggle has, of course, less "merit" than another who reaches a similar decision only after a prolonged contest with baser inclinations. The first moves so steadily toward the good deed that his or her conduct seems governed by necessity; the will of the second, vacillating between good and evil, appears to be less subject to causality. Hence the opinion that merit depends on free will and would vanish if all volitions were determinate. But the whole concept of merit appears to me to have merely pedagogic importance. We laud the honorable deed of the child or even the stumbling adult in order to encourage such good determinations, and at times we permissibly exaggerate our praise to make it a more powerful stimulus.

The morally awakened person, who has discovered the source of righteousness within oneself and is faithful to it because to do otherwise is to repudiate one's higher self and render oneself vile in one's own sight, is no longer interested in praise or blame, reward or punishment, whether merit is ascribed or whether it is not. Although one may pay attention to praise and reproaches as indication of success in increasing the welfare of those whom one tries to benefit, one realizes that they neither increase nor diminish by a hair's breadth one's moral stature. One has passed the stage at which one's conduct is influenced by sweetmeats and whips. The concept of merit doubtless has a place in ethics because of its usefulness in moral exhortation, but its value in this connection is obviously independent of the decision we reach on the problem of moral freedom.

The attempt to make the worth of things contingent on factors which are highly uncertain is one of the most unfortunate trends in ethics. No sensible person doubts the value of a benevolent disposition, an honorable decision, or a generous deed. But whether, and to what degree, indeterminacy enters into our volitions is a problem involved in the greatest uncertainty; and the most ardent defenders of free will can tell us no infallible method of putting this question to proof. Hence to make moral worth contingent on free will is to throw into the greatest confusion a matter which without this gratuitous complication seems clear enough. This exaggerated insistence on a certain dubious aspect of the moral life appears to result from elevating the means above the end, a phenomenon all too common in other departments of human endeavor.

Morality grew out of our efforts to safeguard certain things, which are not strictly moral, such as life, happiness, the stability of the community, and all those treasures of the spirit which an orderly society is capable of generating. Naturally, we cherish for their own sakes the spiritual qualities revealed in the highest moral endeavor, such as unselfish love, sympathy, generosity, benevolence in its widest sense. Since these are not only beautiful in themselves but a source of continuing beneficence, we esteem them more than the concrete results of any single act to which they prompt us; just as we value a beautiful spring of limpid water more than any single draught we take from it. But when we hold all the other values which life can realize as negligible in comparison with the moral qualities, we lose sight of the end in our admiration for the means; as was done by the Stoics in their dogma that virtue is the only good, and by Kant when he declared that nothing but a good will is good without qualification. If all this were true, there would be nothing external to itself which such a will could blamelessly choose, and it would discover no means to demonstrate its goodness; it would be a sterile, useless will, entangled in its own perfection. Similarly, the exaltation of duty without due appraisal of the values it safeguards promotes self-martyrization and the hardening of life. To lavish praise upon the moral disposition without regard for the ends it serves is like hoarding money for its own sake and might be described as moral miserliness.

The belief that moral worth is dependent on certain recondite qualities and confined to a mystic brotherhood narrows and impoverishes the moral life. The fanaticism that places moral values immeasurably higher than all other values teaches that only moral agents which can generate these values are proper beneficiaries of moral endeavor; and, since animals do not give unmistakable evidence of those peculiar mental attributes which are the basis of human morality, they are not accounted worthy objects of moral effort. The correctives of these narrow views are, first, recognition that nonmoral values of a high order exist and may be realized by nonmoral beings; and, secondly, true appreciation of the place of human morality in the world process and an understanding of the ends it serves. Moral endeavor is one particular mode of harmonization, distinguished from other modes by the intelligence, foresight, and choice it brings to its task. Hence it is linked by the closest bonds to every other expression of harmonization, in the lifeless as in the living world. And just as the value of the moralness of the cosmos and the protomorality of animals is independent of our views on determinism, so the worth of human moral effort is not altered by our opinion about free will.

The measure of the value of any form of harmonization is the amplitude and perfection of the harmonies it produces; and if human morality is to be ranked above the protomorality of animals or the moralness of the nonliving world, it can be only because it yields wider harmonies. Thus, to curtail our moral endeavor in any direction on the ground that only moral beings are its fit objects, is to stunt our morality and limit its worth. As long as the world contains any discords, which humans might correct by the exercise of their peculiar endowments, no one, no matter how highly purified and holy, can soar above morality. The saint or mystic who, unable to choose evil, remits the effort to increase goodness in the world, has not risen to some higher sphere. He or she has retired ignominiously from the battle, and by disdaining to employ in a worthy effort his or her moral accomplishments, rendered them sterile and vain.

Moral acts are not only means, but marks or signs of a certain disposition and character. The highest moral conduct reveals deep understanding, a broad sympathy with the joys and sufferings of other creatures, appreciation of a wide range of values, and the will so to live that the maximum number of beings can perfect themselves. Such a disposition is of inestimable worth and indeed the most precious thing in humanity; for it springs from a richness and fullness of spirit which is valuable in and for itself. Moreover, it is the solid foundation of happiness, as of all the other modes of harmony which people cultivate, including friendship, truth, and beauty. Such a spirit would be precious even in a world so ordered that it found no occasion to labor strenuously for moral ends. Its toils and other acts of devotion are valuable not only for the results they achieve but likewise as indications that such a spirit exists. But it is because of the harmony that pervades it, not because of its works, that the virtuous mind is intrinsically precious.

The excessive emphasis that German moralists have placed upon the will tends to isolate morality from other aspects of the world process and weakens rather than strengthens moral effort. The human will is effective in increasing harmony only because other conditions, wholly independent of it, enable it to do so. Suppose, for example, that like certain other organisms, we could live only in the flesh of a highly organized animal, who died slowly and miserably while we battened on its tissues and fluids. Suppose, further, that one day we awoke to the evil of such a life. All our willing would not improve our situation, for, despite the claims of Jean-Baptiste Lamarck, by no effort of the will can we alter our hereditary structure and intimate physiological processes. Our only alternatives would be to continue our nasty life or to destroy ourselves. Let us, then, gratefully acknowledge that something older than the human will has prepared for us such a world, and given us such efficient, adaptable bodies, that our moral effort is availing, and recognize that, at its best, it is but a way of cooperating with cosmic trends.

6. Free Will and Self-improvement

To believe that our acts are the inevitable outcome of causal sequences reaching us from the immeasurably distant past sometimes brings a feeling of helplessness and oppression. We have gone astray and disgraced ourselves, and we could not have done otherwise because the whole course of cosmic events was leading to this result! To escape this sense of helpless subjection to a past over which we exercised no control, we sometimes clutch at the notion of free will. But does it ease our burden of shame and remorse to believe that we have done wrong when we could have done better? Does not this assumption, on the contrary, give us added reason to be disgusted with ourselves?

Remorse for past mistakes is worthless save as an incentive to strengthen our character so that we may avoid similar lapses in the future. One who sets about to improve oneself may legitimately ask whether one is more likely to succeed if mental processes follow determinate courses or if they are subject to the hazards of indeterminacy. Our very desire to lead a more righteous life is an actual determining factor, which we can probably trace to prior causes, such as the wholesome influences of childhood, reading, or the example of a noble character. Does the view that causality rules in the mind as in the external world weaken our faith that our effort will lead to a definite result?

Most human enterprises are begun on the assumption that when all the pertinent circumstances are the same, a given operation will always produce the same effect. The engineer designs a bridge in the belief that steel and concrete behave in a strictly determinate manner. If one doubted this, one could have no faith in one's calculations, and might hesitate to bear the responsibility for a construction whose collapse might cause the death of many people. The physician prescribes medicines in the belief that they will have predictable effects upon a determinate system; the least suspicion that they will act capriciously should make him or her desist from incurring the risk of killing the patient. Is it only in moral endeavors that the probability of success is diminished if the system with which we deal is subject to strict causality but increased if unpredictable results can be expected? The person who regrets imperfections or past blunders and resolves to improve himself or herself is not embarking upon an unprecedented undertaking, but sets forth on a path which many have trodden before, some of them leaving records which serve for guidance. If one believes in the causality of psychic events, it is reasonable to assume that the same methods which were successful with others will have the desired consequences; but if one believes that volitions or other mental events are subject to unpredictable hazards, one has no ground for making this assumption. Far from discouraging us when we undertake to correct the errors in our early education or to dominate rebellious passions, mental determinism should increase our confidence, whereas the doctrine of free will should make us doubtful of success.

So delicately balanced are our psychic forces that the belief that some achievement is within our power has great influence not only on our volitions but even on our physical performance. If one is confident about jumping across a chasm, one is more likely to succeed than if one fears falling short. In such a complex system, we can hardly predict how our mind will be affected in a novel situation until we actually find ourselves in this situation. Although, from analogy with the scientist's ability to forecast what will happen in certain relatively simple physical systems when all the pertinent facts are known, we contemplate the possibility that an infinitely capacious mind might foresee everything that will ever happen in the Universe, we lack the slightest evidence that such a mind exists in humanity or angel or God. A mind that so far surpassed our own puny intellect would seem to be not only quantitatively but qualitatively different, so that it should be called by another name. Thus, even in a wholly determinate world, there is true creative advance and the emergence of unforeseen splendor. Only the passage of time can reveal what time will bring forth. And in the external world as in the spiritual realm, creative advance consists in the ever more harmonious ordering of the practically infinite resources which the Universe already contains, rather than the influx of radical novelties which reveal themselves to us as indeterminate effects.

7. Free Will and Responsibility

Finally, we must attempt to define the attitude toward moral responsibility which the doctrine that volitions are determinate leads us to take. Society, for its own protection, and as the only foundation for a feasible procedure, imputes to each individual responsibility for his or her own acts. These acts admittedly have many determining causes in hereditary traits, in the influences of childhood, in the companions of youth, in the contemporary social atmosphere. When, as a result of unwholesome influences, a person commits a crime, it would be both logical and just to follow up each of these contributing factors and deal with it separately, wherever possible penalizing parents for their negligence, teachers for their inefficiency, elder brothers for the bad example they set, editors for publishing magazines which cast a glamour over crime, and the public at large for permitting so many noxious situations in its midst. But this would impose upon the court of law an impossible task; and while disentangling these causes contributory to the crime, it would discover that each could be traced to antecedents which diverged in all directions, until lost in a past inaccessible to censure and correction. The only practicable course is to deal with all the contributing factors where they are gathered at a single focus, in the criminal, and deal with that individual as though he or she were the primary source of all of them. This is only a legal fiction but without such a fiction the law would have no basis for procedure.

Not only in courts of law, but in our daily intercourse with those around us, we inevitably treat persons as though they were the primary source of all their deeds and fully responsible for them. Yet we know that we ourselves are not wholly as we wish to be, and we can, in many instances, point out definite causes for our failure to conform to our ideal, in heredity, schooling, or bondage to economic circumstances. Should we, then, indignantly reject the imputation that we are radically responsible for what we do, as contrary to fact and derogatory to our personal dignity? Or should we assent to it, and even insist upon it, as the indispensable condition of our personality? Let us examine the implications of these alternatives.

When we consider the origin of our bodies, it is evident that they are composed wholly of materials that flowed into them from external sources. Since there is nothing in my body for which I am originally responsible, I would not be acting capriciously or irrationally if I repudiated every atom of it, saying this is not myself, but something that properly belongs to my mother's milk, or the food that I ate, or the water that I drank. But by taking this course, I reduce my physical self to a nonentity. If every particle of my body is cast back upon some outside source, in an ideal sense it dissolves into nothing and cannot be said to exist. It is only by conveniently losing sight of the external origins of the particles that compose me that I can claim them as my own; and the justification of this claim is the fact that, whencesoever they came, they have been given a unique configuration by an organizing principle, which did not come to me with the nourishment I took but is the original constituent of my being.

When I examine my mind, I find myself in the same plight: aside from its organizing principle, which determines the form and coherence of everything that enters it, I can scarcely claim anything in it as peculiarly my own. My earliest notions of the external world came to me directly through the senses. Later, by hearing and reading and reflection, I acquired more complex ideas, chiefly by recombining the manifold data of sensation. My appetites and passions I can trace largely to my inherited organization, and the more unruly of them appear to have been foisted upon the human stock by the accidents of genic variation amid the stresses of life in a competitive world. My most cherished ideals were in large measure inherited from my predecessors; if I have elaborated or modified them better to conform to my own temperament, this was effected largely by the selection of materials already at my disposal. My volitions are the necessary result of factors already within me; and if I believed they were not, I would become greatly alarmed, because I could not undertake to control them. Thus, I can follow a considerable share of my thoughts and volitions back along causal sequences to sources beyond myself; and it seems probable that if I understood psychic processes well enough, I could follow all of them in this fashion.

Doubtless in the lives of most of us occasions arise when to take this course, and blame our failings or transgressions on factors external to ourselves and beyond our control, would save us much embarrassment and anguish of spirit. But thereby we would dissolve and repudiate our personality, reducing ourselves to spiritual nonentities; just as we ideally annihilate our bodies when we ascribe all the particles which compose them to the sources whence they came.

Thus, whether or not our volitions originate in us without prior causes, it is to our interest to claim them as wholly ours and make ourselves fully responsible for them; for only so can we constitute ourselves moral persons. When we will an act, the determining factors are ours because we make them ours, freely adopting them as our own and deliberately losing sight of their causal dependence on prior events external to ourselves. If we repudiate the motives of our acts, casting them back upon their causal antecedents, what in our body or mind could we claim as our own because it is more truly representative of ourselves? If our neighbors did not spontaneously ascribe responsibility to us, we should become indignant and insist that they do so, severing all relations with them if they persisted in dishonoring us in this fashion. The instinct of self-preservation should make us assert our sole responsibility for our deeds, for otherwise we are no more than eddies in the stream of events.

We can make good our claim to radical responsibility for our volitions because causality, which appears in general to prevail in mental no less than in physical systems, follows in the former a peculiar course. So far as we know, no physical system makes ideal exploratory excursions into the future before responding to solicitations actually present, as minds, or at least human minds, commonly do. To an observer thoroughly acquainted with physical systems alone, volitions would appear to be indeterminate because they could not be explained by the only understood mode of determination; yet to an intelligence with fuller insight into all the pertinent factors, they would doubtless be seen to obey their own mode of causality. The peculiar nature of causal sequences in the mind gives us a unique control over our destiny, such as no mechanical system enjoys. It enables us to subjugate the peripheral and variable factors in our complex nature to the central and constant factor, our enharmonization. In the measure that we make every thought and deed conform to that process to which we owe our being, we become free; and we cannot understand freedom otherwise than as the capacity to give perfect expression to the central determinant of our being.

Freedom does not consist in the absence of causality, which would make us the playthings of chance, but in obedience to our original or primary cause rather than to secondary causes. For us, freedom signifies glad cooperation with harmonization, for to this process we owe our being; and whenever we permit some disruptive passion to divert us from the cultivation of harmony, we reveal our ignoble bondage to factors external to our true selves.

Chapter Eleven

Right and Wrong

1. The Importance of Analyzing Moral Terms

WE NOW TURN our attention to the meaning of such moral terms as "right," "wrong," "good," "duty," "ought," and others of allied significance. Since these are words which we constantly use not only in philosophical ethics but whenever in daily life we talk about questions which have a moral aspect, a clear conception of their meaning should throw much light on the nature of moral endeavor, how it arose, toward what end it is directed, and its relation to other phases of the world process. Yet there is a widespread belief among moral philosophers that these terms, or some of them, stand for notions which defy analysis. "What definition," asked Sidgwick, "can we give to 'ought,' 'right,' and other terms expressing the same fundamental notion? To this I should answer that the notion which these terms have in common is too elementary to admit of any formal definition. . . . This fundamental notion must, I conceive, be taken as ultimate and unanalyzable."[1] Professor James Tufts, in a review of contemporary ethical thought, took much the same position. "Right, duty, good are not for ethics—to be resolved into something else which is not a moral term."[2] G. E. Moore believed that although "good" stands for an indefinable notion, the meaning of "right" is definable in terms of good.[3]

The teaching of these philosophers is, of course, contrary to that of an important section of ethical thought, which maintains that moral terms and notions can be analyzed into nonmoral characteristics, as when it is said that the good is the pleasant, or that a right action is one approved by the majority of humanity, or which conforms to law, or which promotes the survival of the species or the prosperity of a society, or which obeys the will of God. Ethical systems which hold that moral notions are analyzable without a remainder into nonmoral characteristics, such as pleasure or survival, have been termed "naturalistic," while the point of view exemplified by Sidgwick, Tufts, and Moore is "non-naturalistic." Although it is perhaps stretching the point to include theologically based ethics among the naturalistic systems, this terminology at least calls attention to a valid distinction and has the advantage of brevity.

It is a profitable procedure, when approaching the discussion of some difficult question, to ask why each of the contrary opinions has been so warmly upheld by its advocates. Often it is not the simple desire to discover truth, but some supposed advantage of the cherished opinion, which perhaps subconsciously prompts its adherents to support it. But frequently it turns out, on careful scrutiny, that this opinion is not so favorable to the desired end as it superficially appears to be; and it sometimes happens that the contrary opinion, when rightly interpreted, is actually more consonant with our aims. Thus, when we examined the relation of free will to moral worth and merit, we found that, although some philosophers have held that in the absence of free will moral worth disappears, actually free will, when correctly understood, seems to destroy moral worth; for an act that does not follow necessarily from constant traits of one's character can hardly be taken as an indication of the worth of this character. Similarly, when we examine the non-naturalistic view, that moral notions cannot be interpreted in nonmoral terms, it seems at first to fortify morality by raising it to a sublime height, far above all the other human concerns. If the very words which ethics uses are not even to be understood in terms of wider application, moral endeavor seems to stand apart from the common affairs of life, remote and unassailable, cloaked in inscrutable authority. It is then futile to ask why an action is right, why a duty is incumbent on us, or why something is good. Since these terms cannot be adequately analyzed into anything simpler, we are reduced to hopeless circularity, and can only solemnly reiterate that the deed is right because it is right, that we must perform the duty because it is our duty, that the result is good because it is good. By making the language of morality uninterpretable, or at least not adequately interpretable, we shield its commands from reason's prying gaze.

But we place morality on this lofty pedestal only at the price of divesting it of definite content and divorcing it from the concerns of daily life. No serious moral writer has ever done this; for every sensible person recognizes that morality is highly pertinent to practical affairs and the prosperity of individuals and communities. But it is only by admitting, or at least tacitly assuming, that ethical concepts are partly or largely understandable in terms of wider scope that we manage to relate our ethical discussions to everyday life. And the more completely we analyze our ethical terms, the more effective their application to life becomes. Far from strengthening moral endeavor by removing moral concepts to a remote heaven of their own, non-naturalistic ethics succeeds only in weakening it by separating it from its vital and cosmic foundations; and it achieves the absolute, unquestioned supremacy of right and duty at the price of emptying them of their content. If followed to its logical conclusion, this insistence upon the mystery of ethical terms can only lead to moral fanaticism, the rigorous observance of an absolute of duty whose ends have been forgotten.

From whatever side we view the matter, it is to our benefit to understand fully the meaning of moral expressions. Some philosophers contend that the purpose of ethics is to interpret moral phenomena, especially the meaning of moral concepts and for them to leave these finally unanalyzed seems a sorry conclusion of arduous studies. Others hold that ethics loses most of its interest and importance if it does not improve our conduct. As long as its basic concepts are not interpreted in terms of wider scope, ethics is separated by an unbridged chasm from other aspects of the world, a situation at once philosophically unsatisfactory and practically disastrous. If in each of us the feeling of rightness is primary, derived neither from our condition as an animal of a particular kind nor our conception of the significance and destiny of the Universe, it would appear that there can be no common ground for resolving differences of opinion on moral questions and uniting humanity into one moral community, with a single comprehensive purpose. The conclusion that the notion expressed by the words "right" and "ought" are not analyzable into other terms—or, what amounts to the same thing, that it is beyond the province of that branch of philosophy most concerned with them to analyze them—leaves the field in undisputed possession of the unresolved moral relativism which is one of the debilitating maladies of our day. Like all isolationism, this separation of ethics from its cosmic, vital, and philosophic foundations has lamentable consequences, and we have every incentive to bring it into closer union with them.

2. The Intrinsic Probability That Moral Notions Are Definable

The foregoing observations do not prove the case for or against the naturalistic interpretation of ethical terms; for the analysis of concepts is a matter of logic, which should not be influenced by our moral aspirations, save that to find truth. They are intended merely to remove misunderstandings and prepare us to approach the problem without fearing that we shall injure the cause of morality by removing the veil of mystery from the words it uses and permitting them to stand naked before us. From the purely logical standpoint, it is highly probable that the basic concepts of ethics are analyzable into simpler notions. Ethics is the study of moral phenomena; and the object of moral endeavor is to arrange living things and their activities into coherent, harmonious patterns. A pattern is made up of entities joined by definite relations. Since morality is concerned with the relations between the beings it strives to harmonize, it seems likely that its basic notions are of the relational sort.

As Locke pointed out, relational terms are often clearer and easier to analyze than those which refer to the entities they relate.[4] In every relation there are at least two relata which may be distinguished, and a certain kind of connection between them which can be specified. In the case of ethics, the relata are not themselves moral characteristics; for it is generally admitted that humans and other living things, and every act they are capable of performing, can be described without introducing moral concepts. Thus, the mere fact that ethics deals with relations between entities definable in nonmoral terms leads us to expect that its basic concepts can be analyzed without a remainder into nonmoral characteristics. Moreover, since human morality is a late development in cosmic evolution, we should expect that its rather complex manifestations would be understandable in terms applicable to the earlier stages of this evolution.

Before proceeding with our inquiry, it is necessary to distinguish sharply between moral concepts and moral sentiments. Moral questions enter so largely into our daily lives, and their decision is so often urgent, that our thinking about them is necessarily rapid and our judgments are often promptly reached. Moreover, since they are so intimately connected with our welfare, both by the direct consequences of actions and indirectly by the praise or blame, reward or punishment which society metes out to us, we feel strongly about them. Because the thought is often swift and the feeling intense, we are likely to be more acutely aware of the latter than the former; and when we declare that a certain action is "right" or a "duty," or that something is "good," we are above all conscious of a certain sentiment. This feeling, in all its grades and intensities, is indescribable; and we could no more convey an intimation of it to an intelligent being who lacked the moral sentiments than we could give a congenitally sightless person a clear notion of what we mean by "green" or "blue." By concentrating their attention on the affective tones which almost always accompany the use of moral terms, and overlooking whatever conceptual content they might have, the moral skeptics are able to declare that they are merely expressions of emotion or desire, lacking intelligible meaning, thereby not only heaping ridicule on the devoted labors of ethical philosophers but dishonoring the cherished moral aspirations of humanity.

The feelings that hover about these moral concepts, insofar as they have true ethical relevance, seem to be all of the sort that we ascribe to conscience, and as such were considered in Chapter VII, where it was pointed out that conscience is our sensitivity to harmony and discord, which makes us uncomfortable when we perceive any disharmony, especially one for which we hold ourselves responsible, and contrariwise gives us a feeling of satisfaction and repose when we achieve harmony. We have now to consider whether, apart from feeling, we can discover any conceptually clear meaning attached to such moral terms as "right" and "good."

We must, first of all, weigh carefully which of these terms we should take first. Whichever of these two fundamental ethical terms is more elementary, or lies closer to the roots of our moral experience, should have precedence in our treatment. G. E. Moore held that "good," which in his view is an indefinable notion, is the key word of ethics, and that "right" may be understood in terms of it. That course of action is right, he maintained, which of all possible courses most conduces to the realization of the good. A truly philosophic ethic should begin with an examination of the proper end of life, which is often designated as the highest good, thence proceed to consider the best means of attaining this end; and these means constitute right conduct. But morality is older than philosophy; and in the moral experience of humanity as a whole, as of each of us individually; the notion of right precedes that of good. Long before they are prepared to undertake a philosophical investigation of that difficult problem, what constitutes the good, children are reminded a hundred times over that certain acts are right and certain others wrong.

Likewise in primitive societies, the ends of life were taken for granted, without examination, and only the means of attaining them were subject to scrutiny. These ends were the instinctive satisfactions, life itself and all that supported, perpetuated, and made it enjoyable. For an animal so dependent on its fellows as humans at an early stage came to be, the individual could prosper and propagate its kind only in a society; hence the means to be fostered were, from the moment people began to turn their thoughts to them, those which contributed to the continued prosperity of the society. Right conduct was that which promoted the welfare of the community, and through it of the component individuals. It is highly significant that the Bible, for all the elaborate moral or quasi-moral regulations of the Pentateuch and all the fiery insistence upon righteousness of the prophets, contains no sustained discussion of the good. It remained for the analytic minds of the Greek philosophers to tackle this question.

Thus, while a strictly logical treatment of ethics should, as Moore contended, begin with an investigation of the good and pass from that to consider what is right, if we are interested in tracing the moral development of individuals or societies, we must start with the notion of right and proceed from it to that of good. Nevertheless, either of these terms can be understood without the other, when we recognize that morality is, above all, the effort to arrange our activities in a harmonious pattern, an advantage which certain other treatments of ethics lack.

3. Four Criteria of Rightness

By careful observation of any animal, especially of a social species, we are able to decide what constitutes rightness and wrongness for it. *That conduct is right which is compatible with the whole pattern of behavior that brings prosperity to the community or the species, enabling individuals to dwell in harmony with each other and with their environment. That is wrong which is incongruent with, or disruptive of, this pattern.* Everyone who has given much thought to the matter will at once recognize that this definition of what we might call "objective rightness and wrongness" is too simple to be an adequate account of the notion of right and wrong in humans, even fairly primitive humans. But I believe that we have discovered not only the biological origin of the distinction between right and wrong, but what is a far different matter: the solid core of our present notions of rightness and wrongness, as likewise the criterion by which we most often test human conduct.

It will be objected that when we pass from animals to humans, the problem acquires a wholly different complexion, for even the most primitive known races regard as right or wrong many things which contribute nothing to their survival and prosperity. They feel a strong obligation to worship their gods with many and complicated rites, and to omit any of the traditional procedures, or to approach the god in some unconventional manner, is as wrong to them, often far more flagrantly wrong, than to injure a neighbor. Likewise, they owe many duties to the spirits of their ancestors, and to neglect these is also manifestly wrong. No animal, as far as we know, gives a thought to gods or ancestral spirits. But all these elaborate ceremonials still owe their rightness to the contribution they make to the welfare of the individual and his or her community, only now their relevance to this welfare is imaginary rather than real.

Primitive religions are almost wholly concerned with safeguarding the foundations of the tribal life by propitiating factors in the environment which cannot be directly controlled. The purpose of the rites and taboos of which they are compounded is to ensure the regular alternation of the seasons, adequate rainfall, the fertility of the fields, the fecundity of women, success in hunting, victory in war, and at the same time to avert sickness, famine, natural catastrophes, and all the dire calamities which befall mortals negligent of their obligations to the unseen powers. This extension of the scope of right conduct was brought about by humanity's restless imagination, which immensely complicated life, rather than by any change in the ultimate criterion of rightness. As, when we observe an animal, we say that rightness for it consists in conformity to the pattern of behavior which has brought prosperity to its kind, so rightness for primitive people consists in conforming to all those traditional procedures which they *believe* to be essential to the welfare of self and tribe. The fact that a scientific observer considers many of these procedures superfluous or futile is beside the point.

The second criterion of rightness is an outgrowth of the manner in which we learn the rules of conduct that we must obey in order to pass through life without bringing censure on ourselves by antagonizing our neighbors. Animals are innately endowed with at least a solid foundation for the behavior they must observe in order to dwell with success in their ancestral environment and remain on satisfactory terms with their companions. Our own innate endowments are so rudimentary that without much guidance and instruction from our elders we could never meet the demands life makes on us. Our parents and teachers not only tell us what is right for us to do but give unmistakable signs of approval when we conform to their directions, and even more emphatic demonstrations of disapproval when we disregard them. Since, in many instances, we still can detect no real superiority of the preferred conduct over vetoed procedures, we act to win approval and avoid censure rather than from an appreciation of underlying principles. In school and with our playmates, we are sensitive to the approbation and contempt of our companions. It is inevitable that beings educated as we must be associate rightness with the approval of other members of our society and wrongness with their censure.

In a homogeneous and stable culture, there will rarely be sharp divergence between the two criteria of rightness we have so far recognized; for conduct that conforms to ancestral custom will nearly always be praised or at least tacitly accepted, whereas divergent behavior will bring condemnation if not active persecution. In rapidly changing cultures and among people who develop independence of judgment, conduct which an individual sincerely believes to be right will often be resented and condemned by others. Although such adverse criticism may not convince thoughtful individuals that they have done wrong, perhaps they will not have the same confident feeling of rightness that they would enjoy if their neighbors unanimously agreed with them.

The third criterion of right conduct is its effectiveness in producing the good. We learn to distinguish between right and wrong long before we begin to think about the ultimate ground of this distinction. Perhaps the majority of people, even in literate communities, pass through life without a careful examination of its ends. But from time to time arise thinkers who, not content with blindly following the habits of their neighbors, try to discover what supreme good life offers to them and their fellows. When this highest good has been recognized, all the details of existence are examined with reference to it, and actions become right or wrong according to whether they promote or obstruct its attainment. That course is eminently right which, of all possible courses available at a given time, most effectively conduces to the good. The maxim of happiness for humanity as a whole might, for example, be taken as the rational end of all human endeavor. Then every act which tends to maximize felicity will be regarded as right, whereas all conduct that produces a preponderance of misery over happiness is wrong.

The attempt to assess conduct as means to an end will bring us at many points into conflict with the two preceding criteria of rightness, conformity with an established pattern and the approval of our contemporaries. We see this most clearly when we examine, with a mind disciplined by science and philosophy, the customs of some primitive tribe, whose efforts are directed largely to ensuring its own preservation. A large segment of its rites, including many which impose much hardship upon its members, appear to us useless as means to this end, and others weaken rather than fortify the tribe. Yet were we to expostulate with the tribesmen, pointing out how their strength and prosperity would be increased by certain changes in their ways, they might indignantly reject the suggestion; for such departures from the ancestral mores would, in their view, be wrong.

It often happens that an act which appears to be an effective means to an approved end repels us when viewed by itself; and this brings us to the fourth criterion of rightness, that of intrinsic fittingness. When we investigated the economy of the oropendolas, we could discover no sound utilitarian reason for condemning their practice of stealing fibers from each other; for this seemed to discourage careless building and produce a colony of tougher, more enduring pouches. Yet it seemed incongruous that birds on the whole so diligent and peaceable should indulge in thievery; and we were inclined to disapprove the habit, not on the ground that it is detrimental to the welfare of the oropendolas, but because it offends our finer sensibilities.

In our own lives, occasions arise when an act which would be right by all of the first three criteria nevertheless seems wrong to us because it is not fitting. We would hesitate to resort to subterfuge and deceit even if this were the only means to attain some supremely good end, not because we would be breaking a law or disregarding established usage, nor yet because our friends would censure us if they knew, but because it does not seem fitting for a free person to go about his or her affairs in a furtive manner.

If Utilitarians believed that hurting some defenseless creature could increase the sum of happiness in the world, it would be, by their principles, not only right but a duty to do this; yet if a person of fine sensibilities, they might feel that it is somehow wrong deliberately to inflict suffering on one being for the benefit of others; and they might feel so strongly that such a procedure is not right, that they would avoid it even to the neglect of duty. The Royal Lie, which Plato advocated as part of the policy of his ideal Republic, might or might not serve the laudable purpose for which it was intended; but we feel that it is not fitting for rulers to govern their people by perpetual deceit. In all these cases, a thorough investigation might disclose, in its remote or collateral if not in its immediate effects, further reasons for disapproving the conduct which we deem inappropriate. But our disapproval does not depend on the discovery of unsuspected consequences of the reprobated acts; we condemn them because they are unseemly in themselves, or incongruous with the character of the actor.

These, I believe, are our principal criteria of rightness and wrongness; and although others could be named, I think they can be analyzed into these four. Among the others is conformity to law, or obedience to a ruler or any recognized authority. But if we study the origin of the basic laws of a civilized nation, we can trace them back to tribal custom, and this in turn corresponds to the pattern of behavior of a social animal. The fundamental laws of any nation prescribe penalties for certain acts, which have long been recognized as disruptive of society, such as violence, theft, and murder. In the immense complication of an industrial society, with its indirect methods of holding property, the laws have become exceedingly involved; so that it is at times difficult to discern the relevance of some of them to the primary purpose of promoting the welfare of the community by safeguarding life and all that supports it.

We are all too familiar with unjust legislation, which favors a certain section of society to the detriment of the whole, as likewise with stupid laws, that defeat the ends they are intended to serve. Yet every law issued by the recognized ruler or government of a state imposes as such an obligation to obedience, so that one must have very strong grounds to justify its infraction; and the reason for this lies in the fact that some dominant authority is necessary for the stability of human communities as at present constituted, and to show disrespect for any edict of this authority weakens all its laws, good and bad together. It is right to obey a law, then, regardless of its content, because such obedience is essential to the health of every human community. Although appeal to some other criterion of rightness may lead one to break the law, its intrinsic claim to our obedience can never be disregarded. Similarly, the commands of any recognized authority, as one's parents and teachers, have a claim to rightness, if only on the ground that respect for such authorities is part of the tradition on which human society is established.

To the devout, the precepts of religion take precedence over the laws of the state, so that for them it is right to disobey the latter in order to remain faithful to the former. Must we, then, recognize a special form of rightness, whose stringency is derived from its transcendent source? This seems unnecessary, because people appear to judge the rightness of obedience to religious mandates by principles we have already mentioned. If one is faithful to the precepts of one's faith merely because one hopes thereby to win a celestial reward, then one's conduct is right by our third criterion, as means to an approved end. From a higher point of view, it appears intrinsically fitting for a creature to obey the regulations, attributable to the Creator, regardless of consequences; and such obedience is right according to our fourth criterion. In a primitive community, whose religion is primarily concerned with safeguarding the foundations of the tribal life, to neglect its ritual or break its taboos is also to depart, from the customs of the tribe and, in the view of the tribesmen, to imperil its very existence; hence to conform to them is right according to our first criterion. And in every community, savage or civilized, which has a dominant religion, conformity with it is approved and dissidence strongly condemned by one's neighbors, so that the second criterion of rightness is also applicable here. Accordingly, for those who attribute a divine origin to religious mandates, obedience to them is right by all four of the primary criteria of rightness.

4. The Meaning of "Right"

By analyzing the criteria of rightness, I believe we have prepared ourselves to understand why the notion of "right" is so vague and elusive that careful thinkers have taken it to be primary and indefinable. Except for people so dull or fanatic that they judge every claim to rightness by a single test, such as conformity to the mandates of religion or to the law of their country, no one of the four basic criteria is so authoritative that it reduces the others to insignificance. Thus, when we make an earnest effort to determine the rightness or wrongness of some proposed course of action, we continually shift our point of view, judging it now by one criterion and now by another, without any set rules of procedure. For example, the course which I propose to myself appears to be the one, of all that occur to me, which most effectively conduces to an end whose goodness I cannot doubt, but it does not seem intrinsically fitting. Or else by following it I shall depart from the customs of my community and incur the displeasure of my neighbors. The law commands so and so, yet this will have an effect which I strongly disapprove. My friends, whose opinion I respect, unanimously recommend such a course; but to me it appears unlikely to produce the intended effect.

With the exception of a few of the most heinous crimes, there is scarcely anything a human can do which will not at times appear right by one standard and wrong by another. Only in a society far more unified in its purposes, and in a world far more harmoniously integrated than our own, does it seem possible that a course of conduct could appear right by every valid criterion we could apply to it, so that we would recognize it as absolutely right. In our actual world, to make an act perfectly right is often like fitting a board into a space for which it was never intended; we can make it fit snugly on one side or another, but not on all sides simultaneously. And as we go shifting and turning it around, seeking the best possible adjustment, we become confused, and ask ourselves what rightness is.

To discover the meaning of "right," we must look for some characteristic common to every valid criterion of rightness. This common feature appears to be some sort of relationship to a wider context. In the first criterion, conformity with the established usages of a community, it is immediately evident what this relation is. But I believe that we gain clearer insight into the nature of rightness when we assess some innovation or change, rather than merely follow established procedure. If the proposed innovation can be harmoniously articulated with the accepted body of customs, laws, and beliefs, we are likely to approve it as right; if it clashes violently with established usage, we shall probably reject it as wrong.

This becomes clear if one considers, for example, the history of the slavery question, especially in the United States of America, where the Northerners, who did not need slave labor, almost unanimously agreed that the institution was wrong and should be abolished, whereas the majority of the Southerners, whose economic system rested upon slavery, could see nothing morally wrong in holding the Africans as chattels. Similarly, a review of the question of usury shows that commercial societies commonly hold it right to lend money at interest, whereas agricultural societies have often regarded it as an evil. Or to take a question which agitates us today, that of controlling the rate of human reproduction, perhaps the chief objection to the practice of contraception is that it disrupts the normal pattern of animal life, wherein the union of the sexes leads to conception and birth. Similarly, the strongest argument in its favor is that, unless we limit humanity's rate of increase, we shall never realize the ideal of universal peace, in a world which provides enough food and other material necessities for everybody. It is evident from these, and many other examples that might be adduced, that the rightness or wrongness of a practice is judged not by intrinsic qualities so much as its articulation with its context.

When we turn to the second criterion of rightness, approval by society or at least that section of society with which we identify, it is obvious that here again we are concerned with the wider relations of the act we are assessing. One who judges his or her contemplated course by this standard desires the sympathy of neighbors, and wishes to be in harmony with them.

In applying the third criterion, we judge an activity according to its efficacy in producing an approved result. In the crude application of this principle, the end justifies whatever means most effectively conduces to it. But with growing insight, we recognize that the means must not only conduce to the end but likewise conform to it. The wise regard with suspicion every means not in harmony with the end it is intended to achieve. Some people, for example, who make happiness their life's goal, will enter any profession, no matter how distasteful, which promises to yield the money which they believe will eventually bring felicity. But to choose a means so antithetic to one's primary end is an unwise procedure. Life cannot be sharply divided into living and preparation for living. Today is as much a part of one's life as tomorrow, and the preparation for living is itself living. We may not survive to reach the happy years for which we are painfully preparing; and even if we do, the felicity they bring may not outweigh present unhappiness. It would be more prudent to seek some more satisfying if less lucrative employment, in which one might enjoy the "pleasures of pursuit" and taste the sweets of life as one proceeds, instead of hoarding them all against an uncertain future. Similarly, contemporary regimes which promise to lead humanity to utopia, but which meanwhile subject people to dire hardships and outrageous indignities as, it is claimed, an indispensable preparation for this future Elysium, are employing means so little in harmony with their professed end that they are most unlikely to succeed.

When we look at the fourth criterion, the intrinsic fittingness of the deed, it appears that at last we have found a standard of rightness that depends on nothing external to the act itself. But closer scrutiny reveals that this is a hasty conclusion; we cannot so easily attain the absolute. Even if the act is not judged with reference to its wider context, it is still judged with reference to the actor. To be right in the sense of fitting, the very least that we can ask of the deed is that it accord with the character of the doer. It is generally admitted that certain forms of conduct appropriate to a soldier would be shocking in a saint; and Eastern religions, especially Jainism and Buddhism, set far stricter standards for the monk than for the householder. Even from the standpoint of fittingness, the rightness of a deed depends on its relation to something else.

It appears, then, that the terms "right" and "wrong" refer to relational ideas, far too complex for us to suppose that they are primary and indefinable. *If a given act or practice fits harmoniously into the context with reference to which we judge it, we call it "right;" if it is incongruous with this context, we say that it is "wrong."* If we frequently judge the rightness or wrongness of an act so swiftly that our knowledge of these attributes appears to be intuitive, this is because our judgment of at least the simpler cases has been facilitated by long practice, beginning in early childhood before we began to introspect our mental operations. And since relational notions are commonly analyzable and explicable, I see no reason to doubt the possibility of conveying to an intelligent being, quite lacking in moral sentiments, an adequate idea of what we mean by "right" and "wrong;" and if we could do this, it would be proof that these notions can be analyzed without a remainder into nonmoral terms. The pure intelligence we now contemplate would presumably be perfectly at home in mathematics, physics, and allied disciplines wherein congruence, harmony, and similar notions are frequently employed. Accordingly, this intelligence would be prepared to understand that rightness is a sort of harmony between a single act or course of action and its context, and that the act is considered now with reference to a coherent system of conduct, now with reference to the opinions of one's fellows, now with reference to an end approved as good, now with reference to the character of the actor.

Perhaps we would have most difficulty in making our amoral intelligence appreciate what we signify by the fittingness of an act, for exceedingly refined sentiments are involved in such judgments; but this is the criterion of rightness to which we ourselves least frequently appeal. Of course, we who are moral regard rightness and wrongness with peculiar sentiments of approval or disapproval, reverence or reprobation, which an amoral intelligence would hardly feel. But it seems as absurd to contend that such an intelligence could not understand the meaning of right and wrong because of lacking these sentiments, as that we could not convey to a disembodied intelligence the concept of a pineapple, because of not experiencing the peculiar feelings with which we contemplate it, especially when we are hungry. To me the notion of a pineapple seems just as analyzable and understandable as that of a pinecone, which never excites my appetite.

When a moral being judges an act to be right, he or she at once feels a pressure or obligation to perform it; and this peculiar sense of cogency could never be felt by the amoral intelligence. But a little reflection makes it clear that the notion or feeling of obligation is different from that of rightness, although in normal people closely associated with it, doubtless in consequence of early training. We often amuse ourselves or sharpen our ethical judgment by considering what course a figure in ancient history, or a character in fiction, should have taken in certain contingencies, without ever feeling the obligation to follow this right course ourselves. Even our judgment of what is right for our contemporaries is associated with feelings quite different from those which accompany our judgment of what is right for ourselves. If I fail to do what I deem right for myself, my conscience troubles me; if others neglect to do what I judge to be right for themselves, I regard them with indignation, pity, or possibly contempt, which are feelings quite different from an unquiet conscience.

The source of the widespread modern view that the notion of right is not capable of complete analysis into non-ethical terms appears to be the discussion in Chapter III of Book I of Sidgwick's *Methods of Ethics*, wherein "right" and "ought" were considered together. The failure to make an adequate distinction between them seems to account for Sidgwick's conclusion, which I believe to be untenable. The judgment by which we decide that a deed is right appears to me to be quite distinct from the feeling of obligation to perform it. The meaning of "ought" will be considered, along with duty, in Chapter XIV.

Chapter Twelve
Goodness

1. The Meaning of "Good" Revealed by Its Uses

"**G**OOD" IS ONE of the drudges of our language. Few words are more often used, or in a wider variety of contexts. We speak of good people and good animals, good thoughts and good deeds, good books and good tools, good weather and good food; and, when we wish to express approval or assent, we often tersely exclaim "Good!" A further peculiarity of this word is that it seems to affect, or at least to express, the character of the person who utters it; so that, on the whole, people who use it much are pleasant companions, while we are inclined to avoid those who say "good" far less often than "bad" or some other of its antonyms. Nevertheless, a forthright,

honest person is sometimes repelled by the too complaisant nature of one who finds everything good and nothing
bad; for such a person seems to lack character, to have no
standards or preferences of his or her own. This peculiarity of disclosing the speaker's temper allies the use of the
word "good" to a moral judgment, which invariably tells
us something of the character of the person who forms it.
Every utterance of the word "good," even the most careless and fugitive, especially if it has reference to sentient
beings and their predicaments, is a more or less spontaneous moral judgment, by which the speaker reveals an
estimate of that to which the word is applied.

This word which we use so often, at times so feelingly, yet
for the most part so uncritically, is exceedingly difficult to
define. Nearly always it is an expression of approval, which
is an affective state; but does it possess in addition to this
function a determinate conceptual meaning? Can we detect
a constant significance inherent in its myriad occasions? In
particular, what is the status of the word in ethics, where
it is used to denote the goal of the whole moral endeavor,
yet is sometimes declared to be indefinable?

First, we shall consider how humans apply this adjective
to others of their kind. In a rural district, a "good neighbor"
is one with whom we can live without friction, who from
time to time lends us tools, to whom we can look for help
in an emergency. A bad neighbor plagues us with his or
her animals, disputes over the boundary lines, and refuses
assistance when most needed. Sometimes it happens that
the same individual will be called good by one neighbor
and branded as bad by another; and in such cases it will
repay us to investigate closely the nature of the relations

between the several parties. The one who calls this person a good neighbor is on friendly terms with him; but the other, who considers him bad, quarrels with him.

Are we to suppose that this person classified now as good and now as bad, completely alters his character as he walks from the eastern to the western limit of his farm? Why should he not get along just as well with one of his neighbors as with the other? Possibly the fault lies largely or wholly with the neighbor who calls this man "bad." This is most probable; for when simple, unreflective people apply the term "good" or "bad" to another, they signify hardly more than the kind of relation that prevails between this second person and themselves. When one person calls another "good" and another calls the same person "bad;" we can usually discover valid reasons for these diverse judgments; yet it is obvious that they cannot apply to the same person's intrinsic character, which could hardly be simultaneously good and wicked, but rather to that person's relations with others, which on one side may be cordial and on another bitter. By the phrase "a good person," most people mean no more than one whose relations with the speaker are friendly or harmonious.

Even the most disinterested appraisal of a person's character is made by the application of the same criterion, but now from an impersonal rather than an egoistic point of view. How do we decide whether a person is good or bad save by examining that person's relations with family, neighbors, animals, land? Even at the final judgment before a divine tribunal, as conceived by the ancient Egyptians and many later religions, the inquisition would doubtless be concerned almost wholly with the defendant's relations with his or her fellows, and the remaining questions would take account of conduct toward the gods. If we look for some criterion of moral worth other than one's dealings with the persons and things about one, we shall find none save that of internal consistency or steadfastness of character. This is, in my estimation, a most important quality, too often undervalued; but, as H. J. Paton pointed out, a thief or a murderer might be actuated by a will no less coherent in itself than that of a good citizen; and if this were our only criterion, the former might conceivably rank as high in the moral scale.[1] To avoid this difficulty, we would need first to consider individual's relations with the beings about them, then decide whether their whole character is in keeping with their overt conduct.

In our appraisals of the practical abilities of people, we apply the adjectives "good" and "bad" in much the same manner as in our ethical judgments. We hear of this man that he is a good soldier but a poor executive; of another, that she is a good linguist but a poor mathematician; of a third, that he is a good father but a bad businessman. What do we imply by these characterizations save the person's adequacy in some determinate situation the nature of his or her relations in some particular sphere or occupation? Here, again, the word "good" implies harmonious relations.

As with people, so with things and situations. To children eager to set forth on a picnic, the brilliant Sun in a clear sky is "good weather;" but to the farmer anxiously awaiting a shower to revive parched crops, it is "very bad." Food is good if it satisfies our appetite and agrees with us; and since there is truth in the saying that one person's food is another's poison, the same dish may justly be characterized as good or bad, according to the speaker. The goodness of a tool depends on what we are trying to accomplish; if we are in urgent need of a chisel but are handed a saw by a stupid assistant, we may petulantly exclaim "That's no good!" Although it is in fact the best saw in our tool chest.

It has become evident that the goodness of any object is not inherent in the thing itself, but depends on how well it can fill a definite need or fit harmoniously into a given situation. Hence the wisdom of the old saying that we do not desire a thing because it is good, but it is good because we desire it—because it meets the requirements of some particular situation. Schopenhauer, who in my opinion was so often wrong, was correct when he declared that the concept of good is essentially relative, and signifies the conformity of an object to any definite effort of the will.[2] Since goodness is not intrinsic in the object, it could not possibly be good until we begin to think of it in some particular context. If we are sufficiently philosophic or disinterested, we may consider its adequacy for some ideal situation remote from our selfish desires and needs; but most of us call things good or bad from a more immediate and personal point of view.

It should now be apparent why the use of the word "good" or its opposite betrays the character of the speaker. Each of these words denotes a relation, which must have at least two terms, one of which is often the speaker. If I call a neighbor "bad," it usually means that we disagree; the fault may be either the neighbor's or mine or of both; and only an impartial judge could decide this point. Parents who complain that their children are bad often unwittingly accuse themselves; for, in general, good parents have good children, although history records some notable exceptions, which might be attributed to the pranks of heredity. Good teachers are far more likely to have good pupils than incompetent ones. Good workmen usually have good tools, because they know how to select and care for them; and those who constantly complain of the inadequacy of their tools betray their own deficiencies. So, too, good horsemen and women generally praise their steed; while those who abuse their horse reveal their own equestrian incompetence more often than the defects of the poor animals, who can say nothing in their own defense. Individuals who find much good in the people and things around them, or in the world at large, shows their capacity to establish satisfactory relations with a considerable variety of people and situations; but those who condemn nearly everything they encounter confess themselves to be out of tune with the world, and the fault may well be theirs.

As commonly used by people who do not pretend to be philosophers, the word "good" denotes a particular kind of relationship rather than an intrinsic quality of the thing so designated, although the natural tendency of the human mind to hypostatize its concepts may confuse the user on this point. To be good means to be in concord with, to be congruent with, or to be adequate to the purpose of, some other entity. Goodness, then, is a mode of harmony, like truth, beauty, and friendship. The concept of goodness is wider, less specific than that of these other three, and seems almost to include them: a true friend is always one whom we deem a good person; a beautiful picture is a good one; and truth, even when disagreeable, seems somehow to be good.

This common meaning of the word "good" is, as will appear, adequate for ethics, which is concerned with the conditions of the establishment of harmonious relations among living beings. If goodness were an intrinsic quality of things rather than a relation between them, we might take possession of it by acquiring objects in which it inheres, as we amass gold or other property; but we could not become good unless in the sense of becoming more coherent in ourselves. In this case, becoming good could not mean establishing more harmonious relations with other beings; for such relations are obviously external, although they depend on intrinsic qualities. The great purpose of moral endeavor is to become good rather than to have good, to achieve satisfactory relations with those about us rather than to acquire a certain kind of property.

It follows from this that to call an isolated, simple entity "good" is largely meaningless. To decide whether anything is good we must consider it in relation to something else, whether this second entity is ideal or actually exists. If, however, the isolated object is compound, its parts may be more or less harmoniously combined, and we might say that it is more or less good in the sense of being more or less integrated or coherent. The parts would be good or bad in relation to each other; but the isolated entity so compounded could, properly speaking, be neither good nor bad, for there would be no second term by which a relationship could be established. The Universe, as the totality of interacting entities, is by definition an isolated system; hence to call it good—or bad—means something quite different from saying that a person or a tool is good. In the first case, we refer only to its internal relations, and mean that a high degree of harmony exists between its parts; in the second case, we as a rule mean that the person's external relations are harmonious: "nothing is fair or good alone."

2. "Good" Not an Indefinable Notion

Since the same thing may be good in one context and bad in another, it is obvious that goodness is not an intrinsic quality but a relational property of the thing in question. Yet it is equally obvious that this goodness depends on intrinsic qualities. The goodness of an axe is different from the temper of its steel; for this accompanies the axe wherever it goes; but the axe, which is good in the hands of an expert woodsman, is, except as an article of trade, worthless to a clerk who does not know how to use it. Yet since the goodness of the axe depends on the quality of its steel, by the laws of association we come to say that its goodness consists in this. Similarly, the goodness of a person is distinct from his or her character; for the same person, with no change of character, may live in harmony with some neighbors and quarrel with others, displaying goodness on one side and badness on another. Yet the goodness of a person, depends on that person's character, and the more excellent this becomes, the more the person will evince goodness by dwelling in harmony with all beings; hence by association we speak of a good character. Similarly, the will, which is not an entity but merely a mental act, which cannot enter into relations with external things, is not, strictly speaking, either good or bad; and when we talk of a "good will" we mean no more than the prevailing character of a person whose volitions tend to increase the goodness or harmony in the world. If we wish to be precise in our language, we should say not a "good will" but a "benevolent (i.e., good-willing) will," not a "bad will" but a "malevolent (i.e., bad-willing) will."

Our conclusion that "good" as employed in common speech, and as it should be used in ethics, refers not to some intrinsic property of things or situations but to their external relations, is in direct opposition to doctrines long held by European philosophers and now supported by the Realistic Value school of ethics. One of the leading advocates of this view, G. E. Moore, wrote: "My point is that 'good' is a simple notion, just as 'yellow' is a simple notion; that, just as you cannot, by any manner of means, explain to any one who does not already know it, what yellow is, so you cannot explain what good is. Definitions of the kind that I was asking for, definitions which describe the real nature of the object or notion denoted by a word, and which do not merely tell us what the word is used to mean, are only possible when the object or notion in question is something complex."[3] This interpretation of the meaning of "good" appears to have arisen as a reaction against the too narrow definition of seventeenth century philosophers like Spinoza and Locke, who identified the good (in the words of the former) with every kind of pleasure and all that conduces thereto, evil with pain and its causes.[4] Moore's interpretation is obviously incompatible with our view that "good" refers to a peculiar kind of relation; for, as we learned in our previous discussion of right and wrong, relations are invariably analyzable into at least two relata and the connection between them, and it is usually possible to convey the notion of this complex situation to another intelligent being who has not experienced it directly.

But we have also recognized that although goodness is not itself an intrinsic quality, it depends on the intrinsic qualities or internal constitution of the entity which we call "good." Might there not be some peculiar quality common to all such entities, and might not this be what Moore had in mind when he referred to "good" as a simple, unanalyzable notion? When we reflect that, according to circumstances, we apply this adjective to things so diverse as fire and water, animals and vegetables, light and darkness, delicious foods and nauseating medicines, immovable structures and swiftly moving vehicles, it is difficult to imagine what this intrinsic quality, equally present in everything we from time to time call "good," might be.

Undoubtedly, our experiences of goodness are colored by affective tones, but these also seem to be as various as the situations in which good is recognized. So diverse are these affective states accompanying the experience of goodness that it appears impossible to discover a quality common to them all. How different is our emotion in the presence of a truly just and benevolent person from the feelings aroused in us by a delicious fruit or an excellent tool, yet all these things we spontaneously call "good." One wonders how people ever came to apply the same adjective to objects and situations so diverse, the source of such varied feelings. This could have happened only because they recognized some conceptual similarity in all these instances, for all are manifestations of fitness or appropriateness or harmony. If we remove this essential relation, the instances of goodness contain no common property to bind them into conceptual unity and give them a common name. If it be objected that the very swiftness with which we often apply the word "good" to an object or situation shows that it is a quality as simple and easily recognized as a color or a familiar taste, I shall beg the reader to recall how rapidly he or she sometimes decides that some deed is just or some contemplated act impossible; yet justice and impossibility are notions involving relations and at least as complex as goodness.

The affective tone to which a particular experience of goodness gives rise is no more the essence of goodness than the exultation of a scientist who makes a new discovery, in astronomy or chemistry or biology, is the discovery itself. The latter can be communicated without difficulty to all competent colleagues but the exhilaration that accompanied it is ultimate and unanalyzable; for possibly no one else ever experienced that particular shade of feeling. If goodness were not a relation or system of relations which can be analyzed and made the subject of intelligible discourse, the study of ethics would lose much of its value.

Without a concept and definition of goodness, which implies also a concept and definition of its opposite, badness or evil, we could know whether a particular action or object is good or bad only by direct experience of it, as we can know the taste of sugar only by tasting it or something that contains it. It would be useless to try to explain to someone why he or she should avoid an evil, for only by experiencing it could that person understand just why it is to be shunned. With this limitation, ethics might exist as systematized reflection on past experiences, but it would lose most of its regulative function in leading us toward the good and away from evil. Ethics becomes a fruitful guide to conduct in the measure that it recognizes that goodness and badness denote relations which can be analyzed and communicated, and are not ultimate notions which can be known only as experienced. Hence we cannot accept the opinion of John Ruskin that "Reason can but determine what is true; it is the God-given passion of humanity which alone can recognize what God has made good."[5] As though reason were not itself a God-given faculty! Happiness one is constitutionally able to experience, without the necessity of representing to oneself all of this person's shades of feeling, which can at best be communicated only in terms at once general and vague.

3. Perfect Goodness

Thus, when adequately analyzed, the word "good," like "right" emerges from the cloud of mystery with which some thinkers have surrounded it and is found to denote a definite, understandable relationship. Each particular experience of goodness is, as a rule, accompanied by a more or less agreeable affective overtone; but these emotional states are of great variety; and it is not by considering them so much as the situations which produce them that we reach the notion of good. Now that we know the meaning of "good," we are prepared to examine the question "Is anything wholly good?"

I carry in my pocket a watch which, without repairs, has kept accurate time for many years. Naturally, I call it "a good watch." Even when I consider it more broadly, not merely in relation to my need of knowing the hour but in relation to everything it might influence, I find no reason for limiting the force of the adjective "good" as applied to it: it injures nothing, it competes with nothing, it uses no natural product which some other being may need. This watch is a compound entity, consisting of springs, gear wheels, pinions, and other metal parts, which together form complex machinery. Each part is delicately adjusted to those which surround it, and it is the accuracy of these adjustments, which makes a good watch. These parts which act so harmoniously together must be called "good," for this is what we mean by the word. Yet the wheels and other moving parts do not run wholly without friction, which, in the course of time, will wear them out and ruin the watch. Thus the harmony between the parts is not perfect, for in their interactions they injure each other, and they cannot be wholly good. Were they perfectly good, the watch should run forever.

This consideration of the goodness of a watch may seem a barren exercise, devoid of ethical significance; yet it has the advantage of showing precisely what we mean by good without appealing to an example which by stirring our emotions, would obscure our conceptual clarity. Instead of something small we might have taken something great, like the solar system, where the sun, planets, and their satellites move ceaselessly, in such nice equilibrium that they go on for thousands and millions of years without colliding and destroying each other. Hence each of these celestial bodies is a good neighbor to the others, however much strife or evil may exist on some of them. Yet because their gravitational pull on each other creates tides whose friction gradually retards the rotation of each, they seem to affect each other somewhat adversely, so that their goodness falls short of perfection.

When we turn from the consideration of lifeless objects great or small to that of living things, the question of their goodness assumes a more intimate and momentous aspect. We may begin with plants, which in a sense stand between inorganic bodies and animals. They differ from the latter in being less aggressive, never actively pursuing and destroying other living things for food; although we might except those botanical oddities, the insectivorous or carnivorous plants, which entice and entrap many tiny animals, whose bodies they digest. Numerous parasitic forms of vegetation, both green and devoid of chlorophyll, attack other plants and even animals, less violently it is true than animals attack each other, but often with results as fatal. These heterotrophic vegetables obviously fall short of perfect goodness, as do the many vines and creepers which twine around or run over stouter plants in their effort to reach the light, often strangling or smothering the trees and bushes they seize as supports.

The great mass of vegetable forms, rooting in the ground and nourishing themselves on mineral salts, water, and air, which using the energy of sunlight, they synthesize into organic compounds, come much closer to our concept of goodness. But nearly always, when we study these more carefully, following their progress from the germinating seed to the mature flowering plant, we find that they have not grown to full stature without competing with and overcoming neighboring plants of the same or other kinds, which through the accidents of seed dispersion grew up too close to them. Hence these plants, too, possibly through no fault of their own, seem to lack something of perfect goodness. But here and there, chiefly in areas less favorable to vegetable life, one encounters a plant in whose goodness it is difficult to detect a flaw: as some hardy alpine herb, growing alone in the crevice in a rock where no other seed has fallen, injuring nothing yet adding its small, bright contribution to the beauty of the mountain crag.

Animals more obviously violate the concept of goodness, for none can live without tearing and devouring other organized beings, whether vegetables or other animals, or else sapping their strength as noxious parasites. The larger ambulatory animals can hardly move without crushing the herbage and multitudes of small creeping things; and all compete with each other for space and nourishment in the same manner as plants, but often far more violently. Moreover, they struggle for mates in a fashion wholly unknown among vegetables, even the milder herbivores sometimes exhibiting in their quarrels with rivals a fury that astounds us. Thus none is wholly good; yet those which devour only vegetation seem to be endowed by nature with a capacity for goodness lacking in those which kill and tear for food creatures more akin to themselves; while the fiercest kinds, which destroy living things that they do not require to sustain their own lives, fall most conspicuously short of goodness.

No kind of animal except humanity is wholly capricious in its behavior. Each is endowed at birth with instincts which regulate its conduct not only toward other individuals of its own kind but toward those of other species that it habitually encounters. These innate patterns of behavior, on the whole, tend to promote harmony within the species and to diminish strife between species. In this we may recognize a kind of moralness or protomorality pervading the whole living world. Only in animals capable of foreseeing the consequences of their acts and deliberately choosing between alternative courses of action does morality proper arise, doubtless by gradual transition from the protomorality which preceded it. As the moral consciousness matures, it creates for itself the ideal of perfect goodness, of becoming perfectly integrated in oneself and at the same time living in harmony with all things, injuring nothing.

But this ideal is, as we have seen, incapable of realization by any animal, and perhaps by any material entity whatever. Have we, then, defined perfect goodness in a manner which makes the concept an abstraction, useless for ethics and the practical business of living? Far from it! Every religion, every active philosophy, every discipline which over a long period has won the devoted allegiance of many people, has cultivated an ideal which few or none could fulfill. The Stoics could point to no actual sage who quite satisfied their concept of the Wise Person. What devout follower of Christ dares to call himself or herself a perfect Christian? What yogic adept has wholly emancipated self from the promptings and demands of the flesh? What Jain ever followed to the letter the cardinal precept of his or her religion, to injure no living thing? The chief value of each of these doctrines is that it offers an ideal toward which we can continuously strive, not a goal which we can easily exceed, thereby depriving our lives of their highest purpose. It is precisely because the definition of goodness here proposed makes perfect goodness an ideal which at best we approach asymptotically that it is adequate for the purposes of morality. Moreover, since harmony is the foundation of happiness no less than the condition of goodness, and all values arise from it just as all disvalues indicate its failure, an ethic based on this concept can satisfy that thirst for felicity no less than that yearning toward virtue which, as Lecky pointed out, are human needs which must be served by every living system of ethics.

Chapter Thirteen

Ethical Judgments and Social Structure

1. Motives, Intentions, and Deeds

IN THE LAST two chapters, we tried to discover the meaning of two key words of ethics, "right" and "good." We noticed a fundamental similarity in the notions which these words convey; both refer not to a quality we could discover in an act or a thing if it were alone in boundless space, but to its relations with a larger whole. Both "right" and "good" are adjectives which designate harmonious adjustment to a context. In general, we apply "good" to entities which fit harmoniously into their surroundings, as likewise to the ends of action; while "right" is reserved for thoughts and deeds which lead to approved ends. Yet in everyday speech this distinction is not rigidly maintained, for we often speak of a "good deed" or a "right end." And whenever we designate an action as right or wrong, an entity as good or bad, we pass an ethical judgment.

It might be objected that not every assertion that something is right or wrong, good or bad, is an ethical judgment, but only a certain class of such statements. To say that a person is good is certainly to pass a moral judgment, but to affirm that a food or a tool is good seems to be without moral relevance. Similarly, to say that one's treatment of a child or a horse is right appears to be a statement of a different order from saying that handling of tools is right. Ethical judgments, it is maintained, have reference to the character and welfare of living things, not to the quality and uses of inanimate objects. Yet how a person treats tools reveals character no less than how one treats one's fellows, although the traits revealed in one's dealings with the latter seem to be of greater moral importance. And our welfare and happiness certainly depend to some extent on the quality of the instruments we make and how we employ them, although not so much as on the temper of our minds. Although some of the statements in which we use the terms "right" and "good," or their opposites, seem more pertinent to moral endeavor than others, all such statements appear to have a certain relevance to it; and it is hardly possible to draw a sharp boundary between the ethical and nonethical uses of these words.

Were we and our world so constituted that every deed were at once an adequate expression of the motive that prompted it and an efficient means to the intended end, we would doubtless pass a single judgment on both the internal and external aspects of conduct, not bothering to distinguish its component elements. But in the immense complication of life, such a summary mode of judging would not only be frequently unfair to our neighbors, but would fail adequately to train our moral discrimination. It often happens that a praiseworthy motive leads, either because the means were poorly chosen or because of unforeseen developments, to a lamentable result. And conversely, it occasionally happens that a despicable motive has a happy result. Not only is it necessary, in order to make a fair appraisal, to distinguish between the motive of the deed and the act itself, it is convenient to analyze the subjective prelude to action into motive and intention.

The motive is, in the strictest sense, the psychic impulse or spring of action, such as appetite, greed, generosity, compassion, curiosity, or vengefulness, which by gaining control of the mind sets the agent in motion, becoming at the moment his or her will. In all deliberate activity, this psychic impulse exists in intimate association with a definite idea that corresponds to it and promises its fulfillment; as when hungry we often entertain the idea of sitting down to a meal at a certain place and time. This attraction on which the mind is set is commonly called the motive of an act, but it is only one aspect of the motive and we shall gain in clarity if we designate it the "objective." The whole motive, or internal prelude to action, consists then of: (1) the psychic impulse or spring of action, which is affective rather than conceptual, and (2) the objective, which is the mental image of the activity which will fulfill or satisfy the psychic impulse. It may be noticed that sometimes the objective stirs up the impulse, while at other times the impulse gives rise to the objective. The sight of some unguarded treasure, and the notion that one might gain possession of it, may arouse the impulse of greed in a mind which a moment ago was innocent of this affection. As an example of a spring of action giving birth to an objective, we might take the familiar case of hunger stirring up visions of food, or of hatred giving birth to thoughts of injuring one's enemy.

But this contemplated end of action seldom occurs in isolation. It is often part of a wider fabric of foreseen consequences of an action; and these expected consequences merge into unforeseen effects, some of which we might by making a greater effort trace a little farther, but which always flow on and on into distant regions whither the human mind strives vainly to follow. In order to act at all, we must sooner or later abandon the attempt to trace the consequences of our deed to their ultimate and perhaps infinitely remote limits; and the best of us can do no more than hope that our most carefully thought out actions will, on the whole, produce more good than evil in the world. In practice, then, we must separate from the total consequences of our contemplated act that small part which we can more or less clearly foresee, and fix our scrutiny on it as we decide whether we should or should not pursue the course in question. The whole foreseen consequences of a decision are by ethical writers called its "intention;" which will always include the objective, and often a good deal more.

If the world were so ordered that we could, by isolating our objective from its context, make it the equivalent of our intention, it would be a great deal easier for us to lead good and happy lives. But it not infrequently happens, that a commendable objective is inseparable from an evil intention; as, for example, when an investigator, whose aim is to learn how to cure a certain disease which afflicts fellow humans, plans diabolically cruel experiments upon animals, as the only means imaginable for accomplishing the purpose. Even criminals often pursue objectives which are not in themselves wicked. That of desperados who rob a bank is the same as bankers, to acquire wealth; but since they foresee that they can accomplish this only by using violence, and depriving other people of their property, and perhaps killing a clerk or a guard, all this is part of their intention; so that in deciding to rob the bank they become responsible for these results, even if they would gladly avoid them yet nevertheless obtain the coveted money.

Although to become an objective an imagined act must always exert a positive attraction on the mind, the intention very often contains additional elements which repel it, or decrease one's eagerness to perform the contemplated act. Often these repellent or dissuasive aspects are so strong that they inhibit our pursuit of some objective that draws us strongly. We become moral beings in just the measure that we give full weight to the morally undesirable aspects of some course of action whose objective attracts us strongly. But there is an opposite side of the picture: sensitivity to the collateral and remote effects of every course of action may dissuade us from carrying out some duty that we have every obligation to perform.

Moreover, while we are putting an intention into effect, unforeseen opportunities or obstacles may arise, causing us to modify our plan of action, so that the deed itself is seldom exactly as we originally intended it to be. This deed is what other people behold, so that it forms the basis of their judgment of us, and it provides an example which may influence their conduct for better or for worse. When our deed has been accomplished, we may ourselves scrutinize it calmly at our leisure, and in its light pass sentence on the resolution that prompted it. Since our intention can scarcely ever include all the direct and collateral consequences of our action, these, as they develop with the passage of time, become the objects of still further scrutiny, whereby we test the wisdom of the decision which led to them. By means of such multilateral examination, errors of judgment are sometimes corrected. Hence the complete ethical analysis of conduct includes separate judgments on the motive, the intention, the deed itself, and all its detectable consequences, at whatever distance from the primary actor.

2. The Order of Judging Motives and Deeds

It is of interest, and perhaps of some importance in the training of children, to discover in what order we learn to make the several kinds of moral judgments, whether we examine motives before deeds, or deeds before motives. Although philosophers had earlier speculated on this question, it remained for Professor Jean Piaget of Geneva to attempt to solve it directly by the interrogation of young children. His method was to tell the children pairs of simple stories, each of which introduced variations of some little childhood transgression, and to ask them to judge the relative culpability of the chief actors. He found that the youngest children whom he was able to question, six or seven years of age, tended to attach far more importance to the external results of a deed than to its motivation or intention. Thus, a child who had quite innocently broken fifteen cups was held to deserve severer punishment than one who, in the course of taking forbidden food, broke a single cup; and the enormity of a lie was proportionate to the degree of its divergence from probability, without much regard for the motives that prompted it. With advancing age, the children became increasingly sensitive to the intention of the actor; so that the child who, while trying to be helpful, carelessly caused a big damage, was no longer considered naughtier than one who by disobedience caused a small damage. Although at every age from six years to ten were found individuals who judged by the criterion of objective responsibility and others by that of subjective responsibility, the latter group became more numerous with increasing age. As they grew older, the children became increasingly alert to motives and intentions.[1]

These children, as Piaget recognized, learned to evaluate their faults on the basis of the material damage they caused by observing the reactions of their parents or guardians. Because parents in general become more annoyed the greater the loss their household suffers by childish disobedience or carelessness, and tend to make their children more uncomfortable in proportion to their own displeasure, the children learn to judge their guilt by the magnitude of the material damages for which they are responsible and the severity of the censure or punishment they receive. Ultimately, it is the effect of their own transgression on themselves, in parental rebukes, in the deprivation of gratifications, or in corporeal punishment, which makes children aware that they have done wrong, and furnishes the scale by which they measure their misdeeds.

This suggests that if children were never scolded and punished, if their quick sympathy did not even detect sadness or displeasure in the loved adults whom they have hurt or inconvenienced by their naughtiness or clumsiness, they would form their first moral notions by observing the effects on themselves of the actions of those who surround them. Until they had been struck, they could not imagine the painful consequences of a blow. Until their own feelings had been wounded by harsh speech, they could hardly know how greatly the sharp tones of their own voice can hurt their companions. Until some treasured possession had been stolen from them, they could have no knowledge of the pain and hardship thievery may cause. Until they had been inconvenienced by a lie, they could hardly imagine the evil consequences of falsehood. Similarly, until they had been given joy by the kindness and generosity of others, they could have no intimation of the worth of these qualities. And it is largely through their interactions with their contemporaries that they become aware of these consequences of right and wrong conduct.

Thus, without the complication of adult example and constraint, it is probable that our earliest moral judgments would be passed on the deeds of others as they affect ourselves. Then, with expanding sympathy and a growing sense of responsibility, we would judge the deeds of others by their impact upon a third party, and perhaps at the same time our actions as they affect those around us. A few years more would pass before growing inwardness of thought prepares us to scrutinize the motives and intentions of our acts and classify them as laudable or shameful. Motives are known to us directly, and their quality is felt only as we experience them in ourselves. We infer the motives of other people from their overt conduct; insofar as their actions resemble ours when we are driven by a particular impulse, we surmise that they are impelled by a similar motive. Hence we must form the habit of scrutinizing our own motives before we begin to judge those of our neighbors. As our own affections, when we behave in a certain way, appear to us as noble or base, so we infer that those of other people who perform similar actions are worthy of our admiration or censure.

Accordingly, if our moral development followed its natural course, we would become critical of deeds before motives, and of the deeds of other people before our own. Later, when we began to pay attention to motives and intentions, we would judge our own before those of other people. Piaget's investigations revealed that in certain cases children reveal greater awareness of intentions when reviewing their own conduct than when evaluating that of the characters in a story, and that they make allowance for the rightness of their own intentions while still passing a harsh objective valuation upon the clumsiness of their playmates.[2]

The capacity to distinguish between the internal determinants of action and its external effects is the mark of a refined moral judgment, yet it is easy to distort the relative values of these two aspects of conduct. Although it is almost universally recognized that, no matter how favorable its effects, activity which does not spring from right intentions is devoid of moral worth, it is more seldom admitted that praiseworthy intentions which never issue in effective action are of hardly greater worth. Although at times the best of intentions miscarry, because of insuperable obstacles or unforeseen turns of events in the external world, too often benevolent impulses are ineffective because of their own weakness, or because of an unwise choice of means for putting them into effect. Were our good impulses stronger and our intentions clearer, we would take greater pains to make ourselves and our means adequate for the accomplishment of the desired end.

To be satisfied with ourselves because our motives are noble and pure even, if our procedures are blundering and ineffective, is to misjudge the total worth of a human being. The intelligence, perseverance, and strength necessary to give substance to our moral aspirations are products of the same creative process as the aspirations themselves, and to hold that the former are negligible in comparison with the latter is to undervalue the whole achievement of harmonization. If right intentions make beautiful spirits, right deeds create a beautiful world, which in turn provides the milieu most favorable for the production of beautiful spirits. The success of moral endeavor depends equally on right resolves and right action, as the wise have always recognized.

Similarly, when judging other persons, it seems as unfair to give attention only to their motives and intentions as to weigh only their deeds and their effects, for in either case we neglect important components of a complete human being. But I believe that, on the whole, we shall make a truer estimate of people by reviewing their performances than by listening to their apologies; for doubtless, like most of us, they are often influenced by a mixture of motives acting simultaneously; so that even without deliberate falsehood, they may try to raise themselves in our esteem by stressing motives which are generally approved and slurring over others less commendable. Moreover, it is not a wholesome practice to be constantly dissecting our neighbors in an effort to tease apart their intentions and their overt behavior. If we are able to forgive their trespasses, it is almost as easy to forgive an evil motive as the blundering and disastrous execution of a good one, especially if we suffer about equally in the two cases. Either defect may often be traced to flaws in heredity or faults of education.

If we never undertake to punish vindictively, we shall be spared the embarrassment of deciding whether to have meant well and done badly deserves a severer penalty than to have intended a base action and performed it skillfully. It appears to be chiefly when we are responsible for applying remedial measures to a delinquent that the ability to distinguish the subjective and objective aspects of conduct assumes great importance; for the correctives we use will vary greatly, according to whether one meant well but acted ineptly, or was competent in the execution of a wicked intention.

Another reason for assessing the character, motives, and deeds of others is that thereby we sharpen our moral insight and give more definite shape to our ideals. But to pass judgment on the personages of history, and even of fiction, serves this purpose as well as the criticism of our intimates, and perhaps even better; for in the perspective of time or of art we see whole what in the passing scene we glimpse only fragmentarily, without yet detecting those remoter consequences of actions which we need to know in order to pass a balanced judgment. And this is certainly the more charitable method of exercising our faculty of judging. But such criticism of the motives and deeds of others is salutary only if it helps us to bring greater wisdom to the formation of judgments of more consequence to ourselves and other beings, those which determine the ends we seek and the courses we pursue. It is to judgments of this sort that the present chapter is chiefly devoted. By what process do we form them? Are all ethical judgments, as has been held, merely expressions of emotion and desire, or is there a valid distinction between true ethical judgment and a simple assertion of preference? If we can settle this point, we shall gain clearer insight into the nature of moral endeavor.

3. Characteristics of Ethical Judgments

Ethical judgments have several aspects, including the assessment of the motives and intentions underlying conduct, and its effects on self and others. But the most typical and important kind of judgments includes those concerned with the solution of the problems which arise whenever, in the course of growing or striving to perfect themselves or to realize some value, two beings come into conflict with each other. Since, for the morally mature person, the second entity is not necessarily another human, but may be anything which exhibits, or moves toward, some harmonious form, we shall call these two entities *A* and *B*. When they come into collision, three methods of settling the difficulty are possible: (1) *A*, if the more powerful or astute, may impose its will on *B*, without regard for its feelings, aspirations, or perfection of form. (2) *A* and *B*, if intelligent or at least adaptable beings, may try to settle the difficulty in a manner which will permit each to realize its aspirations to the fullest extent compatible with an equal realization by the other; or the more intelligent of them may attempt to work out such a solution in the interests of both. Or (3) *A* may voluntarily yield, effacing itself so that *B* may attain its objective without interference from *A*.

In the first of these solutions, whereby *A* ignores the claims of *B*, the latter may suffer severely but the former also loses. *B* is thwarted and may be destroyed. But *A*, if an intelligent being capable of sympathy, misses the opportunity to understand *B*, and to grow in spirit through this insight. *A* becomes hard and mechanical, a being self-engrossed and out of harmony with surrounding beings. It has taken the course advocated by some who preach the superman; but if we followed their doctrine, what we would develop is not a superman, if by this we understand an animal of deep insight and broad sympathies, but rather a supermonster.

The third solution, by which *A* yields completely to *B*, is almost as unsatisfactory as the first; for it deprives *B*, if an intelligent being, of the opportunity to grow by understanding and sympathizing with *A*, who voluntarily relinquishes legitimate aspirations and may fail to complete his or her growth. If *A* succumbs in consequence of this abnegation, the world will lose the more morally advanced of the two; for *B*, who permits this sacrifice, is evidently not capable of the generosity which *A* displays. Repeated sacrifices of this sort would result in the moral impoverishment of the world by the premature removal of its most valuable inhabitants, and thereby retard the progress of harmonization. This is the course which seems to be recommended by the Sermon on the Mount. Although it may improve one's chance of winning heaven, it is not to the best interest of the living community.

The only solution which we can approve as morally sound is the second, which requires that *A* and *B* try to understand each other and reach an accommodation that does justice to both, permitting each to fulfill itself to the maximum degree compatible with the continued growth of the other; or that one of these beings, if more intelligent than the other, plots a course that will be favorable to both. This is the ethical solution, because it strives to adjust conflicting patterns with the minimum of distortion or constriction to either; and we are led to prefer it because it is the only one compatible with that persistent demand for growth and harmony which makes us moral beings. Whence it is evident that morality is frequently self-limitation in the interest of harmony and the attainment of the greatest perfection by as many beings as possible, but it is only most exceptionally self-annihilation. Good and moral beings are those which create a favorable environment for each other; and to accomplish this end, the first must neither destroy the second nor permit it to harm itself for the benefit of the former.

Just as an ethical judgment is demanded whenever the pursuit of our own legitimate aspirations brings us into conflict with other beings; so, too, a similar mode of reasoning is required whenever two or more of our own desires or aspirations compete with each other. It is almost as immoral to suppress some aspect of one's own nature, without at least giving it a hearing, as to crush out the life of some other creature, without considering its claims to exist. Most, if not all, of our desires spring originally from deep vital sources, which make them worthy of our respect. They are the very pressure of life upon the mind; and without at least some of them we would remain forever inert, because we lacked all incentive to action. Perhaps no natural appetite is unmitigatedly evil, however much it may have been distorted or vitiated by a faulty education, a disordered society, or the vagaries of an uncontrolled imagination.

Probably no two desires of a moderately and sane kindly person are intrinsically incompatible, although they are made so by limitations of time, strength, and resources, or the obstacles which social arrangements oppose to their satisfaction. Hence to avoid repeated frustration, and all those disturbances which arise from failure to integrate the various aspects of our nature, we must strive to reconcile them to each other within the limits of possibility and arrange them in a coherent pattern. To accomplish this, we must first decide which is of greatest value, so that its fulfillment will be most precious to us. Fortunate the person who has some ruling aspiration, such as that for holiness, knowledge, or the satisfactions of an ordered life in the midst of one's family, to which one can assign primacy in the company of one's desires, arranging the others below it in descending scale. Such a dominant aim will, as a rule, greatly facilitate the ordering of one's desires and the unification of one's life. Yet, from time to time, it may become necessary to weigh the claims of some neglected or despised impulse against those of the ruling motive; and this will require the exercise of reason to reach an ethical judgment, employing much the same procedure that we follow when adjusting the claims of two individuals. The use of judgment in the unification of one's personal life is the necessary prelude to the establishment of satisfactory relations with those about us; for, until we are harmonious in our selves, we with difficulty achieve harmony with surrounding beings.

An examination of the method whereby we work out a satisfactory solution of a conflict reveals to us the nature of an ethical judgment of the most important class, that by which we reach a decision which shapes the course of moral progress. It is a judgment, made under the influence of the integrative or moral force within us, which strives to do justice to two, or more, competing claims. These may be two demands of our own nature, as our thirst for intellectual growth and our need to preserve bodily health and strength, or they may be claims of distinct individuals or groups of individuals. In the simplest case, it takes cognizance of my own desires and aspirations and those of some other being whose needs conflict with mine, and it tries to reach a solution which will harmonize these claims and permit both of us to realize our legitimate goals in the fullest measure compatible with the nature of the situation. This criterion will distinguish an ethical judgment sharply from a decision to act originating in some single personal desire, which may or may not be wicked or harmful.

Because of our deficiency in wisdom and knowledge, a genuine ethical judgment may not be the best solution of a difficulty. It may be a very imperfect solution; but if made after a sincere effort to reconcile and do justice to all the competing claims, it is a true ethical judgment. Thus, an ethical proposition is more than a statement of desire, preference, or aversion, and it is not a hypothetical imperative. It is a statement of the fact that, in a definite situation, a rational and moral being has decided, by a special form of reasoning, to act in a certain way, or that someone else should act in a certain way.

It may be remarked in passing that the way we reach an ethical judgment is hardly different from that whereby we form an honest judgment on any difficult or controversial question, even one whose interest is purely theoretical. In the first case, we weigh competing claims and try to strike a balance between them. In the second case, we weigh contrary arguments and, if they contain even a grain of truth, modify our conclusion in their light. Since there is a morality of thought no less than of action, all conscientious judgments are reached by essentially the same method.

4. The Moral Solution of Conflicts Necessitates Social Structure

Every moral solution of a conflict between individuals imposes upon each the necessity of observing certain restraints with reference to the other. Neither can pursue its course just as though the other were not there or, being there, were unworthy of consideration. If the two individuals remain in proximity for a considerable period, they must develop certain habitual modes of treating each other; and their interactions will be on the whole reciprocal; for, as became clear in Chapter V, between finite beings only reciprocal relations can be enduring, because the long continuance of uncompensated trends would lead to the exhaustion of one of them. But when two beings are joined together by reciprocal, mutually beneficial relations, they form a rudimentary society. In a world as crowded as ours, these beings will almost inevitably come into contact with others; and by the moral solution of the problems thereby arising, more members will be added to the society. Hence the formation of societies, which show pattern and structure because of the definite relations existing between their component individuals, is the necessary consequence of moral endeavor. It is not true, as some have taught, that all morality is social;[3] for two beings who came together only momentarily and then separated forever might exhibit moral conduct toward each other, and moreover there is a morality of personal life, even if one dwells in complete isolation; but it is true that morality tends to become increasingly social.

The fact that many societies grew up in the world, long before humanity brought its peculiar intellectual endowments to the settlement of moral problems, is further proof of the moralness pervading the cosmos from its prime foundations. Animal societies are, as a rule, composed of individuals of a single species, but this fact of natural history does not impose a limit on social organization. It seems necessary that beings of a single kind learn to dwell in concord before they extend their harmonious association to other beings. But the forward march of harmonization tends to expand coherent patterns indefinitely in all directions, thereby binding an ever greater diversity of beings into an orderly society. We are led by the very movement that forms our bodies by joining innumerable discrete particles into an organic whole, and likewise our minds by combining countless separate impressions into a coherent system of thought, to prefer the ampler to the narrower pattern and to make strenuous efforts to realize it.

The characteristics of societies, which would be the necessary outgrowth of our moral endeavor even if nature had not given birth to them before humanity appeared on the Earth, must be taken into account in reaching our moral judgments, which too often go astray by overlooking certain of their peculiar features. A society is not a structureless conglomeration of individuals but exhibits a definite and usually intricate pattern. Even a pattern which, when surveyed externally, appears simple and homogeneous takes on a more complex aspect when viewed from within. To one looking down on a sheet of paper covered with dots uniformly spaced, all except the marginal dots appear to stand in the same relation to the others. But if we imagine ourselves in the place of one of these dots, the situation assumes a different aspect, for some of the other dots are closer to us and some farther away. Those lying nearest us have special relevance for us. Hence even if we imagine a society composed of identical units, the principle of harmonious association could not imply that each individual stands in the same relationship to every other individual. Far less could identical relations prevail among the members of any actual society of living organisms, composed of individuals very unequal in age, strength, ability, and kinship.

Each of the special relationships in a society has its own peculiar structure. There is the pattern of the family, defining the relations between husband and wife, parents and children, brothers and sisters. There is the industrial system, defining the relations between employers and employed, between co-workers, between creditors and debtors; there is the complex political structure; there is the pattern of friendships and that of voluntary associations. A society is, then, a pattern of patterns. Far from being weakened by this multiplicity of special relations, the whole social fabric is immensely strengthened by them; for distant units are often linked by special bonds, which interlace with more general bonds. Where wider patterns are formed by the harmonious articulation of two or more societies, the total organization becomes still more complex. The consideration of these patterns in all their complexity is of primary importance in making ethical judgments; for each kind of relationship gives rise to its own peculiar duties and privileges.

5. Moral Qualities of Socially Limited and of Unlimited Relevance

Some moral qualities are displayed chiefly in dealing with members of one's own society, whereas others are significant in relation to beings beyond an organized society.

Thus, veracity is of importance only within the limits of an association of beings between whom there is mutual understanding and some form of cooperation based upon exchange of information. For, obviously, it can make no difference to one who could not discover the meaning of my words whether I tell a truth or a lie. Contracts and promises of all sorts have significance only when made by people within a social structure which can enforce their fulfillment, or at least by beings bound together by a sense of honor. Since there has hitherto been no adequate machinery for the enforcement of those international contracts called treaties, and some nations have shown themselves lamentably deficient in honor, treaties are at best of doubtful value.

Other moral attributes enter into our relations with creatures beyond the society to which we belong; and some of them seem to acquire greater importance when we pass beyond the limits of an organized society; for they alone can bring gentleness and beauty into our contacts with beings with whom our relations are not regulated by law and custom. Compassion is certainly necessary in our intercourse with other humans; yet in its absence our cruel and selfish impulses are at many points held in check by statute law and social censure; so that even without the least tinge of sympathy or pity, the calculating egoist will exercise some restraint in dealing with other people, but beyond the pale of society, compassion and kindred sentiments are often the only influences able to mitigate our treatment of weaker creatures, so that without them morality collapses. In its stead arises an anarchy without parallel even among speechless animals, whose innate modes of behavior not only regulate their relations with others of their own species but in many instances exercise a moderating influence on their treatment of members of other species.

Another moral quality, too often overlooked, which immeasurably elevates our conduct in regions where law and custom impose little or no control, is respect for form as such. Every organized form, not only that of every living creature but likewise that of crystals and geological formations, is an expression of the same creative energy which made us moral beings. Hence respect for form is really an expression of reverence for the source of our moral nature; and to treat organized, and especially beautiful, forms with careless disdain is to reveal a deficiency of moral insight. A growing reverence for form as such transforms and ennobles one's contacts with the natural world.

Another virtue whose chief sphere of action seems to lie beyond rather than within an organized society is charity. Even in our intercourse with those closest to us, there will always be a place for the charity which moderates censure and radiates good will; but that compassionate beneficence that often takes the form of almsgiving or service to the sick and the stricken, which is what we now chiefly mean by "charity," will reach out beyond the limits of an organized society just in the measure that this society becomes perfect. The reason for this will be seen when it is recalled that charity is a nonreciprocal activity, whereas a moral society is founded on reciprocal relations. The truly charitable act is done at the bidding of love, compassion, generosity, or some allied sentiment; and it looks for no reward either on Earth or beyond it, except the satisfaction springing directly from the performance of the deed itself. Thus charity cannot be compelled, and to command it is to destroy it.

But deserving members of a well-organized society should not be left at the mercy of the spontaneous impulses of others for the satisfaction of their vital needs. On the contrary, by their services to the community they earn what they require; so that it is not charity so much as equity which prompts their neighbors to provide for them. In his second or *Magnesian Republic*, Plato forbade almsgiving, declaring that in a state such as he contemplated, no somewhat virtuous or temperate person would be reduced to beggary.[4] Of course, no society however wise, can legislate away disease and helpless senility, so that there will always be individuals dependent on the good offices of others; but it is cruel to leave them at the mercy of the spontaneous feelings of their neighbors. We might say that by their willingness to perform their just share of the community's work so far as they are able, they earn the right to be supported by the community when circumstances beyond their control prevent the discharge of their obligations; and that every member of the community, by agreeing to this arrangement, secures for himself or herself the same benefits if somehow disabled. Moreover, all the members of a society are linked together by so many bonds that the presence within it of much unalleviated suffering will react unfavorably on the whole, so that it is to everyone's interest to safeguard the welfare of neighbors. And where one's private interests are at stake, true charity is scarcely possible.

Beyond the limits of the most comprehensive actual society are living creatures whom our moral impulse bids us to include within our system of organized, reciprocal relations, although up to the present we have found this impossible to achieve. Nevertheless, we can at least reach out to help them when in distress, as by rescuing them from the pools and pits into which they sometimes fall, feeding them when hungry as far as our means allow, perhaps at times curing their wounds. Such charity is the truest sort, because we can never expect any extrinsic recompense nor even an indirect economic advantage from it. When we contemplate the vast amount of mutilation, suffering, and death which hourly occurs among the living creatures on this planet, and the complex relations among them which make it impossible for us to help one of them without perhaps indirectly injuring another, we sometimes suspect that our most devoted effort on behalf of nonhuman creatures is scarcely more than a gesture. Yet it is a gesture which symbolizes the comprehensive society that we aspire to create.

6. Some Principles of Judgment

The consideration of the structure of moral relations suggests a few general principles which should be helpful in forming ethical judgments in difficult cases. A harmoniously adjusted unit of a coherent society which includes oneself seems, other things being equal, to have a greater claim on us than a creature beyond the society or merely on the fringe of it, or than one imperfectly adjusted to it. Whenever there arises between two or more beings a conflict so acute and urgent that it can be resolved only by injuring or destroying one of them, and one of these is included in our society while the other is not, the first should be defended at the expense of the second. Thus we seem to be justified in driving away or killing a wild animal, whose relationship to us is undefined, in order to preserve a domestic animal, who dwells in harmony with us. Similarly, it seems allowable, in extreme cases, to wound or kill criminals to protect a law-abiding member of the society; for criminals have by their very attack placed themselves beyond the pattern in which we live.

Within an orderly society, it should never be necessary to resort to force in order to settle a difference; for the methods of composing disputes are among people well-established by law and custom, while animals of many kinds settle their quarrels by innate, nonviolent behavior. In the absence of such arrangements, harmony would be destroyed, bringing the society in danger of dissolution. When one party in a dispute has recourse to violence, he or she at least temporarily steps outside the social structure, and should be subjected to the mildest force adequate to restrain unruly impulses. The ultimate sanction of these principles is that by following them we safeguard the coherent patterns by which alone the total amount of harmony in the world can be increased.

Even within a coherent society, we occasionally confront moral dilemmas which appear to be soluble only by the sacrifice of one of its members. Any settlement of a difficulty which involves the removal of a concordant element is deplorable, and should if possible be avoided. To sacrifice one's life or health for others is never the ideal solution of a moral problem, although it might be justified if several or many are saved at the expense of one. When one person sacrifices health or life to safeguard the health or life of another, it is always questionable whether the world does not lose more than it gains. Thus, if two people of approximately equal age are adrift in a small boat with insufficient food, and one intentionally starves so that the other may live, it is probable that the person who dies is of greater moral worth than the one who permits the first to make the sacrifice. Nobody is capable of judging whether we are of greater or less worth than our neighbor; and it is doubtful whether even an impartial third party could possess the knowledge of persons and the moral insight to give an infallible verdict on this question. Hence when two or several persons are similarly circumstanced, it is hardly possible to decide who should sacrifice for the others.

7. Veracity Considered in Relation to Social Structure

Even if, in making an ethical judgment, we were called upon to consider only two competing claims of our own nature, or the conflicting demands of two separate beings, in each case abstracting oneself or these others from the surroundings, the task might be difficult enough. But we and they are parts of a complex and baffling world, and our decision will not be wisely reached if we confine our attention to the chief actors while losing sight of the environing complexity. It is doubtless because it is so difficult to give due weight to all the modifying circumstances, that people so often follow blindly some isolated moral mandate which seems to be pertinent to their present problem. Thence arise Procrustean solutions, which do violence to the delicate shades of the actual situation. To avoid such crudities, it is necessary to view moral questions in terms of the patterns which moral endeavor creates, to see every problem in its whole context—a method which often yields a clear solution to an ethical dilemma which baffles more narrow ways of thought. This is a fruitful practice, which can be recommended in all moral dialectic.

As an example of this method of reaching decisions on moral questions, let us consider the mandate of Veracity and possible limits to its application. Should we invariably "speak the truth although the heavens should fall," or are there contingencies when we may with a clear conscience tell a falsehood? If we regard truth-speaking as a categorical imperative, it follows that we must believe it unconditionally wrong to tell a falsehood. This is to attach a certain mystical sanctity to the correspondence between the thought in one's mind and the word on one's lips. When telling a deliberate untruth, we insert into consciousness a barrier or warning sign, separating this statement from our accepted body of "true" information. We do this from time to time, for our enjoyment and even for our instruction, when inventing a fable or when reading wise nonsense like *Alice in Wonderland*. Certainly, a single falsehood does not impair our ability to distinguish truth; although the habitual speaking of untruths may do so, as recognized by the adage "Tell a lie often enough and you end by believing it." We cannot categorically condemn the telling of falsehoods, in certain situations not likely to occur frequently; on the ground that it will distort our internal pattern of true ideas.

When we consider the external or social pattern, the importance of veracity is clear. Language, in its unspoken and written forms, was developed for the conveyance of intelligence from mind to mind in a community founded upon cooperation and mutual trust. If we could not rely on what our co-workers tell us, society would disintegrate. A single falsehood told to a member of one's community, even to shield oneself from pain or disgrace, diminishes the confidence each person gives to a neighbor's words, and is a threat to the order by which we live.

But suppose that bandits point guns at me and threaten to shoot unless I give them certain information of value to themselves. Must I tell them the truth, when by inventing a tale I can safeguard my property, or save an honest person from loss or injury? I reflect that desperados are no longer members of my society; by lawless conduct outside the system in which I live, beyond the social fabric which is held together by the mutual confidence of its members. I disrupt no coherent pattern by lying to outlaws; in the very act of demanding information from me at the muzzle of a gun, they have placed themselves in a relation to me which cancels all my obligation to tell them truly. My duty is to preserve the social order in which justice and veracity are respected, not to aid persons who have made themselves of the society which undertakes to safeguard its members against just such outrages. The only interest I can possibly have in them is to redeem them from their wickedness. If, by adhering with fanatic rigidity to my code of truthfulness, I aid outlaws in finding booty, I make their way of life more attractive to them and decrease the probability that they will resume honest habits; while so long as they continue their lawless career, they remain a standing threat to many of the things that I value, including honesty, security of life and property, the enjoyment of the fruits of toil. Clearly, my duty is to confound them with lies if I cannot otherwise thwart their evil intentions.

May we tell a falsehood to those who are desperately sick, in order to conceal disagreeable information which might diminish their chances of recovery? Sick persons, we reflect, are temporarily in a pattern different from that in which we live—a pattern no longer equitably social but centered about the ailing individual. If they fret over their inability to perform their customary tasks, we remind them: "You have no tasks; your single duty is to regain your strength." If we persist in telling invalids a truth which may be injurious to their health, we are adhering with stupid rigidity to a rule made with reference to a situation which no longer exists. When *invalids* recover and *resume* their normal relationship to their community, we treat them with our usual regard for veracity.

It seems a mistake to adduce arguments similar to the foregoing to justify the telling of falsehoods to children, as, for example, to conceal from them certain biological facts which are often held to be improper for immature minds. Children have not fallen out of the social pattern, deliberately like bandits, or involuntarily like invalids. They are a normal component of every enduring society, and nothing could be more important to them than to have unshaken confidence in the veracity of their guardians and develop the highest regard for truth. If, when they ask embarrassing questions, we cannot shift their interest to subjects more appropriate to their age and understanding, we had better tell the facts as we understand them, as simply and delicately as we can.

The common method of teaching moral rules to children as simple, unconditional imperatives has obvious pedagogic and mnemonic advantages, and perhaps this is the only way that such rules can be taught to the very young and to mentally retarded adults. But it creates a false view that all are equally universal in their application, which, like so many of the habits and prejudices that we acquire in our most impressionable period of life, even the most rational people with difficulty outgrow in later years. Likewise, it tends to substitute moral heteronomy for moral autonomy, the blind following of rules received from others for the exercise of a cultivated intelligence inspired by a wide benevolence that springs from one's inmost self. Moreover, in creating the impression that these simple rules cover all the essential points of morality, this method of instruction tends to exclude from the moral consciousness whole fields of activity where ethical considerations certainly enter, although the complexity of the situations may make it impossible to provide guidance in the form of unconditional imperatives.

Because moral rules are so often taught in the same unconditional form as the most universal natural "laws," and as children we are told that it is wrong to lie just as we are told that water flows downhill, we carelessly conclude that these are equally statements of fact, that neither admits exceptions, and that a moral maxim must partake of the universality of application of a "law of nature." This misconception persisted even in a thinker of the force and originality of Kant, who held that lying is unconditionally wrong, even in an attempt to save a friend from being murdered. But if we decide to model our conduct on the "laws of nature," let us imitate nature as it actually is, not as it is simplified for classroom instruction. No natural object is insensitive to any of the forces to which it is exposed, and, insofar as it is free to move, it follows a course which is the resultant of all of them. Similarly, moral beings sensitive to all the complications of their actual situation often find it impossible to act in strict conformity to a single maxim, but must adjust their conduct in the light of all the pertinent conditions.

We should indeed regard veracity as a universal obligation; but to save innocent beings from injury, especially when we can do so without inflicting harm on any other creature, is a principle of conduct which should also become universal; and which of these two rules has the higher authority seems obvious to me. When these two maxims push us in contrary directions, we shall, if we follow the example of nature, choose a course which strikes the balance between them. If I lie to save a friend from a brigand I injure neither the friend nor the outlaw; for nothing could be ultimately more harmful to the latter than to be successful in illicit endeavors, and nothing more salutary than to find a lawless life so unprofitable that it must be abandoned. But if I provide the information demanded, or keep silent when I might throw him or her off the track, I make truth serve the cause of injustice and so degrade it. In this instance, the claims of justice and veracity, taken together, cause me to divert the outlaw by false information, then to rectify my necessary infidelity to truth by giving an accurate account of my conduct to the guardians of the law, to whom it is due.

A lie which we shall be forced to live with in secrecy is

by all means to be avoided, for it will corrode the mind. Such a lie, told for dishonest or disgraceful ends, is in a sense absolute and difficult to efface. But a falsehood which we shall not be ashamed to avow to all honest people, as one told to conceal from an invalid information that might retard his or her recovery, or one told to baffle a desperate criminal, is only relative; and we wash it from our minds when we admit the circumstances to those whom we respect. This rule might be helpful in deciding when it is permissible to depart from strict veracity, but I doubt whether it would hold in all cases without exception. In morals, as in agriculture and medicine, rigid rules are never an adequate substitute for a cultivated judgment and sound common sense. It is for this reason that the very lifeblood of morality is universal benevolence and the will to do right. The moral being can scarcely live if you remove this rich blood from his or her arteries and fill them with the cold water of maxims; at best you will have a more or less efficient machine. Yet good intentions without instruction are dangerous. It is the combination of right feeling, right knowledge, and cultivated judgment that makes the truly moral person.

8. The Esthetic Appeal of Morality

The motives and values with which ethics is concerned are not created by reason so much as recognized by it. The formation of ethical judgments is, however, a rational process—a function of the so-called practical reason. The problem presented to it is not only to join in a single coherent pattern the greatest possible number of living things, but to do this in such a way that the maximum number of positive values may be realized by these beings, while so far as possible all disvalues are excluded. This pattern must be built up within the framework of the environment, and it must be practicable. A miscalculation of the conditions of its existence may lead to disaster. Notwithstanding the perils which attend this pursuit, the exercise of ethical judgment is as strongly attractive to some minds as the solution of mathematical problems or of puzzles is to others. There is endless fascination in articulating our wholesome desires into ever more inclusive patterns, or in blending the polychrome aspirations of the members of a society into a harmonious picture. Hence our inveterate tendency to moralize; hence the interminable discussions provoked by projects for social reform. And those whose purer inclination leads them to weave a moral arras too bright or delicate to withstand the wear and tear, the soot and grime, of our actual social setting, hang it in the clouds, or place it upon fertile utopian islands set amidst stormless azure seas.

The recognition that moral endeavor is, above all, the attempt to arrange living things and their activities in a harmonious pattern accounts for its esthetic appeal. Since ancient times, the good has been identified with the beautiful, and more recently, the Earl of Shaftesbury declared that "there is no real good beside the enjoyment of beauty."[5] As there is beauty in an isolated note of pure sound, a single color, a curve standing free in space, so, too, we recognize fittingness and beauty in a single act viewed in isolation, as giving water to a thirsty stranger, or holding forth a straw to a drowning ant as the dove did in La

Fontaine's fable. But most of our sustained attempts to create beauty take the form of building up patterns, as of notes in a symphony, of lines and colors in a painting, of masses and shapes in a building, of flowers and foliage in a garden. The joining of human desires, needs, and activities in a harmonious pattern is a creative effort cognate with these, which appeals in a similar way to our esthetic sense. Even to solve these moral problems in theory is deeply satisfying to the spirit; and if we could see our ideals realized in practice, with actual living creatures moving and interacting harmoniously amidst the forms and colors and sounds of the natural world, we would feel that we were in the presence of beauty far transcending that created by any single art—a harmony which by combining the contributions of all the arts into an organic unity gives them fresh and more profound significance.

Our moral structure is at first self-centered. Our own needs and desires are the points of departure of our practical judgments, and we weave the interests of others into our growing fabric only when we recognize their pertinence to our private ambitions. Such a pattern is narrowly limited in space and time; it reaches no farther than our selfish aims; it endures no longer than a single life; it collapses when the individual is removed from its center. By its very nature, an egocentric pattern cannot inspire heroic effort; since it has significance only for one mortal, it would be folly for that mortal to sacrifice self in order to preserve the pattern. The grandest moral endeavor can be called forth only by an ethical ideal which promises to survive the individual. It may exist in God or in the heaven of Platonic Forms; to be most compelling, it should be firmly established in the society to which the individual gives allegiance. In the absence of a moral pattern which transcends the individual self, one would be irrational not to be selfish.

Yet even the selfish person, if wise and prudent, will be faithful to standards of personal conduct, no matter what the price. For, as the ancients taught, life, health, wealth, and fame are not subject to our will alone, but may be taken from us tomorrow by any one of a thousand contingencies over which we lack control. Only our moral purpose and voluntary acts are wholly in our keeping. It would be folly to sacrifice that of which our possession is assured, for some other advantage of which our tenure is precarious.

When we make an ethical judgment, we carry out on the plane of conscious reflection a process as old and widespread as life itself. Almost every living thing, animal and vegetable, is in natural conditions drawn by a multitude of stimuli to which it reacts positively, repelled by perhaps as many others to which its response is negative. Often it is solicited by more opportunities for self-completion than it can utilize, or menaced by more potential dangers than it can flee or prepare itself to resist. In a social animal, the necessity to make numerous complex adjustments to its companions is superimposed on its need to balance its exchanges with the environment. Without the capacity to evaluate, coordinate, and adjust into a fairly coherent pattern the numberless attractions and repulsions, strains internal and external, to which an organism is subject, life would hardly be possible.

This coordination of an organism's responses to the manifold stimuli which assail it is accomplished by the same integrative process which in the first place built up its body. Success in fusing into a coherent pattern all its impulses, appetites, and responses to the lifeless and living things which surround it, brings to the creature, if sentient, a feeling of unity and wholeness which is doubtless satisfying, and is certainly the indispensable foundation of all enduring happiness. When the animal at last becomes reflective, success in blending into a harmonious pattern all the diverse beings, activities, and values in which it takes an interest, and the feeling of integrity which thence ensues, becomes its criterion of moral accomplishment.

Chapter Fourteen
Duty

1. The Relation of "Duty" to "Right" and "Good"

THE EXAMINATION OF the notion of duty or obligation properly follows that of such moral terms as "right" and "wrong," "good" and "bad." A course of action is not right because it is our duty; on the contrary, it is our duty to pursue it because it is right; and we hold it to be right because we believe that it will increase the total amount of goodness or harmony or happiness in the world, or at least because it is customary, or generally approved, or intrinsically fitting. And it is our duty to avoid other actions because we judge them to be wrong; and we consider them wrong because they promise to diminish the goodness of the world, or if we adopt some less rational ethical criterion, because they are forbidden by authority, or condemned by our contemporaries, or intrinsically unfitting.

The notion of duty adds to that of right or good the idea of action. Applying standards supplied by a moral being, an amoral intelligence might decide just as well as ourselves that a certain action is right, but he or she would feel no compulsion or even inclination to perform it; for rightness is primarily a criterion of judgment and only indirectly an incentive to action. "Good" is essentially a static notion; and this seems evident from the fact that Plato assigned to the Form of the Good the supreme position in the Intelligible World, where change never intruded. But Duty would be an alien in the eternal realm of Forms, which because it is static could never contain more goodness than it already possessed. "Duty" is a dynamic notion, which could arise only in a changing, developing world, straining always toward goodness, but still remote from its perfect realization. And before this notion could arise, it seems necessary that this world should already have begun to take shape, producing definite patterns of moral relations, which might be injured by certain courses of action but preserved, or even extended, by other courses. Until people could see that certain activities were in accord with, and others contrary to, the system of relations which supported their lives, they could have no reason, except that of immediate gratification, for preferring one course to another, hence no feeling of duty or obligation.

The sense of duty is, of course, far more than the idea of performing an action which we recognize to be right. We experience it immediately as a certain internal pressure driving us toward the behavior in question; it has an urgency and flavor peculiar to itself. Those who hold that this feeling is primary and undefinable call our attention to a truth which each may test by introspection; but they seem to go too far when they attempt to establish an ethic on this fact. If we search for feelings which we cannot derive from other feelings, nor analyze or explain in such a way that one who has never directly experienced them can appreciate their peculiar quality, then attempt to establish a philosophy on each of these primary and undefinable feelings, we shall have innumerable philosophies and involve ourselves in hopeless confusion. For every distinguishable sensation and affective state is just such a primary, undefinable feeling, and might with equal right be our ultimate datum, the point of departure of our system.

It is not by losing ourselves in admiration of the absolutely unique quality of every separate shade and tint of color that we build up a science of optics, but rather by learning how all these distinct sensations are related to each other in their mode of occurrence, and how the light waves of different lengths affect our nervous system. Similarly, we do not establish a science of acoustics, nor compose a symphony, by going into ecstasies over the altogether unique quality of every different audible note, but by considering the relations between these notes. Although all science and all philosophy must begin with some ultimate principles or primary data beyond which it cannot go, our chief endeavor is to reduce their number; and we consider ourselves most successful when we can derive all phenomena from one basic fact, one ultimate mystery. This, which is the goal of science no less than of ontology, must also be the objective of ethics if it is to become a unified science, worthy of a place beside the other sciences. Instead of resting content with the obvious fact that the feeling of duty or obligation, like the flavor of sugar, is unique, we must attempt to discover how it is related to other mental contents, and to trace its derivation from some deeper and more primary constituent of our being.

2. The Vital Significance of Duty

The primary fact of life is the effort of each living thing to build up all its components into a coherent, smoothly functioning system, and to adjust this system to the environment which supports and preserves it. Not only the material components of the body, but all its activities, whether consciously or unconsciously performed, must form an integrated pattern, adapted to external conditions. But life is not a process that culminates in some magnificent harmony which is thenceforth preserved, with no further effort, in a heaven of static perfection. The pattern which is slowly achieved must be maintained by constant exertion, and defended against a myriad of adverse circumstances. The living organism must possess not only the capacity for growth and adjustment, but likewise for maintenance, defense, and repair, for healing wounds and recuperating from diseases. This applies not only to its tissues and physiological functions but equally to its voluntary activities, which likewise form a somewhat coherent system. And what is true of single organisms is also true of those aggregations of organisms which we call societies: they, too, must achieve coherence and the means of preserving it against internal and external threats, else they will fail to survive. The feeling of obligation or duty in each of its members is to a social group what the capacity for restoring its daily waste, resisting foreign organisms, and healing its wounds is to an animal body.

Every coherent society of animals strives with all its resources to preserve the total complex of conditions, internal and external, in which it prospers. When this effort becomes conscious, as in ourselves, and above all when it demands an exertion contrary to immediate desire or inclination, a feeling of obligation or duty arises. But the sense of duty, it will be protested, is felt not so much with reference to a whole pattern of life as to particular demands upon us, which we are led by spontaneous insight, habit, or persuasion to recognize as valid. These objects of duty are precisely those features which lie at the weakest points of the system; or in a rational animal which foresees the future, those conditions, near or remote, which most threaten its disintegration. The feeling of obligation is commonly directed to the points where the system by which we live is, or appears to be, feeblest or most in peril of attack from without, or where it is threatened from within by the failure of spontaneous inclination to support essential activities.

Thus, if there be sickness in the household, the care of the invalid takes precedence over everything else, and the able members of the family neglect other habitual occupations to nurse and attend him or her; for the sickness, and even more the death, of one of its members will cause great changes in the family's way of living. If there be famine, however, the search for food takes priority over every other activity, even that of attending the sick; for general starvation presents a greater threat to the existence of the community than the loss of a few individuals through disease. In the event of war, the activities essential to the defense of the community are held to be the highest duty, because nothing could be more disruptive to its institutions than subjugation by a foreign invader. Although all the activities necessary for the maintenance of a pattern of life are equally duties, those which run smoothly are, as a rule, performed with little feeling of compulsion; while the consciousness of obligation attaches itself most strongly to the weak or threatened points in the system.

This outstanding concern for the weakest point in the vital pattern is witnessed among animals in general, and even among vegetables, although apparently without consciousness of what is happening. A green plant, if deprived of light, will dedicate all its resources to an attempt to remedy this deficiency. It stretches up tall, pale, and spindling, neglecting to form expanded leaves, to thicken and strengthen its stem, and to produce chlorophyll. These are also essential elements in its system; but the most serious immediate threat is deprivation of sunlight; hence all less pressing activities are reduced or suspended until this lack can be remedied. Or, if a deficiency of water threatens to cause the plant's death, the extension of the roots through the soil takes precedence over all other forms of growth. In an annual herb, the production of seeds at the end of the growing season is indispensable for the preservation of the species; and no matter how depauperate the plant remains in an inimical environment, it will often manage to open a few sad blossoms and set a few seeds.

3. Duty as the Pressure of the Whole on Its Parts

Since every animal must be provided with a means of maintaining and restoring its pattern of behavior no less than its organic form and physiological functions, it appears obvious that it possesses either awareness of duty or something corresponding to this. In humans, the sense of duty becomes particularly prominent and complex because of the manner in which the individual's system of behavior is built up from the outside by social influences, instead of developing spontaneously from within. A large share of our habitual activities were impressed on our nervous system by forceful training, so that from their inception they came to be associated with a feeling of compulsion or duty. As Piaget pointed out, the feeling of obligation first arises when the child accepts a command emanating from someone whom the child respects. Thenceforth, every command coming from a respected person is the starting point of an obligatory rule.[1]

But that which reaches us from outside, whether it be food or ideas or modes of behavior, we eventually assimilate into ourselves and make our own, if it is at all compatible with our nature. Thus habits which were in the first place impressed on us become, with frequent repetition, as much parts of ourselves, and are performed as spontaneously, as though they were innate, as is true of so many of the activities of animals guided by inborn systems of behavior. The fact that we lack such innate modes of behavior, whereby we might satisfy our appetites and fill our waking hours with agreeable activity, makes us seize the more eagerly upon behavioral patterns supplied by other people, and so assimilate them to ourselves that we may finally lose sight of their external source and regard them as originally our own. At least, this is the effect of the best and most natural education, which, although it must at times begin by using compulsion, strives to replace this as early as possible by spontaneous motives.

Thus in humanity, as in other animals, the sense of duty or some equivalent inner tension is not primary, but a product of that vital necessity to build up and preserve a system of harmonious relations which is the original spring of all moral endeavor. Why do little children perform a disagreeable duty imposed on them by their parents or guardians? Either (1) because they love them and their affection is precious to them, or (2) to escape punishment. In the first case, they strive to preserve a relationship which contributes to their welfare and happiness; in the second, they obey in order not to lose the pleasures of which they may be deprived as punishment, or in order to avoid the actual physical pain of a whipping, which in turn arises from the distortion of the normal arrangement of the minute parts of the body by the blow. In either case, they act to preserve a condition that is pleasant to them, or to escape one that is disagreeable. The feeling of obligation, then, springs from the primary vital necessity to maintain the integrity of a harmonious pattern of life.

The obligations which, as judgment matures, we finally recognize as valid and binding were either self-imposed or laid upon us by others. In the first instance, we assign these duties to ourselves in order to achieve or preserve some object or condition which seems good and desirable to us because it is a mode of harmony. In the second case, other persons must have originated these commands to achieve or preserve some object or way of life which seemed good to themselves or to the group of which they were a member. Or else these obligations, never "invented" by any particular person, grew up gradually, as a means of preserving the integrity of a tribe or other social group. In any case, the need to preserve a pattern, or the desire for a good, is primary, the feeling of obligation or duty is derivative.

The intensity of our sense of duty in communal affairs is a function of the strength of our feeling of identification with the group or cause whose integrity is jeopardized by some external threat or our own negligence. If no strong affections bind us to friends and neighbors, and if it appears that our personal interests might survive the disintegration of the society which immediately surrounds us, we are, unless unusually altruistic, not likely to make strenuous efforts or great sacrifices to preserve it. Hence the importance to a nation at war of fostering patriotism, which is a feeling of identification with one's compatriots, often with a complementary feeling of distinctness from, and enmity to, neighboring peoples. Another important ingredient of the sense of duty is the self-respect, or sentiment of equality or justice, which makes us ashamed to reap benefits from the efforts which others make to preserve things which we have an equal interest in maintaining, and for which we are equally able to struggle.

It is often held that the feeling of obligation is engendered by the constraint exercised by a society on its members, but this is only a particular instance of a wider truth. The feeling of duty arises from the pressure which the whole exerts on its parts. The whole may be a community, the parts individuals; the whole may be a program of personal conduct which we have chosen for ourselves, the parts the several activities which comprise it; or the whole may be some complex task which we undertake, the parts the details of this undertaking. I set about to make some bookshelves, a piece of carpentry which I enjoy. But to sandpaper the wood, before applying a stain, is an at times irksome detail, which I would avoid if I could. Yet the desire for completeness, the pressure of the whole on its parts, drives me to finish this tedious task; and this feeling of obligation is homologous with that which impels people to take due care of their health, to provide for their family, or to fight for their country. The variations in the intensity of the feeling of obligation in these several instances cannot be ascribed to differences in source or intrinsic nature; for the root of our sense of duty is always the same; they are a function of the magnitude of the issues at stake and the importance of the consequences to self and others. That compulsive pressure which an organic whole exerts over its parts, and which finally produces the sense of duty, is not an invention or outgrowth of social life; although the peculiar circumstances of human society do much to increase the role it must play in our lives, and to heighten our consciousness of it.

4. Duty and Spontaneous Inclination

Some moralists maintain that duty invariably involves a feeling of compulsion by internal or external forces acting against spontaneous inclination—a struggle between obligation and desire. If we admit this contention, we are led into some strange paradoxes. As has been pointed out by Locke, Hume, Spencer, and others, and is indeed common human experience, acts at first distasteful or painful to us become by repetition less so, until at length we lose all feeling of repugnance, and may even find them pleasant. When, by the formation of appropriate habits, we are strengthened in the performance of customary duties, the strain we feel in performing them is diminished. The sense of obligation or compulsion is replaced by spontaneity. Do duties, then, cease to become duties because, other circumstances remaining unchanged, we no longer discharge them with a feeling of compulsion?

Again, it is a rather common experience that on some days we carry out a habitual task reluctantly and against inclination, whereas at other times we perform it eagerly, and are even vexed if circumstances compel us to relinquish it to others. Our feeling as we approach our tasks varies with health, with energy, with the other things we wish to do. Is to wash one's babies, feed one's animals, or sweep the floor a duty one day and not a duty the next day?

To eat enough to preserve health and strength, to take enough sleep, even to enjoy sufficient recreation to keep in good spirits, are no less necessary for our individual welfare directly, and that of the community indirectly, than to support our dependents, pay our debts, and defend our country when it is attacked. But normal, healthy persons eat, sleep, and amuse themselves with no feeling of compulsion or obligation. Only when in ill health will they feel that it is their duty to eat as their physician directs, even if appetite protests; or, when engaged in some constructive work which absorbs all their interest, they may tell themselves, or be told, that it is their duty to sleep more or to take more recreation, lest health fail. Are we to deduce from this that to eat sufficient food, to get enough sleep, and to take the exercise we need is now a duty and now not a duty?

How shall we resolve these paradoxes? Either we must admit that a large share of our duties are performed with no feeling of obligation, even eagerly and gladly; or, if one insists that in the absence of this feeling duty vanishes, we must recognize that the sense of duty is not the prime foundation of the moral life that it is so often claimed to be. The ultimate foundation of morality is that innate striving of each living thing to build up all that intimately touches it into a harmonious pattern which minimizes discord; and since in performing this constructive work the organism engages in an activity natural to it, it will, even if sentient, ordinarily feel no sense of compulsion or strain. The feeling of obligation is, accordingly, a special phenomenon, which assumes prominence when the process of harmonization is carried on against unusual obstacles, or when the vital pattern is threatened with distortion or disintegration, or when it must be slowly and painfully restored after some disruption.

Thus it happens that although we perform a large share of our right and necessary activities freely and gladly, without regarding them as burdensome obligations, the sense of duty or moral compulsion arises only when we are made aware of the necessity to act against some internal resistance of feeling or inclination. This view reconciles our concept of duty with the teachings of the Stoics, who above all moralists insisted on the primacy of duty, and are even credited with coining the word.[2] Yet they held, as we learn, for example, from the discourses of Epictetus and the Hymn of Cleanthes, that the best sort of people perform all their duties willingly and even eagerly, and by this glad compliance with necessity displays their freedom.

But if the feeling of duty is not the prime foundation of the moral life, we must not too hastily conclude that it is a minor or negligible factor in morality. Few of the larger organisms would reach maturity if they had not, in addition to the capacity for growth, that for restitution and repair. And we humans, in the complex circumstances of a civilization that has been changing so rapidly that it is impossible for us to achieve perfect organic adaptation to its demands, would accomplish little if we had not, in addition to our spontaneous impulses, the capacity to persevere doggedly when inclination fails. Most human relationships are not exempt from contingencies when neither affection, far-seeing self-interest, nor external pressure would suffice for their preservation, so that they would disintegrate unless we carried on stubbornly from a sense of duty. The feeling of duty or obligation is the auxiliary motor of the moral schooner, which keeps it on its course when spontaneous breezes fail. However it might be with a creature provided from birth with vital impulses adequate for all its needs, it seems inevitable that for us humans moral discussions should center so largely about duty, that we are often led to assign to it a foundational position among our moral equipment which does not in reality correspond to it. Yet without this sense of duty, we would often know what is right or good yet lack all motivation to pursue it.

5. Verbal Signs Which Arouse the Feeling of Obligation

Because it is so necessary for the community as a whole to keep constantly in the mind of its members their dependence on it and their interest in preserving its integrity, it was inevitable that, with the growth of language, methods of controlling the behavior of the individual by appeals to their feeling of social solidarity should arise. The forms of speech thus developed are logically confusing and difficult to classify. Since they are not propositions and often they convey no definite information to the hearer's mind, they are sometimes regarded by logicians as mere expressions of feeling. For the most part, they are elliptical forms of speech, shortcuts which from long habit have come to imply more than they denote. If someone tells me simply "You ought to do so and so," or "It is your duty to do that, " he or she has advanced no conceptually clear reason for acting; but if I respect that person's judgment, the statement may cause me to examine more searchingly the actual situation, and in this I may find motives adequate to determine my conduct.

Even if the statement which calls attention to a duty is more explicit, of the form "You ought to do A because of M and N," it never acquires the apodictic force of a valid syllogism or a mathematical proof. The conclusion, or alleged duty, does not follow from the premises, or stated reasons, with the ineluctable necessity of a sound deduction in logic. We come nearest to giving a satisfactory logical form to a declaration of obligation when we express it as a conditional, or hypothetical, imperative: "If you desire X, you will do A, because of M and N." For example, we might remind a farmer of a duty to keep fences in good repair somewhat as follows: "If you value the good will of your neighbors, you will keep your cattle on your own land, for otherwise they will damage the crops of your neighbors, who will become angry with you."

This proposition carries the same intellectual conviction as any other statement of fact based on adequate observation; but whether or not it brings moral conviction and stirs the hearer to active endeavor depends wholly on the validity of the conditional clause. Possibly the farmer does not value the good will of neighbors, and in this case our suggestion falls flat. All that the most detailed statement of obligation can do is to call attention to a weakness, a danger point, or a certain incompleteness in my situation; and as I contemplate them, my enharmonization, which constantly impels me to strive for wholeness, concord, and continuity, may drive me to take measures to counteract these perils or remove these limitations. No moral discourse or reminder of duty can do more than this.

In all moral action, the actual motive power surges up from our inmost depths, and verbal reminders of duty are only conventional devices for releasing this force and setting us in motion. They are often signs like the cries of animals, rather than symbols standing for determinate concepts. If told that I ought to perform some act, yet no reason is assigned, I may do it simply because I have such confidence in the speaker that I obey blindly, feeling sure that if I took the time to examine all the circumstances that the speaker considered, I would reach the same conclusion. This is a short route to an ethical decision for a busy or a lazy adult, or for a child whose judgment has not yet developed. If told that I ought to do something lest I be punished, no properly moral consideration has been presented to me; nevertheless, even in this instance the deep vital urge to preserve my life from that disruption of its integrity which punishment involves is the actual cause of my action; so that it seems that a moral impulse has been aroused, although one at a low level.

6. The Sense of Duty as a Conservative Rather than a Progressive Force

We can hardly doubt that our capacity to experience that particular complex of feelings which we strive to arouse by saying "That is your duty," "It is your obligation," or "You ought to do so and so," has through the generations been greatly strengthened by selection. The earliest stage of human social life which has been available for modern study reveals people living in small groups of closely cooperating individuals, almost constantly hostile to neighboring groups. In the endless feuds between tribes, the submissiveness of the individual to control by the group, which even now is often regarded as the most important aspect of morality and duty, was certainly a great factor in success; so that those clans in which the sense of obligation was strong and widely diffused would be likely to survive and multiply, whereas those in which violent, uncontrollable selfish impulses prevailed over social tendencies would be overcome and exterminated. Even in modern states, that sensitiveness of individuals to the interest of the commonwealth which we call patriotism and a sense of duty is a decisive factor in the survival of the nation.

In addition to this selection of tribes or societies as wholes, there has always been an equally drastic selection of individuals. The most primitive tribes had no statute law and no equivalent of punishment by the state as we now know it; but individuals who violate the ancestral customs and taboos lived in an apprehension of supernatural retribution which might have a most depressing, even a fatal, effect on the suggestible mind of the savage. Or they became an outcast from their clan and faced alone the many perils which beset primitive people. At a later age, after strong governments grew up, the most fearful punishments were inflicted for violations of the king's edicts or the laws of the city; and misdemeanors which we now regard as trivial were often capital offenses. In such circumstances, continued over many generations, it is clear that a very strong feeling, almost the equivalent of an instinct, must have developed in the breasts of humans to strengthen their faithfulness to the local conceptions of rightness and duty. A large share of the individuals in whom this feeling was too weak to inhibit impulses which ran counter to custom and law were eliminated by intense internal selection.

We should not expect that the sense of duty, rooted so largely in the instinct of self-preservation, could give rise to a moral ideal as comprehensive and lofty as might spring from other components of our complex nature, such as love, compassion, or the aspiration toward perfect goodness. It has been frequently remarked that Kant's ethical doctrine, with its supreme exaltation of duty, contains little definite content to make it attractive; and Stoicism was saved from a similar sterility only by its cosmic loyalty, rooted in a profound admiration of the beauty and regularity of the Universe, and a desire to cooperate with the universal Reason in preserving it.

It is easy to overlook the fact that the effort of a society to preserve its integrity, which leads it to impose obligations on its members, has no other source than that force within the individuals themselves which impels them to conserve the wholeness of the system, which supports their lives. This oversight, and the processes by which rules were enforced through long ages of human development, inevitably gave rise to the view that the ultimate moral sanctions are external to the individual rather than within him or her. Thus, unless one follows Kant in making certain speculative assumptions about the practical reason which have never occurred to most of the encomiasts of duty, the morality which assigns a primary rather than an auxiliary position to duty is almost unavoidably one of heteronomy rather than of autonomy.

The chief objection to moral heteronomy is that, when absolute, it is fatal to moral advance. Since the principle of growth resides in the inmost self of each individual, only one who has achieved autonomy can be adequately sensitive to it, and lead one's self and one's fellows toward a more perfect and inclusive moral order. Hence an ethic of heteronomy cannot be the highest or final product of moral evolution. It lies between the protomorality of animals who carry on the activities necessary for the preservation of their lives, and the propagation of their kind, in conformity to innate patterns of behavior, on one side, and the morality of an ideal of goodness, on the other side. Despite great psychological differences separating the morality of duty from the protomorality of animals, it may be, in the scale of ethical values, scarcely higher than the latter.

The widespread modern notion that morality is a grim, depressing business is largely due to the primacy assigned to duty in so much of the ethical thought, religious and secular, of the Christian world. To classical antiquity, which cultivated in diverse forms an ethic of the good rather than one of duty, moral discussions and the moral life were far from forbidding and gloomy. An ethic of the good, which gives full liberty to reason to question and test, represents a higher stage of human development than one of duty, which is appropriate for primitive cultures and children, who accept rules of conduct without examining them. The morality of duty is at best an interim morality; or, insofar as the obligations it recognizes derive from the ideals of individuals now dead or our own past aspiration toward goodness, it may be regarded as a crystallized or fossil morality. Of course, since nobody can live constantly at the level of best insights and highest aspirations, the regulative value of the sense of duty is great—a truth which has nowhere been better expressed than in Matthew Arnold's poem, "*Morality*:"

> We cannot kindle when we will
> The fire that in the heart resides.

The feeling of duty or obligation is on the whole conservative rather than generative, a guarantor of stability rather than a principle of moral growth. In a sense, the whole moral history of humanity might be viewed as a struggle between the doctrine of duty, which is so largely regulative and static, and the aspiration toward an ideal good, which is dynamic and progressive. So-called duties are often shackles on the feet of moral idealism. But, as in no sphere of human endeavor can we wholly throw off the weight of the past in our march toward a happier future, so the secret of the moral life consists in preserving a just balance between the duties imposed upon us by the past and our striving toward a higher and more comprehensive goodness.

7. Plain-Duties, and the Possibility of Discharging Them in Full

Yet, as they acquire form and consistency in our minds, these dreams of a more comprehensive and perfect moral community impose their own authority on us, becoming in turn a source of obligation. Thus the sense of duty, which at lower stages was concerned with the preservation of a tribe and then of a nation, is at last attached to ampler patterns which are created in our minds by a wide benevolence. Accordingly, we may recognize two degrees of duty: (1) conventional or plain-duty, which is rooted largely in the instinct of self-preservation and serves the welfare of a family, tribe, or nation; and (2) ideal or over-duty, which is inspired by general kindly feeling or a noble example, but ultimately by the influence on the mind of the creative energy within us, and which reaches out beyond narrow municipal boundaries to embrace a larger realm.

Our plain-duties spring largely from our weakness, our lack of self-sufficiency, our dependence, material and spiritual, on those who surround us. If we needed nothing from others, we would have no plain-duties. But we depend on our fellows for food, clothing, shelter, and many diverse services, and we must return the value received. We crave the affections of a spouse and family, and in acquiring them involve ourselves in certain additional duties. We look to the government for the protection of our persons and property, for providing schools for our children, roads for our journeys, and other benefits; the acceptance of these services places us under obligation and gives us duties. We cultivate friendships, and friendship also has its duties.

Our plain-duties are, on the whole and in their broad features, as a rule clearly defined, by custom or law or both together, according to the community in which we dwell. We have fulfilled the duties which devolve on us in accepting food, clothing, or any other commodity from other people, when we have paid the current price for them, or an equivalent in labor or goods. If we tried to exceed our simple duty in this respect and paid more than the stated price, our neighbors would regard us as whimsical or mad. Toward one's family, too, a person's duties are, as a rule, rather narrowly defined, by custom if not by law. One is expected to provide dependents with food, raiment, a home, and an education, the quality of which is at least tacitly prescribed by the social group to which one belongs. If one exceeds one's plain-duty in these respects, as by providing family with a finer house or children with a better education than is customary with people of the same income, one may be praised by a few, but criticized by many as an ambitious fool, a social climber, or a slave to the whims of one's spouse. Here, again, one lives most comfortably when one does no more than one's plain-duty.

Toward the state, our obligations are rigidly defined by law, which stipulates to the last cent how much we must pay in taxes, what we may or may not do in the public thoroughfares, how often we must vote, and so forth. Even in time of war, an individual's service to country is left less to one's own sense of obligation than it was a few generations ago, but prescribed by law. Modern armies have been composed of conscripts as well as of recruits. The state is usually most exacting in seeing that citizens fulfill their duties toward it, and at the same time it often frowns on any excess of duty. Reformers, revolutionaries, utopian dreamers—all who would improve or benefit society according to their own notions—are almost universally regarded with disfavor in official circles. If citizens wish to dwell at peace with their government, they should give it exactly what it demands, neither more nor less.

Average citizens perform the plain-duties that were designed for them. Although they may sometimes be under stress to find the means for their fulfillment, usually they suffer little perplexity as to what they are.

Can we finally discharge and cancel our obligations to the parents who gave us life and to the community which protected and nourished us in our formative years? This is a perplexing question to which thinkers have given contrary answers; but it is a most important problem, intimately linked with our freedom and the possibility of untrammeled spiritual and moral growth. Aristotle, expressing a view widespread in early civilizations, declared that for giving them life and nurture people owed to their parents and city a larger debt than they could ever repay, whence it seems that they could never cancel their obligation to their community and withdraw from it. On the other hand, the more modern religions, whose gods were no longer protectors of a single people, as Hinduism, Buddhism, and Christianity, have on the whole regarded our duty to our own immortal part as more binding than our service to the society which gave us bodily existence, and have frequently encouraged retirement from civic affairs in order to cultivate a closer union with a supernal Being, or to win spiritual liberation. Today, we seem to be drifting back again to the earlier view, which has its roots in the pressing need of a small tribe surrounded by enemies to enlist the support of every able-bodied member; we tend to regard our obligations to society as paramount and indissoluble. Between which of these extremes does truth and justice lie?

It is clear that our obligation to society did not arise from a contract into which we freely entered. None of us pleaded to be born, nor had a voice in the selection of our parents or the community in which they dwelt. From our earliest years, we were compelled to conform to their wishes and submit to the education they saw fit to give us. Our existence and the possibility of future prosperity depended on our acceptance of the conditions which our elders prescribed for us. From one point of view, we were throughout childhood and adolescence accumulating a debt, whose cancellation would demand the remainder of our life. Yet a more liberal attitude would hold that there must come a time when we are at liberty to pause and assess these benefits, many of dubious value, which have through so many years been thrust upon us, to assay what they are worth to us, and to decide whether we wish to continue to receive them.

This assessment of the worth of one's culture is a gradual process, which one begins at an age that depends on how rapidly one's character ripens. The horizon of most people is so narrowly bounded by the society in which they dwell that they never pause to examine it from some higher point of view. But if, after mature reflection, we conclude that for fuller development of our spirit, and possibly also greater service to our kind, we must break loose from the social entanglements which from childhood have enveloped us, it would be ungenerous and unfair to hold us accountable for benefits received during our immaturity, when we were unable to judge their worth, when our rejection of any of them, had we dared to make it, would have been scoffed and overruled as childish perverseness. At the same time, we should be held responsible for obligations freely contracted after we reached the age of discernment; and, indeed, just persons will not voluntarily default on these. But if we have no dependent wife or minor children, have paid our honest debts and satisfied the contracts we deliberately made, we should be permitted freely to retire from society—if, indeed we can find a retreat beyond its pale.

Even in acknowledging the binding force of obligations freely contracted in more mature years, citizens concede more to society than it can enforce on any of its members; for we may die, leaving our debts unpaid, our country in peril, and our children unprotected. In bringing new members into its midst and devoting its resources to their nurture and education, society, like all investors, stakes its wealth on a dubious venture: the children may turn out to be imbecilic, or on coming of age they may find their culture so uncongenial that they can scarcely endure it. If a community fails to make itself attractive to its members, it deserves to lose them; for a society held together by force becomes intolerable. Good people will not injure their fellows; nor could they with an easy conscience become traitors and plot against the city which gave them birth and guided their earliest steps, as so often happened in ancient times. But they are not obliged to dwell among their fellow citizens, if they are not agreeable to them.

8. Over-Duties and Their Source

The possibility of effecting the full quittance of our plain-duties leaves us free to dedicate ourselves more fully to our over-duties, which are sometimes incompatible with the former. These over-duties are endeavors which nobody demands or even expects of us. No fellow Athenian ordered Socrates to spend long, unrenumerated years trying to make Greeks more competent and virtuous; neither king nor popular assembly commanded Aristotle to undertake the colossal labor of working out his system of philosophy; no bishop or ecclesiastical superior instructed Luther to correct the abuses of the Roman Church; no governmental official directed John Brown to rise up and liberate the Negro slaves; nobody told Gandhi that it was his duty to devote strenuous years to improving the status of his downtrodden Indian compatriots in South Africa. Yet each of these men believed that he followed the path of duty in his special sphere.

While the strict accomplishment of plain-duties brings one the respect and confidence of neighbors, and those rewards and comforts which usually accrue to the solid citizen, the performance of over-duties frequently brings ridicule, contempt, hardship, persecution, premature death. Apparently it was the sense of over-duty that Wordsworth had in mind when he addressed the "*Stern Daughter of the Voice of God*;" for that voice is hardly necessary to remind us of our plain-duties. The remonstrances of family and neighbors are usually heard loudly enough if we are remiss in them. But what is the voice that bids us perform what nobody expects of us, that which may excite the scorn and indignation of our contemporaries?

Acute sensitivity to the coercive force of commonplace duties seems often to make one deaf to this inner voice. Those to whom the mandates and customs of society appear too venerable and binding ever to be brushed aside are hardly capable of effecting that breach with convention which is the prerequisite of moral progress. It is not those who follow unquestioningly the dictates of traditional morality, but those who act in obedience to an insight into the intrinsic fittingness of things, or to the appeal of a vision of more perfect harmony, who lead us to higher ethical levels. The spiritual heroes of humanity are not notable for their strict compliance with conventional obligations. Whether we see them through the mist of legend or in the full light of history, our accounts of their lives point to the same truth. To give just a few examples: Young Prince Siddartha, the future Buddha, abandoned his wife and new-born child to go forth in quest of enlightenment. Socrates was executed by his fellow citizens on a charge of impiety to the Athenian gods. Jesus was at no age a model of filial piety, and as a lad was guilty of a breach of duty when he alarmed Joseph and Mary by staying behind in Jerusalem to argue with the doctors. St. Francis was a wild, undisciplined youth, who sorely tried his father. Shelley, who in magnificent poetry taught universal love, was expelled from Oxford for publishing a tract in support of atheism. The early waywardness of many saints is not unrelated to their late sanctity. Rebellious to the conventional rules of society, impatient of authority, they are yet capable of intense loyalty to their inner light. Were they more submissive to established rules of conduct, they might find it impossible to follow that larger vision which transcends them.

The commonly accepted duties—the plain-duties—reflect the general scale of values of a nation, a period, or a social group. Most people make their sense of obligation conform to these values, to the end that they may dwell in concord with their neighbors and enjoy the solid benefits that society has to offer. The feeling of duty, as developed in the great mass of humans, leads not to moral improvement and hardly even to material progress, but to a dead and stagnant level, the perpetuation of existing values, a Chinese or Spartan crystallization of society. "It is the reformer," wrote Gandhi, "who is eager for the reform and not society, from which he should expect nothing better than opposition, abhorrence, and even mortal persecution. Why may not society regard as retrogression what the reformer holds dear as life itself?" Without the few exceptional people sensitive to over-duties, no social or moral advancement seems possible.

But whence comes this strange feeling of duty, which goads exceptional individuals to antagonize their neighbors, forsake peace of mind and bodily comfort, jeopardize their fortunes and their lives—to risk, in short, all those advantages which the careful observance of conventional duties would place more securely in their grasp, by strengthening their position in the social order? Does it spring from a feeling of obligation directed, like so many of our obligations, toward posterity rather than toward our contemporaries? Or are we impelled to attempt performances, and to impose upon ourselves tasks, beyond the conventional range of human endeavor, by the remembrance of how large a share of all that is most precious to us we owe to men and women who were not satisfied with the mere fulfillment of their plain-duties? Or is thirst for fame the driving force—for the wise know that although people jeer and frequently kill those who attempt to jolt them out of their ancient ruts of thought and habit, they at last revere the memory of those whom they have stoned or crucified?

These considerations may intensify the efforts which courageous people dedicate to their self-imposed tasks, and make them the more willing to endure hardship and slander, but they do not explain the origin of their wider vision nor its compelling power. For this we must look to that internal source of all moral endeavor, that creative energy within us which constantly impels us to order all our thoughts and feelings into a single coherent system, then to attune our active lives to this inner harmony. The wider moral ideal is a product of the same creative process that has brought into the living world more splendor and beauty than utilitarian principles can account for. Plain-duties are obligations which we owe to society and our neighbors for the many services they perform for us; over-duties are imposed on as by the creative energy which pervades us and to which we owe our being. We owe to our inmost self, which is a ray from the divine source of all the goodness and beauty that the Universe contains, services which no person can rightfully demand of us.

9. Aberrations of the Sense of Responsibility

In common with many of the structures and functions of living things, the sense of responsibility is subject to occasional hypertrophy, becoming overdeveloped at the expense of other faculties. When this occurs, we exaggerate the degree of our responsibility for the consequences, both to self and others, of our own decisions and acts. An overwrought feeling of responsibility may make a sensitive mind, especially one much given to contemplation, unfit for an active life. It may even acquire the intensity of a disease, causing a person to refrain from action because of excessive fear of acting wrongly, so that he or she becomes responsible for sins of omission rather than risk incurring sins of commission. Likewise, an exaggerated feeling of responsibility inclines us to view whatever befalls us, whether pleasant or disagreeable, as invariably the result of our own good judgment or its lack. Such a state of mind not only tends to make one overcautious and overserious, but often renders one excessively pleased with oneself when successful, unnecessarily downcast when things go amiss.

We may correct this tendency to overestimate the weight of our personal responsibility for the consequences of our acts by the reflection that, although accountable for what we do, and especially for the intention underlying our deeds, we cannot control or even foresee all their effects, near and remote. To suppose otherwise is to make gods of ourselves. There are so many accidents, or unforeseeable turns of fortune, even in the most carefully regulated life, that not even the wisest can take all of them into consideration when laying plans. In the performance of our plain-duties, it seems enough that we follow conventional standards of prudence. Whether planning our business, arranging a journey, marrying, rearing children, or serving the community, we may feel that we have done our duty when we take the same precautions as the other reasonably sound people whom we know. The outcome must be left to powers beyond our control.

Another form of aberration of the sense of duty, if such it be, is not so easily corrected. From time to time are born individuals whose notions of right and wrong differ from those prevalent in the society in which they live. They come to believe that their neighbors err in their manner of worshipping God, marrying, eating, clothing themselves, or possibly in their mode of disposing of the dead. According to their personal cast of mind and the age in which they live, they aver that they have been called by God to follow a fresh path, or that they have beheld a vision leading them in the true way, or that they depart from accepted modes of acting merely because theirs is the more decent procedure. Again according to the temper of the age in which they live and the intellectual level of the stratum in which they move, they are called prophets, heretics, visionaries, faddists, or cranks. Some will proclaim that they are inspired; others, that they are mad. They will be told by well-meaning friends that they are ruining their prospects for advancement in career, impairing social standing, or jeopardizing their health. Doubtless they will indeed be damaging themselves in various material ways, and having a lonely time of it, too. Yet if, after examining their conscience as carefully as they can, they still hold their peculiar convictions, they can do no better than to follow their guiding light, under whatever form it reveals itself to their inward eye; for there is no higher authority to which they can appeal for guidance. If they turn away from that inner light, their life will be failure and sham, no matter how loudly the world may acclaim their success. But if they follow bravely the star which may be visible to them alone, their course must be deemed triumphant, whether it lead to social ostracism, poverty, ill health, an early and lonely grave—or perhaps posthumous fame.

Chapter Fifteen

The Relativity of Good and Evil

1. Good and Evil Concepts That Arise in a Developing World

HARMONIZATION, THE CREATIVE activity that pervades the Universe, is the primary source of morality, as of life and all its other manifestations, including society, knowledge, and art. To this constructive principle we owe whatever order and harmony the Universe reveals. Morality is, above all, the endeavor to arrange the constituents of the world in a harmonious system, which excludes strife and discord but admits contrast, which heightens feeling and emphasizes meaning. This process began on our planet long before the advent of rational animals capable of using deliberation, foresight, and intelligent choice to advance this end. Ethics is concerned with only that part of the process in which these mental qualities are displayed, for these are the distinguishing features of morality in the strict meaning of the term. But morality, so defined, is only a late phase of a movement that began on our planet before life arose and gathered impetus as organized beings evolved. The whole world is activated by a moral principle, without which our efforts to promote harmony would be unproductive.

Since life arose from a closer integration of heterogeneous elements than had existed on the lifeless Earth, it was from the beginning associated with an intensification of harmonization, the moral principle. But this close vital integration of elements and processes was feasible only in small units strictly delimited from the surrounding world. The separateness of these living entities or organisms, which soon came to compete with each other for space and sources of energy, introduced conflict of a kind which had been absent from the lifeless Earth. The superior goodness of life over inorganic matter brought much evil into the world. Thus in every creature we recognize not only goodness but a limitation of goodness, which we call "evil." How to expand the system of harmonious relations, pushing back the margin of conflict, is the essence of the moral problem.

Moral endeavor, then, is a phenomenon of a world in process of formation. In utter chaos, if one can imagine such a condition, there could be neither good nor evil; for these arise only with reference to a definite order, and especially one which generates purposes and interests, which, as we know them, are properties of beings with a certain degree of coherence and organization. If there could somehow arise in the midst of chaos an intelligent, purposeful mind, it could find no support for its purposes, and even its existence would be momentary. For intelligence can exist only in a somewhat orderly environment, and purposes can hardly be realized in the absence of all external support. Hence the judgment of such a being, as it felt its momentary gleam of consciousness in the midst of chaos and expired, would be that its world was wholly evil because everywhere it beheld discord, and nowhere harmony and order. But the evil itself would be extinguished along with the purpose which could not be sustained in its midst. There can, then, be no absolute evil; for evil can be recognized only by its contrast with some order or goodness, whose existence is incompatible with unmitigated discord. Yet utter chaos is what would be left if all goodness were extinguished. As evil increases, the world moves toward chaos; but if disorder became total, there would be neither good nor evil.

The opposite of chaos would be a world pervaded, down to the last atom and electron, with perfect harmony and order, in which no purpose was thwarted, no hope remained unfulfilled, no opposition or strife persisted anywhere. In such a world, we would recognize no evil; but with the disappearance of discord, we would probably also lose the concept of its opposite, goodness—unless we retained it as a dim memory of an earlier phase of the world process. With the resolution of the last conflict, the assuagement of the final pang, the dying away of the last motive for improvement, moral effort would vanish in its own fulfillment. Morality is always concerned with the choice between the worse and the better way, or between the better and the best; and where all is perfect, there can be no further choice. It is doubtful whether perfect concord is compatible with life, which, on the physiological side, is a process of continuous adjustment. It is certain that living, as we know it, would lose some of its zest in this placid heaven. Yet, as Plato and Plotinus supposed, intelligences might exist to view and find delight in the prospect of endless static perfection.

It has become apparent that moral endeavor belongs to a transitional world, struggling along at a stage intermediate between complete disorder and finished perfection. Good and evil, as we must apply these adjectives to the things and situations that surround us, are relative terms, designating not absolute harmony and total discord, but signifying a step forward toward perfection, a lapse backward toward chaos. Moral effort belongs to a world containing entities which have not yet been harmonized in a comprehensive pattern. The entities themselves arose in ways obscure to us and largely beyond our control. But the process of harmonization is at certain points subject to our influence; and in the exercise of this ability we can cooperate, in our small way, with the creative energy in bringing order out of discord. Moral endeavor is the field in which humanity can most effectively contribute to the process of creation.

2. The Goodness of Living Things

The primacy of the moral obligation to preserve life in all its forms arises from the fact that the least living thing represents an achievement of harmonization beyond the reach of our creative skill. Not only does the mere presence of life point to the existence of harmony or goodness in every creature; likewise, a measure of goodness is revealed by all the activities of living beings, even those which we account most wicked. For no organism can move or act except by that harmonious coordination of complex parts which is a manifestation of goodness. Moreover, it is possible to recognize elements of morality, in the conventional meaning of this term, even in the conduct of the most reprobated of criminals. We might take as an example the thief who delays to break into a shop until the policeman has turned the corner. To deny oneself immediate gratifications for more comprehensive or enduring advantages in the future is an expression of prudence, one of the widely recognized moral virtues. Burglars defer the realization of their desire to possess the goods in the shop window in order to increase the probability of escaping with and enjoying them; whereas wholly corrupt or immoral persons would give immediate, uninhibited play to their impulses, acting without any regard for consequences or any thought for their own future.

However reprehensible their disregard of the rights and feelings of others, burglars wish to preserve from interference by the guardians of the law such harmony as they have managed to infuse into their poor, disordered lives. Perhaps they intend to share their spoils with a confederate, or to use their unlawful gains to buy food and clothing for their family. Thereby they prove that they can establish, at least for a while, amicable relations with one other person, or with a few, even if they are incapable of fitting themselves into the wider harmony of a society. Hardened outlaws who for years terrify a district and defy a well-organized police force cannot be wholly devoid of morality; for their mode of life would hardly be possible without a modicum of foresight, prudence, consistency, and the ability to endure voluntary discomforts and privations in order to attain a desired end, all of which are qualities of some moral importance. Yet even if their ethical principles are wholly egoistic, they miss their aim; for social life offers many advantages and varied sources of pleasure which solitary outcasts cannot experience, probably cannot even imagine.

While in the interest of scientific accuracy we must admit the fact, doubtless distasteful to everyone whose ideals are high and pure, that even those who commit the most hideous crimes are not always completely devoid of morality and goodness, we must likewise recognize the limitation of the goodness of people whom we revere as noblest and best. As absolutely wicked conduct would exhibit no coordination of any sort and no regard even for one's own immediate future; so absolutely good conduct would cause pain or loss to no being of any kind, at whatever distance from the actor. Utter badness signifies total disorder; perfect goodness means universal harmony. Both are incompatible with the maintenance of animal life, which arises out of order and harmony yet, as we know it on this planet, involves conflict in which other beings are thwarted, injured, or destroyed. The behavior of most living things, from the simplest unicellular organism to the human of most exalted ethical ideals, seems to fall somewhere between the two extremes of utter badness and perfect goodness. This mixed character of the people and things with which we must deal is a source of endless perplexity and much embarrassment. How greatly it would simplify our treatment of them if we could classify them as wholly good or utterly bad! And how much more comfortable would we feel if we were certain that we have nothing in common with those who fill us with ineffable loathing!

We spontaneously designate as "good" whatever advances our purposes, increases our feeling of security, or gives us pleasure. Too often we forget that this valuation is without absolute validity, but relative to a particular interest and point of view. The same event which brings us satisfaction or pleasure may cause pain or loss to some other being, which would then qualify as "evil" the very same thing that we call "good." A third party, viewing the matter impartially, would find it difficult to decide which of these two opposite characterizations of the same event is more valid. That which is wholly or absolutely good would cause no pain or distress anywhere, so that there could be no judgment to contradict the one which called it "good." In the actual world of countless delicately balanced or conflicting interests, it is difficult to point to any occurrence which does not somewhere, to some being, cause unhappiness or loss. Hence, as we use them in daily speech, "good" and "evil" are relative terms, lacking in absolute validity. This must not, however, be taken to mean that they are equivalent or meaningless terms, for they often denote quantitative differences. Ethics, like mathematics, treats of the more and the less; but, unfortunately, it is unable to assign precise numerical values to the elements with which it deals.

3. Attempts At an Absolute Separation of Humanity

The history of human cultures reveals the gradual replacement of standards of conduct and moral ideals by others of ampler scope and higher vision. If we examine a series of expanding moral concepts, we find that each is laudable when compared with that which preceded it, but in many respects deplorable when contrasted with that which followed. Primitive humans had a duplex code of morals: with members of their own clan or tribe they practiced the "law of amity," and with all the rest of the world the opposed "law of enmity." There was apparently a time when people cultivated friendly relations only with those whom they recognized at sight and called by name. A great deal of conduct which we now condemn as wrong was right in the eyes of our savage ancestors.

Although Aristotle, whose moral concepts have had so great an influence on all subsequent ethical thought in the West, had on the whole advanced far beyond these primitive notions, his writings reveal unmistakable traces of their persistence. A widespread trait of primitive races is to regard themselves as intrinsically superior to other peoples. This view was often expressed in the name they gave themselves: Aryan, for example, means "noble;" and Bantu signifies "man above men." This pride of race was still strong in Aristotle, who held that "barbarian" peoples, less spirited than the Hellenes, were naturally intended to be their slaves, as animals of various sorts were created to serve humanity in their several capacities. If the barbarians resisted the servitude for which they were naturally destined, it was right to make war and enslave them by force![1]

In Aristotle's moral writings, more attention is devoted to friendship than to the domestic affections; and this, I believe, reveals that Greek society of Aristotle's day was a little closer than our own to the primitive state in which the men's clubhouse took precedence in many ways over home and family, and the ties between warriors and friends were more sacred than those between man and wife. Aristotle's "proud" or "magnanimous" man spent his money lavishly to win honor and prestige, walked with a slow and stately step, spoke with deep and level voice, took few things seriously, was not likely to be hurried, and was dignified toward people of high position but unassuming toward those of lower rank.[2] This attitude and this use of wealth to acquire status are familiar to the student of tribal society, and would be condemned by any moralist imbued with the ethically more advanced Stoic or Christian traditions.

Ancestral attitudes are exceedingly difficult to outgrow; and none has lurked more stubbornly in the human mind than that which makes absolute distinctions between one's own tribe or race or cult and all the remainder of humanity. Although Christianity substituted for haughtiness the ideal of humility, it did not quite succeed in liberating itself from the primitive habit of separating all humanity into two contrasting groups, different in nature and destiny. It made, however, one important advance: membership in the elect group was not, as with the Jews and other early peoples, determined by natural birth, but by the "second birth" of baptism. Thus all who would renounce their unregenerate ways and embrace the Christian doctrine could gain admittance to the blessed fold, and, if they subsequently maintained a certain standard of conduct, attain everlasting bliss. All who remained outside the fold, or having entered by birth or subsequent choice, fell short in rectitude of behavior—all these were doomed to endless suffering. Eternal bliss, either immediately or after a finite interval of purification in purgatory; eternal torment—a more absolute separation of individuals is difficult to conceive. No primitive tribe ever made a harder distinction between the in–group and the out–group.

So radical a separation of humanity could be justified, on any natural ground, only if some were wholly good and others absolutely bad. But every animal, human or otherwise, falls somewhere between these two extremes. To be wholly bad implies a degree of disorganization, and of disharmony with one's ambience social or natural, incompatible with living and acting; to be wholly good means behaving in such a manner as to cause no pain or loss to any sentient being anywhere; and this, again, is incompatible with the necessities of animal life. The difficulties in the orthodox Christian view were recognized by Origen, John the Scot, and other early ecclesiastical philosophers, who combated the doctrine of the absolute separation of souls. It was their belief that all humans, even "devils," would be eventually purified and attain salvation. But these amendments to the established creed were branded as heresy by the dominant powers of the Church.

In the East, however, these more liberal views had long found favor. Indian sages repudiated the notion of absolute distinctions between people, just as they rejected the idea of an absolute difference between humanity and other forms of life. To them, all beings that lived were alike in origin and destiny, and all contained an element of goodness which ensured their ultimate salvation. It is a Buddhist tenet that finally, perhaps after many reincarnations, every sentient creature will become worthy of bliss. In the Mahayana tradition, the liberated soul may voluntarily postpone entry into Nirvana, enduring further lifetimes of painful toil in order to guide other beings along the difficult path which leads to ultimate release. It is beyond the province of ethics to examine the theological and metaphysical implications of these opposing views. Yet they are based on interpretations of good and evil which it is pertinent for us to consider.

4. Moral Relativism and Its Transcendence

Just as it is inaccurate to characterize individuals as wholly good or bad, so it is perilous to classify customs and moral rules as absolutely right or wrong. The growing recognition of this truth is the perhaps inevitable outgrowth of that comparative study of the customs of the innumerable human tribes which was begun by Herodotus, and has proceeded at an accelerated pace during the last century.[3] Continued investigation has made it evident that scarcely any form of human conduct has not, somewhere or at some time, been considered right, whereas by some other group, or at some other epoch, it has been branded as wrong.

Thus, it seems that modes of behavior are not absolutely right or wrong, but can be so classified only with reference to some code or body of customs whose acceptance is far from universal. This observation has led to much confused thinking. Since it is possible to cite precedent for almost any act to which a person's undisciplined impulses may prompt him or her, there is a tendency among the callow and the rebellious to find in this fact moral support for aberrations from the rules which prevail in their own community. Those who argue so forget that the customs of any society, savage or civilized, must attain a certain coherence if that society is to survive, and that the acceptance of any particular practice depends on its consistency with the whole body of customs to which it belongs. The same considerations which cause some practice to be regarded as right in one social context may condemn it in a different context. All this follows clearly from the discussion of right and wrong in Chapter XI.

The second fallacy of ethical relativism may cause more ultimate harm, because it has been held by careful and mature thinkers. This is the tendency to regard as equally worthy of respect all patterns of culture which have demonstrated their ability to survive. A body of customs which for many generations has given stability and a measure of prosperity to a people can hardly be quite worthless; and it is, at first sight, difficult to see how we can ascribe greater value to the mores of one culture which has successfully weathered the storms of existence than to the very different customs which have served equally well the needs of a different people. This view of ethical relativism has arisen in part from a growing distrust of our own civilization, which in recent years has failed so signally to give us peace and contentment, and in part from a nostalgic yearning, growing largely out of this failure, for the simpler ways of alien peoples, who often seem happier than ourselves.

At the very least, we may say in favor of the doctrine of moral relativism that it has liberated our minds from the habit of measuring all cultures by the yardstick of our own, and condemning all that diverges from the tradition into which we happened to be born. It has awakened us to the possibility of finding fundamental human values under an outlandish garb.

There are two ways in which the value of one pattern of culture may be weighed against that of another. We might judge them by their internal relations alone, or by their extent and external relations. The first method would involve the assessment of the degree of harmony, or the amount of friction, between the several members of a society, and of their happiness. Ethnologists have reported varying degrees of concord among diverse peoples. Thus, in Ruth Benedict's *Patterns of Culture*, we are given a picture of harmonious cooperation and mutual good will among the Zuni of New Mexico; of suspicion, hatred, and many-sided distrust among the inhabitants of the island of Dobu off the coast of New Guinea.[4] The differences between these two races are, however, quantitative rather than absolute; for from no human community is discord wholly absent; nor is any society possible without a measure of cooperation among its members.

It would be hazardous to attempt to assign a numerical value to the harmony or discord among the members of a society. Different cultures have been studied by different observers, and undoubtedly a large subjective factor enters into their appraisals. Even more difficult to measure is the happiness of a people, which can be no more than the sum of the happiness of the component individuals—and an individual's felicity is notoriously difficult to assess. Some societies do indeed impress us as being merrier than others. But the cheerfulness of one society and the gloominess of another may be caused by innate temperament or by climate rather than by customs and social structure. The innate temperament may indeed be more influential in determining the customs than in giving their affective tone to the people. Yet after due allowance has been made for all these difficulties, one can hardly avoid the impression that the moral codes and institutions of certain societies produce happier, or nobler, people than the codes and institutions of certain other societies.

The method of assessing the value of a pattern of culture by its extent in time and space and its external relations is more promising, because here we deal with objective features easy to observe. What are the relations of the society in question with other human communities, with other forms of life, with the land and waters which make all life possible? Measured by this standard, the Spartans, whose polity was so highly admired in ancient times, make a poor showing. The military aristocracy lived only by cruelly oppressing, and deliberately debauching, the Helots, who formed a large part of the total population of Lacedaemonia, and they were almost constantly at war with neighboring states. The Greek cities in general, for all the intellectual and artistic brilliance of Athens and others, suffered in varying degrees from these same two defects: at home, a large class of slaves and freedmen excluded from the benefits of citizenship; between the many petty states, continual quarreling, which eventually led to their undoing. Much as we admire the achievements of the Greeks, we recognize in their civilization grave defects which we would not wish to imitate.

The great modern states have overcome two of the outstanding defects of Greek society. They have, legally at least, admitted the total adult population (excluding criminals) to all the advantages of citizenship; and they have been able to unify and consolidate great areas of land and masses of people, so that cities which in the Hellenic world would have been independent political units constantly bickering, are in the modern world peacefully cooperating parts of a single political system. But this second advantage is offset by the fact that the large modern countries are no more able to dwell in peace than the petty states of ancient times. The wars, although less numerous, have increased in magnitude and destructiveness in proportion to the growth of the nations which wage them; so that it is most doubtful whether, in this respect, we can claim any net superiority over the city-states of antiquity. Although chattel slavery has been abolished in all but a few modern countries, there are in nearly all of them glaring and cruel contrasts between the living conditions and educational opportunities of individuals; while severe economic competition produces much bitterness at home, and makes enduring peace between nations difficult to achieve.

The harmonious adjustment of humans to the land which supports them is no less important to their continued existence and happiness than their relations with each other. In assessing the value of a culture, its attitude toward the Earth and its waters cannot be omitted from the reckoning. Whole cities and cultures, as the Mesopotamian and the Old Mayan, seem to have decayed because they would not, or could not, treat with due care and respect the land that supported them. New nations are likely to be more negligent in this matter than older ones; as a country grows populous and brings into cultivation its reserves of fresh land, it must either treat its fields with greater tenderness or else decline. The United States of America has in the present century been in a stage transitional between the thoughtless exploitation of a new country and the careful husbandry of an old one which, like China, had learned how to endure.

In no respect have human cultures differed more radically than in their attitude toward other forms of life. In many lands, almost every nonhuman creature is an object to be exploited, to be killed for food or sport, to be tortured or mutilated as people's whims might dictate. In others, every form of life is sacred, to be treated with respect. The religions of India have made the greatest advances in this direction; but even where the avowed principles are the same, the way people actually treat other animals is strongly influenced by the density of the population and the severity of the struggle to fill each stomach. In overcrowded India, where it originated, the doctrine of *ahimsa*, or harmlessness to all things, could not in recent times be so carefully observed as in Burma, where it was imported and firmly implanted by Buddhist missionaries.

The far-reaching moral consequences of this attitude toward other forms of life are attested by H. Fielding, who in *The Soul of a People* gave a charming picture of Burmese life (now Myanmar) toward the end of the nineteenth century.[5] He wrote: "That this kindness and compassion for animals has very far-reaching results no one can doubt. If you are kind to animals, you will be kind, too, to your fellow man." It is really the same thing, the same feeling in both cases. If to be superior in position to an animal justifies you in torturing it, so it would do with men.

Although no pattern of culture, with its supporting moral code, is perfect and beyond reproach, and none utterly wrong in all details, it is still possible to recognize higher value in some than in others, because, although they still fall far short, they approach somewhat nearer to the ideal of an all–embracing harmony. Even when due allowance is made for the adaptations of customs and moral concepts to diverse economic arrangements, as food-gathering or agriculture or mechanized industry, and to peculiar local conditions—to the arid desert, to the frigid Arctic, to the warm and humid tropical forest—we can detect in certain cultures specific features of universal worth, and point out in others traits which in any ambience would be deplorable.

Apart from their ecological and economic adaptations, which are temporal and local, cultures support moral concepts which are general and enduring. No single culture of which I have information has succeeded in blending into a coherent pattern all the highest moral values, as none has had the good fortune to exclude all objectionable features. Hence there seems to be no culture that we can praise unconditionally, and none, which we can condemn unreservedly. To achieve a more adequate morality, we must choose here and reject there. But before we can intelligently improve our ethical standards, it is necessary to recognize that, although no culture has attained the goal of perfect goodness, some have achieved a wider and more inclusive harmony than others, and this provides a quantitative basis for preferring them and emulating what is best in them.

Chapter Sixteen

Characteristics of Ethical Systems

1. The Concept of an Ethic

EVERY ANIMAL WHICH lives prosperously, preserving its species from generation to generation, has of necessity a well-articulated system of behavior. Such systems range from the genetically transmitted patterns of behavior of an insect or a fish, which probably never deliberately tries to improve its conduct, to a carefully thought-out scheme of philosophic ethics. Because, as we shall see, all these systems, from the most primitive to the most advanced, possess many features in common and serve the same vital purpose, it will be useful to have a single term to designate the whole range of them. Students of animal behavior now call their science "ethology," because it deals with the *ethos*, the customs and usages, of the various kinds of animals. Thus the terms "ethics" and "ethology" are of cognate origin, and both are concerned with the study and interpretation of conduct.

The great differences between ethology and ethics stem in part from the fact that the former deals with creatures who can be studied only by objective observation, and who reveal relatively slight ability to modify their inborn modes of behavior; whereas the latter deals with animals— ourselves—whom we can examine introspectively and by interrogation, and who possess some capacity to modify their conduct in the light of reason. But these great differences should not make us lose sight of the fundamental similarity of the subject matter of the two sciences; and in view of this similarity it probably would not be stretching the word too far to call any system of behavior, human or nonhuman, actual or contemplated, an "ethic." If we use the term in this sense, it becomes obvious that every ethical theory is not an ethic, because as presented by its author, it may be limited to the interpretation or the exposition of a few broad principles. But if it could be worked out in sufficient detail to provide actual guidance through life, it would become an ethic.

In the widest sense, then, an ethic is the body of habits and practices, with its supporting theories or beliefs when these are present, by which an animal carries or might carry on its necessary activities, meet the emergencies of its life, and fulfill its nature. And every species of animal, no less than every human who does not live at random, borne along by the broad current of the society in which he or she happens to live, has a more or less adequate ethic, which may be innate or acquired. Chapter III demonstrated that the inherited behavior patterns of certain animals bear a broad resemblance to human moral codes, in that they exhibit many features which serve admirably to minimize the friction between individuals and permit them to live together with a measure of harmony; hence it seemed permissible to say that these animals who, as far as we know, never discuss principles of conduct nor frame explicit rules, are, if not moral, at least protomoral.

Our most carefully elaborated ethical doctrines are substitutes for the innate patterns of behavior of these protomoral animals, or attempts to improve on them and to regulate our lives by principles that are ideally satisfying. Such doctrines are as diverse as temperaments, social habits, and metaphysical speculations. Yet it is obvious that all which are neither mere vaporous theorizing nor the expression of a hedonic mania, but give guidance to conduct and lead life to its fulfillment, must possess features in common; for all have roots in our primal nature, and all depend for their motive or appeal on deeply imbedded impulses, appetites, or aspirations. Unless it derives force from some vital impulse, the most carefully reasoned system of ethics may command our admiration by its careful logical articulation but it can never move us to act.

2. Vital Impulses the Points of Departure of Every Ethic

The primary source of a living system of conduct can be no other than the original principle of life itself, that creative activity at the core of our being which we call enharmonization. Without this constructive process within us, we could never achieve that unity of organization and fixity of purpose which finally issues in a coherent system of behavior. Philosophic ethics itself, however, need not, except perhaps for purposes of interpretation and wider orientation, reach back to this fountainhead of life. It finds adequate points of departure in certain features of the psychic organization of animals, themselves the product of the operation through long ages of this integrative process, but more readily revealed by introspection of ourselves and observation of other creatures. Among these are the instincts and impulses of animals, their will to exist, with the addition, in some of the more highly endowed of them, of such traits as sympathy, love, and aspiration.

We might picture the situation to ourselves by imagining a subterranean river of pure water rising from the depths of the Earth in a single powerful stream, but before reaching the surface breaking into a number of veins, some of which retain most of their original purity, while others are discolored by the silt and mud through which they seep, and all at length gaining the outer air by a number of mouths and fissures, often widely separated from each other. These emergent streams are the impulses or motives which are the springs of all voluntary action, on which all activity depends for its driving force. Without at least one of them, the most coherent system of ethics would be like an intricate engine, complete with all the necessary pistons, rods, and wheels, but with no fire in its furnace nor steam in its boiler.

The distinctive features of an ethical doctrine depend, in the first place, on which of these springs are chosen as points of departure, and how many of them. Just as we have monistic and pluralistic systems of ontology, so we have monistic and pluralistic theories of ethics. One of the most famous of the ethical theories using several points of departure is that of Plato, whose tripartite soul suggested a multiple derivation of the moral virtues, one corresponding to each of its divisions. The immortal rational soul, whose seat is the head, when sound and of good quality possesses the virtue of wisdom; to the spirited or "irascible" soul that resides in the heart correspond the virtue of courage or fortitude; while the appetitive or vegetative soul of the nether parts of the body when of a superior grade displays the virtue of temperance. Finally, Plato completed his theory by adding to these three a virtue which preserves the balance between them and keeps each to its proper tasks—justice. In this scheme we have the origin of the four cardinal virtues that have figured so prominently in all subsequent discussions: wisdom or prudence, fortitude, temperance, and justice.[1]

3. Single Motive Systems Exemplified by That of Hobbes

More often, philosophers have preferred to set their ethical system on a single support, which permits them to display their constructive skill by deriving all their conclusions from a solitary first principle, and thereby achieving that unity and neatness so dear to the speculative mind. The complex reality of human nature offers, at the level where it is available to inspection and introspection, a number of points of departure for a system of conduct, and moralists are free to choose that which is most congenial to their own temper, or best serves their purposes. Among these may be mentioned the will to survive or the effort to preserve one's own being (Hobbes, Spinoza), the desire for pleasure or happiness (Epicurus, Locke, Bentham, and many others), the esthetic appreciation of beauty and balance (Shaftesbury), the thirst for virtue or moral perfection (Stoics), the autonomy of the will (Kant), the will's tendency toward coherence in its willing (Paton), parental love (Sutherland), the yearning for immortality (Christian and Mohammedan ethics), the thirst for final peace (Buddhist ethics), and numerous others. That from the same point of departure one may reach diverse destinations is evident when one compares the socially oriented ethic of the Utilitarians with the Epicureans' creed of retirement from active life, both derived from the thesis that pleasure or quiet contentedness is the end of human existence and its pursuit the most powerful spring of human actions.

It is highly gratifying to our sense of unity and symmetry to follow the derivation from a single first principle of a full complement of moral virtues, and doubtless the philosopher who accomplishes this is proud of his or her achievement. No one has to my knowledge done this more concisely and—if you grant the correctness of his premise—convincingly than Hobbes in the fourteenth and fifteenth chapters of the *Leviathan*. According to this seventeenth century materialist, the first and fundamental law of nature, which in psychological terms is the most compelling motive in human conduct, is "to seek peace and follow it." That this is merely another way of stating the fact that self-preservation is the first law of nature, and that peace is sought as the surest means of prolonging life and safeguarding its supports and satisfactions, is clear from its accessory rule, the "Right of Nature," which is "By all means we can, to defend ourselves," when we or our possessions are jeopardized.

From this "fundamental law of nature" follows the second law: "That a man be willing, when others are so too, as farre-forth, as for Peace, and defense of himselfe he shall think it necessary to lay down this right to all things; and be contented with so much liberty against other men, as he would allow other men against himself." In conformity to this natural law, individuals enter into the agreement often known as the social contract, which puts an end to the perpetual war of each against all which, in the view of Hobbes, is the condition of humanity in the state of nature. Whether or not human society is of contractual origin, there can be no doubt that, once it has been established, certain modes of behavior, which may be regarded as the practice of certain virtues, will be advantageous to the person whose ruling principle of conduct is to live in peace with one's neighbors. The first of these is justice, which causes us to respect the contracts into which we have entered, and in particular that supposed social contract whose abrogation would plunge us again into the perpetual warfare of humanity's natural state, with all its disagreeable consequences. The second virtue is gratitude, which leads us to requite the favors we have received; for all of us, Hobbes held, give to others only with the intention to benefit ourselves; and if we are often disappointed in this expectation, we will be reluctant to extend mutual help, society will dissolve, and war prevail as at first. Similarly, it will be to our advantage, as strengthening the bonds of society, to be complaisant or sociable, not striving to accumulate superfluous possessions to the detriment of others; to pardon those who repent after having offended us; to refrain from revenge; to avoid hating or showing contempt for others; to be humble, acknowledging every other human as one's equal by nature; to be modest; to judge with equity; and to be fair in the distribution of property. And the sum of all these "laws of nature" is simply the Golden Rule: "Do not that to another, which thou wouldst not have done to thy selfe."

I believe that every unbiased judge will admit that, whatever the motives of those who carefully obeyed all these "laws of nature," their conduct would be admirable, almost impeccable, from the moral point of view. And I think it also obvious that perfectly rational and self-controlled persons, determined always to enjoy peace in the only possible way, within the context of a society, would behave very much as Hobbes describes, giving every outward sign of gratitude, humility, forgivingness, and the other virtues, however foreign they might be to their temperament, and however much they might have to dissemble their feelings in order to bear in public the character of virtuous people and practice the Golden Rule.

In fact those whose estimate of human nature was no higher than that of Hobbes would, for their own safety, be more than ordinarily careful to avoid giving their neighbors the least cause for taking offense. Many of us go through life counting on the sympathy and uncalculating kindness of our fellows to overlook our trespasses and give us more than we deserve; but if we believed that other people refrain from harming us only out of calculated self-interest, we would always feel constrained to act with the suave prudence of a sycophant in the presence of a selfish and irascible autocrat, or with the studied gentleness of a trainer in the cage of a half-wild tiger. The question which concerns us here is simply the matter of fact, whether humans are generous, just, grateful, and the rest, because they ardently desire peace and are convinced that these attitudes will help to preserve it, or whether at least some of the moral virtues are not more direct expressions of human nature, rather than derived by experience and reflection from some other spring of action.

4. The Value of Monistic Systems

Although we examined the system of Hobbes because it is a concise and peculiarly illuminating example of the deduction of the whole of moral conduct from a single motive, the same considerations apply to every other monistic system of ethics. If philosophers persist in deriving from one determining principle others which are of coordinate rank and equally constituents of human nature as we find it, they are not only wasting their effort and giving us a distorted view of ourselves, but what is more lamentable, they in most cases limit the height and amplitude of their ethical structure by narrowing the foundations on which it rests. When we daily have the demonstration that the physical person walks better on two legs than on one, and most other animals move more efficiently on their four, six, or even more legs, we wonder why philosophers take such perverse delight in trying to make the moral person limp along on a single foot, and what value there can be in this mode of progression, save as a demonstration of acrobatic skill. In *Life Ascending*, I tried to show how the general characteristics of humans, and indeed of all living things, arise from the action of a single creative principle; but this operates in the depths of our being, and when it emerges into the light of consciousness it has already been transformed into several motives or springs of action, of the sort that we can take as the points of departure of an ethical rather than of a cosmological system.

Still, we should be grateful to the philosophers who have lavished so much ingenuity on the derivation of all the virtues and the whole duty of humanity from a single psychic trait or a single motive. Many of these system-builders do succeed in erecting a fairly comprehensive structure; and the surprising point is that, despite the great diversity of their points of departure, the several finished edifices so closely resemble each other. Insofar as their construction is sound and contains no false joints that fail to bear the weight imposed on them, this similarity of the final products teaches us a valuable lesson. If these superficially so distinct points of departure of ethical theories are as unrelated as appears at the first glimpse, the convergence to which we have called attention may be due to a highly improbable coincidence; or else we may suspect that the builders of moral systems, influenced by their prejudices and the general tone of their cultures, have been guilty of grave psychological and logical blunders, of Procrustean feats in fitting the most diverse bodies into the same bed.

A more probable inference is that these first principles of ethical systems, as the will to survive, the thirst for happiness, the desire for moral perfection, the tendency toward coherence in willing, and the rest, are so many diverse expressions of a single more fundamental principle, so many separate mouths through which an originally simple subterranean current issues forth to the light. These springs give birth to streams which, by virtue of their common origin and cognate nature, flow over the surface in the same direction, forming a network of intercommunicating channels. No matter which of these little streams we happen first to stumble on, by following its course we are introduced to the system and are able to map its form and whole extent—or at least a significant part of the whole, for most moral philosophers seem to have missed some important branches of the network.

There is no close relationship between the point of departure of an ethical system and its final form, which is tremendously influenced by the moral stature and breadth of sympathy of the thinkers who constructed it. Since an ethical argument can never be as closely articulated as a mathematical proof, they will always find sufficient flexibility in their material to shape the final structure into conformity with their prejudices. How different are the edifices which Hobbes and Spinoza raised on the same fundamental principle! Actually, the only method of judging the relative value of the several possible determining principles of ethical theories is the grandeur of the moral concepts to which they lead, the amplitude and coherence of the societies which they contemplate, and the nobility of conduct of those whose lives are inspired by them. The best ethical system is that which would produce the widest and most harmonious pattern, providing the maximum "length and breadth of life" to the greatest number of beings.

In his review of the ethical theories expounded in the first half of the twentieth century alone, Hill distinguished five main types (excluding the views of the skeptics in ethics), which in aggregate furnish fourteen distinguishable varieties of ethical doctrines.[2] Some of these theories appear to me to have little foundation in psychological or cosmological fact, but the majority do contain at least a solid core of truth; and I believe it obvious that one who sincerely endeavored to guide his or her conduct by any of these theories would lead a life more satisfactory to self, and more beneficial to neighbors, than a person devoid of ethical doctrine.

Far from being discouraged by this multiplicity of ethical theories, I believe that we should rejoice in them; for, unless some of our most respected thinkers have gone far astray, they demonstrate that beings such as ourselves, in a world such as ours, have a number of motives and incentives for striving to lead good and beneficent lives; and that these diverse springs of action reinforce rather than oppose each other. And if we concede that Spinoza, or Butler, or Bentham has rather convincingly demonstrated that one or two of these principles, if carefully and rationally developed, are a sufficient foundation for a fairly coherent and satisfactory life: how much more adequate a foundation might be laid by taking them all together! If one pillar will somehow uphold a structure, it will be indeed firmly supported by four such columns. To lavish vast ingenuity in demonstrating the adequacy of a single pillar is not wholly a waste of effort, if only because it will increase our confidence in the solidity of the edifice which contains several of them.

Moreover, the diversity of human character will include individuals in whom one motive for moral endeavor is strongest and some in whom another is most powerful. Thus the ethical theory which is convincing to me may appear weak and ineffectual to you; and the great practical advantage of having a variety of doctrines, all pointing in the same general direction, is that one of them may touch a vital spring and release moral forces in a person who would be left unmoved by some alternative exposition. Although it is inevitable that some motives of action should appeal to us as a higher or nobler than others, we should not scorn or deprecate those which seem inferior, so long as they promote conduct of which we can approve. As a person struggling to raise a weight which taxes his or her strength to its limit does not dicipline a child's helping hand; so, in a world which cries out for so much moral endeavor as our own, it would be extravagant folly to spurn or discard any slightest motive that promotes this effort. For my part, I have never studied any well-constructed ethical theory without being instructed and fortified in moral endeavor, and without being grateful to the author.

5. Limitations and Dangers of Monistic Systems: the Ethics of Spinoza

Although we freely acknowledge the advantages of having a variety of ethical theories, each striving to support the whole edifice of morality on one or two principles, we must not overlook a grave danger in this practice. Most writers give the impression that they are satisfied with their own work as a complete and adequate exposition of the moral life. Often the edifice they raise is so high and imposing, and we are so absorbed in admiration of the patience which has so closely fitted the stones together and the architectural skill which has balanced on a single pillar so much solid masonry with such varied ornamentation, that we are apt to forget that with a few more supports a grander structure could have been reared with scarcely greater expense, and one which would be in less peril of tumbling down in the first earthquake of humanity's unstable nature. Thus, while we applaud monistic systems of ethics, and fully recognize their value, we must beware lest they cause us to be satisfied with an ethic whose scope and inclusiveness is narrower than it need be, and to rest content with a doctrine less able to withstand the corrosion of skepticism and the blasts of passion than is some more broadly founded ethic.

The fairness of these remarks will become apparent when we apply them to the *Ethics* of Spinoza, one of the most famous and closely knit of all ethical systems, hence one which best displays the logical advantages that the philosopher derives from starting with a single principle. Like the majority of the strictly monistic ethical doctrines, it is egoistic or egocentric; for although one may make some pretense of deriving altruistic motives from egoistic motives, the reverse process is more difficult, if not impossible, to achieve. Of these egoistic, monistic systems, the Spinozan is one of the most attractive and lofty, so that by examining it we may form an unbiased notion of the best that is to be expected from doctrines of this sort.

Against a pantheistic background, Spinoza considered the origin and nature of the mind and its emotions. By pleasure he signified "a passive state wherein the mind passes to a greater perfection;" by pain, "a passive state wherein the mind passes to a lesser perfection." "The mind, as far as it can, endeavors to conceive those things which increase or help the power of activity in the body," and at the same time "it endeavors as far as possible to remember things which exclude the existence of . . . things which diminish or hinder the body's power of activity." By "good," Spinoza understood "every kind of pleasure, and all that conduces thereto, especially that which satisfies our longings, whatsoever they may be; by "evil" . . . every kind of pain, especially that which frustrates our longings." Note carefully that he states: "No virtue can be conceived as prior to this endeavor to preserve one's own being." "The effort for self-preservation is the first and only foundation of virtue."

These quotations from Parts III and IV of the *Ethics* might prepare the reader to expect an antisocial rule of conduct which wholly disregards the rights of others and recognizes no obligations to them. But reading further, we learn that "to man there is nothing more useful than man—nothing . . . more excellent for preserving their being can be wished for by men, than that all should so in all points agree, that the minds and bodies of all should form, as it were, one single mind and one single body, and that all should, with one consent, as far as they are able, endeavor to preserve their being, and all with one consent seek what is useful to them all." Thus, the recognition of the usefulness to self of concord with one's fellows leads the formally egoistic philosopher to socially positive behavior—leads him, in fact, to advocate a degree of uniformity among people that even those whose first principles are more altruistic might find insipid.

But farseeing self-interest failed to bring Spinoza to the recognition of ethical considerations in humanity's relations with nonhuman creatures. "As everyone's right is defined by his virtue, or power, men have far greater rights over beasts than beasts over men. Still, I do not deny that beasts feel: what I deny is that we may not consult our own advantage and use them as we please, treating them in the way which best suits us; for their nature is not like ours, and their emotions are naturally different from human emotions." Whereas complete concord with fellow humans conduces to the increase of one's own perfection and power, no advantage of this sort was anticipated from achieving harmony with nonhuman creatures, because their nature was conceived to be different from ours. Hence the ethical system was tightly closed about the human species, leaving all other created things beyond reach of its mitigating influence.

The grandeur of Spinoza's philosophy lies in his demonstration of the power of the intellect, when equipped with adequate ideas, to control the passions and free us from bondage to them, and in his conception of "the intellectual love of God." This last might have led him to moral principles more liberal and inclusive than those he adopted. It is a pity that he, who reasoned so closely, did not follow this love of the creative power to its logical conclusion in love of all creatures.

6. Diverse Methods of Guiding Behavior

Just as an automobile needs not only a motor but also a steering wheel, so the behavior of animals, including humans, requires not only motivation but likewise some means of guidance. Systems of conduct, using the term in its broadest signification as the whole body of habits and practices, with supporting beliefs when present, which guide the life of any animal, differ no less in their mode of control, actual or contemplated, than do the motive or motives which are their points of departure.

The behavior of nonhuman animals, especially the less social species, is largely self-directed, although not without some pressure and guidance by the environment. A spider, a solitary wasp, a nongregarious bird or mammal, procures its food, fashions its nest, nourishes and defends its young, almost wholly in conformity to an innate pattern, with or without some addition of learned behavior, but with no prodding by its fellows, no threats of punishment for laxness, no promises of reward for efficient performance, no fear of censure, and no thirst for praise. Even in such populous and coherent societies as those of many termites, ants, bees, and wasps, the individual appears to be innately equipped for the special part it is destined by its peculiar structure to play in the life of the community, so that it requires little or no instruction, nor any threats or social sanctions, to keep it at its appropriate tasks; although, of course, the very presence of so many fellows, closely surrounding it on all sides and subject to mass impulses, may cause it to behave otherwise than it would if, with the same inborn endowment, it found itself in solitude or with only a few others of its kind.

Humans, even in quite primitive societies, are more in need of, and subject to direction by, their fellows. With the decay of innate patterns of behavior induced by human social life, it is doubtful whether they could carry on life-supporting activities, to say nothing of rearing their children, without the instruction and example they received from their parents and others during their formative years. Since their pattern of conduct has been impressed on them from the outside rather than grown up along with their bodies, throughout life most people require more external guidance than any other free animal of which we have knowledge. In the most primitive, unstratified societies, still without definite ruling and priestly classes, the control of the individual is by the community as a whole, its customs, traditions, prejudices, and mass impulses. Yet even here the more experienced elders and most competent leaders and warriors, precursors of the chiefs and rulers of more advanced societies, play a special part in guiding the rank and file of the clan; just as, among certain gregarious birds and mammals, the older and possibly more intelligent individuals greatly influence the behavior of their fellows, without bearing any insignia or title of rank. Although in primitive human societies there is control of the individual by the group, there is little coercion or compulsion, no adequate method of forcing compliance with the tribal will and tribal customs; so that, while their neighbors look somewhat helplessly on, forceful, self-willed individuals flout conventions with an impunity that no advanced society would permit.

Although at every level of society, from the lowest to the highest that humanity has yet attained, the conduct of the individual is powerfully influenced by the habits and prejudices of his or her neighbors at large, as societies evolve we find a steady increase of regulation from above, with a corresponding diminution of the necessity for what we might call direct lateral control. On the one hand, there is the central authority, whether vested in a single ruler, a popular gathering, or an elected assembly, which, through its arbitrary edicts or constitutional laws exercises by mere prescription a powerful control over the conduct of individuals. On the other hand, there is the priesthood, at times closely associated with the state and at times quite independent of it, which, by appealing to motives of a different sort, everywhere strongly influences the behavior of all but a minority of the individuals in the most highly literate societies. Where, as in all the older civilizations, the priestly and the secular powers are not sharply separated, we may call the ethical system "socio-religious." From this primitive matrix have been derived, by evolution with differentiation, religious systems on the one hand and social systems on the other.

When we turn from the systems of conduct that actually prevail among large numbers of living things to those merely advocated or contemplated by thinkers, we find a similar diversity in the modes of direction. Those who philosophize within the pale of an established religion perforce recognize the moral authority of its hierarchy. Practically all serious thinkers, aware of the horrors of anarchy and the disintegration of society which would result from disregarding the laws of the state have recommended obedience to them as a general policy; but the part assigned to civil law in regulating the moral life of humanity has varied immensely from system to system. From Hobbes to the Utilitarians, a succession of British philosophers thought that laws could comprise the whole, or almost the whole, of the moral life, and believed that they could be so framed that the individual, in pursuing his or her own advantage, which of course includes avoiding the punishments that might accrue from infractions of the statutes, would benefit the community as a whole.

But perhaps the majority of writers on morals have taken a wider view. Although recognizing the necessity of statute law, at least until people are far better than at present, and the expediency of conforming to it, they have held that for morally enlightened persons the true guides to right conduct are reason and conscience. Such persons will, on the whole, obey the laws of their country; but they will recognize extensive regions of conduct where ethical considerations apply but where statute laws, which after all can establish only minimum requirements of justice and decency, fail to command or to guide. They may at times be led by reason and conscience to disobey the laws, although not without taking into account the socially deplorable effects of disregard for law as such, regardless of the ideal justice of the particular statute in question. They must decide, for example, whether, on the whole, more harm will be done by conforming to an unjust law or by that weakening of the whole legal structure which inevitably ensues from the least overt infraction of its provisions, especially by respected members of the community. And even if the machinery of law enforcement were suddenly to collapse and the community be left in a state of anarchy, persons whose conduct is controlled by reason and conscience would not permit the least relaxation of their principles, continuing to act in the absence of all statute law with greater rectitude and justice than the majority of their neighbors, lacking a high moral philosophy, displayed while they stood in fear of the consequences of breaking the law.

When we survey systems of conduct broadly, we recognize one outstanding similarity between the most primitive and the most advanced of them, but which is not shared by those in between. In animals directed by an innate pattern of behavior, as in humans inspired by the highest ethical principles, conduct is guided largely from within; whereas at the lower stages of their development humans require external control, by fellow tribesmen, by a religious hierarchy, or by statute law, and in the absence of this, society becomes chaotic. Hence it appears that the necessity for external regulation is confined to the stage of development in which humanity is passing from the innate patterns of behavior, which undoubtedly were once possessed by our prehuman ancestors, to the right use of reason in accordance with the creative process within us. External guidance, at least for adults, is a feature of the transitional period in which humans struggle to win mastery of that new and dangerous gift, the free association of ideas, which is the necessary precursor of rational thought. Anarchy, in its literal sense of absence of a government which enforces laws, may be the ultimate, as it was the primitive, state of the human stock; but anarchy is disastrous except for people whose principles and self-control are far superior to those of a large proportion of our contemporaries.

7. Diverse Sanctions of Conduct

The control which we considered in the last section is, on the whole, directive rather than compulsive, and it may impose no penalties for aberrations. The application of sanctions and punishments, especially when this is done by some external agent, adds to the compelling power of a system of behavior but is apt to lead to an unfortunate rigidity. These sanctions or modes of enforcement are the complements of definite internal motives, and without them would, in many instances, be ineffectual. They may be either intrinsic or extrinsic, natural or artificial; and the several kinds of sanctions may together dominate the whole conduct of a single animal.

Although the psychic life of nonhuman animals must remain for us largely a matter of conjecture, we suppose that pleasure and pain play important roles in ensuring conformity to their innate patterns of behavior, for otherwise they would seem to be scarcely more than organic automata; but even with them, the sanctions may be either intrinsic or extrinsic. As was pointed out in Chapter III, it seems likely that at least the higher animals experience a feeling of satisfaction, if not of stronger pleasure, in carrying out activities that conform to their innate pattern of behavior, which means merely that they act in obedience to impulses which are the spontaneous product of their psychophysical organization; while they feel discomfort or a sense of frustration if, because of internal derangements or external interference, this pattern is distorted or thwarted in its expression. Thus it is not improbable that, in building its nest or attending its young, an animal enjoys pleasant feelings which are in themselves sufficient incentive for the continuance of the activity. On the other hand, it may avoid trespassing on its neighbor's domain because of the painful consequences of a clash with this neighbor; and in this case the sanction would be extrinsic rather than intrinsic, although it is hardly factitious or artificial.

At every stage of culture, people who retain a vestige of vital sanity carry on many of their necessary and morally commendable activities simply because of the gratification which they find in performing them. But as societies that grow more complex burden the individual with more restraints and more varied obligations, this intrinsic sanction becomes increasingly inadequate, and additional forces are necessary to ensure conformity to the established norms of conduct. At every stage of cultural development, the approval of one's fellows is a strong incentive to follow the established customs, whereas fear of blame and anger is a powerful deterrent to unconventional behavior. In at least some of the more primitive societies, individuals' sensitivity to censure appears to be stronger than it is in many civilized people; so that, as among the Trobriand Islanders, they may be driven to suicide merely by hearing their lapses from the tribal mores proclaimed aloud by their compeers.[3] Such a sanction is extrinsic rather than intrinsic, but it seems a natural outgrowth of human nature rather than a deliberate contrivance.

In advanced societies, the methods of ensuring conformity of conduct are many and various, and different departments of the behavior of the same individual may be controlled by different means. Thus, the same person may be deterred from burglary chiefly by dread of legal punishment, from drunkenness by apprehension of social disgrace, from adultery by fear of punishment after death; yet exemplary treatment of children may spring directly from a strong parental affection and sympathetic participation in their pleasures; so that in this department of life, at least, he or she requires no external sanctions to compel doing what is right.

Legal punishment is an extrinsic and artificial method of enforcing conformity to a social code of behavior. Because, from our earliest years, those of us who grow up in civilized communities have the police force and the prison constantly held before us, punishment by the state seems the most natural and obvious method of deterring people from crimes, whether against certain individuals or society at large. Yet humanity required long ages to discover this mode of correction; for in the more primitive societies, including not only barbarian communities but even states that had acquired the rudiments of civilization, individuals were left to seek personal satisfaction for the wrongs they had suffered from their neighbors, although by means that were increasingly defined by law, until finally the state undertook to punish the more flagrant offences against individuals.

Threats of supernatural retribution, or of punishment after death, are likewise an artificial expedient for procuring conformity to a code of conduct, but one erected on a natural foundation. Wherever exists a vivid apprehension of a powerful, all-seeing anthropomorphic god, it is difficult to resist the suggestion that this god's displeasure will soon be felt by living people who have disobeyed ordinances or been deficient in humility. Likewise, the belief that some part of the human personality survives physical death is a spontaneous development of thought common to practically every branch of the human family. And doubtless, with growing reverence for justice and righteousness, it would occur to thoughtful people that their future happiness must be affected by the moral quality of their conduct in this life. But the elaborate eschatological schemes of many religions, with their ingenious torments, graded punishments, and possibilities of advancement from purgatory to realms of bliss, appear to be the deliberate invention of a priesthood determined to employ every possible device to enforce obedience to its mandates.

Although social and religious systems of conduct invariably make full use of external pressure to enforce obedience, a philosophic ethic finds no such extraneous props at its disposal. So long as it remains pure and independent of civil or ecclesiastic entanglements, it must find within each adherent sufficient incentives for following its precepts. One who propounds such a system must appeal to moral inclinations deep within the human mind, which prefers certain modes of conduct to certain others because of their greater fittingness, beauty, or adequacy to satisfy the demands of the most constant and enduring part of our complex nature. Such modes of behavior may be chosen because they bring a sense of satisfaction, happiness, or fulfillment, not to be gained from other competing modes; but the preference for them will be independent of any external rewards or penalties that might accrue from them. One whose conduct is self-directed, and nowise influenced by legal, social or religious sanctions, may enjoy full moral autonomy; in the measure that such considerations control his or her behavior, autonomy gives place to heteronomy.

Kant believed that moral autonomy is exhibited only by those whose will is determined by nothing except respect for the moral law itself, so that in making their choice their only care is to conform to a principle which they can regard as a law of universal application. To permit one's choice to be influenced by love, sympathy, desire for happiness, or even the wish to be virtuous, is, according to this view, a mark of moral heteronomy; for none of these things is the content of a law which the practical reason can recognize as binding on every rational being.[4] If we admit Kant's contention, it follows that none of the ancients had reached the altitude of moral autonomy; for none knew anything about such a law; and even few moderns have recognized it. Moreover, although reason might discover a moral law, the purely rational cognition of this law could not determine the will to action; for reason itself is never a motive, but only a moderator and guide. The respect or reverence for this rationally discovered law, which might move us to obey it, is not, properly speaking, a function of reason but an expression of the affective side of our nature, wherein lie true springs of action; so that in any case something more than bare reason is necessary to determine the will.

In Chapter X, I pointed out that freedom consists in conforming to our original nature, but is lost when our actions are determined by passions and attitudes which, in the long struggle for existence, have been foisted on animals, until at times they cover over our primary nature so densely that we can hardly recognize its character. Since the original determinant of each person's being is enharmonization, which is a segment of the universal harmonization, we are free whenever we strive to promote harmony by whatever means appear most effective to us; but when we act from some other motive, we are enthralled to secondary accretions of our complex nature. But it is not indispensable that we recognize the relation of our moral effort to our enharmonization; for were we to contend that this is the essential condition of moral autonomy, we might question whether anybody has hitherto been autonomous. It is sufficient that our determining motive be a pure expression of harmonization. Among such expressions are unselfish love, sympathy, the yearning for that happiness which can be known only by one who has achieved perfect harmony within himself or herself and with surrounding beings, or admiration for the modes of conduct or moral virtues which experience has shown to be most effective in producing and preserving harmony. In short, whenever the motive of our act is the increase or preservation of some form of harmony for its own sake, we exhibit moral autonomy; whenever we obey a moral mandate from fear of punishment or censure, or to win some extrinsic reward, we are subject to heteronomy.

Judged by this standard, all who conform to moral rules to avoid punishments or win rewards promised by society in this life, or those promised by religion in a future life, are still far from attaining the height of moral autonomy. Nor can any ethical system, like that of Epicurus, which

recommends actions called virtuous simply because by following them we increase our contentment or avoid pains,
aspire to the dignity of autonomy. But an ethic directed to
the cultivation of a happiness of which an important component is the feeling of wholeness and soundness which
is furthered by a course of conduct that meets the highest
demands of our nature, and is on the contrary impaired
by deviations from the course which we hold to be right,
is an autonomous system. And even more the Stoics, who
chose virtue for its own sake, cultivated moral autonomy.
Moreover, it seems to me that an animal who, solely in
obedience to impulses which spring up within it and without the least external compulsion, refrains from dangerous
excesses in all the manifold activities of its life and dedicates
itself to the long and arduous task of rearing a family of
young which will return no thanks and bring no material
benefit, exhibits moral autonomy or something closely
analogous to it. From this autonomy, or strong promise
of it, humans fell away under the disintegrating influence
of their nascent and still hardly manageable intelligence,
and aspire to return with the help of philosophy.

8. The Plasticity of Ethical Systems

A few other general characteristics of ethical systems
remain to be noticed. The first of these is plasticity, which
includes not only the capacity for growth and change of
the system itself, but also the degree to which it permits
individuals to work out their own solutions to the moral
dilemmas which confront them. The innate systems of
behavior of animals are on the whole rather rigid, and

incapable of changing to meet situations that fall beyond the range of variation which the species normally encounters. A slight accident may upset a delicately coordinated series of activities and cause a fresh beginning; a marked change in the environment, to which a more intelligent animal might adjust itself and survive, may result in the extinction or migration of a species whose behavior is governed largely by heredity. But, even if the behavior of the individual is rigid and inflexible, that of the species may be capable of relatively rapid modification in response to changing external conditions, effected in part directly by the natural selection of random genetic mutations, in part by genetic assimilation (organic selection), a process in which innovations in behavior arising from individual insight or initiative are supported and fixed by alterations in the germ plasm, for which they prepare the way.

The available evidence points to the conclusion that during by far the greater part of its existence, humanity, despite the dangerous gift of inchoate reason, was hardly more capable of modifying behavior than other vertebrates, and apparently much more conservative than many species of insects. The alluvial and glacial deposits reveal that for vast stretches of time people of the Old Stone Age chipped their flints by much the same techniques, to produce forms hallowed by tradition, with only slow and minor alterations in pattern. The stability of form of their more enduring artifacts suggests a corresponding conservatism in the more perishable aspects of their culture. It seems that only in relatively recent times, with the dawn of the Neolithic Period, possibly ten or fifteen thousand years ago, did the human mind acquire sufficient flexibility to permit rapid changes in arts, institutions, and moral maxims.

Since then, different societies have changed at different rates—the Eastern world, for example, having been for a considerable period more conservative than the West—and, within a single society, different aspects of human behavior have exhibited diverse rates of change. That which most concerns us here, the modes of conduct of greatest ethical significance, have on the whole remained more constant than economic and political activities. The reasons for this are fairly obvious. In no society can people deviate much from the pattern of behavior established among their neighbors without incurring censure and persecution, which may be violent or insidious. The more primitive and homogeneous the society, the stronger its opposition to divergent behavior; and in many savage and barbarian communities any outstanding innovation, especially if it give evidence of ingenuity, is likely to evoke an accusation of witchcraft, with all its terrible consequences to the supposed sorcerer.

Moreover, in nearly all human societies above the grade of savages, and including those far advanced in technological achievements, the priesthood have claimed the right to dictate morals; and they everywhere stubbornly resent changes in ethical standards. The reason for this is clear: the mere concession that improvements might be made in maxims of conduct which for generations they have held as the immutable laws of God, is an admission of fallibility injurious to their prestige, and tending to undermine their authority, together with all the material advantages that accrue to them from it. Only in their infancy, when still plastic beneath the hands of an inspired founder, and perhaps those earliest associates who drink the founder's wisdom from its source, are religious systems of conduct susceptible to much modification in the light of changing values and needs. And, just as they are slow to change their norms of conduct in response to changing social conditions, the upholders of a religious system of ethics are usually reluctant to grant to individuals freedom to use their judgment in applying guiding principles to particular instances. The more powerful and firmly entrenched the hierarchy, the more violently it opposes the free exercise of conscience.

The most adequately modifiable systems of ethics are the philosophical, especially if they can avoid fossilization as a tradition too ponderous and ancient to admit criticism and alteration, but preserve their capacity for growth as a body of living thought. More than all other ethical systems, they possess the tremendous advantage of providing clear and universal principles, and at the same time encouraging each individual to apply these principles to daily living in the light of a cultivated moral judgment. Thus they can, on one hand, remain ever acutely sensitive to the deepest springs of moral endeavor within us, expanding with each increase of sympathy and insight, and, on the other hand, preserve wide-eyed alertness to the changing conditions of the surrounding world, so that this moral energy may be adjusted to the actual circumstances of life and not dissipate itself in fruitless or anachronistic endeavors. This capacity of reason to mold action to its ideal ends gives sufficient adaptability to living systems of philosophic ethics, and makes them our best hope for the moral advancement of humanity.

9. The Varying Scope of Ethical Systems

Not the least important of the features in which ethical systems differ is their scope; scarcely any other characteristic provides so sensitive an indicator of their relative value. A nonhuman ethic often achieves admirable mutual adjustment among the members of a family or reproductive group, but fails to prevent fierce strife between adult, self-dependent members of the same species. Despite the close internal cohesion between all the diverse members of a colony of ants or bees, each closed society exists in a state of war with all similar societies. In birds, however, as was pointed out in Chapter III, we find numerous traits of behavior which reduce or eliminate strife between neighboring families that are quite independent of each other, as well as a general mildness of temper which permits many kinds to dwell in peace in the same small area and share the same foods. Moreover, although we lack evidence that nonhuman animals take a deliberate interest in the welfare of the organisms of other kinds which surround them, as members of a single living community all are likely to thrive or languish together; so that through the ages they have, by mutual interaction, become so adjusted that on the whole they do not needlessly or wantonly injure each other.

The tribal or socio-religious systems of conduct of the most primitive human groups embrace only the few score or perhaps few thousand individuals who comprise the tribe, and perhaps extend with reduced force to a few surrounding groups with whom relationship is claimed and friendly intercourse cultivated. Within this little society the law of amity prevails, but all beyond its narrow pale are treated according to the law of enmity. Philosophers of past centuries who viewed the "state of nature" as a condition of perpetual warfare of each against all other would find little support in the newer ethnological studies; but they would have been correct if for individuals they had substituted petty groups, far too small and weak to establish a high culture. Indeed, the situation with primitive people is hardly different from what we find among ants and other social insects, in which the admirable cooperation between individuals sprung from the same near ancestor contrasts with fierce enmity toward similar societies.

As improved economic conditions permitted tribes to remain intact until they grew larger, or as after their fission the several divisions of a clan retained the same customs and language along with the tradition of a common ancestry, the socio–religious ethic became more inclusive, although there was still the sharpest contrast between the conduct deemed proper toward a member of the same nation and that permitted toward outsiders, who were often looked upon as scarcely human. But as civilization softened manners and increasing trade occasioned more frequent and prolonged contacts with representatives of other nations, this exclusiveness was mitigated. There was a growing tendency to regard all people as brothers, and to apply to individuals of alien races the same norms of conduct as prevailed within the limits of the nation. Nowhere is this process better illustrated than in the ancient Hebrew literature, in which we can trace the gradual expansion of moral sentiments from the fierce tribal exclusiveness of the Israelite invaders of Canaan to the Messianic visions of Isaiah and the doctrine of the brotherhood of humanity, which began to take shape in such pseudepigraphal writings as the *Books of Enoch* and the *Testaments of the Twelve Patriarchs*. That this process was by no means completed by the Augustan Age is evident from the reluctance of Jesus to "cast the children's bread to dogs" when implored by the Canaanite woman to heal her daughter.[5]

Only when a religion ceased to be the peculiar possession of a single people, when its doctrines were spread abroad by itinerant teachers in addition to being transmitted from parents to children, and when its god became the father and protector of all humanity or all beings instead of the custodian of a tribe, did socioreligious systems give way to religious systems properly so-called. Perhaps a strictly religious ethic, as opposed to a socio-religious system, can exist only where religious freedom prevails and the church is divorced from the state. The close alliance between the ecclesiastic and secular authorities throughout medieval Europe, or rather the domination of the latter by the former during much of this period, permitted the enforcement of religious mandates by secular punishments and disabilities, and gave to the whole of Western Europe much the character of a single extended tribe in which, as in all primitive tribes, the religious and secular interests were still interfused. Although the European tribe had become too sprawling and heterogeneous for the law of internal amity to be maintained, the law of external enmity continued in full force, as was all too plainly demonstrated in the conduct of Christian Europeans toward other races, and in particular the American aborigines.

Despite certain obvious shortcomings in practice, all of the great living religions teach an ethic which enjoins the same mild treatment of all members of the human species, conceived as one great brotherhood. In this, Christianity was in the West preceded by several centuries by the Stoic philosophy, which had so powerful an influence on the liberal policy of the Roman Empire at the height of its glory, and has left its permanent imprint on Western thought. Although alike in advocating equal treatment of all people, the more advanced religions differ vastly in their attitude toward other living things. Christian ethics has practically nothing to say about human treatment of other animals; the West's growing, but still far from adequate, tenderness toward nonhuman creatures owes more to its poets and students of nature than to ecclesiastical sources, and it can find stronger support in the *Old Testament* than in the *New*. The more universal scope of Eastern religions, such as Jainism, Hinduism, Buddhism, and Taoism, includes concern for all living things. One could hardly ask for an ethic more inclusive than that of the Jaina ascetic, whose every movement is regulated with a view to avoiding injury to the least sentient being.

A survey of Western philosophic ethics reveals the same slow broadening of scope, and the same present limitations, as we find in Western religious ethics; but as we have already touched upon this subject in Chapter I, it need not detain us longer here.

10. The Propagation and Survival of Ethical Systems

Finally, systems of conduct, like the species of living things, differ in their means of propagation and length of life. As with animals and plants, their survival depends largely on the efficiency of their method of reproduction. Since innate patterns of behavior are transmitted genetically in the same manner as the physical characters of animals, they tend to survive as long as the species itself. They may change slowly, or at times even somewhat swiftly, just as bodily characters change; and their disintegration by genetic accidents is no less likely to cause the extinction of the species than physical malformations that arise in the same way. If we gauge the value of an ethic by the length of time it has survived without radical alterations and the number of lives to which it has brought stability and perhaps also a measure of happiness, none ranks higher or is more worthy of our respect and earnest study than some of the instinctive systems. Perhaps only a poet can bring home to our imagination the antiquity of some of these systems of behavior, beside which our most ancient human institutions are the creations of yesterday, and none has to my knowledge done this better than John Collings Squire in the following verses:

> O let your strong imagination turn
> The great wheel backward, until Troy unburn,
> And then unbuild, and seven Troys below
> Rise out of death, and dwindle, and outflow,
> Till all have passed, and none has yet been there;

> Back, ever back. Our birds still crossed the air;
> Beyond our myriad changing generations
> Still built, unchanged, their known inhabitations.[6]

It might repay us to devote more attention to the deep vital roots of the instinctive behavior of animals, to strive to discover still lurking stubbornly within ourselves vestiges of similar impulses and motives, and to try whether on such strong and wholesome organic foundations we can erect an ethic broader in scope and more adequate to our needs than those which have hitherto been offered to us.

In tribal or socioreligious systems, continuity of tradition supplements the continuity of the germ-plasm. The traits of behavior are still passed from parents to children, but example and instruction now play the leading part, and genetic transmission is correspondingly pushed into the background. The ultimate survival of such a system of conduct is closely linked with that of the society which practices it; and the peculiar rites and customs of many a tribe have been utterly lost with the extermination of the people to whom they failed to bring prosperity.

When the church has been separated from the state and a variety of religions spring up in a community, the perpetuity of any one of them is less assured than when the whole society is permeated by a single cult and modes of conduct having a religious sanction are scarcely to be distinguished from those imposed by the state. Even where religious toleration prevails, children are likely to retain the faith of their parents, which has saturated their earliest and most impressionable years. But, as they grow to maturity, they may come under the spell of rival creeds and hear the persuasive discourses of their expounders; so that where full religious freedom prevails, the survival of any particular faith depends in larger measure on the intrinsic appeal of its doctrines, the attractiveness of its ritual, and the eloquence of its ministers.

Even more than with religions under a regime of fullest liberty, the propagation and survival of a philosophic ethic depends on the persuasiveness and example of its exponents. Lacking rites in which even children can participate, lacking the continuity provided by a temple and a congregation, these doctrines which can hardly be understood without some sustained mental effort, first make their appeal to youths striving to discover the significance of life, or to older people who have outgrown their inherited beliefs. In the absence of teachers to persuade by their words and win respect by the example of their conduct, a philosophic ethic remains a mere academic exposition which rarely determines the course of a life. In ancient times, when devoted individuals not only thought philosophy but strove to live in conformity with its doctrines, systems like those of the Stoics, the Peripatetics, and the Epicureans were powers in society. In modern times, when philosophers are for the most part only investigators and expositors, satisfied if they can write books or discourse learnedly from an academic chair, philosophic ethics can scarcely be said to live, but remains a field for abstract and largely sterile speculation.

Despite the unavoidable brevity of this comparative survey of ethical systems, certain important conclusions stand forth clearly from it. Although we have given reasons for believing that all moral endeavor springs from a single source at the core of our being, this escapes our ordinary introspection, and at the level of consciousness has already become transformed into a number of impulses or motives, which together determine our moral effort. But, in the interest of logical conciseness and neatness of exposition, philosophers have often preferred to single out one or two of these possible points of departure for an ethical doctrine and to support their whole system on them. Although, in many instances, we cannot but admire the coherence they achieve, and the skill they display in balancing a vast superstructure on a slender foundation, this structure is never as adequate as it might have become if they had deigned to rest it upon all available supports. Hence it rarely satisfies the demands of our inmost nature, and for this reason it fails to arouse the moral energy requisite for active endeavor; so that ethical systems remain subjects for academic discussion rather than the inspiration of a devoted life, as in ancient times. Without teachers who bring conviction by their example no less than by their words, these systems fail to win disciples, who exert a powerful influence on their times. Given the conservatism which has long prevailed in the field of religion, if philosophic systems of ethics, more sensitive to new influences and better able to employ reason for the adjustment of means to ends, do not become a living force, the moral life of a community tends to stagnate rather than to advance steadily to higher levels.

Chapter Seventeen

The Foundations of a
Universal Ethic

1. The Necessity of Recognizing All-pertinent Motives

THE PHENOMENA OF inorganic nature, and even more those of life, are so complex that the human mind can hardly think about them without great simplification. We like to assign to each event a single cause, conveniently forgetting that scarcely anything happens without a number of cooperating circumstances, and that our so-called "cause" is merely the last, or the most conspicuous, or the most inconstant, of the contributing factors. Thus we are in the habit of saying that the tides are caused by the Moon, overlooking the Sun's great influence on them.

In vital phenomena, especially, our inveterate habit of assigning to each event a single cause leads to loose and careless thinking. We would often go astray if we attempted to correlate the blossoming of a tree solely with changes in temperature, paying no attention to such important influences as rainfall, length of daylight, composition of the soil, and interval conditions still more difficult to analyze. Biologists have become increasingly skeptical of single-factor explanations. Yet for several centuries, there has been in Western philosophy a persistent attempt to attribute one of the highest endeavors of one of the most complex of organisms to a single factor, establishing whole systems of ethics on the instinct of self-preservation, the calculating pursuit of personal happiness, the sense of duty, or whatnot. No wonder that none of these systems has succeeded in comprising the whole breadth and richness of moral endeavor or of satisfying our ethical needs, and that the increase of systems has led only to increasing perplexity and doubt.

The only remedy for this unhappy situation appears to be resolutely to forgo the satisfaction of attaining monistic neatness by drawing deduction after deduction from a solitary premise, like children playing with wooden blocks and trying to raise a high tower on a single one as base. Our method must be quite the reverse; we must begin with a survey of human nature in all its complexity, picking out every one of its components, which has ethical significance and might serve as a support for moral endeavor. What matter if, at the level where we first surprise them, we cannot discover their interconnections nor trace their development from a single source, so that our self-regarding impulses seem unrelated to our altruistic impulses, our desire for perfection distinct from our yearning for happiness. As biologists or psychologists, we may never be content until we have traced every aspect of human nature to one source; as moralists, our business is gratefully to accept, just as we find it, every impulse and every appetite which might contribute to moral endeavor, and to employ our skill, not in time-consuming dissections, but in guiding these impulses to fruition in a morally satisfying life.

In earlier chapters, I tried to show that all psychic traits of moral significance, including conscience, love, sympathy, the sense of duty, and esthetic appreciation, are outgrowths of that integrative activity at the very foundation of our being which tends always to arrange all things in coherent aggregates. Whether the reader accepts this conclusion is, for our present purposes, not entirely necessary. It is enough if we recognize the presence of these modes of thought and feeling within ourselves, and agree that, in the broadest terms, the whole endeavor of morality is to increase harmony among the components of the world, creating a coherent pattern not only as ample and inclusive as we can make it, but also as perfect in all its details. In the present chapter, we shall muster in review all those components of human nature, discussed in earlier chapters, which may serve as the foundation for a wider ethic.

2. Virtues Derived from the Will to Live

It is a trite remark that self-preservation is the first law of nature, and it is equally true that the preservation of one's own being is the first principle of ethics. A number of moralists including Spinoza and Hobbes have based their whole system on this motive. The Stoics, too, gave this principle a foundational position in their doctrine, and one of their most prolific writers, Chrysippus, is reported to have said, "The dearest thing to every animal is its own constitution and its consciousness thereof."[1] In more recent times, Spencer gave full recognition to the moral importance of this deepest impulse of our nature, and of all animate nature.

The moral importance of preserving oneself is not only that we cannot be good and virtuous unless we exist, a truth too obvious to detain us; it is that life is hardly possible without that harmonious coordination of all the parts and functions of an organism which we may take as the prototype of goodness and a standard for moral endeavor. Even if the mere prolongation of life could satisfy us, we could not achieve it without a certain amount of moral effort, or some innate equivalent thereof. Temperance and prudence, as was pointed out in Chapter III, are natural virtues, which we find exemplified in every animal that stops eating when its need is satisfied, or refuses to jeopardize its life for the immediate gratification of appetite. If in them these reactions are unreflective and automatic, our own self-conscious temperance and prudence are achieved largely by opposing to the appetite that tempts us to present indulgence or gratification the imagination of disagreeable consequences. Patience, too, and fortitude are essential for the preservation of life amidst the difficulties and perils which often beset it, and they have their roots deep in animal nature. Without putting the least strain on the principle of self-preservation, we can support on it roughly half of the moral virtues; but we should beware lest this easy deduction tempt us to pile the remainder upon the same vital foundation.

Few people are content simply to exist, reproduce their kind, and thereafter pass into nothingness. They find satisfaction in the efficient performance of the activities necessary for the maintenance of life in whatever circumstances they are placed, and they are pleased when this proficiency is recognized by their fellows. Although the particular skills and accomplishments most highly valued vary greatly from culture to culture, and from class to class in the same society, each takes pride in his or her competence in them, and this is a powerful incentive to the cultivation of virtue. Moreover, we thirst to fill our lives with agreeable activities and significant experiences, even when these are not essential to its preservation. This desire to complete and fulfill our lives may take the form of an insatiable thirst for knowledge or a burning aspiration for holiness, or it may spur us to dedicate all our energies to acquire outstanding skill in one of the arts, or it may lead us to surround ourselves with agreeable friends and beautiful objects. We develop an ideal of personal perfection, which certainly owes much to our desire to win a respected place in society by the display of the accomplishments and the exercise of the virtues which it most appreciates, but which at its highest far transcend the demands of society and substitutes for the approbation of other people the inspiration of some archetype of perfection, or at times merely the approval of conscience. Although it is difficult to conceive an ideal of perfection that has not grown out of the experiences of communal life, such an ideal is by no means limited by the needs or approval of society. Like so many other manifestations of life whose form has been in the main determined by the pressure of the environment, our ideal at last far transcends the demands of the environment, impelled to greater heights by an internal force.

3. Virtues Derived from Parental Impulses

Although the same immanent activity which causes us to grow into complex organisms and to exert all our strength to preserve life impels us also to crown life with an ideal perfection, the form of this ideal is profoundly influenced by our relation to a larger whole. We are driven by the most powerful impulses not only to complete ourselves but to give ourselves; and unless we weave this second demand into our ideal of perfection, we shall hardly rest satisfied with it. These two contrasting motives undoubtedly spring from the same source, the creative activity to which we owe our being; but, at the level where they enter consciousness, it is scarcely possible to trace the connection between them; for the instinct of self-preservation and the attitudes to which it gives rise often seem diametrically opposed to the impulses which reach beyond ourselves and culminate in altruism. Indeed, in many organisms self-preservation and reproduction are incompatible and mutually exclusive; the laying of eggs leads promptly to the death of the parent. But in humans, as in most warm-blooded vertebrates, a higher integration has been effected, with the result that the self-regarding and other-regarding motives exist side by side and complement each other, although often not without a struggle to strike a balance and come to terms.

Some thinkers have attempted to derive this second aspect of our nature from the first, tracing all our apparent altruism to farseeing self-interest; but to prove their case, they would have to demonstrate not only that our human zeal to protect and defend our children, but the corresponding behavior in every nonhuman animal, is so derived. Since this would make vast assumptions about the ability of such animals as wasps and fishes to unravel intricate relationships, we must reject it in favor of the simpler view that the other-regarding impulses are an innate component of our nature, and that in the animal kingdom they first appear in the form of parental solicitude. Just as, without performing feats of verbal jugglery, we derive such virtues as prudence, temperance, and fortitude from the instinct of self-preservation, so, in an equally direct and unstrained manner, we trace love, sympathy, generosity, compassion, and charity from this second side of our nature. And so much are these affections and attitudes parts of ourselves, that we can hardly be satisfied with an ideal of personal perfection, which omits them.

4. Love of Beauty and Respect for Form as Moral Motives

The two foregoing motives of human endeavor, one impelling us to preserve and perfect ourselves and the other driving us to consider the welfare of others, must certainly be given coordinate positions in the foundation of any system of human conduct because the attempt to pile one upon the other can only result in a distorted and unstable structure. But other motives, scarcely inferior in importance, will give added breadth and stability to our moral edifice, yet cannot easily be derived from either of the foregoing motives, so that they, too, must be placed in foundational positions. These are our love of beauty and our respect for form and order, which are closely allied and doubtless are diverse expressions of a single primitive psychic quality. From ancient times, philosophers have recognized that the good is also the beautiful; and Shaftesbury established his ethic on this identification.[2] Because we spontaneously love beauty, appreciation of the beauty of a harmoniously ordered life might impel us strenuously to cultivate it, even in the absence of all other incentives.

Had we no other motive for moral endeavor, reverence for form might make us moral. Life imposes form on the crude materials of the world and cannot exist in the absence of such organization. When we view ourselves externally, we are a definite form. Each of the living things which surround us is above all a specific form with an associated process, and that it is something more is largely an inference. Moreover, nearly everything useful to us, whether made by us or furnished by nature, is so by virtue of its form. Thus, as we grow in insight and sensitivity, awareness of what we are, no less than reverence for the source of our being, make us reluctant to destroy forms which it is beyond our power to create. If we cannot prove to the skeptic's satisfaction that we inflict pain on other living things when we tear or maim them, respect for their marvellously intricate forms should make us hesitate to injure even the least of them, except under the pressure of the sternest necessity. Moreover, every moral situation has, as a reciprocal relationship, an ideal form, which we cannot perceive without regarding it with that respect and admiration which every balanced form inspires in us, so that we are pained by its distortion or destruction, even when we suffer no personal loss. Justice in particular is an aspect of form, usually symbolized by the weighing scales; in addition to all other attractions, it has a strong esthetic appeal.

If some think that we have admitted too many incentives to good actions, and that all genuinely moral conduct can be reduced to the operation of a single primary motive which assumes diverse guises as it ramifies through our life, let them pass in review their deeds of the past day or month and see whether all those of moral worth can be so explained. If they live, not in a crowded city, but in contact with the wider world of nature, as on a farm, such an examination will be more convincing. Now they refrain from eating too much of some tempting but rather indigestible dish, and such prudent temperance is motivated by self-interest. Now they help a sick neighbor much poorer than themselves, doubtless without the reflection that some day they may find themselves in similar plight and require the return of their kindness; and their conduct in this instance seems to be inspired by unselfish altruism. Now they release a butterfly that has blundered into a room and cannot find its way out, and this is charity or compassion. Now, in the course of cleaning their grounds, they take pains to preserve a shrub or tree of no economic importance, simply because it is beautiful; since it adds something to the loveliness of the world their effort to save it is certainly a moral act, inspired by love of beauty. Let anyone take the trouble to subject some brief interval in his or her life to similar scrutiny, and I believe that he or she will agree with Martineau that "no constant aim, no one royal faculty, no contemplated preponderance of happy effects, can really be found in all good action."[3]

5. Conscience the Cement of the Moral Structure

The will to live and to perfect ourselves, an innate altruism, love of beauty, and respect for form—these are the foundation stones on which an ethic can be built foursquare; and we cannot relinquish one of them without narrowing and imperiling our structure. Although no ethical system can dispense with conscience, I have not given it a foundational position, because as an integrative principle it is the binding force of our structure rather than one of its supports. One might call conscience the cement of the moral edifice. We have as the basis for our system four motives, separate where they appear above the level of the ground, and often seeming unrelated or even antagonistic to each other, as when self-interest impels us one way and altruism another. Without conscience to mediate between them and bring them into harmony, they could never become the supports of a coherent structure.

Conscience is the expression in consciousness of the enharmonization which acts ceaselessly to bind into a coherent whole all the diverse constituents of our bodies and our minds. We are aware of it chiefly as the disquietude that we feel whenever any of the perceived and recognized components of our active life, especially those under voluntary control, as our deeds and our principles, our words and our ideas, are out of alignment; and it does not permit us to rest content until such disharmonies have been rectified. One might say that to relieve oneself of the distress caused by a troubled conscience is a motive for action, an aspect of the pleasure-pain motive; so that conscience should be given a foundational position in our system. This distress that we experience whenever we detect disharmony among the constituents of our life, especially those to which we assign moral significance—this calmness and peace which we enjoy when no disharmony is evident—are just conscience itself; so that it must be recognized as a spring of action. But even if we choose to consider it a motive, it cannot be a primary motive; for unless we already had moral impulses, which we failed to heed, or carried out imperfectly, or which came into conflict with each other, we would never experience twinges and pangs of conscience.

Nor can a foundational position be conceded to the sense of duty, which is hardly to be distinguished from conscience. If, as was contended in Chapter XIV, we do not feel the pressure of duty until the structure of our lives, individual or social, is imperiled either by external threat or the failure of spontaneous inclination to support the demands of the situation, duty presupposes this structure hence it cannot be part of its foundation. Likewise, we refrain from placing at the ground level such powerful auxiliaries of the moral life as reverence or attachment to goodness for its own sake, and love of knowledge and truth. Before we can revere goodness we must form the ideal of goodness, and this must grow out of those more primitive components of our nature which we have set in the foundation. Humans first value knowledge because it helps us to satisfy our desires and avoid perils, and only gradually does it become precious for its own sake. Reverence for goodness and love of knowledge are outgrowths of that preference for coherence, order, and form which is an original constituent of our nature and undermines them. It is not surprising that, on such contracted and corroded foundations, the utmost skill of moral philosophers scarcely avails to raise an ethical structure that commands our admiration and satisfies the demands of our nature.

6. The Intuitive Element in Every Satisfying Ethical Doctrine

In addition to those primary motives of action which are the mainspring of all moral endeavor and the conscience which demands coherence in our lives, certain other points must be considered before we attempt to build an ample and satisfying moral edifice. The first of these is whether we have moral intuitions, and, if so, what is their importance. Scarcely any serious thinker, I believe, still maintains that we possess moral intuitions in the form of specific rules of conduct, such as "Thou shalt not kill," or "Thou shalt not steal." Nor is it demonstrable that we possess innate moral principles in a more general form, such for example, as might determine us, prior to all experience, to make the maximum happiness of humanity, or the cultivation of personal perfection, the guiding principle of our lives.

Nevertheless, I believe that, in its broadest terms, the contention of the Intuitive School contains too much truth to be lightly brushed aside or neglected in the construction of an ethical doctrine. We are so constituted that certain determining motives and modes of conduct appeal to us as higher, nobler, or more worthy of ourselves than certain other determining motives and modes of conduct, some of which appear intrinsically petty, ignoble, or vile. This evaluation does not grow out of our experience of the effects on self and others of the motives or the conduct in question, but is an intuitive appraisal of the decision or the act itself, according to its intrinsic qualities. It is hardly necessary to point out that we can pass no judgment on the aspects of a deed prior to our experience thereof; yet the form of the judgment is determined by something within ourselves that owes nothing to our individual experience.

A moral intuition, then, does not enter consciousness as a general principle or maxim, nor yet as a commandment to act in a certain way, but is more vague and indefinite. It gives a general direction to our moral endeavor without determining its details; it imposes a condition, which our ideals and conduct must fulfill in order to satisfy us. As long as our professed maxims conflict with our intuition, we feel restless and ill at ease; when they correspond, we begin to find peace. As to what this moral intuition is, I hold that it is basically the recognition that harmony accords better than discord with our nature, whence it follows that we prefer the wider harmony to the narrower, and of two patterns of equal scope, the more coherent to the less coherent.

Nevertheless, humans often delight in strife and discord, as the warrior in battle and the contentious person in heated argument. But perhaps the chief source of the warrior's delight in the fray, in the days when a battle was not a diabolical exhibition of mechanical ingenuity but a hand-to-hand conflict between adversaries who respected one another's martial prowess, was skill in handling arms and parrying an opponent's thrusts, the exultant display of vigor and courage. Strength resided in the harmonious constitution of the body, skill in the close cooperation of eye and nerve and limb. Since from boyhood training had probably included little beside martial exercises, the warrior perforce had to find in battle the satisfaction in coordinated activity that the artist or craftsman derives from the exercise of special skill. Similarly, to argue convincingly requires a well-organized mind and the coherent flow of ideas, which is itself a source of gratification. Even in much of our violent strife, our joy in harmony asserts itself; the external opposition gives play to the internal integration; and every other motive for engaging in contests, as in the desire to hurt or to humble one's adversary, is a revelation not of our primary nature but of modifications imposed on us by the struggle to survive in a competitive world.

Most schools of ethics tell us we should do this or that because the world, including human society, is so constituted that such and such consequences will flow from our behavior. Instead of making our conduct conform to our inmost nature, we are directed to regulate it with a view to what might happen in the external world. It is natural that a being who looks ahead as we do should guide activity by its expected effects, to oneself or to those in whom one takes an interest. But an ethic based wholly on the foreseen effects of certain behavior places too much confidence in our ability to predict the future, and too little faith in the hidden potentialities of the coming years. Unlike the other schools, the Intuitive moralists insist that we act in certain ways because such behavior conforms to our nature—that we should regulate our conduct by what we are rather than with a view to what might happen to us. Had we the strength and courage to follow our most impelling intuitions with less fear of their foreseen consequences to ourselves, they might lead us to a future more satisfying than we can imagine.

7. The Cosmological Principle and Its Correspondence with the Intuitive Principle

While giving full recognition to the place of intuitionism in ethics, we can hardly afford to neglect what we may for brevity call the cosmological principle. Not only is it of importance for us to discover what kinds of conduct most closely conform to our own nature when we are most truly ourselves; it seems also of consequence to learn what kinds of conduct, if any, are most in keeping with the structure, the purpose, or the dominant trend of the universe in which we find ourselves. Does the study of the world and its evolution suggest that certain aims or modes of behavior are more incumbent on us than others? I doubt if many people would demur to the proposition that if there is a Creator and we can with certainty know the Creator's will it is our duty to obey it. And if there be no transcendent Creator, but an immanent purpose or dominant trend in the universe, discoverable by us, it would seem to be equally incumbent on us to act in harmony with this process or activity which made us. Indeed, it might be difficult to do otherwise.

This places us in a dilemma. We have recognized the validity of two apparently unrelated ethical principles: (1) the moral obligation to be true to our most central intuitions, and (2) the similar obligation to conform to the will of a cosmic Creator or at least to an immanent cosmic purpose, if either of these exist. But suppose that we should find these two guiding principles radically incompatible, so that we could not conform to the external standard without violating conscience, and we could not conform to the central impulse of our nature without embarking on a course of conduct directly in opposition to the will of God or the cosmic trend? In such a situation, our morality would stand abashed and bewildered, and ethics might become fantastic.

But that our innate principles of conduct should be at odds with the cosmic process seems so improbable that we cannot seriously contemplate such a contradiction. Not only are we products of this process, we are parts of it. In any system, the principle which determines the whole determines its parts. The activity, which pervades the Universe and governs its evolution, is also immanent in us and stamps its impress on us. The whole possibility of leading a good and moral life depends on this congruence between our own constitutive process and the process, which pervades the

Universe, between our individual enharmonization and universal harmonization.

What could be more pathetic and futile than to discuss ethics and develop an ideal of conduct in a world which refused to support moral endeavor? Often, no doubt, we feel that our effort to lead a harmonious life is inadequately supported by our total environment—who does not wish that it were easier to be good? But the fact that we do at least partly succeed in living in accordance with our moral ideals proves that they receive a certain amount of external support, and this in turn demonstrates a measure of moralness in the wider Universe. Thus ethics deals with a complex situation, embracing the human spirit and the environing world. The situation is, in fact, so complicated that the most adequate analysis presents us with a single, or at best a few, cross-sections of the whole; and many ethical theories which seem to be true as far as they go fail by a long way to give us an adequate account of the moral life.

One of the gravest dangers that beset the thinker in search of some trend in the wider world which might serve for moral orientation, is to suppose that this can be found in the study of organic evolution. It is to harmonization, not to evolution, that we must look for moral guidance; hence it is necessary clearly to distinguish the two processes. Harmonization is the driving force in evolution, so that without it there would be no evolution, yet it is not the equivalent of evolution. In the growth of an organism, harmonization builds up the crude materials of the world into patterns of ever increasing amplitude, complexity, and coherence; if it could avoid all complications it would produce an ever more perfect harmony, unmarred by any discord. But it was necessary for harmonization to proceed simultaneously throughout extensive regions of the Universe, if not the whole of it, imposing some sort of order upon all the included materials. Thus it began to build up innumerable patterns, many of them so close together that, in continuing to grow, they inevitably impinged upon each other and competed for the materials essential for their further development. This strife of entity with entity in an overcrowded world has had an immense effect on the course of organic evolution, and has imposed on the beings which slowly evolved numerous modifications contrary to their original nature. Thus, far from being a perfect expression of harmonization, evolution has become so complex that it tends to mask the essential character of harmonization; and it requires much penetration to discern the primary direction of the movement beneath all its complicated secondary effects.

Harmonization might be compared to a broad stream whose surface is disturbed by many eddies and crosscurrents, which for all but the skillful pilot conceal the direction of the deeper flow. If we confine attention to the stream's troubled surface, which is evolution, we might be unable to discover any prevailing drift. While certain evolutionary lines exhibit a growing perfection of organization, others show reduction, often ending in parasitism. If on one side a steady increase in the beauty and friendliness of organisms, is evident, on another side hostility has intensified and aggressive weapons have become more effective.

An evolutionary ethic is faced with the embarrassment of deciding which trend in evolution is predominant, or at least of discovering valid reasons why we should prefer and strive to promote one trend in evolution rather than another; and the grounds for such preferences are hardly to be found in the study of evolution itself. But an ethic of harmonization is not an evolutionary ethic, and it avoids this perplexity by looking beneath evolution to the process of which organic evolution is a confused and imperfect expression. Since this process is the source of our moral aspirations and endeavor, we have no difficulty in deciding that our ethic must conform to it. One of the grand objectives of morality, then, is to make the course of evolution, insofar as we can influence it, a more perfect expression of the process which underlies it. Humanity's moral nature might be regarded as one of the instruments which harmonization has developed for overcoming some of the difficulties in which it has become involved, as an unavoidable result of the course it was driven to pursue.

8. The Correspondence between Goodness and Happiness

Not the least of the difficulties which confront the architect of an ethical doctrine is the question of happiness. Some authors have held that the whole aim of morality is to attain happiness, for self, for humanity, or for all sentient beings; whereas other thinkers have believed that deeds done for the sake of personal happiness are devoid of moral worth. It would be most paradoxical if we and our world were so constituted that the greater our moral endeavor and the more closely we approached our ethical ideal, the more miserable everyone became; while, on the contrary, the more wicked or immoral our conduct seemed to us, the happier we grew. Such a situation might make us pause and ask ourselves if we had not founded our ethic on false premises, badly in need of revision.

Even when we recognize that our moral effort springs primarily from a demand of our inmost nature rather than from something outside us or from our thirst for felicity, we must further admit that it would be confounded if we discovered that it led only to increase of sorrow, just as it would stand abashed if we discovered that it worked in opposition to the dominant trend of the surrounding world. The whole possibility of an effective and satisfying ethic seems to rest, then, on the congruence of our moral nature with the world process on one hand, and the compatibility of goodness and happiness on the other.

The situation is saved by the intimate connection between goodness and happiness. Goodness, as we decided in Chapter XII, is a relative term, denoting the harmonious coexistence or interaction of two entities. Such entities are said to be good in relation to each other; and a being absolutely good would dwell in concord with everything and clash with nothing. As organisms, we are products of harmonization, a process which unites the crude elements of the world in harmonious patterns, and our continued existence depends on the preservation of harmony among the myriad constituents of our total selves. When this harmony is disturbed, we ail in body or mind, or in both; with the further decay of harmony, we die. Not only does life depend on the harmonious integration of body and mind, it demands a high degree of concord with the environment in all its aspects. Life arises from harmony, it endures only so long as harmony is maintained, hence its dominant effort is the establishment and preservation of harmony.

The same pervasive activity which gives form to the body also makes itself felt in the mind as a demand for harmony in thought and action, in our relations with everything that surrounds us, and finally even in the relations of these external things with each other. Thus it happens that the moral imperative is to strive ceaselessly for goodness, which is just another name for harmony. But the same process which made us moral beings also gave us sentience; and it has so fashioned us that we experience happiness in the measure that we achieve harmony among all the components of our total selves, whereas we feel pain and sadness when this harmony is impaired. Since happiness and goodness are determined by the same active principle, there is necessarily an intimate connection between them. One might almost say that our will to be good and our desire to be happy are adjusted to each other by a preestablished harmony in the sense of Leibniz; but actually their correspondence is due to common origin.

Thus, under ideal conditions, it would seem to make little practical difference whether we made goodness or happiness the professed end of all our endeavor; for we could not be happy without being good, and we could not be good without being happy. But, in our actual world, it is most difficult to be neither perfectly good nor thoroughly happy; therefore, it may be of some consequence to decide whether we should make goodness or happiness our primary goal. Moreover, although goodness and happiness are closely associated, one might be easier to describe, to recognize, and to regulate than the other. As a subjective state, happiness is known to us immediately only in ourselves, and its presence anywhere else in the world is largely an inference; whereas we are often able to observe directly whether the conditions which determine it, in self and others, have or have not been achieved. Still further, since harmony and happiness are related as cause and effect, the rational person will endeavor to establish the causal foundation, confident that its usual effect will follow from it. This causal priority, no less than the objectivity which makes it so much easier for us to recognize and assay, are compelling reasons for choosing the cultivation of goodness or harmony as the primary goal of moral endeavor.

Although the immediate aim of our moral effort should and must be the cultivation of goodness, we cannot wholly neglect happiness even as a proximate goal. The reason for this is that, although on the whole the objective condition of harmony is more readily examined and regulated than the subjective state of happiness, a living being, and above all a thinking animal, is exceedingly complex, containing so many aspects accessible neither to inspection nor to introspection, that when all the recognized conditions of life have been harmoniously adjusted, there may still remain subtle undetected disharmonies that are reflected in unhappiness. In sentient beings, happiness is the most sensitive index of harmony; and when it is conspicuously deficient, we may be sure that hidden discords or maladjustments escape our notice. Just as where there is persistent pain or discomfort, we are certain that there is some bodily derangement, despite the physician's failure to discover it by the most careful examination; so, where there is much unhappiness, we must suspect lurking disharmonies, even when all the evident conditions of harmony have been satisfied. Although omniscience might possess a more certain criterion of goodness than that provided by happiness, so inconstant in oneself and so difficult to assess in other creatures, we whose insight is imperfect must look even to this elusive index to correct our errors of judgment.

Although we freely admit the importance of considering happiness when making ethical judgments, we cannot adopt the attainment of maximum happiness as the guiding principle of morality, for two compelling reasons: (1) This criterion is too difficult to apply; and (2) it makes the scope of ethics too narrow. As to the first point, it is difficult to learn the circumstances in which our personal happiness is greatest. When young, we often sadly misjudge the conditions of our own felicity, and only with advancing years do the wisest of us discover the mode of life which most conduces to it. It is reasonable to suppose that another person quite similar to oneself would be happy in the same circumstances; but the more another differs from oneself in temperament and education, the more difficult it is for us to know the conditions in which he or she would be happiest. Contented people who strove to bring happiness to their children or their employees, by insisting that they live just as they do, might succeed only in making them miserable. And if it is so hard to know the conditions of greatest happiness for other individuals of our own species, how much greater is the difficulty of determining this point for animals so different from us as quadrupeds and birds!

Although every benevolent person may subscribe to the Utilitarian's pious resolve so to act as to promote the maximum of happiness among all sentient beings, actually this objective is so vague that when we attempt to extend it beyond humanity it dissolves into thin air; and for all its noble intentions, Utilitarianism has done very little to regulate by moral principles human dealings with the vast nonhuman world. But an ethical system closed about humanity fails to satisfy us, and this is our second reason for rejecting the principle of maximum happiness as the regulative ideal of ethics. Happiness had best remain a subsidiary consideration, serving, where we are able to assess it, as an index of our success in attaining harmony, and when deficient warning us of the persistence of disharmonies that we had overlooked. But our moral efforts must extend far beyond the narrow range of the beings most like ourselves who can inform us of their feelings, and in these more distant regions we must endeavor to preserve harmony even if we can learn nothing of the felicity of the beings which we affect. Yet the known dependence of happiness on harmony assures us that when harmony is at a maximum, creatures will enjoy all the felicity of which their nature is capable.

9. The Correspondence between Self-regarding and Altruistic Motives

In addition to the congruence between the intuitive and the cosmological principles and that between our aspiration for goodness and our unquenchable thirst for happiness, still a third correspondence seems indispensable for the effectiveness of moral effort. We have become aware that we are driven by deep vital impulses not only to preserve and fulfill ourselves; but also to serve others; and it is certainly not impossible that these two sets of motives should so drive us in contrary directions that we could never reconcile them. In fact, when we examine their primordial foundations in living things, we do find that self-maintenance and reproduction, from which our self-regarding and other-regarding impulses are respectively derived, are often very much opposed to each other. We see this most clearly in many plants and animals, including all annual herbs, many invertebrates, and a few vertebrates like salmon and eels, which so exhaust themselves in producing seeds or eggs, and perhaps also guarding the latter for a period, that they never recover from the effort, but die to make way for the next generation. And even in animals, which produce successive broods, and perhaps survive for a considerable period their last reproductive effort, the conflict between self-maintenance and reproduction is clearly evident. In forming and perhaps also nourishing their progeny from the substance of their own bodies, and often, too, in making active efforts to feed and protect them, they frequently lose weight, so that they require an interval of rest and recuperation, before they can with safety to themselves undertake to rear additional offspring.

Thus, when we consider their origins in living things, we find the self-regarding and the other-regarding motives often in direct conflict with each other. If this opposition had continued undiminished throughout their subsequent history, so that in ourselves we found egoistic motives always conflicting with altruistic motives, we would be in an embarrassing predicament. In the measure that we obeyed our persistent demand to improve ourselves, we would perforce disregard our hardly less insistent urge to devote ourselves to others; and, in the measure that we dedicated our energy to advancing the welfare of others, we would neglect ourselves and perhaps deteriorate. How, then, was this contradiction overcome?

As service to others called for psychic qualities rather than physiological processes, the opposition was diminished and even reversed. Insofar as the production and rearing of progeny involves dedicating part of the substance of the parents' body to them, the parents suffer a loss, which is often difficult, and sometimes impossible, to replace; but insofar as parents exercise their mind or spirit on behalf of their offspring, they may enrich themselves by this effort. While, in our ignorance of the subjective life of nonhuman animals, we cannot be sure that any of them is spiritually enhanced by its parental activities, we must recognize that in birds and mammals, as likewise in a number of cold-blooded vertebrates and even numerous invertebrates, the stage is already set for this enhancement. The bird who for weeks sits patiently hatching out her eggs, warms her nestlings with her own body, gives them food from her own mouth even at times when she is herself hungry, shields them from burning sunshine and beating rain, perhaps defends them against predators larger and more powerful than herself, and educates them by example if not by word, is certainly in a situation most propitious for the development of such moral qualities as patience, fortitude, hopefulness, sympathy, and unselfish love. Although she certainly acts as though well endowed with these virtues, we cannot be sure that she ever has the sentiments that we would feel in corresponding circumstances.

Among humans, service to others, whether one's own children, other humans, or beings of other kinds, has not only ceased to be antagonistic to self-development, but, on the contrary, has become so favorable to it that we may doubt whether any human can attain his or her full spiritual stature without devoting some thought and effort to the welfare of others. By approximately our twentieth year, our body has reached its full measure of size, strength and beauty, and soon afterward it begins a long and slow decline in vigor and grace. Thereafter, continued growth and increase in perfection is possible for us only in the mind. But the mind is formed by its experience, and the broader and richer this experience; the more it fulfills its own nature. It may increase its representative knowledge of the surrounding world; and since it is the nature of the mind to know, the more comprehensive and accurate this knowledge, the more perfect it becomes. But representative knowledge is always external to the object known, probably a symbol rather than a replica of it; and we can never discover the degree of correspondence between a percept and its object in the external world.

However, an alert mind strives to supplement representative knowledge by sympathetic understanding, by means of which the objects revealed superficially by sensuous perception are endowed with life and feeling. This second kind of knowledge, so necessary to supplement the cold formality of the first kind, is greatly enhanced by the sort of interest in the beings which surround us that leads us to help them, as by promoting their growth, lightening their burdens, assuaging their sorrows, or settling their conflicts. By such altruistic efforts, we grow in sympathy and understanding; and this mode of growth is open to us in our later years, long after other kinds have ceased.

Thus, in humans, the primitive antagonism between self-maintenance and reproduction, between service to self and service to others, has been largely overcome. On one hand, until we have taken great pains to cultivate our minds and acquire certain skills, we cannot effectively serve others; to rush into altruistic enterprises before we have adequately prepared ourselves for them shows misguided zeal. On the other hand, by dedicating ourselves to the welfare of other beings we identify ourselves ideally with a larger whole, thereby growing in breadth of vision and depth of sympathy. But if the primitive opposition between self-maintenance and service to others has been so largely overcome, it has not wholly vanished. Work for others usually makes certain demands upon one's strength; and if this drain of energy is too prolonged and severe, health suffers. By devoting to others more strength than they can spare, altruistic people sometimes give less than they might have given if they had proceeded more moderately.

10. Should the Number of Individuals or Their Quality Be Our First Consideration?

Another question, which powerfully influences the shape of an ethical doctrine, is whether it looks toward the perfection of the individual or the size, efficiency, and power of a society. Practically everyone who has given thought to the question recognizes that it is scarcely possible to produce good individuals except in a good society, and that the quality of a society is in turn determined by that of the individuals who compose it. Whether we give primary consideration to the individual or to the state is largely a matter of emphasis, but the placing of this emphasis can make a profound difference in the type of person and the kind of society we produce.

We may make it our goal to create a state as wealthy, industrially efficient, and powerful in war as we possibly can, and for this end we shall find it advantageous to have a population as great as the land can support. The individuals who compose this teeming multitude should be industrious, amenable to authority, and not addicted to independent thinking; their other qualities may be indifferent to us. Or we may make it our aim to produce people of the highest type that we can conceive, all as far as possible perfect and complete in themselves, and we may look upon the state as an arrangement for fostering the life of such people. In the first case, the state is regarded as an end, individuals as instruments in its service; in the second case, individuals are an end in themselves, the state a community of ends. Such a state will not endeavor to increase its population beyond a certain point; for it is well known that when organisms of any kind become so numerous that they are chronically undernourished, the quality of individuals deteriorates, although up to a certain point their total mass and power may become greater. Each of these two concepts of society will have its appropriate ethic; and the two doctrines, despite a broad similarity impressed upon them by the fact that they apply to an animal whose nature and needs are everywhere fundamentally the same, will contrast sharply in many important features.

Humanity faces no decision more momentous than which of these two concepts of society it will adopt and support. Before making the decision, it will be well to consider which of the two ends, the creation of excellent individuals or the production of the greatest possible number of individuals, even at the sacrifice of quality, is more in accord with the trend of life as a whole, and with that of our own branch of the animal kingdom in particular. If we decide that numbers take precedence over quality as the goal of life, then the example of the ants, which swarm in such incredible multitudes in the warmer regions of the Earth, leaves little room to doubt that a society in which individual completeness is strictly subordinated to collective efficiency is, for a multicellular animal, one of the best means of building up a teeming population.

When we contemplate the hosts of toiling ants and termites, the bewildering array of parasites, so many of them blind, misshapen, and disgusting in our sight, we may suspect that the one goal of life is to propagate its brood at any price. It seems willing to sacrifice independence of movement, organs of sense that it has taken countless generations to perfect, the greater part of the nervous system, beauty of form and color, the very possibility of a rich and varied experience, to say nothing of the integrity of the organisms that serve as hosts or prey, in order to increase the number of living things, regardless of their quality. But if we look at trees, flowering plants, butterflies and many other classes of insects, the majority of birds and mammals, humans at their best, we can hardly doubt that there is also in the living world a strong tendency to perfect individuals, even at the price of supporting fewer of them—that mere survival is not the only end of life and that the number of units is not the only measure of success.

Among the warm-blooded vertebrates, parasitism in any form is rare and full parasitism unknown. Each individual tends to be complete in itself; and there are only slight traces of that structural and functional specialization (other than sexual) of individuals within the species that has proceeded so far among certain ants, termites, and other insects that no individual is complete in itself and able to carry on alone, or as a member of a pair, the life of its kind. Moreover, the system of holding breeding territories, widespread among vertebrate animals, often imposes a check on the rate of reproduction and helps to ensure sufficient space and food for the full development of each individual. In our own division of the animal kingdom, we detect an unmistakable trend toward the perfection of the individual, rather than the unlimited multiplication of the species regardless of consequences to the individual. We shall be safest if we take our cue from our nearest kin and make the fullest development of individuals our goal. To this end, we must try to avoid that overcrowding which, despite the best social arrangements, inevitably leads to severe competition among individuals, thereby exacerbating the egoistic passions. Since competition for the means of supporting life is the primary cause of moral evil, we must make every effort to avoid creating a community in which such competition is acute.

11. Two Coordinate Aspirations of the Human Spirit

Although the study of the animal kingdom, of which we are a part, can provide valuable orientation to our thinking, the springs of moral endeavor are within us; we are moral in response to a demand of our own nature, and this is what our ethical doctrine must ultimately satisfy. Deep within us we find two yearnings, which, on a superficial view, appear incompatible. The first is the desire to be a complete and enduring entity, an individual human, distinct from all the rest of creation, viewing the world from a definite center with a particular bias, enjoying the values which thence arise, and recognized as a person by those around us. This is the deepest of vital necessities, for only by rather effectively insulating themselves from their environment by selectively permeable integuments and maintaining their distinctness can organisms survive. The second is the yearning to merge with a larger whole, to be identified with it and to serve it. This, in its less ardent form, is the social impulse, while at fullest intensity it becomes a religious aspiration.

These two spiritual needs can be satisfied simultaneously only in a society in which individuals strive to fulfill themselves without impeding the similar endeavor of those around them, but even more seek to improve their own nature by helping others to fulfill theirs. The alternatives to such a community are monadic isolation; a condition most nearly realized by the solitary outlaw, rebellious to society and defiant to God, and, at the opposite extreme, mystic absorption in the One or the Absolute. The first of these conditions strengthens the feeling of individuality at the expense of unity; the second heightens the sense of unity by the renunciation of individuality. Yet the first rarely achieves complete isolation; the second commonly falls short of perfect selflessness; and neither satisfies the average human being.

Although, apparently, neither of these yearnings is wholly absent from an awakened spirit, they differ in intensity from individual to individual, and, in the same person, at different stages of life and with varying moods. Their strength powerfully influences moral doctrines. Where the impulse to realize one's own potentialities is dominant, the ethic will stress the attainment of fullness of life or perfection by the individual; where the demand for unity with something greater than the individual is more urgent, social solidarity or social progress will be strongly emphasized. It seems possible to classify ethical systems according to whether they are directed primarily toward the fulfillment of the individual or the perfection of social arrangements. Nevertheless, the two categories differ chiefly in emphasis; for no thoughtful person can fail to recognize how powerfully the social milieu influences the characters of individuals, nor the necessity of developing adequate individuals if a good society is to be realized.

Even within the limits of the same formal doctrine, the emphasis shifts now to this side, now to that, with the thinker who expounds it. Thus, among the later Stoics, Epictetus, the liberated slave, was more concerned with the spiritual freedom and integrity of the individual; the Emperor Marcus Aurelius, who had vast social responsibilities, thought more about the interactions of individuals and society, and of the human state with the Cosmos. The basic moral rules attributed to Moses were, in ancient Judaism, intended largely for the stabilization of a tribal community; whereas in Christianity they became part of a discipline for the moral purification of individuals who aspired to preserve their personal identity through all eternity. And even within the Christian community, the same basic rules have been binding on the mystic who yearned to become one with God, and the ordinary mortal who hoped for immortal life in a resurrected body.

Still, with these limitations, we can separate ethical doctrines into those which assign first importance to the perfection of individuals and those which aim primarily at the improvement of society. As emphasizing first and foremost the need of cultivating spiritual perfection in the individual, I would place the ethical teachings of the *Bhagavad-gita*, Buddhism, Stoicism, Christianity, Spinoza, Kant, and T. H. Green. I would call this emphasis on the cultivation of the spiritual perfection of the individual the "Grand Tradition" in ethics. On the other side, as leaning more strongly toward the ideal of social integration, I would place Plato (in the *Republic* and even more in the *Laws*), Aristotle, the Utilitarian, Spencer, and many recent writers. In general, modern thought tends to stress the importance of social arrangements to the neglect of individual completeness. Although the Stoics taught that individuals could preserve their virtue and happiness even if the world collapsed around them, Spencer declared that a perfectly good individual could exist only in an ideal society. Both doctrines are true, but they are based on different concepts of perfection: the first, that of a person enclosed within the self, the second that of a person in dynamic equilibrium with his or her surroundings. The Confucians, with their usual moderation, took an intermediate position. Although fully aware of the importance of the social order, to the stabilization of which their teachings were directed, they believed that if individuals would first of all be true to their own moral nature, then cultivate proper relations with their family and those about them, the welfare of society would be assured. They conceived the moral order as spreading out from personal centers to embrace the whole world. Like Aristotle, they placed no sharp boundary between ethics and politics, as their ends were considered to be identical: to define the good life and to discover the conditions of its realization.

If we adopt this view and conceive the moral order as extending outward from personal centers to include an ever-expanding sphere, we become aware that moral endeavor must, in the first place, be directed to the improvement of the individual, then to the cultivation of harmonious relations between wisely beneficent individuals and surrounding beings. In order to embark upon this great undertaking with some probability of success, we must first of all have clearly in mind the goal toward which we strive: we must live under the inspiration of a moral ideal. The foregoing chapters have been devoted largely to the investigation of the resources available to the moral philosopher who attempts to formulate such an ideal, which are all those innate features of human nature that determine the direction of our moral aspirations and impel us to strive for goodness. Prophets and philosophers cannot create such propensities in the human mind; they must take them as given and employ all their skill in leading them forth into the full light of consciousness, and then to adequate expression in a lofty doctrine and a noble life. They are gardeners who attend a seedling that they did not sow, using their art to assist the sprouting plant to grow and spread its blossoms in the greatest perfection.

12.Summary

Briefly to summarize the conclusions we have reached: It will hardly be possible to create a satisfying ethical doctrine without founding it upon every motive which is capable of promoting moral endeavor, although by this course we renounce the monistic neatness attained by ethical systems deduced from a single first principle. The first of these motives is the will to exist and to perfect the self, whence we derive such virtues as prudence, temperance, patience, and fortitude. Of coordinate rank, and wholly distinct as it enters consciousness, is the social impulse, which has its biological root in the parental instincts and is the source of such altruistic virtues as sympathy, generosity, compassion, and charity. To these two we must add, as foundation stones of our ethical system, love of beauty and respect for form and order, which, as developed in finer minds, might almost in themselves support a lofty moral life, but are in many people too rudimentary for this, and serve merely as auxiliaries to the primary egoistic and altruistic impulses. Although these primary motives of conduct appear at times to be in opposition to each other, the fact that they all have their origin deep in our being affords a ground for believing that they are not ultimately irreconcilable. Conscience and the feeling of duty are not, like the foregoing, primary springs of action, but integrative and conservative forces, which impel us to bind all the aspects of our lives into a coherent whole and strive to preserve it.

The ethical structure, which we erect on these innate foundations, will perforce have an intuitive basis, because it must, above all, satisfy a demand of our nature, prior to all experience, which determines our valuations and gives direction to moral endeavor. At the same time, our ideal must be in accord with the whole trend of the world process, or at least not directly opposed to it; for nothing could be more pathetic than an ideal of conduct, which the cosmos refused to support. The goal of our moral effort should be goodness or harmony rather than happiness, for we can know very little of the latter except in the people most like ourselves; hence, whatever it professes, an ethic which makes happiness its aim has necessarily so limited a scope that it fails to satisfy us. But since harmony is the foundation of felicity, in striving to increase it we shall be preparing the way for greater happiness; and happiness, wherever we have means of knowing its quality or amount, serves as a valuable indicator of our success in promoting harmony.

The form of our ethical doctrine will be powerfully influenced by our view of the relation of the individual to society, whether we hold that individuals are of little importance except as they serve a state regarded as an end in itself, or that the whole function of the state is to create conditions which will help individuals to fulfill themselves. Although in some branches of the animal kingdom the completeness of individuals has been sacrificed to the needs of social integration and the creation of a sort of superorganism, among the vertebrates the course of evolution is directed toward the production of individuals whose completeness is rarely diminished for social ends; and for us the safest course is to follow the lead of our closest kindred. But our ethical ideal must, above all, satisfy the spirit's yearnings, in obedience to which we strive not only to become complete and perfect individuals, but at the same time to identify ourselves with a larger whole. Hence our problem is to perfect ourselves without interfering with the similar endeavor of all the beings which surround us, and the dual demand of our inmost self will be even more adequately satisfied if we can increase our own perfection by helping others to increase theirs.

Notes

Preface

1. Spencer, *The Principles of Ethics*. 2 vols.

Chapter One

1. Hartmann, *Ethics*. 3 vols.
2. Green, *Prolegomena to Ethics*, 372-373, 376, 394, 406.
3. Gore, *Philosophy of Good Life*, 58.
4. Lecky, *History of European Morals*. 2 vols.
5. Sutherland, *Origin and Growth*. 2 vols.
6. Since this was written two decades ago, the world has been deteriorating in this respect.
7. Hume, *Treatise of Human Nature*, bk. 3, pt. 2, sec. 9.
8. Schweitzer, *Philosophy of Civilization*.

Chapter Three

1. Schaller, *Year of the Gorilla*.
2. Plutarch, in the dialogue of Gryllus and Ulysses on the reason of animals.

3. Hume, *Treatise on Human Nature*, bk. 2, pt. 1, sec. 12; pt. 2, sec. 12.

4. Spencer, *Principles of Ethics*, vol. 2, chap. 1.

5. Sutherland, *Origin and Growth*.

6. Darling, *Naturalist on Rona,* 57; *Herd of Red Deer*.

7. Grey, *Charm of Birds*, 275.

8. Armstrong, *Birds of Grey Wind*, 57.

9. Selous, *Realities of Bird Life*, 67.

10. Grey, op. cit.

11. Durango, "Territory in Red-backed Shrike," *Ibis* 98 (1956): 476-484.

12. Howard, *Territory in Bird Life*.

13. Pickwell, "Prairie Horned Lark," *Acad. Sci. St. Louis* 27 (1931): 1-153.

14. Tinbergen, "Snow Bunting in Spring," *Trans. Linnaean Soc. New York* 5:16 (1939).

15. Erickson, "Population of Wrentits," *Univ. Calif. Publ. Zool.* 42 (1938): 247-334.

16. Lorenz, *King Solomon's Ring,* 26-27.

17. Selous, op. cit.

18. Chapman, "Courtship of Gould's Manakin," *Bull. Amer. Mus. Nat. Hist.* 68 (1935): 471-525.

19. Miller, "Behavior of Bewick Wren," *Condor* 43 (1941): 81-99.

20. Selous, op. cit.

21. Crèvecoeur, *Letters from an American Farmer,* 232.

Chapter IV

1. Cicero, *De Natura Deorum*, bk. 3, 26-32.

2. Thorpe, *Learning and Instinct*, 177-78.

Chapter V

1. Santayana, *Realms of Being*, 791-97.

2. On reciprocity as the binding force in primitive law and

morality, see Malinowski, *Crime and Custom*.

3. An equally impressive but less widely known example of keeping faith with the enemy is that of Egas Moniz of Portugal, as recounted in the third canto of Camoens' *The Lusiads*.

Chapter VI

1. Sidgwick, *Methods of Ethics*, bk. 3, chap. 13.

2. Secondat and Montesquieu, *Spirit of Laws*. 2 vols.

3. Duncan-Jones, *Butler's Moral Philosophy*, 47.

4. Sutherland, *Origin and Growth*. 2 vols.

5. Wheeler, *Social Insects, Their Origins*, chap. 9.

6. Sutherland, *Origin and Growth*, chap. 10, where reference is also made to the observations of Lubbock.

7. Hingston, *Naturalist in Himalaya*, 38.

8. Hume, *Treatise of Human Nature*, bk. 2, pt. 1.

9. Willetts, *Aristocratic Society in Ancient Crete*, 69-70; Plato, *Laws*, 925-926.

Chapter VII

1. Nietzsche, "Genealogy of Morals," in *Philosophy of Nietzsche*, 702.

2. Locke, *Essay Concerning Human Understanding*.

3. Martineau, *Types of Ethical Theory*.

Chapter VIII

1. Seneca, Letter 92, "On the Happy Life," *Ad Lucilium Epistulae Morales*. 3 vols.

2. Jer. 31:29, 30; Ezek. 3:17-21, 14:12-23, 18:1-32.

3. Locke, *Essay Concerning Human Understanding*, bk. 2, chap. 28, 5.

4. Ward, *Amiel's Journal*. 2 vols., 258.

5. Kant, *Critique of Practical Reason*. Passim.

Chapter IX

1. Mill, *Utilitarianism*, chap. 2.
2. Bergson, *Time and Free Will*.
3. E.g. *Laws*, bk. 2, 662 B-663 D; bk. 5, 732 E.
4. Locke, *Essay Concerning Human Understanding*, bk. 2, chap. 21, no. 51.

Chapter X

1. Skutch, *Life Ascending*, chap. 11.
2. Hobbes, *Leviathan*, chap. 6.
3. Boethius, *The Consolation of Philosophy*.

Chapter xi

1. Sidgwick, *The Methods of Ethics*, bk. 1, chap. 3, par. 3.
2. Tufts, "Ethics," in *Twentieth Century Philosophy*, 20.
3. Moore, *Principia Ethica*.
4. Locke, *Essay Concerning Human Understanding*, bk. 2, chap. 25, 8.

Chapter XII

1. Paton, *The Good Will*, chap. 7.
2. Edman, ed., T*he Philosophy of Schopenhauer*, 289.
3. Moore, *Principia Ethica*, chap. 1. no. 7.
4. Spinoza, *Ethics*, pt. 3, prop. 39, note.
5. Ruskin, *Sesame and Lillies*, lecture 1, 28.

Chapter XIII

1. Piaget, *The Moral Judgment of the Child*.
2. Ibid., chap. 2, 131.
3. Dewey, *Human Nature and Conduct,* 314-31.
4. Plato, *Laws*, 11.
5. Martineau, *Types of Ethical Theory*, vol. 2, 498.

Chapter XIV

1. Piaget, op. cit., 44, 193.
2. Laertius, *Lives of Eminent Philosophers*, vol. II, bk. 7, 107-8.

Chapter XV

1. Aristotle, *Politics*, bk. 1.
2. *Nicomachean Ethics*, bk. 4, chaps. 2 & 3. I should be sorry if the above remarks prevented any reader from studying Aristotle's moral writings for the many insights of perennial value that are to be found in them.
3. How keenly the "Father of History" appreciated the fact of moral relativism is demonstrated by an anecdote in bk. 3, 38.
4. Benedict, *Patterns of Culture*.
5. Fielding, *The Soul of a People*, 275-276.

Chapter XVI

1. Plato, *The Republic*, bk. 4.
2. Hill, *Contemporary Ethical Theories*.
3. Malinowski, *Crime and Punishment*, 77-79.
4. Kant, *Critique of Practical Reason*.
5. Matt. 15:26, Mark 7:27.
6. Squire, "The Birds," in *Poems about Birds*, 360-362.

Chapter XVII

1. Laertius, *Lives of Eminent Philosophers, II,* bk. 7, 85.
2. Anthony Ashley Cooper Shaftesbury, in Høffding, *History of Modern Philosophy*, 392-96. 2 vols.
3. Martineau, *Types of Ethical Theory*, pt. 2, bk. 1, chap. 6, no. 15.

Index

Retail Orders

Individuals are encouraged to ask for Axios Press titles at their local bookstores. Our books are also available online at **www.amazon.com** and at our website **www.axiosinstitute.org**.

Retail orders can also be placed using the form below. All books ordered in this way may be returned for a full refund if not satisfied. Mail the completed order form to:

Axios Institute • P.O. Box 118 • Mount Jackson, VA 22842

AXIOS PRESS RETAIL ORDER FORM

☐ A Question of Values: Six Ways We Make the Personal Choices That Shape Our Lives

☐ The Beguiling Serpent: A Re-evaluation of Emotions and Values

☐ Alternative Values: For and Against Wealth, Power, Fame, Praise, Glory and Physical Pleasure

☐ The Words of Jesus

☐ Alexander Skutch: Selected Writings of an American Naturalist

☐ Nonsense: Red Herrings, Straw Men and Sacred Cows: How We Abuse Logic in Our Everyday Language

☐ Bohemia: Where Art, Angst, Love, and Strong Coffee Meet

☐ Ethics Since 1900

Each of the above books is $12.00 in the U.S., $14.00 in Canada.

☐ Are the Rich Necessary? Great Economic Arguments and How They Reflect Our Personal Values (hardcover)

Are the Rich Necessary? is $20.00 in the U.S., $23.00 in Canada.

Name _____

Address _____

_____

City _____

State, ZIP _____

Subtotal of order $ _____

+ shipping $2.00 / bk + $ _____

5% sales tax (VA only) + $ _____

Total enclosed $ _____

www.axiosinstitute.org ■ 1-888-54 AXIOS